Kristin E. Larsen

# Community
# Architect

THE LIFE AND VISION OF

## Clarence S. Stein

CORNELL UNIVERSITY PRESS

ITHACA AND LONDON

First published 2016 by Cornell University Press

Printed in the United States of America

Library of Congress Cataloging-in-Publication Data

Names: Larsen, Kristin E., 1962– author.

Title: Community architect : the life and vision of Clarence S. Stein / Kristin E. Larsen.

Description: Ithaca : Cornell University Press, 2016. | Includes bibliographical references and index.

Identifiers: LCCN 2016009141

ISBN 9781501702464 (cloth : alk. paper)

Subjects: LCSH: Stein, Clarence S. | Architects– United States–Biography. | City planners–United States–Biography. | Garden cities–United States–History.

Classification: LCC NA737.S638 L37 2016 | DDC 720.92–dc23

LC record available at http://lccn.loc.gov/2016009141

Cornell University Press strives to use environmentally responsible suppliers and materials to the fullest extent possible in the publishing of its books. Such materials include vegetable-based, low-VOC inks and acid-free papers that are recycled, totally chlorine-free, or partly composed of nonwood fibers. For further information, visit our website at www.cornellpress.cornell.edu.

Cloth printing          10 9 8 7 6 5 4 3 2 1

# Community
# Architect

FOR MY FATHER,

TORBJORN JARLE LARSEN,

AND MY HUSBAND,

GLENN ACOMB

# CONTENTS

# ILLUSTRATIONS

## MAPS

## FIGURES

Illustrations

# PREFACE

Kermit C. (KC) Parsons introduced me to the fascinating life story of Clarence Samuel Stein in the summer of 1996 when as a Ph.D. student at Cornell I offered to assist him with a project, and he was completing *The Writings of Clarence Stein*. Through KC I met Jan Parsons, who after KC's death in November 1999, asked whether I might be interested in writing the biography of Stein, which KC had intended as his next project. Over the years, as I drafted the manuscript, it became more of a professional assessment and thematic history than a full biographical treatment of the architect. During this time, I examined a range of themes regarding Stein and his colleagues in conference papers and articles. This work, as it explored related areas of planning history, has informed this study even as I broadened certain elements, introducing myriad new ones and taking them in new directions here.

I initially explored Stein's early years, education, and training, concluding with his service on the New York State Housing Committee in 1919–1920, in a conference paper entitled "Clarence Stein's Formative Experiences and Unbuilt Projects—Transforming Classical Training into Modern Design and Planning Sensibilities." The opportunity to do so came via the International Planning History Society 2008 Chicago conference and the conference proceedings. More recently, I assessed colleagues Henry Wright and Raymond Unwin's advocacy of government housing in relation to Stein's in "Planning and Public–Private Partnerships: Essential Links in Early Federal Housing Policy." Finally, my earliest published article on the contributions of Stein actually reviews one of the later chapters of his career, his role as consultant on the new town of Kitimat in Canada from 1951 to 1953 and his postwar ideas on regionalism as evidenced in his incomplete manuscript entitled *Cities to Come*. Both of these articles appeared thanks to Sage Publications in the *Journal of Planning History*. I very much appreciate the opportunity these venues provided to reach an audience regarding Stein and his colleagues prior to the publication of this book.[1]

Clarence Stein, and the wealth of themes, places, and people that informed his work, has been a focus of my academic life for a number of years, and I owe a great deal of thanks to those who have supported me and provided opportunities for me to visit his projects and learn more about his work. First and foremost, I thank my mentor and former director of the Clarence S. Stein Institute for Urban and Landscape Studies (Stein Institute), Michael Tomlan, who devoted countless hours to reviewing and discussing early drafts, offering insightful comments that pushed me to think in new ways about Stein's contributions and twentieth-century planning, architecture, and urban history in general. Thanks also to everyone who participated in the 2009, 2010, 2011, or 2012 Stein Institute symposiums Michael Tomlan organized, especially Herbert Reynolds, Laurence and Felice Koplik, David Vater, Dorothy Fue Wong, Lauren Bricker, Emily Goldman, and Abraham Thomas. The tours of Sunnyside Gardens and Phipps Garden Apartments by Herbert Reynolds, of Radburn by Laurence and Felice Koplik, of Chatham Village and Shaler Township by David Vater, of Hillside Homes by Abraham Thomas, and Baldwin Hills Village by Steven Keylon, provided a unique and extremely informative perspective. Thanks also to Angelique Bamberg, who guided me through Chatham Village (the subject of her book), Shaler Township defense housing, and what remained of Stowe Township defense housing. Your book is a great contribution to understanding Stein in Pittsburgh, especially at Chatham Village.[2]

The Stein Institute provided financial support for this project, as did the University of Florida through a Faculty Enhancement Opportunity Grant, through travel and research funding, and through a subvention from the College of Design, Construction, and Planning. The librarians at the Rare and Manuscript Collections at the Kroch Library, Cornell University, consistently offered their expert services and made my frantic efforts to collect as much information before I had to return home again a pleasant experience. A big thanks also to Christine Fruin at the University of Florida libraries for providing considerable support in securing background information on the images in this book. John Paul (JP) Weesner applied his considerable expertise in design to make the dark and at times damaged drawings and images significantly clearer, enhancing them so that even the fine lines are evident. He also developed the "Stein font" and used it to create the wonderful maps of Stein's New York in this book. Sonja Larsen, herself an accomplished author and editor, reviewed sections of the manuscript and recommended revisions. Also a special thank you to Jan Parsons for her generosity of spirit in sharing what KC had collected over years of research and writing, of opening up her home when I visited the archives at Cornell, and of imparting her deep interest in Stein, which sustained me as I immersed myself in this material.

Finally, thanks to my friends and family, who have patiently listened to extensive stories about Stein, his colleagues, and their projects. To my friends Lisa, Laura, Carol, and Simon and countless others who exhibited a keen and sincere interest in Stein, and especially my progress on the book. To my siblings Karin, Bjorn (wife Marit), and Sonja (husband John); my mother Inge; and my uncle Dieter—your intelligence and warmth mean the world to me. To my wonderful husband Glenn, himself a skilled landscape architect and expert on sustainability and new town design, who lived with Stein on a daily basis—a third member of the family, whom he graciously accepted into our household. What a gift it is to have you in my life as well as your vibrant and welcoming family, now part of mine—Libby, Mason, Nancy, Greg, and all the rest in Georgia and Louisiana. Finally to my father Toby, who despite suffering from dementia in his final years remembered enough of his profession as a civil engineer and his interest in history to engage in countless discussions about my research and my progress and to encourage me along my way. You are a profound source of inspiration to me.

# INTRODUCTION

Environmental designer, humanist, houser, policymaker, town planner, and regionalist, Clarence Samuel Stein, whose influential career stretched
from the Progressive era of urban reform through the post–World War II era of
postcolonial international planning, was all these and more. In 1956, close friend
and urban critic Lewis Mumford championed the relevance of Stein's work to
future generations. Hailing Stein "as one of the three or four influential architects
and civic designers of our time," he specifically recognized Stein's communities
as informed by "a more profound study of human needs and their architectural
expression" and emblematic of a new age of "social architecture."[1] Consistent with
this characterization, Stein himself preferred to be called a "community architect."

By the mid-1920s, as a member of the Executive Committee to the International Garden Cities and Town Planning Federation, he helped organize the federation's first conference held in the United States. Decades later, when he received
the Sir Ebenezer Howard Memorial Medal for his "notable advancement and
practical application" of the Garden City movement,[2] Stein reflected on the 1925
federation conference. Particularly memorable was a weekend party he coordinated to bring the leading lights of new town design from Europe together with
their American counterparts. He remarked, "A large conference with set speeches
is no place to get acquainted and swap experiences. So we invited a small group of
our visitors from abroad to spend a long, informal weekend with an equal number
of American planners. We went out to the Hudson Guild Farm in the country.
There we could sit under the trees, or roam the woods as we talked." Amidst
dinners in the rustic camp buildings and folk dancing one evening, where "Raymond Unwin took off his coat and in his shirt-sleeves joined in the dance," Unwin,

1

Ebenezer Howard, Barry Parker, and C. B. Purdom of Great Britain, Ernst May of Germany, Eric Keppler of Holland, and Auguste Bruggeman of France joined Stein, Mumford, Henry Wright, Benton MacKaye, Stuart Chase, Frederick Ackerman, and Alexander Bing, all members of the Regional Planning Association of America (RPAA), to discuss the current status and future vision for Garden Cities.[3] This critical moment in the community architect's career attests not only to the stature Stein had already secured in the profession but also to the power of his collaborative approach and networking skills.

Several years later, as the crisis of the Great Depression unfolded, the journal *Architecture* featured Stein as a housing expert to address government responsibilities and potential interventions. By way of introduction, the author noted, "Mr. Clarence Stein, who has spent many years in the study of housing and community planning, has won for himself a reputation as an authority on these matters which is equaled by few American architects. No one has a broader understanding than he of the difficulties which these problems present, nor has any one clung more persistently to the belief that they would eventually be overcome and so striven more determinedly to bring this about."[4]

His prominence in housing, though, was eclipsed by his remarkable community design expertise on display at Radburn, New Jersey, planned in collaboration with Henry Wright. It remained a touchstone throughout his career. Stein termed the holistic approach to design, function, management, financing, and community engagement, demonstrated by the project begun in 1927, as the "Radburn Idea." An early 1931 article outlines the project's primary principles: "For the whole idea of this city [Radburn] is as unique as its plan of interlacing streets and parks, and the plan, interesting as it proves, is merely the surface indication of a carefully thought out concept of new town building that is as much concerned with the economics, the social aspects and the government of cities as it is with their engineering and architecture."[5] Translating these principles into a variety of projects, from garden apartments to commercial centers to new towns, energized Stein for the remaining decades of his career.

Heralding Stein as a humanist and pioneer of environmental design, an exhibition of his life's work held in 1976, just one year after his death, outlined the community architect's multidimensional legacy: "His concerns embraced the problems of all classes and kinds of city people and their children, their desperate need for dignified shelter and vital recreation. He faced their environmental problems at every scale, from the residential community and new towns to the regional scale of the river valley and the 800-mile long Appalachian Trail." Further, colleagues such as Mumford highlighted the relevance of his work for future generations, concluding his introduction to Stein's *Toward New Towns for America*, "Let the planners of the coming generation ponder this testament." Indeed, many of the problems of planning, housing, and design with which Stein grappled, sometimes successfully and sometimes not, are still with us. Stein's agenda is implicit in movements that are shaping the design and planning professions today, including sustainability, smart growth, green infrastructure, and the new urbanism. Rediscovering and reexamining his contributions then takes on new urgency.[6]

Born into a life of relative privilege, Stein benefited from an advanced education, extensive travel, and the luxury of being able to seek out and choose projects rather than being compelled to take them. Although slight and soft spoken, his confidence in his ideas permitted him to collaborate with prominent designers and thinkers who shared his progressive ideals. Stein had an uncanny ability to recognize and appreciate the talents of others and effectively engage those skills.

The architectural and planning influences on him were varied. He was educated in the classical tradition at the École des Beaux Arts in Paris when that venerable institution was at the peak of its design influence. His subsequent training in the office of Bertram Goodhue, an established New York City architect with a prestigious portfolio of large-scale and landmark projects throughout the country, encouraged Stein's appreciation of revival and regional styles. Goodhue also reinforced Stein's interest and proficiency in community design and cultivated his collaborative management skills.

Stein created a variety of model communities, or as he called them "complete communities," that integrated design within a larger planning structure to enhance living, leisure, and work. He considered himself a community architect, in that he showcased the complexity and power of site design and open space to foster social connections. Further, through his friends and colleagues, particularly his closest friend, the conservationist Benton MacKaye, he fostered and integrated a regional perspective (see maps 1 and 2).[7]

Meticulous, dedicated, and focused, Stein demanded the highest quality in workmanship and materials, remaining loyal to an expert group of collaborators,

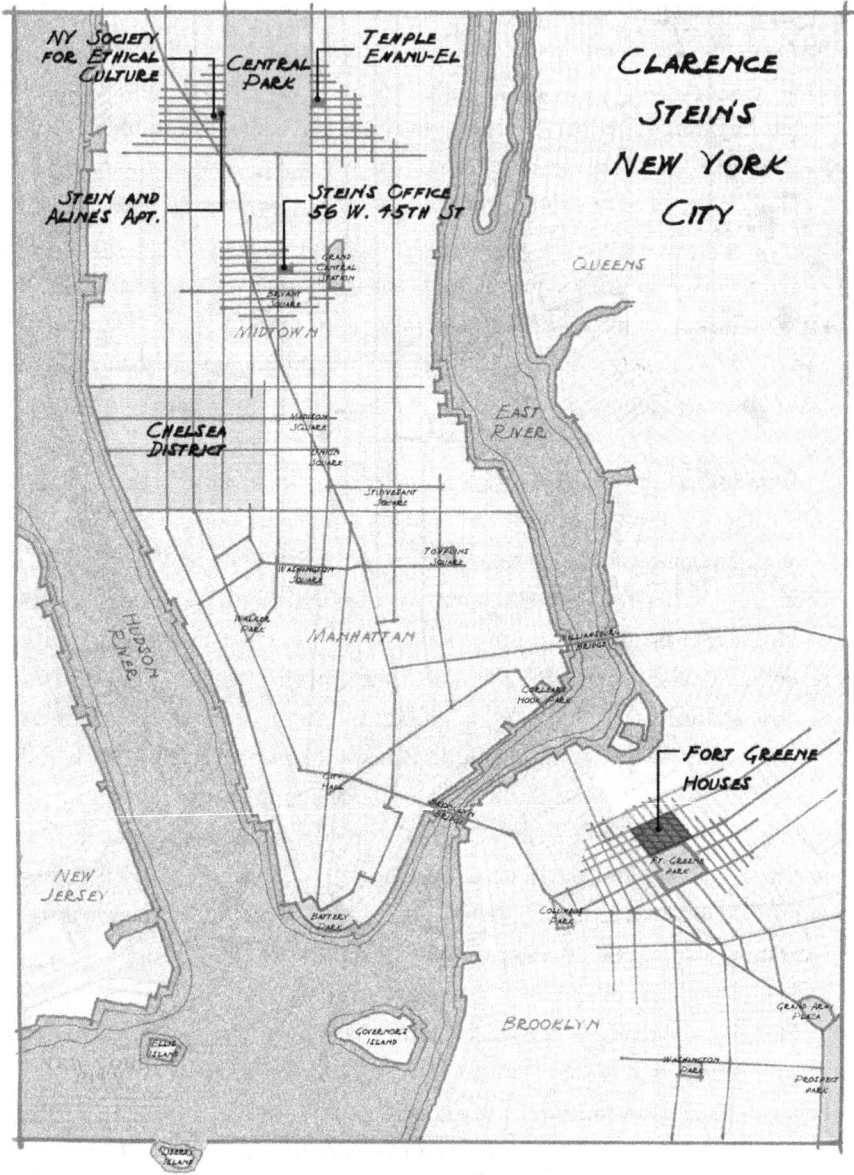

**MAP 1**  Clarence Stein's New York City. Conceptual map of the city ranging through the period of Stein's early residence through his professional years, circa 1900–1950 and showing his home, office, projects, and other sites. Graphic drawing by John Paul Weesner.

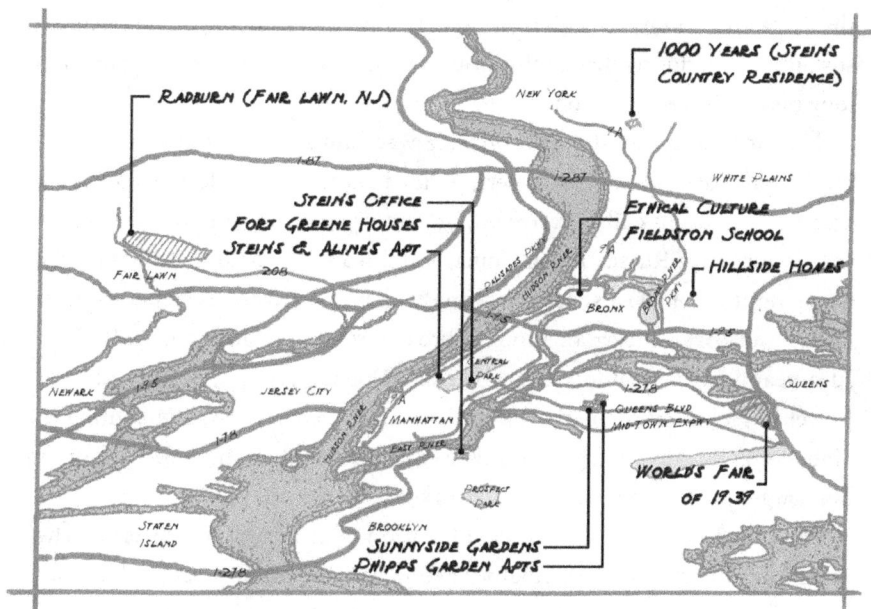

**MAP 2**  Clarence Stein's New York Region. Conceptual map of the region ranging through the period of Stein's early residence through his professional years, circa 1900–1950 and showing his homes, office, projects, and other sites. Dawing by John Paul Weesner.

often discerning and fostering the emerging genius in others or relying on those who had already earned a national reputation in their respective fields. Among these were people like Catherine Bauer who went from her fieldwork with Stein, identifying potential sites for new housing developments, to being a national leader in the advocacy movement for public housing. Similarly, Benton MacKaye, who met Stein while he was grieving his wife's recent suicide, shortly thereafter refined his ideas for the Appalachian Trail with Stein's insight and support. Others included Andrew Eken, one of the primary contractors for the Empire State Building, whom Stein engaged to construct one of the earliest federally funded housing projects; and John W. Harris, one of several developers of the Rockefeller Center whom Stein partnered with over a ten-year period on various town building and planning initiatives. In return, Stein earned an abiding loyalty and respect, particularly among his inner circle. Those closest to him provided the community architect with considerable support, promoting his projects and sustaining him during devastating bouts of depression and illness that required long periods of recuperation.

His income and lifestyle not only allowed him access to some of the most influential artists, designers, writers, policymakers, and intellectuals of his era, creating significant collaborative opportunities, they also supported extensive travels abroad to Russia, India, China, and Europe. Stein immersed himself in these months-long visits, delighting in the detailed design of the pavers in the Gardens of Sochow (Suzhou) and the broader reinterpretations of the Radburn Idea near postwar London and in Sweden. Not surprisingly, he alluded to the power of globalization in his *Toward New Towns for America*, highlighting the "Increasing Equality of Opportunity to enjoy the goods of the world ... [for] an ever-larger proportion of American workers."[8]

Mumford called him, "a rare combination of artist and organizer; ... [he] combined an extremely conciliatory manner with a will of steel; and he had a happy faculty of being all things to all men: he was capable of smoking a long black cigar with Governor Smith or admiring a Renoir that Alexander Bing had recently purchased; of chewing over contractors' estimates with his engineer and man-of-all-work, Frank Vitolo, or of reacting intelligently to the latest idea MacKaye or Wright had evolved overnight." Stein certainly also dedicated much of his career to advocating for reduced development and maintenance costs to make decent housing more accessible to lower-income and working-class families. Yet he remained apart from his target audience eschewing his early mentor John Elliott's call to live and work among them. Even though Stein recommended that the town planner "live in the places he helps to create," he spent most of his adult life in a spacious penthouse apartment on the Upper West Side overlooking Central Park and prioritized the feedback and insights of technical experts on his projects rather than seeking those of the residents. He was most comfortable among his circle of friends, many of them lifelong friends, though the circle widened over the years. His wife, Aline MacMahon, the notable stage and screen character actress, reinforced his intellectual and cultural mindset lending monetary and personal support when job opportunities waned or became too frenzied. She also joined him for many of his overseas travels.[9]

His projects span a period of four decades, reimagining the housing design, delivery, and finance process that engaged an interdisciplinary team of public and private sector experts. His alarm about the "Dinosaur Cities," as he called them, reflected his reformist sensibilities. Indeed, during the opening decades of the last century he witnessed firsthand the deterioration of the American metropolis, particularly the working-class and even some of the middle-class residential areas, into crowded, polluted, unhealthy, and unsanitary places. The images of a Pittsburgh of massed, rickety workers' housing against a smoldering industrial landscape featured in his 1939 World's Fair documentary *The City* bear little resemblance to the dynamic urban neighborhoods of Jane Jacobs that are celebrated today. His proposals, even at the lowest densities achieved at Radburn, New Jersey, presented a very different alternative to the homogenous postwar suburbs of cookie-cutter homes. Density was higher—at Radburn twice as high as typical suburbia; housing types were diverse; parks defined neighborhoods—aesthetically, socially, and functionally; a carefully integrated mix of uses created the complete community; roads were carefully designed to offer functionality for motorized traffic; housing was clustered strategically to create the illusion of greater space (despite increased density) while accommodating cost savings on infrastructure.[10]

Further, a pragmatic element ran throughout these projects because they did not simply illustrate a vision but demonstrated the practicality of that vision by establishing best practices. Stein's publications and lectures, capital and operating cost evaluations of his projects, and continuous monitoring of them reflect this desire to document and promote their practicality. He intended these projects to test the validity of his and his colleagues' ideas and demonstrate their applicability to policymakers, developers, and the general public.

Forces beyond his or any one planner or designer's control resulted in the large-scale, developer-driven residential patterns that characterized the postwar landscape. The Federal Housing Administration (FHA) guidelines combined with assurances of government-backed residential financing and government-sponsored highway construction resulted in formless sprawl rather than the thoughtful integrated design Stein practiced. Notwithstanding these broader sociopolitical and economic forces, Stein advanced innovations in community building that continue to resonate today.

∽

While other books on Stein's work, including his own, have explored his most renowned designs and partnerships, the focus here includes more obscure and unbuilt projects, his intellectual influence, and connections with lesser-known yet noteworthy associates. It establishes Stein as a significant transitional figure during a critical period of urban growth and development in the United States. Looking through the lens of Stein's lifework, this book addresses emerging concepts in site design, housing finance and management, town building, regional development, and community planning and explores a nascent governmental role that influenced these fields. In particular, this examination of Stein focuses on four critical themes that informed his career and legacy—his collaborative approach, promotion and implementation of "investment housing," distinctive interrelated community design epitomized as the Radburn Idea, and his advocacy of communitarian regionalism. The book is arranged around these themes.

The Garden City as introduced by Ebenezer Howard and implemented first most notably by architects Raymond Unwin and Barry Parker, forms the essential thread that ties these themes together. Stein adapted and advocated a distinctively Americanized version of Howard's Garden City, embracing a technocratic planning ethic for the modern age. During the interwar era, Stein and his colleagues in the RPAA formulated a vision of the Garden City that differed radically from that of their counterparts under Thomas Adams who headed the Regional Plan of New York and Its Environs (RPNY). The RPAA used the term *Regional City* to describe their vision of a balance between each distinct town and the countryside with a network of these towns building the region. The RPNY considered Garden Cities satellite communities in service to the metropolis of New York City. For Stein, the Regional City was a foundational principle for all planning; for the RPNY, it was not. While these two streams did much to broaden, modernize, and popularize the Garden City ideal, Stein's dedication to doing so resonated throughout his life as he reintroduced his vision for a postwar era. He began by tracing the implementation of his ideas in his best-known projects, a process he called "steps toward creating New Towns." These elements consisted of "The Garden City, the Radburn Idea, and the Neighborhood Unit."[11] Together these town building principles incorporated the balance of city and country; the design elements of clustered housing, connected parks, and hierarchical street systems; and neighborhoods configured to foster community.

First published in the United States in 1951, *Toward New Towns for America* celebrates Stein's iconic projects, which integrated the essential elements of the "complete community" designed for living, working, and leisure. He completed the draft documenting his life's work at Wyldes, Unwin's home in Hampstead Garden Suburb, drawing inspiration from Unwin's 1905 design that Stein and Wright had visited many years earlier when they were gathering ideas for their first project together, Sunnyside Gardens. In essence, *Toward New Towns for America* disseminates the lessons of the British Victorian Garden City as imported and adapted for the interwar automobile age in America to a post–World War II generation of international architects and planners. Stein considered this testimony to new town design an essential guide for other "explorers"—town planners and community architects—who "progress from one experience and experiment to the next, on the basis of the realities of living communities."[12] He intended in his next volume, *Cities to Come*, to more fully develop his theories of the Regional City. It was never completed.

For Stein, professional networks, often initially formed outside the office and formalized through ongoing collaborative partnerships, provided a critical means to achieve community building and policy goals. Early family connections and friendships through the Ethical Culture Society in New York City and education at the École des Beaux Arts in Paris, committee work through the progressive City Club, service on a statewide housing board, and the formation of a thinkers' network via the RPAA all offered a powerful foundation by the mid-1920s for Stein and his colleagues to spearhead significant changes in design, planning, housing, and real estate development. By the post–World War II era, Stein proposed that a nationally prominent team of consultants form public-private partnerships to build new towns with a range of housing types. This early proposal for an interdisciplinary approach reflects an economic development strategy that is widely used today, though Stein's efforts were much more ambitious in scope. As Mumford noted shortly after Stein's death, "His special facility was to evaluate important ideas, to choose congenial associates, seize imaginatively on their special talents and put them to work on tasks of research or design or construction that drew forth their best qualities."[13] His intent was to maximize the skills and resources among a diverse array of experts and agencies—philanthropic, corporate, and governmental—to design, build, and monitor his projects.

An essential component of Stein's personal and professional life, these partnerships advanced a new type of housing and community that benefited from innovations in design, construction, finance, and management. In the 1920s, Stein along with a range of partners, most notably Wright, led the way in large-scale residential design. Through the City Housing Corporation (CHC), the implementation arm of Stein and his colleagues' new town aspirations, development with limited profit, efficiencies in construction methods, and innovations in financing products made quality housing accessible to a broader population, including working-class families. In addition to savings to lower the initial cost of housing, the CHC introduced design and construction interventions intended to ensure reduced operating costs. Overall, while the initiative of a single company could not survive the onslaught of the Great Depression, many of these innovations later came to define private residential development. These included rental housing design for modest incomes in the garden apartment, large-scale construction techniques and standardized units to ensure more efficient use of resources, and a fully amortized mortgage to make home ownership possible for more households.

With the introduction of new federal housing programs in the 1930s, the public sector contributed new resources; administrative and programmatic capabilities; a holistic viewpoint, as opposed to that of "irresponsible, unskilled, small-scale builders"; and unique powers, such as eminent domain.[14] Stein had advocated for this public sector role, drafting proposals for legislation to address critical housing needs in the state, as part of his chairmanship of a prominent New York State housing and regional planning board in the mid-1920s. At the same time, Stein acknowledged the professional expertise of the private sector. Insurance companies, unions, foundations, and large investment corporations seeking a safe haven for investments at a decent return favored housing designed to accommodate working-class people for the full length of the amortization period and beyond. Well-constructed with appropriate community amenities— open space, services, and commercial uses—as well as safe and well-connected transportation networks, this "investment housing" generated limited dividends while meeting the target population's needs over the life of the project.

Stein firmly believed investment housing offered the greatest opportunity for the architect to design the complete community in collaboration with key partners. He consistently sought to use government powers to harness the profit motive. Yet the cost and design limitations that came to characterize fully subsidized government housing frustrated him. Since speculative housing did not offer viable solutions, he turned to investment housing, which he considered "limitless" in its potential impact and further characterized as follows:

"Its scope depends on its increasing ability, through experience, to use the advantages and businesslike financing of large scale operation under technical leadership to cut costs and improve housing." Stein considered planning "an integral part of housing." He elaborated, "Good, permanent urban housing is only possible as a part of broad planning. For it is obvious that decisions in regard to housing must be governed by considerations of location, surroundings, and transportation."[15]

By definition, the community architect assumed a central role in these projects. Only s/he could coordinate and integrate the various elements to ensure "functional and articulate architecture with a minimum of extravagance," community centers with "complete functional independence of each element and at the same time the common and varied use of structure," ample surroundings for "the evolution of new requirements and changing programs of community life," and buildings grouped "to form simple but beautiful gathering places." Through public-private partnerships, each participant could lend unique strengths to more effectively and efficiently seek solutions. Mumford characterized Stein's approach to advocating and building such partnerships as being one that exploited "the power and wealth of the State to co-ordinate all the forces that create communities and to make them serve public, rather than private and selfish ends. ... First private initiative to test the validity of the new planning; then public enterprise to extend it and co-ordinate it, when private enterprise lagged or retreated or proved impotent."[16]

Stein considered Hillside Homes in the Bronx a prime example of investment housing realized via public-private partnerships. One of the first projects to be built under an early New Deal housing program, "Hillside at the beginning consisted of nothing except my idea that a community of apartment houses should be built so that it would be an example of how urban areas in such cities as New York should be rebuilt. There was no land. There was no client. There was nothing but an idea. Radburn was well under way and I was anxious to see whether the Radburn idea of a community developed around common interests, large open green spaces, and safety of number, could be built into a community consisting entirely of apartment houses." He spent months looking for a site and a suitable partner/developer interested in constructing investment housing. At Hillside Homes and later Baldwin Hills Village in Los Angeles, he realized three important elements were necessary to achieve the complete community as investment housing: a large tract of moderately priced land and "government cooperation but not necessarily direct action, along with adequate sources of investment finance at low rates of interest."[17]

Public-private partnerships as a means to develop assisted housing targeting working-class households anticipated the Low Income Housing Tax Credit (LIHTC), the primary remaining program in the United States that finances the development of affordable housing. Established in 1986, the LIHTC program, with its incentive for private sector, limited partnership development of lower income rental housing, most closely resembles the early limited dividend programs. Yet the 1992 Housing Opportunities for People Everywhere (HOPE VI) program more accurately reflects the goals that Stein and other housers were seeking—focusing on improved design, innovations in management, and enhanced social services offered as part of mixed income, mixed use communities—though Stein and his colleagues preferred vacant rather than developed sites. In recent years, HOPE VI has been underfunded and subsequently subsumed by the federal Choice Neighborhoods initiative that broadens the focus to the communities surrounding the assisted housing units, explicitly targeting public and private reinvestment in essential areas such as education and commercial activity. Overall, while public-private partnerships are a more central consideration in housing policy today, the resources required to integrate long-term affordability, design innovations, and community building continue to be significantly constrained.

With each project, regardless of cost and time constraints, Stein worked to incorporate the clustered housing, integrated parks, roadway and pedestrian paths associated with the Radburn Idea while making adjustments for site constraints and pushing himself to learn something new regarding the adaptability of these linked concepts. "The unit of design in New Towns," he maintained, "is no longer each separate lot, street or building; it is a whole community; a co-ordinated entity. This means that the framework of the community and every detail down to the last house and the view from the windows must be conceived, planned and built as a related part of a great setting."[18] From the beginning, Radburn was widely promoted—in school textbooks and in government documents—and even initially considered so successful that it would survive the Great Depression. Architects emulated aspects of the design, typically cul-de-sacs, in their projects.

The FHA, which set the standard for postwar suburban residential development, as well as contemporary designers, seized on Radburn's street design, redefining it as a means to establish homogenized residential islands rather than the dynamic communities Stein and his colleagues imagined.[19] As the years passed, the cul-de-sac eclipsed the integrated components that comprised the Radburn Idea and came to symbolize Radburn to the exclusion of all else. In the process, the cul-de-sac transitioned from being a service road with a primary focus on accommodating the automobile to a play area and a community space where bicyclists, pedestrians, as well as the automobile, now vied for control.

For his part, Stein insisted again and again that open spaces, not just the traffic circulation system, were essential physical and social considerations. "The Garden City Idea and the Radburn Idea both accentuate the importance of open spaces.... Why? ... Breathing ... Beauty ... Recreation." From the regional to the local levels, open green spaces played essential and diverse roles. A distinct natural entity, such as a river basin, could define the region. The interweaving greenbelts separating the towns included "farm, forest & range," allowing agricultural products proximity to markets as well as "protect[ing] water and soil" and leaving "space for future change, growth and redevelopment." At a more localized level "the grouping of houses in relation to each other [would] take the utmost advantage of sun and wind for every residence, and to open up pleasant, spacious and varied views.... [The community architect] will in part be guided by the form and nature of the land, and how its trees and streams and rocks can best be used or preserved." Stein recognized "going places" and "enjoying places" as two complementary aspects of living that required coordination despite their conflicting use of space. "Spaciousness will banish congestion when an orderly relationship is established amongst circulation, buildings, and open spaces." These designs anticipated the large-scale residential developments of the postwar era while reflecting a sophistication that many of these projects lacked. With its focus on encouraging an enhanced community life through design, mixing uses and housing types, clustering housing to reduce infrastructure costs and creating interconnected green spaces, projects like Radburn engaged many of the principles later associated with sustainability, smart growth, green infrastructure, and the new urbanism.[20]

Both the Radburn Idea and the Regional City outlined the conceptual approach for town building initiatives—the former emphasizing civic design and the latter regional planning applications. The Radburn Idea consisted of siting and design recommendations for a new higher density suburb to accommodate leisure and work and to incorporate integrated park and hierarchical street systems. Meanwhile, the Regional City emphasized land use and planning concepts applied from the block and neighborhood levels (where aspects of the Radburn Idea are most evident) to the regional level. With a humanistic focus, the building blocks of the region revolved around the community with educational, cultural, health, and commercial enterprises designed at all scales to define and strengthen social connections.

In this way, communitarian regionalism provided the lens, allowing the designer to view the overall construct of the place as a means to understand local culture, topography, and environmental networks and to guide plans that encouraged community building. Each complete community then was in balance with the surrounding countryside and interconnected, through a network of what MacKaye called townless highways. As Stein described it,

> We need the close community grass root relation that grows up in a limited sized town—But we must have proximity to larger open places and to neighborly centers of culture, education, everyday affairs such as marketing and local associations.... There is a need of planned development and administration on a large enough scale to make possible all the central facilities and the varied opportunities and occupations which only a great city can afford or support. This combination of the "grassroot" community and the Big City is what I have in mind for in my proposal of a Regional City.[21]

In fact, Stein formed his "thinker's network" in the 1920s to conceive, implement, and advocate town building ideas within a regional framework that balanced the built and natural environments.

While a retreat from communitarian regionalism characterized the postwar era, as objective, quantitative assessments gained prominence through the new field of regional science, recently planners and architects have again advocated a more normative regionalism to promote balanced and integrated development of distinctive, diverse, and interconnected communities. Scholars have returned to the early regionalists to address their intellectual legacy to the postmodernist or "new" regionalists.[22] Yet the complex nature of this earlier regionalism—its connections and contributions—is not fully understood. Regionalism as conceived today often considers just a single icon or limited group from this early period, typically Howard, Patrick Geddes, and/or Mumford, failing to fully grasp Stein's contributions. In addressing Stein's Regional City, and how his regional vision compared to and integrated that of his colleagues, a fuller understanding of communitarian regionalism as it relates to the new regionalism is realized.

⁓

Drawing on Ebenezer Howard's Garden City and Clarence Perry's Neighborhood Unit, Stein redefined community in a salient way to accommodate American culture and the automobile. In advocating for new towns as a superlative alternative to urban housing, Stein laid the groundwork for a "social architecture" that continues to resonate among design and development professionals today. To appreciate the significance of Stein's contributions, this book explores his approach to design and community as it evolved throughout his career. The first two chapters examine Stein's professional and personal identities as underlying elements that inform the four themes addressed in this book. Chapter 1 provides context for Stein's engagement with and translation of Howard's Garden City and for his advocacy of these ideas in his projects, service, writings, lectures, and consulting activities throughout his career. It does so by reviewing the concept with a focus on its adoption and evolution in the United States during the first half of the twentieth century. Chapter 2 then introduces Stein from a more personal perspective, exploring his formative years, including the foundations of his work ethic, engagement in learning by doing, community design skills, and commitment to housing affordability.

That Stein had a gift for identifying his colleagues' strengths no doubt helped him to establish the RPAA, the self-styled planning atelier, at the same time that the famed Algonquin Round Table composed of New York's literary elite was meeting just around the corner from his office in midtown Manhattan. Stein fostered this thinkers' network to address critical planning and community building ideas. Chapter 3 reviews Stein's collaborative approach with a specific focus on the formation and initiatives of the RPAA.

Stein adopted the term *investment housing* to reflect homes designed and constructed to flexibly respond to tenants' needs over the life of the community while ensuring a reasonable profit for the owner due to efficiently planned capital costs and, more important, strategic operational outlays. While not public housing designed for the working poor, something that Stein ultimately argued required more significant government subsidy than was available, investment housing through partnerships with the government resulted in a rent accessible to the working class and emerging midlevel white collar office worker.

Chapter 4 explores Stein's contributions as a houser lending consistent support for a government role in order to more effectively engage the private sector while charting his transition to promoting investment housing as a preferable alternative to public housing.

In chapter 5, Stein's interrelated community design is examined. This design strategy reflected sensitivities to connecting private and public realms and creating hierarchical and networked community spaces. The community architect's attention to these connectivities is especially evident in projects like Radburn and Baldwin Hills Village, yet it is also clear in individual and unbuilt projects such as the Pasadena Art Institute. His linkage of floor layout, private yards or terraces, smaller shared garden spaces, community parks, and regional greenbelts attest to this approach and offer new insight into what Stein called the Radburn Idea.

Communitarian regionalism was a central tenet of Stein and his colleagues' town building ideas. The theme behind his postwar concept of the Regional City is most fully described in his unpublished manuscript *Cities to Come*. Here, in this companion to his seminal *Toward New Towns for America*, Stein envisioned the culmination of lessons learned from these projects. Chapter 6 addresses the maturation of his Regional City and town planning ideas, including his contributions in shaping higher education and his efforts to form design and development partnerships among noted architects, engineers, planners, and urban experts.

His ideas manifested in a community design practice that intervened in the landscape to weave together physical and social networks with the goal of creating complete communities that formed complexes of new towns. Chapter 7 synthesizes Stein's postwar engagement in international town planning initiatives with his reexamination of Garden City principles. The final chapter concludes by assessing the community architect's legacy as embodied in significant current planning, design, and housing movements. The seeds of this legacy were sown early in Stein's career. Chapter 1 examines this foundation of Stein's work, the Garden City and its transformation into the Regional City, tracking the evolution of Stein's town building principles.

# 1

---

# THE GARDEN CITY IDEA

Throughout Stein's life, his excitement about the promise of the Garden City radiated from his manuscripts, letters, publications, and lectures and illuminated his housing philosophy. What struck Stein about Ebenezer Howard's proposal was its spirit of cooperation and community, the balance between open spaces and development, and the notion that distinctive planned new towns served as the building blocks of the region. Rechristened the Regional City by Stein and his colleagues in the RPAA, this network of complete communities was achieved by effectively applying planning tools that engaged the expertise and resources of entrepreneurs and the government to create places that integrated living, leisure, and work.

Early in his career through a series of lectures with the first Garden City of Letchworth near London as the exemplar, Stein promoted this "ideal system" for neighborhood preservation, housing reform, traffic congestion mitigation, and park design.[1] For the next forty years, his commitment to the Garden or Regional City remained constant as he designed, developed, and reframed the concept. This commitment was most evident in his formation of the RPAA to refine these ideas; his founding and investment in the development arm of the RPAA, the City Housing Corporation (CHC); his leadership roles promoting statewide regional and housing policy and advocating for these at the federal level; his promotion of these ideas to a broader public through the documentary film *The City*, which premiered at the World's Fair of 1939; his postwar publication of *Toward*

17

*New Towns for America*; and his subsequent consultations around the world to make the message of the Garden City known. The conceptualization, translation, and transition of the Garden City into the Regional City emerges more clearly when examined through the critical junctures of Stein's career. Stein's central role in these broader discussions and initiatives reflect his efforts to highlight and elucidate this vision, which remained a preeminent facet of his life's work.

## The Garden City Becomes the Regional City

Many scholars have documented the translation and evolution in the United States of Ebenezer Howard's Garden City principles as outlined in 1898's *To-morrow, a Peaceful Path to Real Reform*, reissued in 1902 as *Garden Cities of To-morrow*.[2] A British stenographer and inventor from a modest background, Howard envisioned an alternative to the atrocious living and working conditions of the crowded late nineteenth-century industrialized city. His Garden City offered a balance between free enterprise and cooperative commonwealths as much as between the city and the countryside. Essential principles included land reform with a public trust owning all land, local management and self-governance, and a greenbelt to bound and buffer each self-sufficient community beyond which other distinctive Garden Cities existed, separated, but within an easy train commute. Consistent with this spirit of cooperation and community, the town architects, planners, and engineers designed the Garden City as a team, locating housing, shops, schools, parks, and other amenities within easy proximity to each other. While embraced in Great Britain as a new town development concept, it did not catch on in the United States until the 1920s when two very different regional planning groups appropriated this vision to propose radically distinct models for future settlement patterns in New York.

To promote his vision, Howard formed the Garden City Association in 1899, which expanded by 1901 to include many professional men and influential supporters, such as George Cadbury who had financed the development of Bournville near his chocolate factory in Birmingham just six years earlier. W. A. Harvey, first estate architect and planner of Bournville, described Cadbury's motive for developing this model industrial village: "[A]lleviating the evils which arise from the insanitary and insufficient housing accommodation supplied to large numbers of the working classes, and of securing ... the advantages of outdoor

village life, with opportunities for the natural and healthful occupation of culti-
vating the soil."[3] Cadbury also supported a mixture of income groups from the
"factory-worker to the brain-worker" in the same district.

As an architecture student at the École des Beaux-Arts, Stein visited the
model industrial village with his roommate and fellow student Henry Klaber in
1908. He admired Bournville as a pragmatic reflection of Garden City principles
employed to improve the housing conditions of the working class. With the support of progressive businessmen such as Cadbury and W. H. Lever who funded
the development of the model industrial village of Port Sunlight, the association
formed a company in 1903, shortly after the reissuance of Howard's book. This
company developed Unwin and Parker's design for Letchworth. Critical missing
elements included the lack of a cooperative community and land reform necessary to support housing for the working class and an insufficient mixture of land
uses and infrastructure to accommodate self-sufficiency.

With the opening of Letchworth, the promotion of Garden City principles
in a variety of reform and professional publications, and the widespread circulation of Howard's reissued book, leading reformers in New York established
the Garden Cities Association of America in 1906. Felix Adler, founder of the
Ethical Culture Society, which played such a large role in Stein's education and
early career, and Elgin R. L. Gould, president of the City and Suburban Homes
Company, among the earliest to specialize in large-scale limited dividend residential projects in the United States, were among the founders of the organization. Despite ambitious plans to develop Garden Cities in a variety of places,
primarily in the northeastern United States, the organization did not initiate
development of a single Garden City and officially shut down in 1921.[4]

Another civic reformer and philanthropist, Margaret Olivia Sage, launched
the Russell Sage Foundation (Sage Foundation) in 1907, funded with her late
husband's considerable fortune to "improve social and living conditions" across
the country. Based in Manhattan, the Sage Foundation invested one year later
in the planned community of Forest Hills Gardens in Queens with Grosvenor
Atterbury as architect and Frederick Law Olmsted Jr. as town planner. Initially
intended as a limited profit development based on Garden City design and
land use planning principles, by 1920 Forest Hills Gardens was promoted as "a
high-class suburban residential community." While not a Garden City, Forest
Hills Gardens still made quite the impression with its balance of commercial,

residential, and recreational land uses; its "self-contained and garden-like neighborhoods" appealed to residents like Clarence Perry, who lived in the community and worked for many years at the Sage Foundation. In fact, Perry's conception of the neighborhood unit with its centralized school serving also as a community center and with residences defining a cohesive, walkable community owes much to Forest Hills Gardens. In this way, certain elements of the Garden City movement were initially adopted in the United States.[5]

Connecting the Garden City more tangentially to broader planning initiatives, the City Club attracted reformers like Stein and fellow Ethical Culture Society members who sought improved living conditions through the development of decent housing, quality neighborhoods, and new towns. Founded in 1892 as part of the good government movement to fight political corruption and introduce objective and scientific methods into city management, the organization had several thousand members by 1911 when Stein returned to New York City from his studies in Paris.[6] The City Planning Committee of the City Club specifically focused on the emerging profession, including comprehensive zoning, adopted by New York City in 1916, and neighborhood surveys and plans, which Stein drafted for his former community of Chelsea. Despite initiatives such as these, planning practice in the United States in general was embryonic and fragmented.

While the nascent Garden City movement languished in the United States during this time, the association remained active in Great Britain, promoting passage of the Housing and Town Planning Act of 1909. Yet the leadership of the British organization increasingly embraced more mainstream ideas, such as the so-called "garden suburb," that diluted and obscured Howard's more radical socioeconomic message of land reform and cooperative, self-contained communities. Even Unwin, who in 1912 published his seminal *Nothing Gained by Overcrowding!* with the subtitle *How the Garden City Type of Development May Benefit Both Owner and Occupier,* bowed to a more moderate approach when he focused on "garden city design principles" that intended to foster desirable lower-density housing while incorporating efficiencies to maintain affordability.[7] His role as a government official during and after the war continued to focus on promoting these Garden City principles for improved working-class housing communities.

During the interwar era in the United States, the Garden City movement became reenergized primarily due to the efforts of Stein and his colleagues in the

RPAA as well as Thomas Adams through his work on the Regional Plan of New York and Its Environs (RPNY) funded by the Sage Foundation. Adams had done much to advance the Garden City movement in his native Great Britain when he was appointed secretary of the expanded association in 1901 and shortly after development commenced, estate manager at Letchworth. At the same time, his pragmatic approach and promotion of various design elements also evident at Bournville and Port Sunlight diffused the more radical components of Howard's vision. Elected in 1913 to Great Britain's newly formed first professional planning organization, the Town Planning Institute, Adams left for Canada the following year to become town planning advisor to the national government until 1921. By that time, his reputation as an expert on Garden Cities and town planning was well recognized. The following year he relocated to the United States as a visiting lecturer at the Massachusetts Institute of Technology and, upon Charles Dyer Norton's untimely death in 1923, was appointed general director of plans and surveys for the RPNY. Some of the most prominent planners, architects, landscape architects, economists, and social scientists were employed to consult on the RPNY, and work had begun in 1921 to gather the data necessary to assess development challenges and opportunities in the New York City metropolitan region. In his encyclopedic history of American planning, Mel Scott attributes the roots of the RPNY in part to a 1917 conference held by the City Club to address regional cooperation, which attracted representatives from fifty area cities and towns to participate.[8]

With its roots also in the City Club, the membership of the RPAA, formed by Stein in 1923, connected Garden City principles, housing reform, and regionalism together to offer an alternative not only to the dinosaur cities, as Stein called them, but also to the garden suburb. Unlike the typical planner's focus on zoning and managing land subdivision, the RPAA promoted a vision of modern communities that combined a carefully controlled command of open space networks and circulation systems with regional planning and cooperative living for a rapidly modernizing country.

Charles Whitaker, the reformer, architect, and editor who made the new monthly *Journal of the American Institute of Architects* (*JAIA*) a center for exchange regarding innovations in site design, housing, and planning, fostered the connections and provided an initial forum for the writings of Stein and many of his colleagues who played a central role in the RPAA.[9] These colleagues included architect Frederick Ackerman, landscape architect Henry Wright, urban critic Lewis Mumford, and the conservationist Benton MacKaye.

Ackerman, probably the most radical of the group, was a disciple of economist Thorstein Veblen who, like Howard, favored the single tax approach of Henry George to diminish the speculative value of land. Ackerman emphasized a restructuring of the economy through fundamental changes wrought by experts, or "technicians," who would overthrow the current capitalist system and use their expertise to change land policy, and thus urban development, to equitably house the lowest income.[10] His role as chief of housing and town design for the U.S. Shipping Board's Emergency Fleet Corporation during World War I, and his visit to England during that time to assess that country's efforts to address postwar housing needs, reinforced his advocacy of the Garden City as a tool to realize these goals, a tool that included land reform. Wright, also affiliated with the Emergency Fleet Corporation and with Stein's mentor Robert Kohn, who oversaw the federal community building program during its few months of implementation, combined site analysis and design skills with a housing reform sensibility.

Mumford and MacKaye contributed the broader, more theoretical, regional vision. Mumford engaged most notably with the regional ideals of Patrick Geddes, the Scottish biologist and geographer who advocated surveying and assessing areas before planning for them and encouraged a broader conception of the region—culture, climate, topography—to relate individual settlements with their function in daily life. While Mumford was an urbanist, MacKaye, trained as a forester, saw the region in a different though complementary way. Approaching the region with a focus on the rural, MacKaye drew on American pragmatism rather than Mumford's more urban and European foundations. Like his spiritual guide, Henry David Thoreau, MacKaye was intrigued with the relationship between people and the landscape. He called this "human ecology," or the optimization of human "needs and welfare ... in relation to environment."[11] Thus, while a certain harmony with the landscape was important, so too was realizing what it had to offer. A central theme of his seminal book, *The New Exploration*, involved the need to conserve natural resources while strategically extracting and controlling their benefits and accommodating development where appropriate. His proposals for the Appalachian Trail and then the townless highway address these challenges. As such, he introduced critical elements for broader regional thinking among the group. Other RPAA members, such as the economist Stuart Chase, further refined these ideas to include the notion of market regions and transportation efficiencies.

A key component associated with the RPAA's reimagining of the Garden City involved Perry's neighborhood unit, which he first introduced at a national sociological conference in 1923 and fully articulated in the RPNY volume entitled—*Neighborhood and Community Planning*. While never an official member of the RPAA, Perry did participate in several key meetings that included discussions of the desirable elements of the neighborhood unit to foster community connections. Perry viewed the neighborhood primarily as a social unit with the school forming its physical and civic center shaped by the number of students that could be accommodated, the density of housing, and the walking distance to the school. His proposal for self-contained neighborhoods unified around a school and bounded by major streets also included an element of residential homogeneity, which RPAA members sought to diversify.[12]

Stein tied these concepts together, connecting site planning ideas under the rubric of Perry's neighborhood unit to new towns consisting of superblocks and linked by townless highways and interconnected open spaces to form the Regional City. As editor of Whitaker's community planning section of the *JAIA*, Stein directed the group's examination of these ideas.[13] As the founder and informal sponsor of the RPAA, Stein often hosted their meetings in his Central Park apartment or nearby office, and he helped fund a number of their initiatives. In this way, he did much to bridge these distinctive and complementary philosophies.

While representing a variety of professions, the RPAA membership shared certain key viewpoints. They believed that through enlightened, collective action a distinct type of urban form could be developed in the middle ground between the industrial cities and the remote rural hamlets, founded on the attributes unique to each place and the opportunities afforded through new technologies. The essential issue then involved understanding and effectively utilizing environmental resources to shape the region consistent with a more fully realized community life. Their new American town reconnected people to place and to the land and was planned with reference to location, design, and function, incorporating the technological innovations of the new century. This small group, particularly Stein, Wright, Mumford, and MacKaye, advocated a communitarian regionalism that reflected and reinforced the "local character" of both the human and natural systems associated with the place to facilitate cooperation and community building. Stein argued that the community architect additionally needed to know, "How big must a city be to best do its work for human welfare and happiness (good living) and also how to develop it so as to locate home as close as practical to work and all the essentials for profitable leisure and human development." While the group initially used the term *Garden City*, they increasingly referred to the "Regional City" as their proposal for interconnected new towns.[14]

Stein also sought a way to incorporate the RPAA's ideas into policy. As chair of the New York Housing and Regional Planning Commission (HRPC) from 1923 to 1926, he not only advocated for housing reform, but housing reform from a regional perspective and with government support. Because of this holistic approach, he believed that nothing less than a state plan was needed to guide efficient decentralization of the largest metropolitan populations into a healthful arrangement of Regional Cities. Gathering critical information on the geography, environment, climate, topography, and culture offered a starting point with the resulting report intended to guide a board of experts in its preparation of a state plan.

The report was overseen by Stein who engaged MacKaye to conduct background studies and then encouraged Wright, in his capacity as planning advisor to the HRPC, to connect key concepts, articulated in part through the numerous diagrams he drafted. Given the scale of MacKaye's proposal for the Appalachian Trail, which connected individual, cohesive villages across a significant geographic feature that crossed several states, it is no surprise that Stein asked MacKaye to gather and assess statewide data. As they embarked on the report, Stein reflected, "In regional planning we must consider—first, nature's resources; second, what man has done with nature's resources, and then what man can do to make more efficient use of nature's resources." The International Garden Cities and Town Planning Federation's 1925 conference in New York City offered a significant opportunity for the RPAA membership to present their vision of communitarian regionalism realized as a statewide plan. While the program named a considerable number of national organizations responsible for coordinating the conference, the HRPC, which Stein chaired, was the only group specifically acknowledged as a conference organizer that did not have a national presence. In addition to the informal weekend coordinated by the RPAA membership, the CHC hosted a conference dinner and showcased its first project, Sunnyside Gardens. As a member of the Executive Committee of this international organization, Stein played a key role in coordinating these efforts to ensure that the RPAA's ideas were prominently featured. Of course, the RPNY was prominently featured as well with Frederic A. Delano, chairman of the Committee on the Regional Plan serving as the U.S. vice president to the federation.[15]

Speaking at the conference, Stein outlined the goal of state planning to capitalize on improvements in road design and power distribution and more effectively survey the landscape to properly locate Garden Cities and their associated greenbelts. Adams acknowledged similar motivations channeling the ongoing efforts on the RPNY, including concerns about congestion and densification and the need for "regional treatments of urban problems." Yet the solution involved "a more natural and less cramped system of living" in the metropolitan area by accommodating new centers of industry and growth dispersed around the region, though not necessarily in the form of Garden Cities.[16] Thus seven years before Mumford and Adams's more celebrated debate on the regional vision of the RPAA versus the RPNY in *The New Republic*, Stein and Adams outlined the fundamental differences.

In their writings and advocacy then, the RPAA explicitly connected, in a way that the RPNY did not, the neighborhood unit, Regional or Garden City, and a statewide plan, rather than targeting a single metropolitan region, albeit a significant one. In many ways, the RPAA vision was more focused on each essential idea building on the next to create their ambitious vision for a state with a balanced network of Regional Cities. Meanwhile, across the ten volumes of the RPNY that were published beginning in 1929, the motivating focus was on how to more effectively serve New York City and accommodate future populations by determining the location of growth centers based on current development patterns and targeting infrastructure improvements to accommodate those growth centers. As Mumford argued in his 1932 denigration of the RPNY, political expediency informed the metropolitan plan rather than a fundamental reimagining of the region to improve quality of life throughout the state.[17] Fundamentally then, the two organizations differed in the significance the Garden City played in their missions.

In a series of articles designed to coincide with the International Conference and issued just one month later in May 1925, Mumford explained, "The regionalist attempts to plan such an area so that all its sites and resources, from forest to city, from highland to water level may be soundly developed, and so that the population will be distributed so as to utilize, rather than to nullify or destroy, its natural advantages. It sees people, industry and the land as a single unit." At the core of this special issue of the *Survey Graphic* was Howard's Garden City. Upon reading the series of articles, Howard wrote Stein, "I read almost every word in Survey Graphic—and the more I read the more I was impressed with the grasp of the subject shown, by none of the authors more than yourself [Stein] and Mumford." This critical endorsement of their reformulation of the Garden City into the Regional City, formally presented at the International Conference and personally vindicated by the founder of the Garden City movement, activated Stein and his colleagues to embark on further promoting and developing their ideas.[18]

## The Endurance of the Regional City

Under Stein's leadership, the RPAA adapted the survey methods of Geddes to design distinct, complete communities and regions in balance with nature. In so doing, they assessed and adjusted their approach in response to residents' needs. The result of these efforts, begun with the development of Sunnyside in 1923, was the Radburn Idea, which came to fruition beginning in 1927–1928 with the design and development of the proposed new town within commuting distance of New York City among the farmlands of Bergen County, New Jersey. The Radburn Idea represented the RPAA's, and especially Stein's, transformation of Howard's and Perry's proposals, which Stein then tied to the Regional City. Although the RPAA disbanded in 1933 and the CHC declared bankruptcy just two years later, Stein and his colleagues kept their ideals alive through individual and shared projects, publications, lectures, and advocacy. The Regional City endured in the postwar era as Stein reestablished the RPAA as a national network of notable planners and designers devoted to regionalism and as he published and promoted the outcome of his decades of practice as a community architect for a national and international audience.

At Radburn, the neighborhood unit became a key building block of the RPAA's Regional City with the school serving as a unifying social element.

Limited dividend development to allow greater affordability and cooperative organization resonated with the memberships' brand of Garden City community building. A mixture of housing types and tenures accommodated greater resident diversity. Rather than seeking reduced densities, clustered design allowed the CHC to reduce infrastructure costs, introducing a level of affordability into the design while also incorporating communal open spaces to further facilitate community building.

Tying the Radburn Idea to their continuing advocacy for communitarian regionalism resulted in efforts by the RPAA to connect with allied groups such as the Southern Regionalists, consisting primarily of academics informally led by sociologist Howard W. Odum. While they shared an affiliation with Geddes's call to envision the region more broadly based on life-work-folk, the Southern Regionalists' goal lay in a somewhat different direction—to document the distinct culture of the South, including its arts, people, topography, and climate and to analyze and safeguard these elements. Mumford clearly aligned his thinking with Odum but never attempted the close data collection and analysis that the University of North Carolina professor employed to understand and document the region. In this respect, Odum more closely approximated MacKaye's approach to regionalism. Further, while Odum primarily focused on rural areas, particularly rural poverty, and safeguarding and celebrating the culture of the South, the RPAA incorporated an urban focus—advocating decentralization into new towns—with an emphasis on professional expertise and new technologies to achieve this goal.[19]

In particular, the short-lived Greenbelt Town program of the New Deal, as administered through the Resettlement Administration came the closest to emulating their ideal of the Garden City in America. Construction began in the summer of 1935 and continued until 1938. In that short time, the program sponsored the design of four and the development of three new towns. The program's primary goals involved relocating working-class residents from the congested substandard housing of the city into new communities outside major cities with ample open space, a mixture of uses to accommodate working and living, a population of limited size, and a surrounding greenbelt to define the growth boundary and buffer residents from adjacent development. The program materials specifically referenced the Radburn Idea as a guiding principle.

Many former RPAA members and colleagues worked on the towns, including Stein as program consultant; Wright; Ralph Eberlin, engineer at Radburn; and fellow housing advocate Catherine Bauer. Mumford had introduced Bauer to the membership of the RPAA toward the end of 1930, and she, fresh from a tour of housing projects and programs in Europe, engaged eagerly in the intellectual discussions and advocacy of the group. She worked as the organization's executive secretary from 1931 to 1933 and earned an income as an assistant to Stein conducting housing research from 1932 to 1934. Published in 1934, her landmark book *Modern Housing* documented government housing programs and design in Europe. She went on to play a critical national role as housing advocate, policymaker, and later, administrator during the 1930s and early 1940s.

Toward the end of the decade, Stein decided to promote the RPAA's vision to a broader audience through production of a documentary entitled *The City*, depicting an alternative to urban life featuring Radburn and the Greenbelt Towns, particularly Greenbelt, Maryland, which he felt most closely emulated the development patterns, mixture of uses, and cooperative spirit of community that made them a superior choice. Stein secured funding from the Carnegie Foundation, formed a nonprofit to advise on making the film that included colleagues Kohn and Ackerman, engaged the leading social documentary filmmaker of the day, Pare Lorentz, and persuaded Mumford to assist in drafting the narrative, garnering support from the American Institute of Planners to have the film premiere at the World's Fair in New York City in 1939.

Lyrically filmed by Ralph Steiner and Willard Van Dyke, with Aaron Copeland supplying the orchestration, and a voiceover contrasting the harmonious family life possible in these new communities with the cacophony, pollution, and stress of the metropolis, *The City* directly urges the viewer to demand a better way of life, a modern way of life that ensures clean industry nestled in open countryside but conveniently linked to nearby homes and commercial districts with all the amenities to secure healthful living. The image of the "green city" reverberates throughout the final passages of the film. The narrator intones, "Around the town a belt of public land preserves its shape forever and keeps the earth for the children's use. It's time to bring green nature back into the heart of Every City." And later, "Green cities designed for living, the chance to live on friendly terms with nature with other men, feeling the life flame up again within us." As Howard Gillette maintains in his review of the film as a planning artifact, the filmmakers' goal was no less than "to reorder existing urban forms out of the congested central cities into a regional framework of small urban nodes, each tied together by new forms of transportation and communication." *The City* then reflects the endurance of the modern Garden City as envisioned by the RPAA and particularly Stein during this interwar era.[20]

After the demise of the RPAA in 1933, the federal government became more directly engaged in housing and new town development, and emerging planning professionals presented a broader national network of potential colleagues. Stein continued to formulate his conception of the Regional City during World War II and believed that the postwar era would present a renewed opportunity to advocate for new towns. Following the war, new educational programs as well as opportunities and models overseas offered to Stein's eyes a critical role for a revived RPAA.

In October 1948 Stein had recently returned from the late Raymond Unwin's home, Wyldes, where he had completed the articles that were to become his book, *Toward New Towns for America*. Energized by the opportunity to share his projects, which he viewed in various degrees as the realization of the Radburn Idea and exemplars for what he hoped represented a new era of new town development not just in the United States but abroad, Stein enthusiastically seized on the fiftieth anniversary of the publication of Howard's iconic book, the twenty-fifth anniversary of the founding of the RPAA, and the occasion of the national planning conference, hosted in New York City, to relaunch the RPAA by bringing its former core membership as well as new members together. While he used the Garden City as a rallying cry, and a party in his penthouse apartment overlooking Central Park to attract attendees, the broader planning picture across the United States overwhelmingly tilted toward economic expansion and urban redevelopment with little consideration for the new town model that Stein promoted.

In fact, several of his colleagues advised for either a more focused approach or for no revival of the organization at all. Mumford noted that the RPAA had done much during the 1920s and early 1930s to advocate for regionalism, new towns, and housing availability and affordability, but the federal government had not done enough to realize their goals, and at this point, their good work was all but forgotten. Stein's mentor Kohn was even more direct, "Maybe I am all wrong but the good old U.S.A. seems to be going in quite another direction nowadays." Despite these concerns, the group voted to move forward, and over the next four years, the organization explored regionalism through the lens of international planning, population redistribution, and human ecology. Their adopted mission ultimately was "to discuss, study and make recommendations for the design, development and operation of regions including urban, rural and wilderness areas." If indeed planning practice was moving in new directions, Stein considered them opportunities to reintroduce the Regional City.[21]

Rechristened the Regional Development Council of America (RDCA), the organization embraced advocacy, engaging more directly and actively with federal and regional governments. In addition, the larger membership of planners working throughout the United States represented Stein's ambitious goal of creating a national syndicate of new town and regionalist planners, engineers, and designers. The organization's international perspective was reinforced by several colleagues embracing international consulting as well as momentum for new town planning and development overseas.

Stein's companion to *Toward New Towns for America*, optimistically entitled *Cities to Come*, reflected the maturation of his Regional City ideas, combined with a much more detailed outline of the mixture of land uses necessary to effectively accommodate people in these alternatives to the rapidly developing suburbs. Connecting humanism to design and interrelating the built environment and open spaces from the block level to the region, Stein energetically pursued all possibilities to promote the Regional City as the answer to a host of postwar planning issues. For instance, he advocated that the new housing act proposed in 1949 require complete communities, not simply urban redevelopment and/or inexpensive government housing, to ensure that all Americans enjoy an improved quality of life. When the federal government sought to divest itself of the Greenbelt Towns, he championed their cooperative ownership to maintain affordability, the endurance of their master plans, and their role as models of community building. The immediate postwar concerns with dispersing concentrated development, particularly in the nation's capital, due to concerns about vulnerability from nuclear attack called for scattered new towns.

For Stein, an established public sector role meant new opportunities for public-private partnerships. Such partnerships could affect broader changes across the country by assembling interdisciplinary teams to propose design solutions for a range of income groups. To this end, he successfully engaged planners who were doing important work in rapidly growing regions in the United States, advocating for a coordinated approach to planning along river regions and conducting new town work in India and other countries. In fact, the ideas outlined in *Toward New Towns for America* resonated more internationally as the Radburn Idea found adherents in places as diverse as Sweden and Israel. Stein's postwar advocacy took on a different tenor as he consulted overseas, lobbied on Capitol Hill, and recommended a universal planning pedagogy, which embraced a diverse range of social sciences as much as design. Stein continued to promote an interdisciplinary humanistic approach to creating complete communities, even as planning was undergoing a paradigm shift toward a logical positivist approach that focused on economic development, regional science, transportation planning, and environmental engineering; and even as the maturation of the planning profession meant a disconnect from the allied fields of architecture and landscape architecture, which both increasingly focused on design. Throughout, Stein saw the Regional City of networked new towns as a pragmatic solution to a range of interconnected urban, suburban, and rural challenges. His faith in its flexibility to respond to diverse circumstances both in the United States and abroad was unwavering, only ceasing when frailty, ill health, and old age overcame him. His final promotion of the new town as a planning solution occurred as Congress considered including new towns as a component of housing legislation in the mid-1960s.

With normative regionalism, smart growth, sustainability, green infrastructure, and new urbanism revisiting these ideas, the time is ripe for an examination of Stein's collaborations, advocacy, and projects. It is the arc of Stein's career that provides a context to better understand the impact and endurance of the Regional City. Moreover, the key themes embodied in Stein's contributions build on each other and follow a rough chronology through his life. But how did these themes come to dominate and define his work? We can begin to find the answer in Stein's education and architectural training, which formed the foundation for his later projects. For in the end, while his contributions are seen in the modern era of professional practice, it was his Progressive Era education and sensibilities that uniquely shaped his approach.

# 2

---

## EARLY YEARS AND
## ARCHITECTURAL TRAINING

Born in Rochester, New York, on June 19, 1882, into a loving and up-
wardly mobile Jewish family, Clarence Samuel Stein was the third child of Rose
Rosenblatt and Leo Stein behind older brother William and sister Clara, followed
by younger brother Herbert, and sisters Gertrude and Lillie. His birth must have
been an occasion of special joy following the acute grief of his family over the
death in May of his sixteen-month-old sister Clara. In fact, his mother's nickname
for him was "Clare" an abbreviation of Clarence that also referred to his sister.

In the 1880s, Rochester, located on the Erie Canal, was a dynamic city supportive of the arts and civic reform with a rapidly expanding and diversifying
industrial base. Frederick Law Olmsted won a bid to design a park system for
the city in 1888. While the Stein family initially lived in a new northern suburb
of the city, by the time Clarence was two, they had moved near the downtown to
90 South Union Street. When the Stein Manufacturing Company consolidated
with two other firms in 1890 to form the National Casket Company, the Stein
family moved to the Chelsea district in New York City. During this time, the
neighborhood was undergoing a transition from a wealthy and middle-income,
lower-density neighborhood into a high-density, lower-income immigrant community. With the move, Leo Stein became "second vice president" and assumed
management of the New Jersey casket manufacturing facility.[1]

Both of Stein's parents had strong ties to New York City. His fraternal grandfather and namesake, Samuel Stein, a German immigrant cabinetmaker, worked in the city before moving the family to Rochester, where he and Leo Stein opened a casket-making business, the Stein Manufacturing Company, in 1872. His mother Rose grew up in New York City in a German Jewish family and was an early member of Felix Adler's Ethical Culture Society. The movement attracted primarily Jewish intellectuals in major cities of the East and Midwest, including Philadelphia, Chicago, and St. Louis. The society emerged at a time when the majority of the Jewish community in New York City had a German background and Reform Judaism predominated. In 1878, two years after founding the society, Adler opened a kindergarten, with the Workingman's School in Chelsea following in 1880. Rose Stein hosted Adler when he visited the Rochester group of the society and, upon returning to New York City, became involved with the school he had established for children of the working class, enrolling her own children in the institution. A historian later noted the significance of the schools—they "complemented the Society, making Ethical Culture a place for young and old, for Sunday and weekday, for social service and personal growth." The society formed a critical part of Stein's life, from his education in the classroom to his involvement in urban reform initiatives and clubs to a network of friends, colleagues, and mentors who supported his architectural practice.[2]

## The Ethical Culture Society and Growing Up in New York City

In 1890, New York City's population stood at 1,515,301. That year, Jacob Riis published his influential book *How the Other Half Lives* documenting in words and photographs the wretched living conditions in the tenements he estimated at 37,316 buildings. With the establishment of the elevated train line in the 1870s, Chelsea had already undergone significant commercial development, which rapidly increased as the garment industry grew just north of the area. This was the city of Clarence Stein's childhood, a teeming, multicultural industrial powerhouse that offered the worst and best of urban life—the slums, overcrowding, noise, and congestion mixing with a diverse population, dramatic skyline, and cultural riches.

Stein grew up within the progressive intellectual Jewish society of New York City. As the family quickly prospered, they moved to a series of increasingly affluent newly opened residential neighborhoods on the Upper West Side.[3] From his father and grandfather, Stein learned about the craft and art of cabinetmaking—an essential skill for a casket maker. From his mother, Stein gained his social consciousness and an appreciation of art and music. John Lovejoy Elliott, one of Stein's most important teachers at the Workingman's School, involved him in a variety of clubs and activities, broadening his progressive reform sensibilities and introducing him to avenues to realize his goals.

The president of his class at Cornell and a recent graduate of a doctoral program in Economics and Philosophy at Halle, Germany, Elliott joined the Workingman's School in the fall of 1894. He moved into the Chelsea district to investigate the sweatshops and within a year, opened the Hudson Guild Settlement House, which grew into a number of bureaus, clubs, and agencies to support lower-income residents. Here under Elliott's tutelage Stein gained a sensitivity to the deleterious impacts of the tenements, to the vibrancy of urban neighborhoods with their diverse land uses and people, and to urban reform politics.

When the family moved to a brownstone facing Morningside Park on the Upper West Side, Stein continued to attend the Ethical Culture School in the Chelsea neighborhood. A snapshot book he and his brother Herbert put together in 1897 reflects his growing interest in municipal art. Documenting statues and monuments in Central Park and City Hall Park and stately buildings such as Temple Emanuel, St. Luke's Hospital on University Heights, the Metropolitan Museum of Art, and the new library at Columbia University, the booklet also included "landscapes" and "farming views"—images from Niagara Falls and the Catskills where Clarence and his brother Herbert attended summer camp. By 1899, the brothers traveled a greater distance to Center Lovell, Maine, to partake in the Hudson Guild summer camp. Here, they swam and fished in Kezar Lake, extolling the view in the distance of New Hampshire's White Mountains. They reported back to their father, "The people who spend the summer here almost without an exception artists, teachers or musicians. Just the class of people Mamma would like to meet, a good many of them. All in all it is an ideal place for the summer."[4]

These summers in upstate New York and Maine, may have exposed Stein to the Arts and Crafts movement; certainly his grandfather's cabinetmaking did so.[5] At the time, the social and aesthetic ideals of the reformer William Morris as realized in the Arts and Crafts movement were gaining traction in the United

States.[6] The movement reacted against the industrial machine, which advocates believed had exacted a terrible toll on workers both in the factory and in nearby crowded and unhealthy neighborhoods and resulted in the mass-production of shoddy products. Their solution embraced the return of craftsmanship—a stronger relationship between worker and product—and a closer connection with the land untouched by the negative effects of industrialization. These ideals appealed to the young Stein.

At the age of seventeen, Stein began to think of college. Yet his intensive preparations and a bout of appendicitis interrupted his efforts. In October 1900, Elliott wrote his mother to ask whether Stein could stay with her or family friends in New Mexico. Elliott explained, "He worked too hard last year preparing for college and broke down. Had nerves and appendicitis. Now, the doctor says that he must get out of town where it will be quiet." Yet in the end, the Steins sent Clarence to a family friend's farm in Jacksonville, Florida, for several months to recuperate.[7]

Upon his return to New York City, Stein resumed his work at the Hudson Guild Settlement House. He considered himself more a member of the Ethical Culture Society than an adherent of any organized religion. In fact, members of the society became lifelong friends, colleagues in architectural practice, and provided access to some of his most important early architectural commissions. For two years, he joined his brothers Herbert and Will working with his father at the National Casket Company and learning an appreciation for design, craftsmanship, and materials as well as management. In 1903, Leo Stein became first vice president of the firm.[8] Clarence Stein meanwhile decided the time had come to pursue an advanced education. His father supported his decision.

Shortly thereafter, in the summer of 1903, an opportunity arose for Stein to accompany his father and a family friend to Europe. On their three-month trip, they visited Italy, Switzerland, Germany, Holland, France, and England. While Stein took numerous pictures of classical sites and monuments, modest village squares and guild structures of the medieval era also appealed to him. He was particularly taken with Paris, though the amount of time spent there was the most limited. In his diary he passionately enthused about the city's charms:

> It has not made merely things, many things, of beauty, jewelry, furniture, pictures, statues, buildings—it has made itself a thing of beauty. I do not mean picturesqueness, such as time and nature have given to Florence or the remains of an ancient

beauty which lies partially in its age as at Rome.—No it is an artificial beauty, a modern beauty. It tells what man, man of today, can do to replace nature, not in natures way but in his own.[9]

Within two years, the city lured him back to study its "modern beauty."

Arriving home in early September 1903, Stein resumed his club work with a focus on neighborhood conditions and municipal improvement. In March 1904, he, his two brothers, and their friends who lived on the Upper West Side and shared interests in progressive reform through their connections with the society formed the Young Men's Municipal Club. They included Eugene Henry Klaber, who later joined Stein at the École des Beaux Arts; Julius Henry Cohen, who created the legal framework for the Port of New York Authority; and Alexander Bing, who partnered with him on some of his most important projects. With the goal to bring together those "who aim to study and improve municipal conditions," the roughly twenty young men pledged to examine municipal ownership, forms of municipal government, and "the city beautiful." Regarding the latter, Stein clarified, "what the Municipal Arts Society of New York is doing." Inspired in part by the Columbia Exposition in Chicago and the desire to promote public art in public spaces and buildings, New York City's Municipal Arts Society was established in 1893 and reorganized and incorporated in 1898. But it really secured its distinctive voice separate from the other art and architecture societies in the city by the early 1900s when it broadened its focus to address municipal improvement as reflected in the City Beautiful movement.[10]

To better understand the lower income immigrant areas of the city, Stein took walks and documented what he saw. While empathetic to the living conditions in these tenement neighborhoods, he clearly saw himself as separate from the community's orthodox Jewish culture. Following a walk through Little Italy, the Jewish district, and the Bowery in July 1904, with his father and brother Herbert, the young Stein wrote a letter to his mother respectfully recording what he observed, though clearly from the perspective of an outsider:

> We passed through streets inhabited by Jews. There were Jews of every age. There were old men in their Sabbath Costumes, long coats and high hats some; most of them bearded.... We saw two or three temples. Through the windows of one, a second-story room on one of the business streets, we could see the old rabbi facing a small congregation of old men, all hatted and all seated and moving backwards and forwards, seemingly as they repeated some prayer or catechism.

His notes on the walk also reflect his sensitivity to urban conditions and his awareness of the benefits of community facilities: "In most [streets] are rows of tall tenements. And here are the children, watched over some of them by their mothers.... What a place ... to grow up in! But there are rays of light even in this darkness. One is the outdoor gymnasium and playgrounds in Hamilton Fish Park. Another is, or will be before long, the summer gymnasium and playrooms which will be open in the splendid school buildings."[11] Thus he was already documenting communities to better understand them, particularly the neighborhood amenities that supported quality of life and enhanced community building.

During this time, he enrolled in design and furniture making courses at Columbia University. Yet within a year, Stein decided to move on. At the suggestion of a family friend and a leader in the society, architect Robert Kohn, he went to Paris in the summer of 1905 to prepare for entering the École des Beaux Arts with the objective of studying interior design. A graduate of the École and prominent New York City architect, Kohn entered into architectural practice with Stein in the early 1920s and later headed the New Deal federal housing program.

In the early twentieth century, the École offered a strong tradition of architectural education with a focus on fostering excellence in design and drafting. At the École, Stein quickly shifted his focus to the more comprehensive study of architecture. While Stein chose well in deciding to go to the prestigious architecture school, he faced significant obstacles before being admitted for entry. The majority of Americans seeking entrance into the program had completed high school and even had some college preparation in architecture; Stein lacked this background. Further the school admitted only a small number of foreigners. In addition to learning French, he needed to fill in these gaps while preparing for the entrance exams in drawing, mathematics, descriptive geometry, history, and architectural design.[12] Stein's tenacity served him well here. His formal training in architecture was about to begin.

## The École des Beaux-Arts

Stein's life was transformed in Paris. He quickly became enamored with its broad boulevards; medieval quarters; crowded, vibrant neighborhoods; great and small parks; museums; and rich urban life (see figure 2.1). And so, the city itself contributed to his development as an architect. Further, Paris became a

FIGURE 2.1 Picture of Stein from his days at the École des Beaux-Arts—a museum membership card circa 1907. Box 27, Clarence S. Stein Papers, #3600, Division of Rare and Manuscript Collections, Cornell University Library (CSP/CUL).

launching ground for trips to other parts of Europe. Support from his family, particularly the funding to pay for his lodging, instruction, and extensive travels, made it possible for Stein to afford an advanced education. Over the next six years, he augmented his preparation for and training at the École with travels in England, France, Italy, Austria, and Spain. These experiences contributed to his growing interest in site, park, and city layout. Meanwhile, his classical, formal architecture education at the École equipped him with design skills and an appreciation and understanding of form.[13]

Shortly after arriving on July 1, 1905, Stein settled in the Latin Quarter, home to the Sorbonne and thus traditionally an area of students, artists, and academics. Though disappointed over having just missed the entrance exams, he began to more fully explore his surroundings, praising the ease with which cultural institutions, squares, and parks were woven into the urban fabric so close to his lodgings:

> The hotel is well situated, within two blocks of the École—I wonder if it will ever be my school—and the École is just across the narrow Seine from the Louvre.

Then behind, about two streets away, is the Boulevard St. Germain, where one may eat at innumerable places, and near which one may buy innumerable things. Then the Luxemburg Gallery and the delightful gardens of the same name—I like to go there evenings and sit under the big trees. And the Luxemburg is near the Pantheon, as the Louvre is near the Garden of the Tuileries, which leads one to the Place de la Concorde and so on—an endless chain of beauties all linked together by great avenues of trees.[14]

In excitedly describing these early impressions, he was already moving away from his interest in interiors to the study of architecture and urban design.

Though he admired the vitality of street life and mixture of uses with three to four stories of apartments typically above the cafes and shops, he found the facades and overall effect of buildings constructed to the property line monotonous.[15] Less than ten years earlier, a committee of architects had been appointed under the new Prefect of the Seine to review the city's building regulations with the goal of introducing flexible controls to accommodate a more varied and picturesque streetscape. Height restrictions were also relaxed, provided the buildings were set back at the higher floors. Those who participated in making the changes, many of them architects, were motivated to create a distinctly modern urban design aesthetic. Approved in October 1899, these new regulations were not implemented until August 1902. By the time of Stein's arrival, a period of intensive development had resulted in quite a number of apartments being constructed under these new regulations. Yet they did not meet the designers' expectations, resulting in buildings of taller, but consistent height that many believed did more to obscure picturesque views than beautify the structures themselves.[16] The parks were another matter. Large and small, scattered throughout the city and the surrounding countryside, they offered repose for rich and poor alike often on lands and gardens formerly reserved for the enjoyment of the wealthy alone. Stein praised these well-used refuges from the urban environment.

In an early letter home to his parents, he remarked on the intensity and strangeness of the city but noted that he had begun to grow accustomed to it, probably in part due to the large number of Americans in the district. Stein attended the school when its reputation was at its peak. In describing the prestigious architectural school to his family, he noted the dichotomy between its design and the instructional focus of the institution:

The school is very insistent in the examples it shows, upon the classic—the antique and the Italian Renaissance that in a sense forms a part of the classic. But the buildings themselves have nothing of classical regularity in their arrangement. They seem to have happened rather than to have been arranged. To a number of old private houses have been added new buildings from time to time. The whole is very picturesque.[17]

Though the modernist movement was certainly underway in Europe, the École continued in its long tradition of emphasizing the classical orders and grand design problems. Consistent with this mind-set, Stein praised the municipal art movement occurring in the United States—"City after city is working out schemes for the beautifying of their public places." Still he did not support simply the "rehashing of old work" noting that people "are going to require something different." To achieve that "something different," the architecture profession called on those with the skills to apply the qualities of the old "with the purpose not of copying it" but making it distinctively their own.[18] In this reasoning, Stein was consistent with fellow American students who attended the school at this time "in his effort to find a means of architectural expression consonant with traditional theories of composition and design while at the same time suited to modern needs."[19]

Armed with letters of introduction, he searched for an atelier so that he could enroll at the École as an aspirant and begin preparing for the challenging entrance exams. As an aspirant, he received all the benefits of being a student. The ateliers had a long tradition as an integral component of architectural instruction at the École. While the school was responsible for the lectures, design assignments (programs), and review of the final projects (*concours*), the instruction took place in the atelier. Each atelier was a private school of architecture connected to the École and affiliated with a particular patron—a master architect responsible for teaching the thirty to eighty students whom he had accepted into his studio. The students got their programs at the École but did the work in the atelier. The patron visited the atelier two to three times a week to provide individual critiques of his students' work. Two critical themes typically informed his instruction: "The importance of the plan, and the importance of a vague quality often called 'character.' ... A building with character was one that fulfilled its purpose."[20]

In the hierarchical studio system, the newer students of the École (*nouveaux*) assisted and learned from the advanced ones (*anciens*).[21] This collaborative approach and strong identity with a particular atelier and master made choosing one that much more important. Stein called this approach "mutual assistance," because he considered it similar to the concept of mutual aid he had been exposed to through the Ethical Culture Society. This collaborative work environment informed his architectural practice throughout his career.

Within a month of his arrival, Stein was providing some drawing assistance for an advanced student named Figarol, studying French, and taking a life-drawing sketch class. He also joined a preparatory atelier in the Latin Quarter to prepare for the entrance exams that December, though he clearly was not optimistic about passing them. The culture and sense of place in the district was a critical consideration in his decision, though the hotel, and later the apartment he lived in, along the Rue Jacob lacked services and conveniences that he was accustomed to in New York. In addition to offering the advantage of being able to stay in the Latin Quarter near the École, choosing the atelier of Eugene Chifflot also had the appeal of more American students. The programs that he had received weekly he now received as *equisse*, the twelve-hour design problems that mimicked the circumstances of the most difficult part of the entrance exam, which assessed architectural skills.[22]

Like most aspirants with his level of education and training, he did not pass the exam on his first try that December. These preparations though heightened his expertise in architectural design, including "first a knowledge of motives, of different forms that have been and can be used for design; second, the ability of thinking, reasoning; third, taste—the ability of choosing the best among the many motives one has in mind.... My work here has given me a much broader as well as a more exact knowledge." Of these three, architectural reasoning represented the most critical skill, one that he felt distinguished education at the École from other architecture schools. Feeling the need to justify his parents' financial support of him until he could take the exams again six months later, he clarified that the jury upon reviewing his design marked it as "plan unfinished" because he did not work quickly enough. This decision placed him among a pool of aspirants who might have passed had they been given more time. With more training, he argued, he would be better prepared to complete the architecture design exam within the time allotted. "I do not myself in any way see the results of the examination as a criterion of my ability." His father agreed, pledging support until Stein had "all the preparation [he] needed."[23]

At the beginning of 1906, Stein made a critical change, joining the slightly more expensive atelier run by Gustave Umbdenstock, an architect from Alsace-Lorraine who had a number of American students, many from the Midwest. While Stein hesitated joining this new atelier due to the forceful personality of the patron whom he feared would "prevent your individual growth," he appreciated Umbdenstock's creative, independent, and "up-to-date" ideas and his ability to express them in his drawings.[24]

After a bit of melancholy that first spring in Paris, Stein's mood brightened considerably upon hearing that a good friend of his from the Ethical Culture School, Henry Klaber, had confirmed his plans to study architecture in Paris. As fellow students, roommates, and traveling companions, their friendship deepened and lasted a lifetime.[25] The rigors of Stein's preparations for the exams and his later studies at the École were lightened by trips into the French countryside to nearby medieval villages, such as Chantilly and St. Denis, and nights at the theater or opera, often accompanied by Klaber.

When he again failed the exam in June 1906—due, he believed, to his inadequate draftsmanship—he decided it was time for a break. That break came in the form of a visit from Adler and Elliott. Their visit encouraged his continuing work toward entrance in the École and offered him a fresh appreciation of the city and surrounding sites. In addition, that summer he and Henry traveled for a month taking in the walled cities of France and the work of Viollet-le-Duc, whom Stein praised: "He studied the architecture and the life of the Middle Ages with such thoroughness—that he could not only copy their work with accuracy, but could build in their spirit, things they had never constructed." Stein considered such license a reflection of Viollet's mastery of the historical material.[26]

His education in Umbdenstock's atelier continued with mathematics, architectural research, and at least two architectural programs, critiqued by the patron, each week. The following summer brought the arrival of more friends from New York City. Recently graduated from the architecture program at Columbia, Ely Jacques Kahn sought entrance to the École. Lee Simonson, whom Stein knew from his connections to the Ethical Culture Society, arrived in Paris shortly thereafter to study painting at the École. Both rose to prominent positions in their fields, Kahn as an architect and educator, and Simonson as a theater and set designer.

Stein and Kahn were the only aspirants in their circle of friends to pass the exam in December 1907. Initially, Stein was certain that he had again failed the twelve-hour architecture portion. "I was too careful, and therefore did not work as quickly or as freely as under ordinary conditions." His strong showing in drawing and fair mark in modeling allowed him to advance, along with 127 fellow aspirants, to the written and oral mathematical exams and then the history exams. Of "four to five hundred competitors," only the sixty with the highest scores gained admission to the École, and of those only fifteen foreigners could enter. Stein placed fourteen among the fifteen foreigners who successfully completed the exam.[27]

Following more than two years of preparation and disappointment, Stein was a "full-fledged eleve de École des Beaux Arts" with the right to officially begin his studies at the prestigious institution. Just to be sure that his family understood, Stein emphasized the significance of his accomplishment, "Everybody here is interested in the results, whether they have taken part in the fray or no." In fact, the proprietors of his favorite restaurant in the Quarter, where he, Kahn, and Klaber regularly had dinner, "seemed as joyful at our success as anyone else"— probably due in part to the fact that among the celebrations was a tradition for the successful candidates to buy champagne for their friends, so that "everyone drank to their heart's content." His mother expressed the family's pride at hearing the happy news and her hopes for her son in his chosen profession: "We feel all the more satisfied with your success now that we know what an effort there is to attain it. May you always enjoy your work as much as you do now." In the early glow of his success, Stein eagerly, and somewhat irritatingly as only an older brother giving unsolicited advice can do, wrote to Herbert, "if you can't put your whole heart and energy into your job … that is, if the thing that it leads to is not definite and supremely worthwhile, to you, or if you have not faith—I mean faith, not hope—that it will be worthwhile, will bring out the best in you and good for others—you have not found your calling." And that is exactly what architecture as Stein practiced it became, his calling.[28]

By February 1908, Stein had decided to enter the atelier of Victor Laloux, a graduate of the École. "Design skill and drawing ability" were essential ingredients of instruction, and the programs given to the students "usually did not involve specific social and functional requirements nor did they relate to specific locations." Consistent with the culture of the École, Laloux emphasized the architectural plan "with an intuitive balancing and proportioning of each part so as to contribute to the whole." Reflecting on his patron's teaching style, Charles

Butler, another student of Laloux's and a future partner in Stein's architectural practice, stated, "He would often keep us so long on the study of the plan of a project that the elevations and sections were hurriedly worked out in the last days of the competition." In fact, Butler remembered the professor succinctly articulating his philosophy as follows, "You can put forty good facades on a good plan, but without a good plan you cannot have a good façade." Stein remained in Laloux's atelier for the remainder of his years at the École.[29]

Stein also continued his studies through his travel (see figure 2.2), often accompanied by his roommate, Klaber. One of the more significant trips was to Bournville, England, in August 1908. The prospect of visiting the model industrial village, just four miles from Birmingham, particularly excited Stein who saw it as a fairly successful alternative to the overcrowded tenements. Along the broad, tree-lined streets stood the houses that accommodated two to four families each and were developed in a variety of historicizing modes with small, attractive gardens in front. "Bournville is like a park," he exclaimed. Calling it "the most inspiring thing I have seen in England," Stein considered Bournville far superior to typical workingmen's villages. At the time of Stein and Klaber's visit, roughly 586 houses stood on 456 acres of land and accommodated a population of approximately 2,800 residents, half of whom were Cadbury employees. An inexpensive rail line transported workers from the village to the city of Birmingham.[30]

A book on the community published just two years before Stein and Klaber's visit highlighted the significant role the architect could play in realizing opportunities for reform through the development of these model villages. William Harvey, the architect of the community at the time, noted, "Now that politicians and economists, as well as sanitarians, are identifying themselves with the movement, it is clear that if it is to result in lasting good, the attention of the builders of these new homes for the people must also be engaged; and the field that thus presents itself to the efforts of the architect is a large one."[31]

While Stein appreciated the physical design, he admired the ideals of the model town as well. In the design of the homes and the concept of living close to the land, Bournville reflected the influence of William Morris, the late nineteenth-century leader of the Arts and Crafts movement. Upon reading Morris's *News from Nowhere* the year prior to his visit, Stein had expressed general admiration for Morris's views but critiqued his vision that proposed elimination

FIGURE 2.2 Watercolor by C. S. Stein showing a European street scene circa 1907. Box 38, CSP/CUL.

of existing economic and governmental systems. He elaborated, "The dead dull sadness of the poor of today, along with the unsatisfactory extravagance of the rich—which he so well contrasts with the healthful joyful life in his communistic society—is really an insane way for men to live together. And yet as long as human nature remains, those of us who would better things can only hope to repair here and there and always under the old rules of the nature of man. I doubt if we will ever be able to pull down and rebuild society."[32] For a pragmatist like Stein, Bournville exemplified the ideals of Howard, and Morris before him, realized within the current system, and at a reasonable 4 percent profit to the trustees.

In fall 1908, as his first formal year of study at the École was drawing to a close, Stein began to think ahead to how best to focus his course of study. Students received points in architecture, mathematics, drawing, modeling, and archeology as they worked toward the *diplôme*. As Stein described to his parents, the school management was not particularly interested in "how one acquires the knowledge necessary to make these points" provided each student "finish two architectural problems or an equivalent in the school year."[33] When one attained the requisite number of points, he moved from the second into the first class. Stein had already received four mentions for his project work and was considering taking the mathematics necessary to get promoted to the first class. Because no student could continue after his thirtieth birthday, Kohn advised Stein that rather than devoting time to studies for a major mathematics and construction exam, he focus on architectural design. Specifically, he should continue working on the projects, even inducing his patron to allow him to do several first-class projects so that he could get advanced experience.[34] Thus Stein steadily continued work on his studies at the second level.

In the summer of 1911, at the age of twenty-nine, he returned home after four years of formal architecture education at the École. While various members of his family had visited him in Paris, and he had gone home for one visit during the six-year period he was pursuing his education, he missed his family. Further, his longtime roommate, Klaber, had earned the diplôme the previous year in November and was already home, and his good friend Kahn, with whom he had traveled extensively in Spain the previous summer, was ready to conclude his studies also. His years of study in Paris meant much more than training in architecture. "I have been broadened a great deal, in coming in contact with a different class of people than the few with whom I always associated at home, with Frenchmen as well as Americans, and more in being able to see everything, life and work, looked at from an entirely different point of view."[35]

Before returning to the United States, Stein and Kahn devoted the months of August and September to traveling in Italy, with several weeks in Rome, and Austria, visiting museums and sketching significant architectural sites. They were both apprehensive about their job prospects, convinced that they would be competing against unemployed draftsmen and many other new architects who had traveled as they had. Yet that fall Stein secured employment with the prestigious firm of Cram, Goodhue, & Ferguson.[36] Over the next six years, he refined his professional skills and collaborative work ethic and gained valuable experience with large-scale site planning.

## In the Office of Bertram Grosvenor Goodhue

Although the firm of Cram, Goodhue, & Ferguson still existed, the two founders had drifted apart architecturally and intellectually well before Stein joined the New York office. In 1891, Bertram Grosvenor Goodhue had begun work in Ralph Adam Cram's Boston office lending his already exceptional drafting skills to the firm's design work. The two architects shared an enduring interest in Gothic architecture and craftsmanship evident in the writings of John Ruskin and the work of William Morris. While asymmetrical and generally less prescriptive design appealed to the architects, Goodhue in particular did not agree with Ruskin's strict adherence to antiquarian construction methods. Instead, he advocated "the proper balance of machine-made and handcrafted elements." In 1903 with the commission for substantially expanding the complex at West Point, Goodhue relocated from the firm's main office in Boston to a new branch office in New York City to be closer to this major project. Over the next ten years, the two architects increasingly functioned independently of each other and the sense of rivalry and separation between them intensified. In fact, Goodhue considered the New York City office his primary place of business throughout the remainder of his association with Cram.[37]

In January 1911, Goodhue was appointed consulting architect for the Panama-California Exposition in San Diego, based on his connections with the Olmsted Brothers, who were hired to design the layout of the fair, and on their recognition of his expertise in the Spanish Colonial style. Considered by architectural critics as a master in combining traditional designs with a modern sensibility, Goodhue also preferred more regional influences, such as the Spanish of the American Southwest and Mexico, particularly in his secular structures. The site was the fourteen-hundred-acre Balboa Park. While the Olmsted Brothers recommended that the fair be located proximate to the downtown and thus on the park's border consistent with the vision of landscape architect Samuel Parsons who had recently designed the city park, Goodhue strongly advocated a much more dramatic site near the center of the park on a four-hundred-acre mesa. With the San Diego Panama-California Exposition Board of Commissioners' approval of the latter location and the Olmsteds' subsequent resignation from the project in September 1911, Goodhue became responsible for the layout and architecture of the fair. Shortly thereafter, Stein began to work for the architect.[38]

Due to its strong association with what Goodhue considered the binding stylistic rules of classicism, the École did not impress the architect. Apprenticed in James Renwick's office, Goodhue favored this approach to professional training. Stein's detailed drawings of building ornament, structures, and urban spaces while traveling in Burgos, Cordoba, Seville, Toledo, Avail, Zoragosa, and Majorca impressed Goodhue much more than the four years spent at the École and seemed directly applicable to the work already underway on the exposition.[39]

The strong-willed Goodhue encouraged a collaborative and cohesive office environment in some ways similar to what Stein had experienced at Laloux's atelier in Paris. During the annual Twelfth Night Revels, a party held January 5 that typically included the architects of the office staging a play, Goodhue noted how much he "valued their various abilities," elaborating:

> Of this force I am but one ... with this difference; that I have the power of veto. I believe it makes for happiness that men's work should be interesting and not always mere work, like that of the men ruled by an "efficiency" fanatic. ... And everybody is free to differ with me in my solution of any given problem, (mind you, I always possess the veto power), so that, setting a man a job and then going away for a morning or a day, or even longer, I often come back to find my own solution drawn out, with another, and distinctly better one, alongside.[40]

Though he admitted to having no head draftsmen, he assigned architects increasing responsibility as their tenure with him lengthened, eventually putting them in charge when he was out of the office.

Given Stein's understanding of Spanish design, evident in his sketches of Churrigueresque detailing that had caught Goodhue's attention during the interview, it is no surprise that in less than two years Stein was preparing drawings of the California Building, the central building at the fair. Hardie Phillip, another junior architect in the office, also contributed his efforts to the building, and in the process, he and Stein became fast friends. Stein associated with Phillip again in subsequent decades on designs associated with their years as colleagues in Goodhue's office.[41]

At Goodhue's side, Stein also began to deepen his understanding of site layout beyond the strict classical arrangements of the Beaux Arts. The dramatic entrance to the fair over the Cabrillo Canyon with the California Building as the anchor certainly was consistent with classical sensibilities. Yet Goodhue also grouped the buildings with a studied irregularity to take advantage of the site and to create a variety of intimate spaces off the main boulevard. He bound them together using the strong orthogonal central axis and creating a cohesive whole through the buildings' architectural unity.[42]

In *The Architecture and Gardens of the San Diego Exposition*, issued to coincide with the fair's opening in 1915, Goodhue decried the classical tradition:

> From the first to the last of such expositions there has been apparent an almost constant progress in size and in magnificence. ... To house such enormous congeries of exhibits enormous groups of buildings have become necessary, and so all local, ethnic, and fitting character has been lost, and the architectural scheme and style, following the "easiest way," has taken on a rather colourless, classic character with rows of columns, triumphal arches, courts of honour, and the like—all very magnificent and often very beautiful indeed, but quite unrelated to anything inherent in the exhibits, or to the great event which the Exhibition has, as a rule, commemorated.

The fair popularized the Spanish Colonial Revival. Goodhue also emphasized the relationship between buildings rather than an overwhelming grandeur noting, "We are beginning to find that the display of fewer things, well chosen and well related one to the other, is far more likely to arouse joyful appreciation. An artist, in creating a work of beauty, whatever it may be, chooses and eliminates his elements until he has formed a unified whole."[43]

Stein wrote the only other essay in the book, reflecting the esteem in which Goodhue held the architect's contributions to the project and his ideas on design and layout. In fact, Stein took the opportunity to celebrate "the varied symmetry and underlying order of Latin cities" and to address the integration of this approach in American city planning practice:

> For some time city planning has come to mean to us a great open place surrounded by colonnades.
>
> We have imitated the Piazzo San Marco in Venice, the squares of St. Peter's and the Capitol in Rome. But in so doing we have perhaps forgotten the charm of the approach to these big places. Their impression gains in force from the contrast with the narrow streets that give access to them, whose interest is due not to any symmetrical unity, but to the accidental variety of daily life. On the one hand, the great focal points and the main arteries of traffic speak of the dignity of government and the easy movement of commerce. But we need also the more intimate side of city planning, the by-ways with their little shops, the occasional drinking fountain at a street corner, the glimpse of some secluded garden through a half-open gate.[44]

His comments here parallel his appreciation of the urban fabric of Paris, with its broad boulevards and formal gardens and the more intimate medieval quarters with their narrow, meandering streets. Although early in his career, Stein clearly understood the relation between layout and function and the methods to integrate grander and more intimate designs within a harmonious whole. The next major project, Tyrone, New Mexico, offered Stein an opportunity to hone his site planning skills and to learn about cost savings for affordable housing design.

Goodhue secured the subsequent commissions for the town of Tyrone, the Throop College of Technology (as of 1920, the California Institute of Technology) in Pasadena, and the Naval Air Station and Marine Corps Base in San Diego in part due to the strength of his work at the Panama-California Exposition. In all cases, he adapted and simplified Hispanic-inspired designs and site planning from the exposition to these projects. Goodhue tapped Stein's experience on the exposition and his growing skills as a site planner to work on these subsequent commissions.[45]

Shortly after the exposition opened, the executives of Phelps-Dodge Corporation hired Goodhue to design a model mining town for them near one of their mines in the Burro Mountains of southwest New Mexico. As in other company towns, company executives, including James Douglas (president 1909–1916) and his son Walter Douglas (president 1917–1930), believed that introducing certain amenities while retaining total control over the town would address labor unrest and increase worker efficiency. Owners of the largest copper mine in the country—the Copper Queen in Bisbee, Arizona—in a state that led the world in copper mining production at the eve of World War I, Phelps-Dodge had decided to build their model mining town in New Mexico, away from the prolabor legislation in the newly formed state of Arizona.[46]

In 1904, Phelps-Dodge had bought a significant interest in the Burro Mountain Copper Company (Burro Company) and began to buy smaller holdings in southwest New Mexico territory. By June 1913, the company had started construction of a railroad that would provide access to the area. James and Walter Douglas intended to replace the two older mining camps with a new town and relocate company headquarters from the county seat at Silver City to what became Tyrone. In addition to being much more amenable to mining interests, New Mexico had a ready, and cheap, labor pool of Mexicans coming across the border and did not have the union pressure to bar these workers from the mines. When Goodhue visited the site for two days in July 1915 at Walter Douglas's invitation, development was already underway. Housing for the Mexican workers was being constructed; design specifications for the store had been finalized, and the location of the warehouse directly behind the store had been fixed. Still, Douglas was convinced that it was not too late to bring Goodhue on as the architect for the company's $1 million town project.[47]

Goodhue certainly felt that Hispanic influences were appropriate for the site, but he had a much different image in mind than the ornate style of the California Building. Douglas explained, "Mr. Goodhue seemed to be horrified at the ornate types of architecture and it appears is a strong exponent of extreme simplicity in design. He distinctly favors the Mexican type of architecture, provided it is pure and unadorned by modern so-called improvements."[48] Goodhue intended to substitute the Spanish revival style he had used on the main building of the exposition with a regional design consistent with the modest adobe structures that characterized the villages of the Pueblo Indians and that the Mexicans had subsequently adapted.

Goodhue's office began work on the project almost immediately. Douglas reminded his father,

We discussed the question of the unavoidable delay through this contemplated change in plans and you thought it was worth while rather than initiate an error which we would regret for all time, I have felt that it was wise to make the present arrangement with Mr. Goodhue, which I consider, from a business point of view, an extremely advantageous one. I really feel that Mr. Goodhue will save us far more than his commissions through simplifying the construction costs of the buildings and was satisfied that he was intensely interested in our problem and anxious to be connected with a proposition that so deeply appealed to his artistic sense.

Shortly after visiting the site, Goodhue wrote his office manager Mayers to "put a good man ... at work on restudying the plaza plans" and simplifying the elevations of the cottages for the American employees. "Of course I do not know which men are most available but would suggest Mr. Stein as the best if he is there."[49]

By the time he signed the contract with the Burro Company in late August 1915, Goodhue and his architects had redesigned the company plan, creating a combination of organic and baroque town plan that capitalized on the drama of the surrounding landscape (see figure 2.3). They proposed a formal treatment at the center of the town with the community's significant buildings surrounding the plaza. These included the general store, company offices, bank, and additional shops with offices on the second floor, post office, clubhouse, movie theater, train station, and hotel. To create interest and a picturesque townscape, they varied the massing of these structures with an arcade connecting and unifying them. In addition to a formal axial walkway system within the plaza, the town's major boulevard, Mangus Street, ran parallel to the railroad line and intersected the midpoint of the plaza's shorter sides, continuing to rond points several hundred feet to the east and the west respectively of the plaza. These rond points provided sites for other important buildings, such as the school.

As the community's focal points, the general store and main company office building faced each other across the long side of the plaza. In accordance with Goodhue's proposal, these two buildings were the only ones constructed with any ornate decoration, though clearly subdued in comparison to the main buildings of the exposition in San Diego. In addition to the arcade, Goodhue reinforced the thematic connection between these community buildings by finishing the exterior stucco in various warm pastel colors. In their encyclopedic

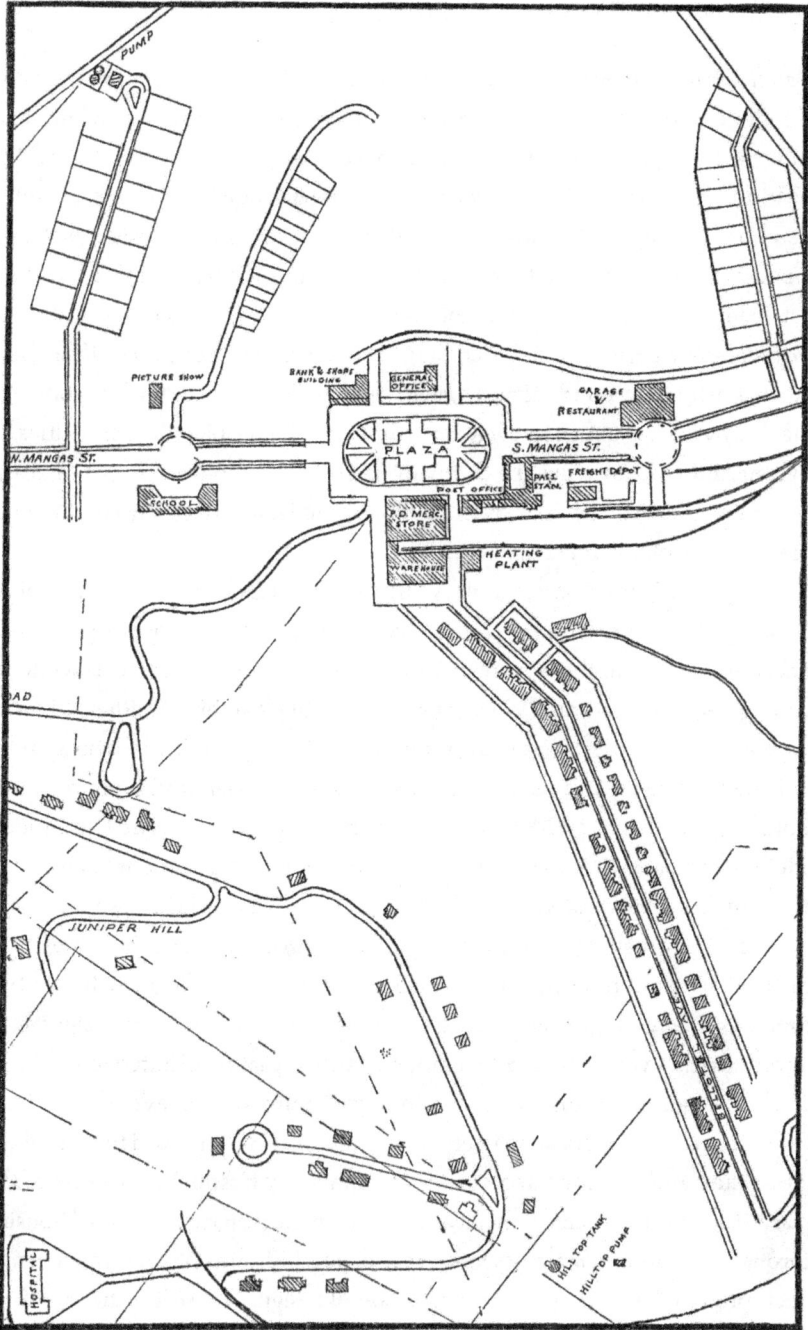

FIGURE 2.3 Layout of Tyrone, New Mexico. *Source:* Leifur Magnusson, "A Modern Copper Mining Town," *Monthly Labor Review* 7, no. 2 (1918): 278–284, figure 1.

*Handbook of Civic Art,* architects Werner Hegemann and Elbert Peets lauded Goodhue's work at Tyrone as an example of harmonious grouping of buildings and "the intelligent use, adaptation, and development of traditional forms."[50]

In addition to Goodhue's modern application of traditional forms, the town also boasted among the most advanced facilities to serve its residents. Community amenities included the state-of-the-art hospital reputed to be the best between Kansas City and San Francisco, impressive school facilities, and a railroad station with rich finishes including "chandeliers and hand-carved benches." Further, an underground exhaust system kept the dust that was the by-product of the nearby mining activities away from the town. Yet despite these amenities, in Tyrone, unlike Bournville, the company had complete control—a paternalistic structure in which "the relation of employer and landlord closely combined in the one controlling interest."[51]

Phelps-Dodge's efforts to improve the quality of its workers' housing while insuring a certain profit provided Stein, who was already an aspiring housing reformer, insight on the hard realities of reducing construction costs while retaining decent conditions. Working with Goodhue's architects, Phelps-Dodge lowered housing costs by reducing room size, increasing residential density, minimizing land costs, and using inexpensive local materials and building labor. Both the American and Mexican workers' housing were patterned on modest adobe structures with no exterior ornament, though the residential areas certainly differed. Segregated from the American workers' housing and located in a minor canyon along a road running southeast of the plaza, the majority of Mexican workers' housing was grouped into attached dwellings, each with two rooms (see figure 2.4). The attached two-room Mexican units were a significant improvement over the tents and temporary shacks that constituted much of the worker housing in the mining camps. In single family and duplex configurations, the homes of the American workers were located on Hilltop Road that ran along a ridgeline and provided access to the community hospital southwest of the plaza. The architects achieved a pleasing effect in the American workers' housing through variations in massing, fenestration, porches, and color. Hegemann and Peets praised the housing as part of the overall design. "These little houses show how the materials and, with proper simplifications, the architectural style used in the public buildings can be employed in the most modest private houses, thus producing a feeling of unity throughout the town."[52]

FIGURE 2.4 Mexican housing in Tyrone, New Mexico, "Bellotal Ave.–'K3,' Double Three Room," dated August 25, 1915. Courtesy of the Silver City Museum, Image #05248.

Within one year of beginning the project, Stein was working on several buildings, including the bank, shops, and warehouse, and was in direct contact with Walter Douglas.[53] In 1916, after having worked in Goodhue's office for five years, Stein began an extended working vacation, traveling to both California and New Mexico with letters of introduction from his mentor and the admonishment to "have a thoroughly good time." Goodhue wanted Stein to see the various projects he had participated on and report back to his employer on their status. In addition to visiting the San Diego Fair, Throop College, and Tyrone, Stein also saw his employer's designs for individual commissions including the Dater House in Montecito, California, and the Santa Barbara Club that Goodhue had secured while working on the company town.[54] Having the opportunity to visit these projects and see the physical form his work had taken must have been especially appealing to the young architect. Further, the responsibility that Goodhue gave him, including supervisory authority while at the site in Tyrone, bespoke Goodhue's trust in Stein's work.

While visiting Tyrone in 1916 and early in 1917, Stein revised the working drawings as needed in response to conditions on the site, including ongoing construction of several major buildings, the plaza, and the housing.[55] At that time, only 230 employees lived in company housing, with the remaining 692 tenants on company land typically in tents or in housing of their own construction, much of it without plumbing, running water, or electricity.[56] Of the buildings proposed for the plaza, the clubhouse was not completely realized and the movie theater and hotel were never constructed. At the close of World War I, the price of copper steeply declined, and the mines shut down. Still a significant part of the town as envisioned was realized. Of all the projects undertaken in Goodhue's office, Stein's work on Tyrone was the most significant in establishing the foundation for his career as a community architect. During this time, his understanding of housing, architecture, and planning also benefited from his ongoing civic reform work.

## Civic Reform in New York City

When he came home in 1911, Stein, at his former teacher John Elliott's urging, began to educate himself on city planning, especially focusing on the Chelsea neighborhood, which was continuing to transition from residential to commercial and industrial uses. Stein's participation in the City Club, particularly from 1915 to 1919 as secretary of its City Planning Committee, provides insight into his early advocacy of the Garden City as a key planning tool. Given his survey work in Chelsea and relatively extensive planning activities occurring in the city overall, which passed the first comprehensive zoning code in the country in 1916, Stein chose to take a leading role in the City Planning Committee. An essay he drafted in 1917 on city planning outlined a simplified version of the neighborhood unit that came to dominate his significant projects: "Think what an interesting group could be made of all these buildings, properly related and surrounded by trees in a small neighborhood park. Such a group would be a symbol of the best ideals of the neighborhood." It was at the City Club that Stein likely first met Charles Whitaker, the progressive editor of the *Journal of the American Institute of Architects* (*JAIA*). Whitaker introduced Stein to some of his most significant colleagues and collaborators: Lewis Mumford, Frederick Ackerman, and Benton MacKaye.[57]

An organization established in part for political reform, the City Club also provided Stein a means to make important political connections such as with future governor Alfred E. Smith. Having grown up on the Lower East Side, Smith knew something of life in the tenements. A recipient of the patronage system so central to New York City politics at the time, Smith was elected to the state assembly in 1904 as a Democrat with strong ties to Tammany Hall. While in office, Smith met and formed a strong partnership with an assemblyman, Robert Wagner, who later became instrumental in the passage of the first federal public housing program.[58]

The Triangle Shirtwaist Factory fire in 1911 initiated Smith's association with Jewish social progressives, namely, Belle Israels Moskowitz, Henry Moskowitz, and Abram Elkus, all key participants in the Ethical Culture Society. They advocated for labor reform and for improved housing and working conditions for the poor. Following the death of 146 workers, mostly teenage girls, in the fire, the legislature established a commission to investigate conditions in factories across the state. As a key member of the Factory Investigating Commission, Smith traveled widely, reinforcing what he was learning from his new associates; assisted in assembling an extensive report; and championed groundbreaking labor and welfare legislation. During this time, Smith probably met Stein, who was beginning to make speeches and work the political connections of the society in his planning and housing reform efforts. As governor beginning in 1918, Smith drew to him experts in various fields to advise him and then used his strong oratorical skills to sell these ideas to the people. Belle Moskowitz, Elkus, and Stein were among these experts.

Though his employment in Goodhue's office introduced him to large-scale community design, Stein's work in the Chelsea neighborhood allowed him to grapple with more complex issues associated with development that had accreted over time and reflected his efforts to integrate his architectural training and experience with his ideals concerning community architecture. In 1918, Stein and his longtime friend and colleague Klaber worked on a neighborhood plan for the area to address whether housing could or should be retained given burgeoning commercial and industrial development and large-scale public projects that had significantly diminished the residential areas.[59] Undertaken for the City Planning Committee of the City Club, the survey examined housing needs and projected future land uses in the area. Stein's training had taught him to first observe and assess existing conditions before drawing conclusions or making recommendations. Though crude, the approach he employed was consistent with the concept "survey before plan." Despite the significant changes occurring in the neighborhood, Stein and Klaber justified the retention of housing precisely because it was near major employment centers.

As the United States entered the war in early April 1917, Stein applied for commissions first in the Officer Reserve Corps, then the Signal Corps, and finally in the Army Corps of Engineers. Initially, he highlighted his recent experience working on the Goodhue military base projects to secure a position in France building aviation bases and then proposed lending his expertise in designing hospitals there.[60] A letter of recommendation from Robert S. Binkerd, secretary of the City Club, touting Binkerd's connections to former New York City Mayor John P. Mitchel and Frank L. Polk, counselor to the State Department, highly recommended Stein for an officer's appointment. Shortly thereafter, on August 30, 1918, Stein received and accepted his commission as first lieutenant in the Army Corps of Engineers, reporting to Camp A. A. Humphreys in Virginia just southwest of Washington, DC, for Engineers Officers Training School.[61] While stationed at Humphreys, he traveled to Washington, seeing the newly completed Union Station and major civic improvements along the mall as part of the 1901–1902 Senate Park Commission or McMillan Plan. He also had the opportunity to visit Whitaker and see his mentor Kohn, the latter busy at work as head of the U.S. Shipping Board's Emergency Fleet Corporation. Along with the U.S. Housing Corporation, these agencies represented the federal government's last-minute effort to provide much-needed housing for war workers proximate to centers of war industry.[62] He was naturally drawn to these large-scale community projects near job centers designed by prominent landscape architects and architects.

During this time, Stein wrote a series of articles for the *JAIA*, the first connecting his and Klaber's work in Chelsea with the emerging national crisis regarding inadequate labor near war industries. The broader and more significant second article outlined his support for government participation in meeting housing needs, particularly given the housing crisis anticipated with veterans returning to a housing market that had come to a standstill during the war. This October 1918 article responded in part to Frederick Ackerman's calls to address the expected postwar housing emergency by modeling a federal program on the temporary war housing programs. Rather than the federal role advocated by reformers such as Ackerman, Stein argued that state-run government housing programs created a greater opportunity "to try out various methods of building, aiding and financing housing," by being more responsive to local conditions as opposed to a standardized national program. In his submittal letter to Whitaker, he discussed the City Club's efforts to induce Smith, then running for governor, "to favor the appointment of a commission by the next legislature to investigate the whole question of housing in New York State and what has been done elsewhere to solve the problems of housing."[63]

With his participation in this and subsequent committees, Stein had the opportunity to formulate and refine his ideas regarding the types of activities the state government should undertake. If he had not already met Ackerman, Stein probably took advantage of his visit to Washington to do so either through his connections to Whitaker or to Kohn. He also met another architect who was working for the Emergency Fleet Corporation at the time, Henry Wright, who became Stein's partner on Sunnyside, Radburn, and Chatham Village.

Following his brief stint in the military, Stein decided not to return to Goodhue's office. With his training completed, he wanted to establish his own architectural practice, allowing him to pursue his interests in large-scale community design, broaden his efforts in housing reform, and explore the potentials of regionalism. As he formulated his ideas and implementation strategies, Stein tapped the considerable resources and collaborators he needed to realize his goals as a community architect.

# 3

## A THINKERS' NETWORK
## AND THE CITY HOUSING
## CORPORATION

Stein's collaborative skills flourished in the postwar period, allowing him to connect with key thinkers in housing, regionalism, and design. He built on the networks already formed through the Ethical Culture Society and a widening circle of notable designers and urban thinkers. Shortly after his discharge from the military, Stein was elected into membership of the American Institute of Architects and affiliated with his mentor Kohn, forming Architects Associated.[1] The firm included Frank Vitolo and Charles Butler. Butler, like Kohn and Stein, was educated at the École des Beaux-Arts. He partnered with Kohn in 1917. Vitolo, also trained as an architect, joined the firm about one year later.

As an architect who firmly believed in collaborative practice to meet the needs of the broader community, Kohn reinforced Stein's work ethic and further enhanced his network among progressive reformers.[2] While his architectural practice provided a means to realize his reformist goals, Stein's contributions to community planning, housing, policy making, town building, and regionalism outside the office were often as critical, perhaps more so, than any individual contract or project he directed. Stein shared Kohn's fervent belief in creating collaborative structures to enhance community building. "Learning by doing," as the Ethical Culture Society advocated, formed a key component of Stein's philosophy. He then monitored and adjusted his approach to improve outcomes in his efforts to design a new type of American community.

Kohn's mentorship played a crucial role in Stein's life, and the senior architect's offices at 56 West Forty-fifth Street became Stein's throughout the remainder of his career. As he launched his professional practice, Stein immersed himself in discussions and recommendations to establish state housing policy, supported and fine-tuned MacKaye's vision for the Appalachian Trail, assembled an interdisciplinary team of experts to model and advocate a distinctive variation of Howard's Garden City ideal, helped found a development firm to implement his community building concepts, and worked to place his collaborative initiatives at the cutting edge of national and international considerations in housing and town building. His closest colleagues in these endeavors were among the leading designers, planners, urbanists, economists, regionalists, housers, and ecologists of this era.

## Early Connections in Housing Policy and Regionalism

Following World War I, Stein turned his attention to the postwar housing crisis, which he believed was more permanent than the general public and many policymakers realized. In November 1918, newly elected Governor Alfred Smith promptly established a bipartisan Reconstruction Commission to reform government and address critical state needs, including housing conditions, availability, and affordability. Stein recognized this opportunity to shape housing policy. His regionalist network also grew significantly over the next few years with his introduction to MacKaye and Mumford.[3]

During the campaign for governor, Smith sought to detach himself from his old image as a Tammany Hall politician. With his backing, key New York City supporters formed the Independent Citizens' Committee for Alfred E. Smith. While a counselor to the Factory Investigating Committee, Abram Elkus, the social reformer and judge, had become a friend of Smith. He chaired the Citizen's Committee, drawing anti-Tammany Democrats, former Bull-Moose Republicans, and former Fusionist supporters of New York City Mayor Mitchel as well as "liberal businessmen, lawyers, intellectuals, and social workers to lend the campaign an air of a crusade for reform." Following Smith's election, many of these supporters joined the governor-elect in Albany. Belle Moskowitz recommended the formation of and directed the Women's Division within the Citizen's Committee to establish and maintain ties with a variety of women's groups active in politics and social issues. A veteran of successful political campaigns, she represented two previously underrepresented groups in state politics—women and Jews. She first suggested the bipartisan Reconstruction Commission as a means for Smith to advance his government reform campaign. Smith appointed Elkus as chair to the Reconstruction Commission and Moskowitz as executive secretary. Robert Moses, just beginning his career as a public administrator and engineer, signed on as research director.[4]

In 1919, Stein, who had served as vice president of the Fusionist Committee and strongly supported Smith in his campaign, volunteered his services as secretary to the Housing Committee of the Reconstruction Commission. Smith accepted the proposition, recognizing Stein's political skills and his insight on housing issues. Stein's mentors Adler and Kohn and colleagues Ackerman, architect Andrew Thomas, and businessman Alexander Bing all served in an advisory capacity to the committee. The committee had its work cut out for it—the great postwar shortage of housing drove rents so high that tens of thousands of tenants could not afford them and were evicted, requiring them to double up with friends and relatives or ultimately end up on the street. Even though Smith opposed rent controls in principle, he urged the legislature to continue wartime emergency rent controls in response to a series of rent strikes in New York City.

Early in their 1919–1920 studies of New York City's housing problems, Stein, Thomas, and other reformers such as housing expert Edith Elmer Wood advised the Housing Committee that regulatory approaches, including rent controls, building codes, and turn-of-the-century tenement house laws widely championed by Lawrence Veiller, were not sufficient. Veiller strongly supported regulation as a means to address housing issues, which he viewed primarily as overcrowding and poor housing conditions. He opposed government funding and a broader government role, believing that the private sector could address housing need. Stein and his colleagues argued that these regulatory approaches could not increase housing production or sufficiently improve housing quality for working-class New Yorkers. Stein maintained,

> The poor of New York—half the population—has always lived in unwholesome, dark, left over dwellings because it did not pay to build new homes. The only

difference between the present and so-called normal times is that a large and more articulate part of the population is suffering. . . .

The provision of adequate housing in decent surroundings for all the people is a public service. Until this is generally recognized we can not set up the necessary machinery, either to meet the present menacing shortage—or the shortage of decent homes for working people that has existed at all times. This can not be attained without the use of every possible economy.

Stein's appeal for a public sector role was made within a context of continued poor urban housing conditions and crowding due to the postwar housing shortages, but also amidst improved accessibility to relatively inexpensive land and innovative large-scale residential development strategies that philanthropists and progressive architects had already introduced in model projects, many in New York City.[5]

That city was a significant center of the housing movement with the most progressive of the housers, like Stein, arguing that adequate policy formulation and program implementation required technical expertise working in partnership with the government. Social critic and economist Thorstein Veblen maintained that the objective technician, or "technocrat," untainted by the profit motive was better qualified to address the needs of the general public. These technocrats included progressive architects, who applied "cost analysis, standardization, and social surveys, to inform design and development." An avid supporter of Veblen, Ackerman argued that restrictive laws would no longer be necessary if professional architects directed housing design and development. Stein certainly subscribed to this characterization of the architect as technocrat. In a 1921 speech before the City Club regarding the "housing problem," he emphasized the significance of a scientific approach: "Science is not afraid of being cast out. It does not progress through the emotions. It seeks the truth."[6]

As the New York State Housing Committee began meeting in 1919, Great Britain and Holland offered models of government intervention. The most recent iteration of a series of housing acts, Great Britain's Addison Act of 1919, granted "local authorit[ies] with national oversight, financial support, including ongoing subsidies, and recommended site and house plans." Repealed just two years later primarily because the "blank check" offered for construction led to rapidly increasing costs for materials, the act did encourage local governments to produce approximately 170,000 dwellings with an additional 44,000 from private enterprise. In Holland, the government contributed a significant amount of aid to address an immediate housing shortage estimated in 1920 at 100,000 dwellings. As Catherine Bauer later documented in her book *Modern Housing*, "From 1919 through 1922, one [Dutch] family out of every thirteen was housed in a new dwelling." Stein enthused, "Housing in Holland—anyhow for the manual worker—has for many years been looked upon not as a speculative business but as a service essential for the welfare of the community."[7]

While Stein's article comparing Old and New Amsterdam discussed financing and the government administrative structure that oversaw development, the images of housing in Amsterdam included perspective drawings and photographs showing modernist apartments and site plans documenting perimeter development. This early return to Europe in search of models for applying housing lessons learned from the war to the challenges facing the United States reflected not only Stein's attention to the role government might play in financing housing but also to emerging design movements. Clearly, there was no use providing housing assistance if the resulting housing was poorly conceived and developed.

The "limited dividend housing" model also made quite an impression on Stein. Dating back to late nineteenth-century Great Britain, limited dividend housing delivered affordable units through philanthropic sector interventions. Housing companies formed and financed by upper- and middle-income social reformers developed and maintained model housing at a certain return to investors. As the largest limited dividend housing developer in the United States made clear, proper management was essential to "offer to capital a safe and permanent investment and at the same time supply wage earners improved wholesome homes at current rates." Though the ideal tenants were the regularly employed working class, many advocates of limited dividend housing also served the most destitute through their involvement in the settlement house movement. With government controls and support relatively nonexistent in the United States and demolition escalating the problem of crowding in slum dwellings, limited dividend housing directly addressed the insufficient supply of adequate housing with the expectation that market demand for working-class housing would ensure a profit and attract additional investors. While limited dividend housing represented a small percentage of the overall number of units produced during the late nineteenth and early twentieth centuries, Eugenie Birch and Deborah Gardner in their study of philanthropic housing note that these "projects had a

profound effect on the design and philosophy of American housing ... germi-
nat[ing] ideas relating to architecture, management, and tenant selection which
later shaped the course of the twentieth-century housing movement."[8]

Some of the earliest and largest limited dividend housing corporations in the
United States were established in New York City, most notable among them, the
City and Suburban Homes Company founded in 1896. With initial capital of $1
million the company developed a number of large-scale projects, establishing a
reputation for consistent dividend earnings and professional management. By
1931, the company had developed more than 3,500 apartments, and by 1933 had
assets worth over $9,880,000. Thus, when Governor Smith's Housing Committee
of the New York State Reconstruction Commission first met in 1919 with Stein
as one of its members, several priorities of the housing movement had already
been realized or explored. These included housing code reform, a brief foray by
the federal government into housing subsidy and development during World
War I, and limited dividend housing strategies.[9]

Though the elements were in place, the members of the Housing Committee
were not yet ready to advocate for direct state engagement in the housing delivery process. In March 1920, they issued a report to the Reconstruction Commission outlining their findings and recommendations. Key recommendations
in their "Message to the Governor" included the following:

- Establishment of a central state housing agency to coordinate the work of
  local housing boards;
- "Enactment of a Constitutional Amendment permitting extension of
  State credit on a large scale and at low rates to aid in the construction of
  moderate priced homes....;
- Exemption of the bonds of the State Land Bank from state and federal
  taxation; [and]
- Passage of an enabling act permitting cities to acquire and hold or let adjoining vacant lands, and if necessary to carry on [develop] housing. This
  legislation would permit conservation of the increment of land values for
  the benefit of the community creating it."

Regarding the proposed constitutional amendment, the official report to the
governor further stated, "It does not mean that the State is to offer subsidy for
the construction of houses. It does mean that the State shall be enabled to loan

money on its credit to limited dividend corporations or to individuals or other organizations of individuals to build houses to be controlled and the loans to be secured by adequate mortgages."[10]

Thus the recommendations focused on encouraging the private sector, with some governmental incentives, such as low interest loans and tax exemptions, to build housing for workers. At a special late summer meeting called by the governor to push the initiatives through, the majority of legislators approved extension of emergency rent controls, some revisions to the wartime rent laws that had led to rapid evictions and other tenant hardships, and limited municipal real estate tax abatements to encourage "moderate-priced" housing construction. However, without the comprehensive adoption of all the initiatives, particularly the system of government oversight and controls, the tax exemptions fed a boom of poor-quality, speculative home building in Queens, Brooklyn, and the Bronx, which did not sell or rent at prices that working-class families could afford.[11]

In November, Smith was narrowly defeated by Nathan Miller in his bid for reelection as governor. Many pointed to the resurgence of the national Republican Party as the reason for Smith's defeat, though his Catholic background, stand against prohibition, and refusal to be involved in the Red Scare—a postwar backlash against Marxists and socialists—probably also contributed to his loss. With Smith no longer in office, Stein continued promoting his housing ideas in articles, many for the *JAIA*, and in speeches before groups such as the Greenwich Village Settlement House. Although acknowledging the necessity of government involvement in affordable housing production, Stein emphasized the role of the private sector primarily through the participation of limited dividend corporations. "Cities or the State should take by the right of eminent domain land best fitted for housing. They should let the land for long terms to limited dividend corporations with restrictions that would save for the community all increments of land value." Stein, who had served concurrently on a committee that had formulated a housing program for the New York Labor Party, considered community development and design key components of such a program and recommended that these efforts "be used toward building new centres of population—garden cities." So from a relatively early date he envisioned a housing program that tied together financing, design, and regional planning.[12]

He was not alone in his perspective. The American Institute of Architects, particularly the New York Chapter, advocated for continued government support of housing into peacetime. As editor of the *JAIA*, Charles Whitaker led the effort with a focus on planned communities, both metropolitan and rural, and offered Stein a means to publicize his ideas beginning in 1918 via an associate editorship with a special focus on community planning and housing.[13] Whitaker also sponsored travel to visit and report on model legislation, programs, and projects, and made key introductions of leading thinkers that shared his housing, community planning, and regionalism sensibilities.

Consistent with this role, Whitaker introduced Stein and Benton MacKaye in July 1921 at his rural northern New Jersey home near Netcong. Stein was working nearby on the site of the Hudson Guild Farm project, a five-hundred-acre farm in the state's Watchung Mountains that had been donated to the Hudson Guild in 1917. The farm provided fresh fruits and vegetables to the guild's cooperative store in the city and campgrounds for summer programs, but officially opened as the Hudson Guild Farm family camp in 1921.[14] At the time, MacKaye, a Harvard-educated forester, was working on several ideas for postwar social colonies, a continuation of the "Lumberjack Utopias" he had planned while with the Forest Service.[15] The lanky New Englander's conservation background and deeper understanding of regionalism complemented Stein's interests.

Like Stein, MacKaye found the idea of Ebenezer Howard's Garden Cities appealing. MacKaye applied the Garden City concept to the Appalachian Trail with a utopian proposal using the labor of former city dwellers to complete the unfinished sections of the fragmented trail along the eastern coast, forging a comprehensive trail system stretching two thousand miles from Maine to Georgia as a series of connected community camps. MacKaye intended to introduce "a base for a more extensive and systematic development of outdoor community life … a project in housing and community architecture." Consistent with the back-to-the-land movement, MacKaye advocated his utopian proposal in part on the basis of improved health, recreation, and employment. Over the next three months, Stein and MacKaye worked together on the *JAIA* article outlining MacKaye's Appalachian Trail proposal, forming a lasting bond.[16]

After publication of the article in October, the project secured endorsements from key allies including the American Institute of Architects' Committee on Community Planning, the National Federation of Settlements, and key players such as Allen Chamberlin, a founder of the New England Trail Conference (NETC). Reporting on the December 9, 1921, NETC meeting, MacKaye explained to Stein, "It will be comparatively simple to push the trail proper portion of our program, the main problem will be how to handle the community feature." This community building issue, in all its various permutations became a key topic of discussion among the members of the informal planning atelier that Stein organized within the next year.[17]

In 1922, Whitaker introduced the two men to another key member of the future atelier, Lewis Mumford. Already a well-known social and architectural critic, the twenty-six-year-old had just published his first book, *The Story of Utopias*. He shared Stein and MacKaye's interest in the ideas of Howard and was himself a disciple of the Scottish biologist and regional planner Patrick Geddes. As a student at City College in New York in 1914, Mumford had discovered the work of Geddes one day in the biology department's library. The brilliant and energetic botanist had turned to studying social and economic issues at a relatively early stage in his career. Due to his commitment to the city, Geddes chose to live in a tenement district in Edinburgh from 1888 until 1912, learning from what he observed and becoming a tireless crusader for housing reform. According to his biographer, Donald Miller, Mumford adopted Geddes's "observational sociology that studied communities as an outgrowth of the organic interaction between place ... work ... and family [folk]." Stein, MacKaye, and Mumford transmuted this "observational sociology" into a key practice requiring them to "survey before planning" to discern the relationships between these three factors before developing and implementing a plan.[18]

Stein's personal life was also thriving during this time. He was dating the young actress Aline MacMahon, whom he had met through his sister Gertrude (see figure 3.1). By 1922, the recent graduate of Barnard had already appeared on Broadway and was part of the repertory company of the respected Neighborhood Playhouse. Mumford met her shortly thereafter while at a dinner in the Stein's home, where Clarence still lived. Mumford described "her dashing performances in the Neighborhood Playhouse 'Grand Street Follies,' where her takeoffs on a series of Broadway stars were sometimes better than the original exemplars.... all too quickly the Shuberts would recognize Aline's abilities with a handsome Broadway contract, without having enough sense later to pick out a play that would do justice to her ripening talents." Attracted to her stunning presence, talent, and intelligence, Stein courted her for six years, although she later laughingly commented that Stein had asked her to marry him within the

FIGURE 3.1 Aline MacMahon, promotional photo for the play
*Winter Bound*. White Studio, circa 1929.

first few months of meeting. Though they often found themselves on opposite coasts, as she pursued a career from Hollywood and Stein continued to run his architectural practice from the New York City office at 56 West Forty-fifth Street, their letters testify to her loving personal and financial support that allowed Stein to launch a series of nationally prominent projects and to evolve and disseminate the modern Garden City concept nationally and ultimately internationally.[19]

# The Planning Atelier as
# Community Builder

As he turned forty, Stein began to consider how new professional connections might translate into a thinkers' network to reconceptualize the Garden City for a modern era. He traveled to England and then Holland with his colleague Ernest Gruensfeldt after they completed designing a client's home in the summer of 1922. As associate editor of *JAIA*, Stein had included a story in the May issue by Edith Elmer Wood regarding the recent International Garden Cities and Town Planning Association conference held in London and Welwyn. Wood enthusiastically discussed the growth of the movement—thirty-eight nations were now members of the association. Yet her disappointment was palpable when she simply stated, "The United States was not represented."[20]

The trip invigorated Stein, feeding his interest in the complex relationships between community building, regional development, and the location and form of urban growth. During that summer trip, Stein also met with representatives of the Garden Cities and Town Planning Association in England, which inspired his proposal to establish a city planning atelier. As he traveled home, Stein ambitiously outlined the topics that would engage him and his colleagues—"man's physical environment as influenced by social, economic and aesthetic needs and the technical means of creating new environments serving those needs."[21]

During the fall of 1922, Stein clarified the organization and functions of what was to become the RPAA, which he conceived as an atelier of architects, social reformers, designers, urban critics, and writers to address housing policy, community design, and regional planning. At the same time, he devoted much of his time to working on Alfred Smith's campaign for governor, overseeing the development of the camp buildings at the Hudson Guild Farm, and again turning his attention to MacKaye's work on the Appalachian Trail. In November, he spent three intensive days meeting with his friend at his Massachusetts home to discuss the next steps for the Appalachian Trail, a meeting they later laughingly referred to as "the Shirley Conference." Early in December 1922, Stein wrote MacKaye noting that the group would address "the bigger part of the work" on the Appalachian Trail, the community building part. "Can we put together that group? I think so, and I am going to try."[22]

In 1923, a variety of opportunities that Stein had worked hard to create came together. A reelected Al Smith returned to Albany at the beginning of the year determined to resume his progressive reform work. Responding to pressure from his office, the legislature established the HRPC in the State Architect's Office to study housing needs and conditions, examine the status of the housing emergency, and make recommendations for the adoption of legislation to address these needs and conditions.

With the mandate to address housing more broadly throughout the state, Stein, as HRPC chair, and the commission membership agreed from the outset that "regional planning" was an essential component of the group's directive. The challenge was not so much the immediate housing emergency but the need to promote a regional perspective in seeking long-term solutions for housing affordability and availability. Notwithstanding this broader approach, the HRPC confined itself during its first year to assessing the current status of the housing emergency and recommending extension of the rent laws. Yet Stein did not lose sight of the more ambitious goals of the HRPC as he began exploring with his friend Julius Cohen, the attorney responsible for the administrative structure of the Port of New York Authority, the establishment of a State Housing Bank as part of an overarching statewide assistance program.[23]

Stein's work on the commission slowed his efforts to establish the proposed city planning atelier. The principles endorsed by the proposed atelier, initially called the Garden City and Regional Planning Association, paralleled the interests of the HRPC. As outlined in Stein's March 7 proposal to the membership, the organization's overall focus was "to improve living and working conditions through the comprehensive planning of regions including urban and rural communities and particularly though the decentralization of vast urban populations by the creation of garden cities."[24] To that end, the new organization affiliated with the International Garden Cities and Town Planning Federation in London and began to consider the realization of their vision through the development of a Garden City.

Members typically met over lunch or dinner held at Stein's home, his office, the City Club, or the Hudson Guild Farm. At its first meeting in April 1923, the organization voted to amend its name to the RPAA, but otherwise adopted Stein's March 7 proposal with few changes. In addition to Stein, those present included Mumford; MacKaye; Wright; Ackerman; Whitaker; Klaber; Kohn; Bing; Stuart Chase, an economist and a good friend of MacKaye's; and

Frederick Bigger, a Pittsburgh architect and former classmate of Henry Wright's at the University of Pennsylvania. The small group of nine members elected Bing chairman of the organization.[25] A real estate attorney and developer, Bing knew Stein from his days at the Ethical Culture School and his more recent advisory activities on the Housing Committee of the Reconstruction Commission. Alexander Bing and his brother Leo owned the successful real estate firm of Bing and Bing, which had made them a fortune in Fifth Avenue development. They had built their reputation on quality design and development marked by their expertise in financing and management. Stein recognized Al Bing's considerable skills, and Bing recognized the opportunity to lend both his financial support and knowledge to the RPAA's goal of building a Garden City.

Just as they had begun to meet and formulate their ideas, Geddes decided to visit the United States, and Mumford persuaded him to attend several RPAA meetings. Having the input of someone who shared their passions for reform and whose work they so admired appealed enormously to the RPAA. Mumford later observed, "Though few of our associates had had any direct contact with Geddes himself or with his varied planning initiatives, they recognized him as the authentic Father of regional planning: so his presence cast a symbolic halo over that first conference." Geddes continued his stay in the United States into the summer of 1923 and turned his attention to MacKaye's work on the Appalachian Trail and his proposed book *The New Exploration*. While also supporting MacKaye's efforts, Stein, Wright, and Bing energetically continued formulating a means to develop their Garden City.[26]

It was probably frustration with the legislature's obstructionist response to the more progressive recommendations of the previous state Housing Committee, particularly government oversight and controls to incentivize the development of decent housing, and their desire to promote the ideas emerging from the current HRPC that spurred the RPAA members to develop their own model community. While Stein and Wright designed the prototype (see figure 3.2), Bing established the CHC to finance and develop the project. In 1923, the three outlined CHC's community building and design strategy, advocating their approach as an effective means to address "New York's housing difficulties" and to "demonstrate the social and economic advantages of—developing self contained communities in which industry and business will be within walking distance of homes." Their proposal incorporated new planning tools and efficiencies associated with wartime

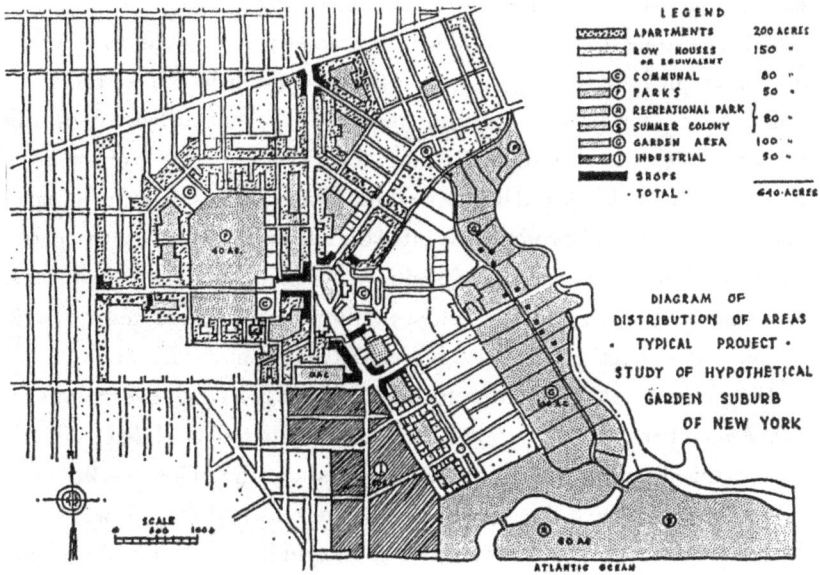

FIGURE 3.2 Preliminary Study of a Proposed Garden City in the New York Region, Alexander Bing, Henry Wright, and C. S. Stein (unpublished manuscript, 1923). Box 1, CSP/CUL.

and philanthropic housing—large-scale development techniques, street design based on the intensity of adjacent land uses, recapture of increasing land values to benefit the entire community, cooperative ownership and/or management, and the establishment of a greenbelt to restrict sprawling growth. Their descriptions, designs, and cost studies of a prototypical Garden City and its application to a site in Long Island formed the core of their report. Upon seeing this proposal in 1924, Thomas Adams, the former director of the Garden City Company that developed Letchworth in England, commented that while he agreed with the overall concepts and feasibility of the garden community development, the proposed site was too costly, percentage of apartments too high, and the likelihood of attracting industry too minimal to realize the vision on the Long Island site. Indeed, the ultimate purchase price was substantial, and CHC did not secure the property.[27]

In the absence of state-authorized loans to limited dividend corporations to develop housing as the HRPC recommended, the CHC sought funds based on the philanthropic model. In their study outlining a proposed Garden City,

Bing, Wright, and Stein stated, "The building of such a garden community will also demonstrate that philanthropic funds can be utilized in financially sound investment in good housing in such a way as to gradually release the original funds so that they may be used again in similar or other constructive measures for social betterment." In the fall of 1923, Bing circulated the proposal for the CHC to elicit feedback and begin the fund-raising process with the initial goal of raising $2 million. His proposal limited the return on investment to 6 percent; anticipated an increase in land value due to development with subsequent sale of out-parcels funding additional phases of the project; and adopted innovations in mortgage financing to increase affordability for homeowners.[28]

Bing aimed high; in addition to soliciting and receiving investments from RPAA members, social reformers such as Simkhovitch and Lillian Wald, and fellow Ethical Culture Society members, including John Elliott and Felix Adler, he also contacted V. E. Macy and John D. Rockefeller. In fact, it was Colonel Arthur Woods of Rockefeller's office who brought the proposal to the attention of Herbert Hoover, then secretary of commerce, in November 1923. More immediately significant was the feedback of Richard Ely, a noted economist at the University of Wisconsin in Madison and director of the Institute for Research in Land Economics and Public Utilities. While he questioned the capacity of philanthropic organizations to undertake housing projects, he acknowledged that "some of the best land settlements that I know of have been those where the men concerned in them have hoped through business conducted according to the best practices to confer benefits upon others as well as to gain a legitimate profit." Further, he maintained, "a concrete demonstration near New York City would attract a great deal of attention and ... would make a profound impression upon the country if the plans should be carried out successfully." Within a year, Ely was on the CHC's Board of Directors, and in July 1925 Rockefeller committed $150,000 to the project.[29]

With support assured, the CHC was incorporated as a limited dividend corporation in mid-March 1924 and began purchasing property near an elevated station in Long Island City that provided rapid transit service for residents to employment centers in Manhattan for a five-cent fare.[30] The CHC defended its decision to develop the site using the limited dividend model by noting the importance of securing sufficient capital and making the enterprise self-sustaining—the goal of ultimately developing a Garden City always in view. In

FIGURE 3.3 Aerial photo of Sunnyside Gardens circa 1927. "Sunnyside: A Step toward Better Housing," pamphlet dated March 15, 1927, n.p., front cover, Box 1, CSP/CUL.

its brochures for the community (see figure 3.3), the CHC made clear that its aim was to provide better housing for less cost than those "put up by speculative builders since the war" while recognizing that "two-thirds of the city's families receive incomes so low that any commercial housing erected in the past five years is quite beyond their means."[31]

Thus the CHC intended to build quality housing with community ameni-ties priced for less than $15 per room—the lowest rate that speculative builders offered at this time for cheap housing in the outlying areas of the city—but still more than what those living in the "old-law tenements" could afford. Running from roughly $10 to $12 per room, the number of rooms ranged from 4 to 8 and 10 (for the two-family houses). A 1927 survey of 566 property owners at Sunnyside found that 150 had "come from actual tenements or old railroad flats." Of the principal wage earners surveyed, 37 percent were mechanics, restaurant workers, chauffeurs, domestic servants, or manual workers while 56 percent were office workers, small business owners, salesmen, government employees, professionals, or teachers.[32]

The ownership structure differed significantly from what was typically available. At that time most mortgages required a considerable down payment with the remainder financed at high interest rates. Further, most households renegotiated the mortgage every five years when full payment on the remaining principal amount became due. The CHC offered something radically different, making homeownership accessible to a wider range of households. The houses in Sunnyside's first unit were sold for 10 percent down or less with the CHC essentially insuring the first and second mortgages in order to allow owners to amortize the payments over an eighteen-year period, a considerably more liberal arrangement than most mortgages offered during this time. The First Annual Report to the Stockholders in the CHC further described the ownership structure for the apartments based on the cooperative model with "tenant owners receiving stock in the cooperative company." In addition, the owners of the two-family houses rented the second unit as a means to fund their mortgages. Thus, though the intent of the CHC was "to be a builder of homes, not a landlord," from the first phase of development, the project mixed housing types and tenure. As Stein later noted: "In spite of the speculative operators' fear of such indiscriminate grouping, and the zoners' preoccupation in keeping dwellings of similar types together, we found this did not cause sales resistance. I have heard of no social difficulty resulting from it." Further, the density of twenty-seven units per acre "helped reduce the land cost per dwelling unit to a third of the cost per dwelling compared to a project comprised entirely of one-family row houses." Due to concerns about speculation, resale restrictions were placed on the units with owners required to offer the unit first to the CHC at cost.[33]

Construction of the second phase began in the fall of 1924 as work on the first phase was completed. This relatively fast completion rate and constant development activity was intended to cut costs typically incurred due to downtime and to the carrying cost of the land and infrastructure improvements. It also allowed the architects and financiers to observe the strengths and weaknesses of the project and make necessary adjustments in subsequent phases. Because the cooperative apartments did not readily sell, they were not included in the second phase of development. In addition, adjustments were made to the mortgage structure so that in the second phase, a single first mortgage at 90 percent of the purchase price amortized over a period of twenty-two years.[34]

According to a CHC report generated in 1928, when "neither individuals nor banks were interested in buying participations in these large first mortgages ... the company [CHC] was forced to carry most of the load itself." In response, CHC established a "new plan" with the same down payment requirements but now a first mortgage of 60 percent structured consistent with lending practices at the time—due in five years with the option to renew for another five—and a second mortgage for the remaining 30 percent fully amortized over a twelve- to fifteen-year period. Because they mirrored the current mortgage instrument, CHC could sell, or "place," these first mortgages. The more unusual second mortgages were financed via mortgage bonds. The CHC maintained, "These mortgage bonds of a limited dividend corporation secured by a large number of mortgages on small houses, constitute a sound investment for the funds of foundations and individuals, and has created a possible means for such capital funds to serve a social purpose." Among the bond holders were Ackerman, Kohn, Herbert Hoover, and the Russell Sage Foundation.[35]

The CHC's experiences, particularly in raising funding for Sunnyside Gardens, convinced them anew of the critical need for government assistance. As Bing indicated in February 1924, if sufficient financial support was not forthcoming from investors, he planned to argue before the legislature "that the State must act, since neither private funds nor benevolent funds would."[36] While they now had valuable experience in designing and building a new type of community with innovative construction techniques and mortgage products, the CHC and the broader RPAA membership recognized that securing statewide policy changes, advocating a regional vision tied to Garden City settlements, and deepening ties with their international counterparts were essential next steps in fine-tuning, promoting, and implementing their vision.

## The HRPC and an International Town Planning Conference

For their part, the HRPC members continued their advocacy of a comprehensive housing program beyond the reactive emergency rent laws and the tax exemptions that continued to be exploited due to a lack of restrictions on affordability. The HRPC issued its final report in 1926. Its recommendations "for permanent housing relief" acknowledged the need to "reconstruct the worst tenement areas" but also to "adopt a method of providing adequate housing for families of limited income which commercial enterprise cannot serve, applicable not only to the worst tenement areas but as well to any part of a city or cities in which the need is manifest." The recommendations focused on encouraging the private sector, notably limited dividend corporations and insurance companies, to supply such housing with incentives such as low-cost loans and tax exemptions from the state. The State Housing Bank would have eminent domain powers and provide the financing by issuing bonds in the public interest, in this case for the development of affordable housing. The State Housing Board would conduct studies to determine housing needs, review project proposals, and monitor the assisted projects for compliance with the rent limitations and other requirements of the law. In their report, the commission assured minimal involvement of government, "This statute does not put the state nor any of its cities nor any of their funds into housing construction or operation."[37]

In 1926, based on the recommendations of the HRPC, the New York legislature established a State Housing Board, authorized the creation of limited dividend corporations to build and manage housing at reduced rents, and exempted them from state taxes, though it did not approve of a Housing Bank to provide the loans. Governor Smith and other supporters of the HRPC's proposed legislation voiced some significant concerns regarding the lack of a specific public agency, such as the State Housing Bank, to oversee the lending process and the authorization of vaguely termed "public limited dividend corporations" to undertake these projects.[38]

Another key initiative of the HRPC in 1926 was their proposal to the governor and legislature for statewide planning, including the establishment of a permanent planning board in the state's Executive Department. Stein, Wright, and MacKaye outlined the significance of the underlying physical characteristics of the state and of the forces shaping them, applying Geddes's approach to survey regional resources and to assess the relationship between town and countryside. Understanding natural, historical, cultural, economic, physical, and social features allowed "men to harness nature to their need" with the ultimate goal of creating more desirable development patterns.[39] A state planning board would oversee implementation of the state plan through regional planning boards authorized to act in an advisory capacity to local governments. Though their recommendations were not realized, the document reflects the skillful coordination of survey concepts and planning strategies at the regional and state levels with decentralization into Regional Cities as an implied goal.

While they developed their proposal for state planning and continued work on the model community of Sunnyside, RPAA members participated in the 1925 International Town Planning Conference (ITPC) held in New York City and contributed to a special issue of the *Survey Graphic* to promote their vision of the Regional City. As they prepared for the conference, Mumford expressed his trepidation to MacKaye about the special *Survey Graphic* issue and more generally his concerns regarding the lack of focus he sensed in the group:

> The damned regional planning number lives up to my worst misgivings. I have a feeling that you and I and maybe Bruere might write a wopping piece, if we could do it after our own fashion: but for the rest of the crowd the idea is still a little unbaked, and in a busy world which gives no one time to think, it is destined for some time to remain so. The regional planning idea exists for the present in a negative state of criticism, criticism of the big city and of "city planning." It is not yet sure enough of itself to offer anything positive: or rather, we are not as a group united on a positive program.

Mumford also expressed his impatience with what he perceived at the time as a lack of vision in both Stein and Wright, who were in the middle of working on Sunnyside, as opposed to MacKaye's visionary proposal for a series of towns connected together along the Appalachian Trail. He continued, "Both Wright and Clarence, a couple of weeks ago, made the confession that they could plan the physical garden cities, but had nothing to put into them—couldn't visualize them on their social and civic side. This is where you come in, Benton, and this is why I hark back again and again to the Appalachian and the New Colonial ideas."[40]

Despite Mumford's concern, within a month Stein presented his proposal for housing reform in a speech that clearly conveyed a regional vision involving the state, the enlightened developer, and the planning of infrastructure to address short- and long-term costs. This approach required securing a "large amount of capital at low cost ... through State loans"; creating "large limited dividend corporations [to] carry out the work" by "reorganiz[ing] [the] methods of production"; cutting the "cost of streets and public utilities ... through better planning and organization"; and considering the "cost of transportation of men, materials, and food ... by better relation of homes to industry and to sources of supply of food and materials. This means Regional Planning."[41] Hosting the premiere thinkers on regional planning and Garden Cities to exchange ideas a few months later provided a way to move forward.

With Ackerman as the RPAA representative to the Council of the International Federation for Town and Country Planning and Garden Cities, Stein a member of the council's Executive Committee, and along with Bing, a member of the council's General American Committee, RPAA members were very much involved with the April 1925 ITPC. At the conference, U.S. progress in establishing zoning and city plans (including recreation and transportation plans—the most common) were outlined as well as the work under General Director Thomas Adams on the RPNY. As Adams outlined, some of the major commercial interests in New York City had come together to address how the region, consisting of New York State, New Jersey, and Connecticut, and particularly the metropolis at its center, would and should grow over the next several decades. The intent was "to advise government authorities and to co-ordinate their activities for planning for the future—after making comprehensive surveys and plans to enable it to give advice and promote co-ordination." With work already underway, but the first volume not issued until 1929, the plan assessed the current conditions of the city and its surroundings and projected how the metropolis might grow by 1965, recommending infrastructure improvements to accommodate that growth.[42]

International topics were also addressed at the 1925 conference. Representatives from other countries contributed papers on broader planning issues such as metropolitan decentralization and the establishment of satellite communities. As chair of the HRPC, Stein addressed statewide planning, while cognizant of this broader audience: We are "entering a period of decentralization over a wide area—a period that calls for a new and broader planning—the planning of states and nations." Stein considered it antithetical to state planning to focus on a metropolitan area to the exclusion of addressing the needs of the region and state in balance with that area. Stein wasn't the only planner who held these views. Other planning groups active in different parts of the country supported regionalism. For instance, Alfred Bettman, president of the United Citizen's Planning Committee of Cincinnati, Ohio, reinforced the need for an integrated planning approach that included the region: "What we now most need to build up and create is the regional mind, so that there shall grow up in the true regional area a consciousness of the organic nature of the problems of the region and an interest in and enthusiasm for the development of the region pursuant to an intelligent and attractive plan."[43]

To promote their perspective, the CHC hosted a preconference dinner, and Sunnyside was featured on the Housing and Town Planning Tour during the second day of the conference. Further, to ensure that they had a better opportunity "to discuss the possibilities of the development of a Garden City in America," RPAA members planned a weekend retreat at Hudson Guild Farm following the conference to which they invited Ebenezer Howard, president of the organization, and Raymond Unwin as guests of honor and other foreign and U.S. delegates who shared their interests in "regional planning and garden cities."[44]

Issued less than a month after the International Town Planning Conference, the May 1925 *Survey Graphic* has become a landmark in planning literature.[45] Stein, Wright, and MacKaye along with RPAA members Mumford, Ackerman, Chase, and Bruere prepared a series of articles on the topic of regional planning that addressed the need for and effective practice of such planning and discussed ideas and challenges associated with this approach. The proposal for a state plan, which Stein had eloquently presented at the conference the previous month, offered a demonstration of the foundations of regional planning practice. In this series of articles, the RPAA members critiqued the "Dinosaur Cities," outlined the potential for demographic changes—the Fourth Migration—spurred by new technologies, recommended more appropriate patterns and planning practices, and specifically addressed the modern Garden City as a model for current and future regional development.

With the 1925 conference and publication of the series less than a month behind them, RPAA members began discussions of how they could capitalize on the energy and insight gained from these significant activities with calls for a permanent budget, broadened activities, increased membership, and an analysis of the necessary features of a Regional City.[46] Yet their energetic participation at the recent conference and coordinated series of articles for the Survey Graphic did not translate into a sustained effort to move the ideas of the group forward. The significant number of delayed individual projects and the need to focus on personal agendas resulted in the RPAA's diminished organizational activity following the conference. Further, the individual members' goals may not have coincided as neatly as originally envisioned.

Looking ahead, Mumford and MacKaye assembled an ambitious, if vague, list of studies that the RPAA could embrace, including a "Study of Giant Power," an examination of "The Economic Basis of Civic Institutions," and a "Study of Regionalism in Europe." Meanwhile, Stein, Wright, Bing, and Ackerman continued work at Sunnyside, choosing to devote their skills to a concrete project that offered a means to fine-tune mortgage financing arrangements, hone large-scale development practices, and explore the relation between floor layouts, the configuration of buildings, and the arrangement of open space. As a result, Mumford noted, that the cohesive "spirit" of previous years was missing; further, every time he saw Stein, the architect "seem[ed] to have a new architectural job."[47]

By this time, the firm's letterhead had Stein's name prominently positioned at the center with "Associates" listed as the architects Robert D. Kohn, Charles Butler, Frank H. Holden, Frank E. Vitolo, and John J. Knight with engineer Eugene W. Stern. Based on the firm's ledger, a number of draftsmen and a secretary and accountant also worked at the firm. Certainly, Stein had access through his family to resources to position himself as a principal in the firm. Further, the firm did quite well during the 1920s. In fact, by the end of the decade, Associated Architects' total commissions were practically eight times what they had generated in their early years of 1921 and 1922.[48] The projects too were quite prominent, ranging from the Chemistry Annex Building at the California Institute of Technology to the Temple Emanu-El in New York City. But with Radburn, Stein soon channeled his collaborative energies to transcend the Victorian Garden City, creating a new type of community for an urban nation increasingly dominated by the automobile.

## Refining Regionalism and Developing the Radburn Idea

As Stein anticipated the CHC's next project, he maintained that community planning—or as he called it from his perspective as an architect, "community building"—was critical. He also expressed concerns about regulations in service of property values and the limitations of the city block, an issue he was becoming only too familiar with at Sunnyside: "We are hedged in on every hand by restrictions that we have made for ourselves through planning, not for beauty or use, but with the thought of return in real estate investment. Even on the side of cost we plan poorly. Our city plan builds up a multitude of unnecessary costs through wasteful streets. To these, the restrictions of place, are added in our cities a multitude of restrictions of law."[49]

In 1926, Russia offered an attractive alternative—a rejection of, or at the very least a deemphasis on, private profit combined with an authority and long-term vision necessary for the individual architect to carry out regional planning. For Stein, like other artists and thinkers of the era, these beckoning qualities appeared to offer an opportunity not available in the United States. Harold Ware, a U.S. agricultural reformer, was working with the government there through his Russian Reconstruction Farms, Inc., to establish small farming communities, or artels. Stein was intrigued with these as another form of the new town or Garden City and offered to provide input on the RPAA experience. MacKaye's expertise in cooperative farming and his proposal for indigenous settlements along the Appalachian Trail recommended him as the best choice to draft a report. Further, this project provided the conservationist income while he was between jobs and working on his book *The New Exploration*.[50] In late September, after reviewing a draft of MacKaye's report, Stein excitedly acknowledged that the proposal was nearing completion.

That summer other RPAA members were continuing their regional planning efforts, exploring models and opportunities overseas as well as in the United States. Wright traveled to the ITPC in Vienna with drawings and photographs of Sunnyside and the RPAA's initial ideas for a new Garden City. Upon his return, he enthusiastically noted that the conference's significance lay in the "new amalgamation of Town Planning and Housing bodies into a single federation which may better cope with the increasing problems of the monster city and its nebulous and unregulated spread."[51]

Anticipating his next project, Stein decided to see Russia himself, embarking on a trip there in May 1927 as a representative of the RPAA. He wanted to "see Harold Ware and his farms" and to personally deliver and confer about the report MacKaye had prepared. While there, he spent a week on a collective farm, but seeing them personally, he questioned the transferability of regional planning ideas from America to Russia.[52]

Meanwhile, Mumford and MacKaye were examining the concept of the region, not based on new towns but from a broader spatial and systemic perspective. Gaining notoriety with his most recent book, *The Golden Day*, a study of the New England literary tradition of the nineteenth century by examining five writers, among them Ralph Waldo Emerson and Henry David Thoreau, Mumford increasingly took MacKaye under his wing. He offered to use his publishing house connections to "peddle it [*The New Exploration*] as hard as I know how, if you'll give me that privilege," and further provided, as Stein and Wright did, financial support as well as feedback on the draft. MacKaye's manuscript described his philosophy of addressing the imbalance created by the growing metropolis on the adjacent indigenous countryside and culture. Thoreau's "philosophy for remolding human outlooks on the earth" appealed to MacKaye—as a "philosopher of environment: [Thoreau] saw the eternities of the indigenous, and he foresaw the inroadings of the metropolitan." MacKaye identified three critical challenges that grew out of the "needs" of "cultured man": "(a) the conservation of natural resources; (b) the control of commodity flow; (c) the development of environment. The visualization of the potential workings of these three processes constitutes the new exploration—and regional planning."[53]

As he worked on the book, MacKaye described to Mumford his vision of the Appalachian Trail as a potential model of regionalism in an industrial age. Mumford reinforced MacKaye's proposal, further clarifying that "simplification and a good rural economy and an active provincial life and a balanced environment and a harmonious set of vital activities are not really revivals of anything.... it is a fresh growth of something new." MacKaye's ultimate goal was to "guide the flow of population into some form of the indigenous mold (the environment of real living)"—the Regional City—"and to deter it from any form of the metropolitan mold (the environment of mere existence)." During this time, MacKaye also turned his attention to his home state, working to identify and map significant areas emblematic of Massachusetts's environment and to identify opportunities for limited access highway planning, an idea he more fully developed as the "townless highway."[54]

As these various examinations of the concept of "region" were occurring, Stein reflected on the RPAA's "preliminary groping in connection with the problems of the Garden City." He further explained, "We propose calling it the 'Regional City.' I wrote Ebenezer Howard about this suggestion, and he seems to approve."[55] Deciding that it was time to move forward with the next stage of realizing their vision, Stein brought the RPAA members together again to begin discussions about their next project.

In July 1927, the CHC purchased the initial eighty acres in New Jersey that became Radburn with the goal of transforming Howard's Garden City into the modern Town for the Motor Age.[56] On this site within the New York City metropolitan region, the architects believed they had the freedom from prescriptive regulations to realize their Garden City ideals at a limited dividend. With Radburn, Bing, Stein, and Wright engaged the expertise of those who had already participated in Sunnyside, including architects Ackerman and Thomas, landscape architect Marjorie Sewell Cautley, real estate and CHC office manager Herbert Emmerich, and engineer Ralph Eberlin as well as newcomers such as municipal consultant Louis Brownlow. Having previously served on the planning commission for the District of Columbia and as city manager for Petersburg, Virginia, and Knoxville, Tennessee, Brownlow was already nationally recognized in the emerging field of public administration.[57]

Stein and his colleagues began by seeking advice from within and outside their ranks regarding innovations in mortgage financing, site design, construction methods, floor layout, and community building. The experts they consulted included economists, regional planners, architects, banking and real estate professionals, public administrators, and social reformers. The RPAA members started the conversation in early October 1927, convening at the Hudson Guild Farm to discuss "problems connected with a Garden City."[58] Critical issues discussed at the "conference" included the nature of the Regional City, optimal size, land tenure, the kinds of industry to attract (and permit), the role of schools, form of governance, land controls and protection, issues of race and discrimination, and income integration. While some of these were quickly addressed, such as dispatching with Harold Buttenheim's idea for the municipality to oversee a leasehold system, others elicited more intensive discussion, with issues of income integration and race particularly compelling, especially given the minimal consideration or even acknowledgement of racial issues found among the RPAA's later records.

As to income issues, the experts acknowledged the difficulties private developers, even those operating at a limited profit, had in constructing housing for the working poor.

> If the poorly paid workers were admitted to the garden city, the industry that used them would either have to subsidize these workers' housing or advance their wages; there was no other way of providing them with the barest minimum of good houses unless the garden city duplicated the very conditions it existed

to escape from.... Unless this condition was faced, the garden city would have a shanty-town slum on its outskirts.

All agreed that "the wage scale must be adequate to the garden city standard of living."[59] Thus Radburn clearly was never conceived as a community to meet the housing needs of the working poor. Given that limitation, some income integration within the community would be possible.

Any interest in diversity though did not extend to race. The minutes of the October 1927 conference contain the only recorded discussion among the group about "the policy of the garden city in relation to the admission of Negroes and people of other races than white." Elliott maintained that any decision about the admission of other racial groups should be left to the community, once established, not the CHC. Stein countered that "the garden city company's policy would have to be laid down at the beginning." To which Elliott noted his discomfort with the CHC's approach to this issue at Sunnyside. Though he "appreciate[d] the necessity of not endangering the development of Sunnyside by permitting negroes to enter it, in its experimental stages, he felt it would be a great mistake if this remained a permanent policy of the garden city." Mumford raised the "practical difficulty in adopting such a plan in connection with development and sale." And with that, the matter was dropped. Interviews with the community's first manager and with an early resident confirm what is evident in an early survey of the community:

> To create what they saw as a congenial environment, realtors hired by the CHC discouraged Jews—as well as blacks—from moving into Radburn, a policy which met with approval or indifference from the town's financiers, administrators, and residents alike. Shared values and experience, not economic and ethnic diversity, were considered important attributes for a smoothly functioning, attractive community.[60]

This commentary reflects the criticisms that Clarence Perry's neighborhood unit idea reinforced socioeconomic homogeneity.[61] More important though, Stein's lack of a position, at least in public documents or private communications, on race or, frankly, people of his religious faith residing in the community he considered an exemplar of his design ideas—the Radburn Idea—is at first blush rather perplexing. Mentors and colleagues, including Elliott and Bauer, took clear positions opposing segregation. Perhaps Stein's intense focus on his design and community building ideas allowed him the ability to elude one of the most significant challenges of the twentieth century—segregation.

Based on a survey of 336 families in 1934, adult residents in Radburn were predominantly Protestant, college-educated young couples with employment primarily in sales, engineering, teaching, or midlevel management. "Deeds and leases are signed by young married people who wish to make their start in a community where a large proportion of the people are in the same circumstances, where the large majority of incomes range from two thousand to five thousand dollars per year per family."[62]

While they expressed concern about the increased value of land associated with nearby improvements and its subsequent impact on housing affordability, the CHC, used the windfall from Sunnyside to fund the Radburn project (see figure 3.4). They admonished, "In order to obtain the full value of the land increment . . . , they [the developers] should include all such land in their original purchase."[63] Income from apartment rentals was also a revenue generator. "We are . . . making considerable over 6%, and yet are furnishing very much better apartments than the market affords; in fact, we have a waiting list for rented apartments. We are planning to do the same thing at Radburn, and in this way to gradually build up a substantial amount of reasonably steady income." Continuing investment by substantial partners, such as John D. Rockefeller, Jr., was also essential.[64]

During these heady days of expansion, Bing maintained the CHC's innovations in mortgage financing assured a market for the bonds and a means to support development and sales in the new community. "I am in hopes that by the time we are ready to build a Garden City we will have a long dividend record behind us, a very large amount of capital, a good sized surplus, and a mortgage bond record, all of which will make it possible to finance the mortgages in the Garden City by means of mortgage bonds."[65] Not only were "complete public improvements" such as the parks, street paving and lighting, and landscaping included in the cost of the home, the liberal financing established at Sunnyside applied here also with a 10 percent down payment, a first mortgage running for six years, and a completely amortizing second mortgage running for up to fourteen years with the CHC "giving a warranty deed guaranteeing the title."[66]

Yet as the CHC moved forward with purchasing the property and as Wright and Stein began drafting the site plan in consultation with engineer Eberlin

Board of Education is
considering 15 acres
movement for James + Renee's
new High School

Plot 17
Plot 17 + 18
Plot 13
Plot 61 + 62

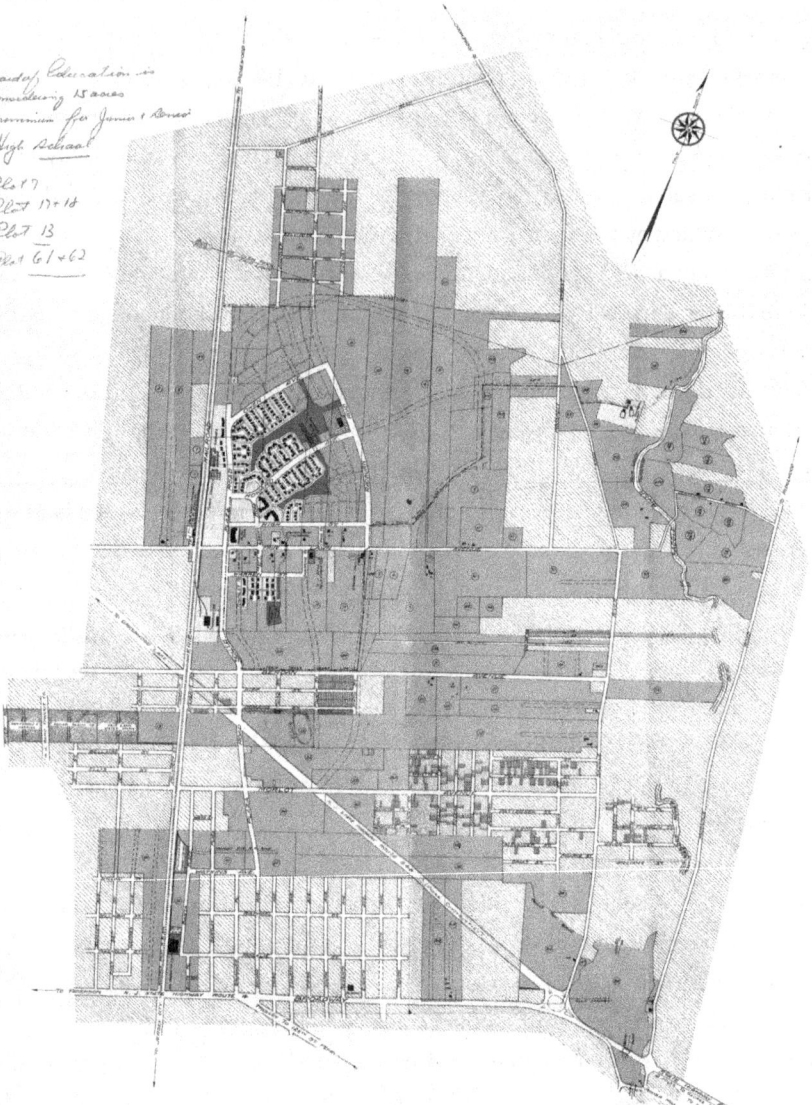

DIAGRAM OF PROPERTY
NOW OR FORMERLY OF
CITY HOUSING CORPORATION
IN THE BOROUGHS OF
FAIR LAWN, GLEN ROCK & PARAMUS
INCLUDING
RADBURN
REGISTERED TRADE MARK
THE TOWN FOR THE MOTOR AGE
BERGEN COUNTY, NEW JERSEY

RALPH EBERLIN
CIVIL ENGINEER & SURVEYOR

CITY HOUSING CORPORATION
RADBURN~PLAZA BUILDING
FAIR LAWN, N.J.

NOTE:
THIS PLAN IS SUBJECT TO
MODIFICATION AND IS NOT
TO BE TAKEN AS THE BASIS
OF ANY CONTRACT

ROAD MAP

LEGEND:
Land not owned by
City Housing Corporation
Land sold by
City Housing Corporation
Proposed Highways or Railways
Property developed by
City Housing Corporation
Parks developed by
City Housing Corporation
Other properties now or
formerly of City Housing Corporation

88

and landscape architect Cautley, Mumford privately expressed his misgivings to MacKaye in a letter drafted less than a month after the RPAA's October 1927 conference:

> The garden city project seems to me a little nearer in New York; but Henry Wright tells me that there is friction and misunderstanding between him and the office—men and lawyers and paperists in the City Housing Corporation; and at the bottom of my heart—this is quite private of course—I don't expect very much good to come out of this new venture. They have found an excellent site, I believe: but the irony of it is, the site is excellent trucking land, now in fullest use, producing early spinach and similar garden produce for the immediate market; and, in the interest of "regionalism" the garden city will probably drive out, if it is placed on this land, a necessary regional use, which should remain exactly in the state it now is![67]

Given its proximity to New York City though, the development of this land was inevitable. Stein and Wright believed implementation of the Garden City on a property at the right price with basic transportation networks in place, but without a prescriptive street system, zoning, or subdivision codes, facilitated a fuller realization of the Regional City.

A subsequent letter from Mumford three months later, as the CHC was preparing to officially announce the project in early 1928, was much more positive. While conceding to MacKaye that this proposal was "only a step towards the regional city," Mumford applauded the "demonstration" as "a great argument against all our existing city plans—namely, that they are obsolete." Wright more forcefully touted the significance of the new community, "The application of this social plan to Radburn was an event, in my judgment, equal in significance to that other social plan of Ebenezer Howard (1898)." Construction began in March 1928, only six months after the RPAA and CHC had convened the conference to discuss the permutations of this proposed Regional City. Some of these notable early participants, such as Raymond Unwin, continued consulting on the plan of the project as the first units began to be sold in the fall of 1928.[68]

The CHC's investment in the physical, social, and economic experiment encouraged self-governance and community administration but required the

---

FIGURE 3.4 Map showing CHC land ownership at Radburn circa 1929. All the land owned by the CHC is in dark grey. The community as developed is at the middle left. Box 17, CSP/CUL.

residents to understand their responsibilities. In addition to advocating the integration of technical expertise and modern efficiencies, these advisors agreed on "the need for interpreting through publicity and education the fundamental ideas for which the garden city stood, in advance of its actual building and occupation." For example, it was important for potential residents to understand that "attaining and protecting beauty" required "some sort of unified control … even at a sacrifice of the sort of liberty that people usually assume with the ownership of a home."[69]

The town of Fairlawn, where Radburn is located, had a population of four thousand and comprised about "3,200 acres of farms and a few hundred cottages of workers from a neighboring industrial city." The proposal to add 1,250 acres and twenty-five thousand people with Radburn would add an area approximately one-third in size to the current town and more important, increase the population more than six times the current number. Further with volunteer and/or minimal services, "no zoning ordinance, no city plan, no assessment map, no full-time paid municipal officials," Fairlawn was not in a position to manage or guide existing or new development in the community.[70]

In March 1929, two months before the community opened, the nonprofit Radburn Association was formed to oversee the development's restrictive covenants and administration of services. It initially consisted of nonresident experts, many affiliated with the CHC, including Charles Ascher, Alexander Bing, Louis Brownlow, and Herbert Emmerich. Based on the progressive mayor-council form of government, with a president (mayor), nine trustees (council members), and a manager to administer the day-to-day issues of the community, this arrangement persisted for more than ten years until residents formed the association's majority. Restrictive covenants were a common tool of new, large-scale developments during this period, particularly in communities that had minimal or no land development regulations. Among the issues the Radburn covenants addressed were fire and police protection; garbage collection, construction and maintenance of storm water systems and roads; constructing, equipping, and maintaining recreational facilities, common open space, and related structures; street tree maintenance; and approval of designs for additions and alterations to structures, including encroachment into setbacks and community spaces. The Architectural Committee administered and interpreted the latter requirements that also ensured building use be maintained as originally established by the

CHC. For these services and oversight, residents paid a fee that could not exceed one-half of their current property taxes.[71]

Compared to Sunnyside Gardens, where resident organizations mobilized to oppose the CHC's handling of delinquent mortgage payments during the depths of the Depression, resident involvement at Radburn during the early years consisted primarily of participation in the Citizen's Association to direct the social, educational, and recreational life of the community. In concert with the town planners and builders and the Radburn Association, the Citizen's Association was the third essential factor contributing to community life. As an early promotional brochure exclaimed, "The community ... must offer not only shelter but an abundant sense of release—a freedom, an opportunity for creativeness, a sense of neighborliness, in short—a new lease on living."[72] Formed just two months after the first family moved in and with membership dues of fifty cents a year, the Citizen's Association and its committees offered a variety of recreational activities for children and adults, a library, music, and adult education. Many in the community participated.

Initially, the RPAA proposed Radburn as a "regional city" with "more complete relations with the surrounding country, industrially and socially, and not [a community] primarily dependent upon the big city." Still, "this point was presently dropped as one which would be chiefly decided by expediency and the necessity for playing safe in the first large venture in the direction of the garden city." Not surprisingly, the developers advertised it based on its "ideal location," "excellent state and county highway" connections, and its "direct line of approach to the new Hudson River Bridge now being built." By 1934, over 70 percent of the working adults in Radburn commuted to New York City. At the celebration of the community's tenth anniversary, Stein observed, "Radburn used many old and tried forms, but it organized them in new functional relations. It was the first town realistically planned to facilitate the use of the auto as well as escape from the auto."[73]

Thus, despite having been conceived by Stein and others as a Garden City, Radburn was not designed or marketed as such. Even in the planning stages, it lacked the greenbelt, communal ownership, and housing for the lower-income factory workers that characterized Howard's proposal for resettling the urban working class. Instead of depending, at least in part, on a surrounding agricultural community and mass transit (the train), the project redeveloped fertile land and redefined the suburb in a salient way consistent with an urbanizing nation increasingly reliant on the automobile. As Stein noted, "Demonstrating the Radburn Idea overshadowed the Garden City idea."[74] As at Sunnyside before it, Radburn tested new approaches in community building. The Radburn Idea promoted superblocks served by roads designed to take into account adjacent land uses and an integrated park system connecting the neighborhoods, schools, and commercial uses so that pedestrians and autos were separated.

With the new town's development underway, the AIA's Committee on Community Planning, which consisted of Ackerman, Bigger, Stein, and Wright, among others, submitted their annual report at the organization's sixty-first Annual Convention in April 1928 on the status of planning in the United States expressing their support for proactive regional planning. They also advocated zoning, provided it "organiz[ed] and relat[ed] the diversified needs of the all-round community with less emphasis on segregation and more upon coordination" to ensure "balanced neighborhoods." To that end, they held up Radburn as a model—"the town is to be built in an orderly and complete sequence from plans fully developed in advance."[75]

With his professional life flourishing, Stein culminated his nine-year courtship of Aline MacMahon with a marriage proposal. The two married on March 27, 1928, and moved into a top floor apartment in Central Park West. Their balcony had a sweeping view of the park, leading them to call the adjoining living room the Sky Parlor. From the outset, Stein depicted their divergent lifestyles in a series of amusing parallel drawings of their respective "typical" days with MacMahon in bed until practically noon and Stein working diligently at the drafting table at that time, having risen at 6:00 a.m. At night, their roles reversed, with MacMahon on stage until late in the evening and Stein already in bed. During the early days of the Depression, Radburn appeared to be untouched by the economic downturn, and MacMahon's work on the stage was earning accolades from notable names in the theater. So it seemed natural to reward themselves with a trip overseas to an exotic location at the end of 1929. The newlyweds traveled to India, visiting Bombay then up to Baroda, over to Jaipur and Udaipur, returning to Bombay, and traveling to Ceylon through Madras and Madura.[76]

Upon returning early in 1930, MacMahon learned that the playwright Moss Hart was working on a new play—*Once in a Lifetime*—and MacMahon was to have a key role in its Broadway performance. Yet, to her disappointment, this role did not come to fruition, and early the following year, she jumped at the opportunity to leave for Los Angeles to appear in a West Coast performance of the play. Given the topic—actors transitioning from the silent screen to talkies— the play garnered significant attention and by the spring of 1931, MacMahon's movie career had begun. Her salary helped sustain the couple during the harshest years of the Depression. In addition, MacMahon negotiated an unusual contract, allowing her to spend at least part of each year in New York City with Stein.[77]

For his part, Stein and his colleagues were all too aware that the RPNY was being heralded as a major planning initiative and the RPAA membership needed to maintain their presence at the state and national levels as key contributors to the discussion on regionalism. They operated during a unique period in history prior to the explosion of fragmented local governments and widespread codified planning, a time when certain architects, intellectuals, economists, conservationists, and social critics "shared a compelling vision of coordinated regional development that, for a [time], seemed just as likely to transform the landscape as burgeoning metropolitan [expansion and formless sprawl] ultimately did."[78] With Radburn garnering substantial attention, the RPAA decided to take the initiative to broaden their constituency.

## Communitarian Regionalism and Metropolitanism

In 1929, as the volumes of the RPNY were being published, Stein began organizing a conference, discussing with other members of the RPAA a means to continue putting communitarian regionalism and new towns at the forefront of planning initiatives. To promote their vision, Stein proposed to involve RPAA members and others such as Adams, Unwin, and Roger Greeley at Williams College's annual international conference, which typically focused on political issues. At the time, Greeley was the chairman of the New England Regional Planning Conference, so a New England location was preferred. While Adams was initially proposed in early 1930 as a participant in the conference, by 1931, because of differences in the visions for urban and regional development between the RPAA and Adam's RPNY, he was no longer being included in invitations to RPAA meetings nor was his name included in subsequent listings of proposed conference participants.

The conference topics Stein and his colleagues promoted all concerned the region, including coordination across political boundaries and economics for a balanced region.[79] Unwin, in his capacity as head of the London Regional Planning Commission and president of the International Federation for Housing and Town Planning, would chair the conference. In these ways, the group hoped to provide an international counterpoint to what they viewed as continued support for metropolitan regionalism or metropolitanism as outlined in the RPNY. The proposed conference never got past the planning stages, but the RPAA, through Mumford, did have an opportunity to directly respond to the RPNY.

Within a month after the issue of the first volume of the RPNY—*The Graphic Regional Plan*—on May 27, 1929, Mumford was corresponding with MacKaye about the opportunity he had been given to assess the plan and the survey reports, summarily dismissing the offer—"There is no need to wade through the whole dismal swamp of reports they have issued."[80] Mumford, MacKaye, Chase, Wright, Stein, and the other members thought the RPNY lacked vision and, in addressing a region of 5,528 square miles that encompassed almost three hundred communities, focused inordinately on serving only one of those—New York City. This metropolitanism was evident in the RPNY's emphasis on transportation networks, especially to ease the increasing congestion caused by the automobile, and on improvements to facilitate the economics of the region serving the City of New York. Alternatively, the RPAA maintained their proposal for distinct Regional Cities linked together by townless highways and overseen by regional governments offered a much more appropriate way to grow.

As Mumford argued in his unyielding critique of the RPNY, "Since it carefully refrains from proposing measures which would lead to the effective public control of land, property values, buildings and human institutions, [it] leaves the metropolitan district without hope of any substantial changes, or more than minor and accessory improvements." In contrast, communitarian regionalism addressed decentralization beyond merely the physical plan of the town but also incorporated "the sociological concept of the city" and the "organic geographical concept of the region" based on surveys and statistical analysis.[81] Yet the pragmatic metropolitanism of the RPNY was more easily and readily adopted.

The RPAA members also continued refining their regional planning concepts such as MacKaye's townless highway, "the complement" of the Appalachian Trail. Essentially MacKaye proposed "to make use of the leverage of the Federal-aided public roads to control future policy in laying out State highways—such policy being to avoid the towns and apply the Radburn principle of culs-de-sac throughout the countryside." While Stein noted that "real estate men are beginning to awaken to the fact that frontage on the through highway has very limited value," Mumford cautioned, "there is one danger connected with it; and that is the danger of forming bad little messes of 'towns' on the townless highway itself: hence the planning of certain necessary services on these roads should be an integral part of the project, or they will come in by the backdoor and create anew the very slum we are trying to prevent." MacKaye began drafting legislation and promoting the townless highway among his contacts in Washington. With federal funding and proper guidance through the United States Bureau of Public Roads, he maintained, "a national system of federal-aided passenger motor-roads [could] take the lead in guiding our people, in accordance with some definite policy, into appropriate communities and settings for furthering the cultural growth, and not merely the industrial expansion, of American civilization."[82]

To address these and other matters, Stein realized it was time to call another gathering of the RPAA. From October 17 to 19, 1930, RPAA members met at the Hudson Guild Farm "to formulate a more definite policy for regional planning"—to outline "the essential elements in a program of Regional Development."[83] The group revisited the 1926 proposal for a statewide New York plan, asserted that regional planning was practically inevitable given current needs and the tools to address those needs, proposed a means to capture the value of land to dissuade the development of open space in certain sectors, discussed their support of the townless highway, and outlined broad steps for moving forward, including statewide (Pennsylvania and New York) and regional (New England) planning.

In reflecting on the outcomes of the meeting, the attorney Charles Ascher cautioned the participants about appearing to be an "inflexibly minded doctrinaire minority group," especially if they criticized the RPNY too stridently. He acknowledged that "Adams [general director of the RPNY] has prepared a plan which compromises the ideals of decentralization to which Adams has heretofore been known to adhere." Yet, Ascher maintained, Russell Van Nest Black, their colleague, planner, and author of the Plan for the Philadelphia Tri-State Region, who had attended the October RPAA meeting, acted similarly. "He [Black] seemed to agree completely with Benton MacKaye's principle of the townless highway, and yet he indicates [in his plan] for the Mercer County of 1970 an intensive development along the New Brunswick Turnpike." In explaining this seeming contradiction, Ascher noted that Black realized "the probability of people actually developing along this turnpike ... was too great for a practical planner to ignore."[84] Idealism, no matter how compelling, could only go so far. Still, the RPAA held fast to their desire to answer the RPNY with their own proposal. If partnering with their New England regionalist colleagues was not going to work at Williamstown, Howard Odum and the Southern Regionalists offered another opportunity for the RPAA members to promote their ideas at a 1931 conference at Williamsburg, Virginia. Their characterization of the region based on shared social, economic, cultural, and natural traits complemented the RPAA's communitarian regionalism in contrast to the RPNY's seemingly random region bounded by a two-hour rail commute from New York City.

In fact, the timing of the conference offered Stein the opportunity to secure a major keynote speaker—New York governor Franklin D. Roosevelt—and again promote statewide planning. Stein had remained in touch with Belle Moskowitz, and she suggested to Roosevelt that he meet with Stein. The governor had just proposed a statewide land survey to aid in the more effective use of farmland. Stein, who defined "Regionalism" as a flexible and responsive approach to foster "the fullest use of natural resources and economic opportunities so as to improve its [the region's] social and cultural life," saw Roosevelt's proposal as much more than an assessment of unused farmland. "On the basis of such information [determined through the statewide survey] approximate boundaries can be laid down of areas in which there appears to be possibility of coordination of economic endeavors. With such maps agricultural and economic experts can proceed to classify the lands of the State and advise, accurately, the use for each classification." The *New Republic* had written an editorial on the proposal that "pointed out the possibilities of national planning in case Roosevelt should happen to be elected president." To Stein's delight, Moskowitz indeed secured the appointment for Stein to meet with Governor Roosevelt. The community architect hoped not only to attract the governor to the July 1931 conference as the keynote speaker but also to "interest him in my old idea of making regional planning one of the important functions of the State and of setting up a Regional Planning Board in the Executive Department." While Governor Roosevelt's thoughts on the topic appeared to mirror his own, following the meeting

Stein still questioned Roosevelt's commitment to the ideas of National and State planning, noting "I think he is a great guy—or a good actor—or both."[85]

In addition to Roosevelt's keynote address and the Southern Regionalists' active participation, MacKaye, Mumford, Wright, and Chase presented papers at the conference. They highlighted the RPAA's advocacy of a new way of harnessing the region through public ownership as a means to maintain open spaces, "the highway by-pass movement," and the "town planning movement." Reflecting back on the event years later, MacKaye noted, "We [the RPAA] opened with one fraternity and closed with another; first with our British brethren and then with our Southern." Despite these accomplishments in securing a national stage for their work in regionalism, community building, and housing, the RPAA faced an immediate challenge closer to home, the survival of the CHC.[86]

## Recognition for Housing Innovations and Hard Times for the CHC

As the CHC began to struggle under the sustained onslaught of the Great Depression, Stein continued to seek opportunities to design new housing developments. One, Phipps Garden Apartments, adjacent to Sunnyside had Stein as sole architect; the other, Chatham Village in Pittsburgh, was in partnership with Wright. As Wright noted, though many considered Pittsburgh to be overbuilt in the late 1920s, that condition did not extend to "dwellings within reach of moderate incomes." To address the welfare of the steel town's residents, the Pittsburgh magnate and social reformer Henry Buhl Jr. had bequeathed an endowment of $13 million upon his death resulting in the establishment of the Buhl Foundation in 1927. Its director, Charles Lewis, decided large-scale limited dividend housing was a worthy initial project for the new foundation.[87]

Later Stein contrasted the success of the rentals at Chatham Village and the ownership model at the troubled Sunnyside Gardens development. "Experience at Chatham Village demonstrated, as compared with Sunnyside, the fallacy of the American faith, almost a religious belief, in what is called 'home ownership.'" During the depths of the Depression, the Buhl Foundation took advantage of low construction and materials prices to develop the first phase, realizing a consistent return averaging 4 percent by targeting those of limited income who could not find suitable housing in the city. Just two miles from the central city on a wooded hillside, the forty-five-acre property was strategically located, but the sloped site was considered a challenge. The innovative hillside project, developed in two phases on sixteen acres, was highly sought after from the beginning, with a vacancy rate of practically 0 percent and a lengthy waiting list.[88]

Stein's commission at Phipps Garden Apartments was also funded by a philanthropic foundation, in this case the Society of Phipps Houses in New York City (see figure 3.5). Developed by the CHC,[89] the site, adjacent to the northeast corner of Sunnyside Gardens, featured more intensive development with four- and six-story apartment buildings. As with previous projects, Stein, in consultation with the CHC, began by determining the amenities possible at the going rent in the neighborhood for the targeted income group and the minimal land coverage needed so that units, appropriately arranged, could be developed and maintained at reduced costs.

Large-scale development practices helped lower construction costs, and solid brick exterior walls, interiors framed with steel columns and beams, and "superior" infrastructure and fixtures ensured lower operating costs. Still, as Wright acknowledged, based on the standard of dedicating no more than 25 percent of monthly income to housing, an "average wage earner could not afford more than a 2-room apartment." To address this issue, the Society of Phipps Houses introduced a cost savings through longer leases, of two or even three years, maintaining that lower vacancies resulted and that longer-term tenants took better care of the property. A discount on rent offered for these longer leases allowed a greater number of units to be within reach of working-class families.[90]

Recognizing the need to generate such strategies, President Hoover assembled experts in design, home building, real estate, and economics, convening the 1931–1932 President's Conference on Home Building and Home Ownership (President's Conference). Those appointed to conduct targeted studies, particularly members of the Committee on Large-Scale Operations (Large-Scale Committee), acknowledged the lessons Stein, Wright, and their colleagues had already learned regarding affordability and large-scale development, including interior design for efficiency, site design to accommodate shared community spaces and the automobile, planning and construction techniques to reduce development and operating costs, amenities and management strategies to address middle-class and working-class needs, and financing methods to make the housing more accessible. Both Sunnyside and Chatham Village were featured

FIGURE 3.5 Main entrance to Phipps Garden Apartments, promotional brochure, circa 1931. Box 17, CSP/CUL.

as models. Further, a number of RPAA members were key participants in the President's Conference. Wright's desire to study these issues and his prominence on the projects undertaken in partnership with Stein resulted in him assuming a major role as a member of the Committee on Subdivision Layout and as the research secretary to the Large-Scale Committee and to the Committee on Design. Alexander Bing participated on the overall planning committee for the multivolume study. Others who played critical roles at Sunnyside, Radburn, and/or Chatham Village also lent their expertise to the Large-Scale Committee, including Klaber, Brownlow, Charles Lewis, and Herbert Emmerich. While Stein engaged in some early discussions relative to the President's Conference, he was not invited, nor did he, actively participate.

Overall, the volumes produced as a result of the President's Conference contained thoughtful reflections and recommendations from an impressive group of experts, though no immediate solutions emerged to deal with the worsening housing crisis. Indeed, John M. Gries, executive secretary of the President's Conference had suggested to Robert Kohn a more incremental approach to implementation "along more or less evolutionary lines."[91] Yet in their call for government support, including tax exemptions and condemnation powers so that limited dividend housing corporations could develop such housing; relaxed financial arrangements, such as longer amortization periods; increased efficiencies and cooperation among the public and private interests involved in housing development; and promotion of model "garden apartment" design and developments such as Sunnyside and Chatham Village, the Large-Scale Committee clearly supported the RPAA and New York's HRPC's ideas.

In fact, the Large-Scale Committee defined "large-scale operations" as "the application of the best technical experience and business practice to the production, ownership, and operation, on a sound income producing basis, of low-cost dwellings of desirable standards, planned so as to provide socially integrated communities." Further, "only a corporation organized for large-scale operations, with ample funds, directed and staffed by experienced and able architects, contractors and manufacturers, and enjoying the cooperation of labor and government, can produce adequate results." Still the Large-Scale Committee clearly favored partnerships where the private sector took the lead, cautioning that "government housing" might be necessary to ensure decent housing for "marginal groups" if "private initiative backed by private capital" did not produce results.[92]

Wright, Stein, Klaber, Ackerman, and Bigger, among others on the AIA Committee on Economics of Site-Planning and Housing endorsed these findings, though they felt the President's Conference had not gone far enough. In their April 1932 report to the annual convention of the AIA, they heartily enthused: "The maximum financial economy, the most efficient planning, and the greatest neighborhood protection are thus far obtainable when large-scale operations are involved, and when the ownership is centralized or co-operative." As always, architects had a critical responsibility to foster partnerships to realize these goals: "Architects should cooperate with land owners, dispensers of credit, site-planners, builders, and others, in efforts to devise and construct well-planned housing projects, so safeguarded that these projects may be (a) community assets and (b) demonstrations of technical skill in the creation of high-standard housing." At the same time, the "economic processes of community development and change" also deserved study to discern "what constructive economic measures can be found to rehabilitate the blighted areas and eradicate the slums." Further, while they endorsed much of what the Large-Scale Committee concluded and recommended, they recognized that the lack of solutions for the lowest income wage earners remained a concern.[93]

Despite their critical role in the President's Conference in seeking solutions and providing exemplars of design, construction, and financing, ultimately the CHC could do little to insulate itself from such a significant and widespread collapse of the economy. As late as the end of 1930, the corporation, specifically its robust development activity at Radburn, gave the appearance that it was miraculously thriving when so many other real estate ventures were already struggling. Though the CHC mortgage product had been innovative and offered home ownership opportunities at much more lenient terms than traditional mortgages during the real estate boom of the 1920s, the lack of government backing for mortgages, which would come with establishment of the Federal Housing Administration in 1934, meant that the CHC assumed responsibility for delinquent payments.[94]

By early January 1931, Bing reported to Colonel Arthur Woods, a key contact at the Rockefeller Foundation, the largest investor in the CHC, that construction activity had come to a "complete standstill" due to the corporation's inability to raise "sufficient working capital to keep on building." Just two months later, Bing met with Stein and expressed his significant concerns about the fate of the CHC. That was all Stein needed to hear; shortly thereafter he pulled his funds and support from the CHC not wanting to be part of the organization as it sold off its final land holdings in the partially completed Radburn.[95]

By March 1933, more than 86 percent of the 520 homeowners at Sunnyside had signed petitions circulated by the Consolidated Home Owners Mortgage Committee at Sunnyside (Sunnyside Committee) demanding relief from the terms of their mortgage agreements. Indeed, the very nature of CHC's limited dividend structure eventually came under attack from the Sunnyside Committee. Since the CHC formed and began construction on Sunnyside prior to passage of the 1926 New York State Housing Law, which the HRPC, under Stein's chairmanship, had drafted, it did not necessarily comply with all the requirements for limited dividend operations that the law established. The key concern was that the CHC's surplus above the 6 percent profit was not benefiting the community. Essentially, the Sunnyside Committee maintained that the operation worked counter to the affordability and homeownership opportunities the corporation touted. Calling these remarks false and malicious, Bing argued that the state law did not provide the flexibility "to build entire communities and Garden Cities." Just two years later, a major petition at Sunnyside to pay only what each homeowner could afford resulted in the decision to declare bankruptcy when the corporation quickly realized it could not retain solvency based on this income stream.[96]

One of the biggest blows Bing faced in his role as president of the CHC came from the criticisms of Lewis and Sophie Mumford. In a June 1935 letter, Lewis Mumford celebrated his family's ten years in the community, noting its "uniqueness" and "success as a living environment" and acknowledged his silence in the controversy. Yet he devoted the next three pages to outlining the fundamental mistakes Bing had made as head of the CHC, notably his decision to "guard their [the bondholders and mortgagees] interests rather than those of Sunnyside [residents]." Further, he charged the CHC with taking the profit above the 6 percent return to support subsequent development at Radburn rather than reinvesting the return to make improvements at Sunnyside. While Mumford did not formally align with either the CHC or the Sunnyside Committee, his lack of support and his wife Sophie's active participation in the Sunnyside Committee clearly still galled Bing years later.[97]

As the CHC's experiment in innovative mortgage products began failing under the weight of the Great Depression, the Roosevelt administration in Washington launched government programs establishing safeguards in the mortgage system. In addition, the recommendations for New York housing spearheaded by Stein's HRPC provided the template for a federal public housing program. Stein's subsequent experience under a diverse range of federal programs reinforced his advocacy of investment housing, which engaged private initiative and expertise using government support, as the most flexible structure for truly enlightened community building. He shared a similar mindset with his friend, fellow houser, and journalist Archibald MacLeish when it came to housing and the role of public-private partnerships. As MacLeish stated in his book *Housing America*, "Since private industry cannot alone acquire the necessary land at the proper prices, nor alone secure the future of that land once it has been built upon, there is every reason both in self-interest and in social interest why a workable cooperation of private industry and public control should be developed. Both have everything to gain."[98]

Stein had entered the 1920s building a substantial architectural practice along with professional and personal networks that reinforced his transformative vision of the Regional City and housing affordability as integrated elements in community planning. His leadership of the HRPC formulated these ideas as policy; his collaborative founding of the CHC implemented these ideas in model communities. Despite the CHC's demise during the 1930s, the Roosevelt administration's support of the housing industry reassured Stein of emerging opportunities to adopt the Radburn Idea and realize the complete community. At the birth of sustained federal housing programs in the United States, the community architect was poised to play a central role.

# 4

## THE ARCHITECT AS HOUSER

Stein and his colleagues enthusiastically welcomed the election of Franklin D. Roosevelt as an unprecedented opportunity to advance regionalism, new town planning, and worker housing. While their expectations were tempered by a concern that Roosevelt was too much of a politician to embrace some of their more radical ideas, their influence in Washington was felt during much of his presidency. Depression-era housing programs targeting large-scale projects offered unprecedented opportunities for design innovations and supportive facilities at affordable rents. Stein's pursuit of an active dialogue between policymakers and implementers reflected a unique understanding of both perspectives. The community architect favored a particular type of assisted housing—"investment housing"—a comprehensive design, development, and management approach to ensure the project's ongoing sustainability at affordable rates.[1]

During a time when most architects did not have the knowledge or skills to design large-scale projects for the working class; when the new planning professionals primarily engaged in zoning and subdivision regulations in reaction to (or anticipation of) development pressures; when most developers did not see a market or specialize in this type of housing; and when housers focused on lobbying and policy making, Stein was in a unique position to take advantage of these programs. Stein's government-assisted, large-scale housing projects designed from 1932 to 1942 provide insight on their implementation. His experience on a diverse range of federally assisted projects reinforced his advocacy of the limited dividend model, which he adopted both in one of the first government assisted projects—Hillside Homes in New York—and a large-scale rental project made possible through the FHA rental program—Baldwin Hills Village in Los Angeles. In addition to these limited dividend initiatives, Stein also collaboratively designed some of the earliest public housing for the Los Angeles County Housing Authority and war workers' housing in Pittsburgh during World War II.[2]

While his partnership with Wright ultimately dissolved during this time as project opportunities and misunderstandings led them in different directions, Stein maintained his association with critical policy initiatives by continued trips to Washington, DC, and his personal connections to key people guiding these early federal programs. These colleagues included Robert Kohn, Henry Klaber, Catherine Bauer, and Nathan Straus, the latter from a family of merchants and philanthropists whose father was a co-owner of the Macy's department store. Straus had been a state legislator from 1921 through 1926 when Stein chaired the HRPC and became director of the U.S. Housing Authority (USHA) from 1937 to 1942.[3] Stein also partnered with major contractors such as Andrew Eken of Starrett Brothers and Eken, builders of the Empire State Building, in the development of Hillside Homes and the nationally recognized firm of George Fuller on Carmelitos in Los Angeles. Stein carefully crafted these strategic partnerships to sustain his implementation goals in the wake of the CHC's bankruptcy. Collaborations such as these reflect Stein's holistic approach to apartment development—design innovations paired with new construction techniques and community building strategies to create a distinctive, low-maintenance (and thus low-cost) project. In addition, unbuilt projects in Pittsburgh and New York reflect the extent and diversity of his efforts.

## A New Breed of Housers

Excepting its short-lived World War I experiment sponsoring housing projects in centers of war-related industry, the federal government's sustained assistance for low-cost rental housing began during the Great Depression. During the period between the end of the war and the Great Depression, progressive housers continued to argue that adequate policy formulation and program implementation required technical expertise working in partnership with the government. For Stein, the public sector offered administrative and program-matic capabilities; a holistic viewpoint, as opposed to that of "irresponsible, unskilled, small-scale builders"; and unique powers, such as eminent domain. Yet he also valued the professional expertise of the private sector. Only the architect could coordinate and integrate the various elements to ensure "functional and articulate architecture with a minimum of extravagance," ample surroundings for "the evolution of new requirements and changing programs of community life," and buildings grouped "to form simple but beautiful gathering places." Through partnerships, each participant could lend unique strengths to more effectively and efficiently seek solutions.[4]

As chair of the HRPC from 1923 to 1926, Stein gained valuable insight on housing policy and program development. Based on the recommendations of the HRPC, the New York legislature authorized the creation of limited dividend cor-porations to build and manage housing at reduced rents and established the State Housing Board to oversee these projects. To make them financially viable, these limited dividend projects were exempt from state taxes, although the legislature did not approve a Housing Bank to "reduce the excessive cost of securing capi-tal." Instead, limited dividend housing corporations could issue bonds directly. Further there were now two types of limited dividend corporations—private and public—with the public having the additional power to use eminent domain to acquire land for housing development. According to Michael Straus and Talbot Wegg, both employees of the Public Works Administration Housing Division, which oversaw the New Deal public housing program, this legislation "is the foun-dation on which all public aid to low-rent housing in the United States is built."[5]

In a March 1932 speech before the New York Public Housing Conference, a group of housers formed earlier that year to advocate for limited dividend hous-ing and the formation of a housing authority in New York City, Stein reaffirmed the need for a public role—"no plan will succeed that does not offer a practical means of securing money at much less cost and on better terms than is possible at present. This means governmental participation in housing either through the use of State or Municipal credit or through direct governmental construction."[6] Given the nationwide social and economic crises of the Great Depression, fed-eral officials had significant reasons to become more directly involved in housing.

Within two months of his speech, Stein was lunching with Carl Stern, who had served as counsel to the HRPC, and Andrew Eken, the builder who partnered with him on constructing Hillside Homes, to discuss "a bill in Washington to spend untold millions on housing—It is almost unbelievable—but it may pass." Senator Robert Wagner, who had served as state senator and justice to the New York State Supreme Court and was familiar with the state's housing legislation, promoted federal support for worker housing. By the end of June, Stein enthusiastically wrote to Bauer who was traveling in Europe, "The Bill has been amended so that monies will only go to those limited dividend housing corporations which are completely regulated by state or municipal laws. This means, of course, that if the Wagner Bill is passed there will be a tendency on the part of a good many states to immediately pass housing legislation. I have been working with Robert Kohn, Carl Stern, and George Gove on an outline of suggestions for laws in other states."[7]

In July 1932, Congress passed the Emergency Relief and Construction Act making it possible for the Reconstruction Finance Corporation (RFC), which had been formed in January, to make loans to limited dividend corporations for the construction or reconstruction of low- income housing. As Stein and his colleagues had hoped, approval and oversight of these loans fell to state or municipal housing boards rather than private entities, such as banks. Initially, the only state to have the legislative and administrative structure in place to take advantage of the program was New York. Other states soon followed New York's example in hopes of accessing this funding. In response to passage of the law, the Public Housing Conference began seeking support for projects in New York City that could be funded with RFC loans; one of those projects was Stein's Hillside Homes in the Bronx.[8]

With the potential offered by new government programs, Stein focused on improvements in unit and building design to realize savings in construction and long-term maintenance costs and to facilitate community connections. To guide the architect, Stein wrote a series of articles outlining "A Community Housing Procedure" "to act as a reminder of the many factors that must be considered in connection with a housing development."[9] Objective analysis of three primary factors—social and civic, economic, and architectural—allowed the architect to understand and properly shape these new communities. Surveys informed the social and civic; cost and market analysis the economic; and functional and comparative studies appropriate architectural treatments.

Despite these critical, emerging initiatives in housing policy and the contributions architects like Stein had already made, the organizers for one of the most influential exhibits on modern design maintained that housing, particularly in the United States, had not garnered the serious attention of architects. According to Henry-Russell Hitchcock and Philip Johnson, who launched the "Modern Architecture—International Exhibition" show at the newly opened Museum of Modern Art in 1932, housing developments in the United States "are seldom examples of sound modern building and never works of architectural distinction." For their part, Stein, Talbot Hamlin, and other architects, who became involved as housing experts working for or in concert with the government, believed that housing, particularly worker's housing, should be a central concern of architects, who could apply their unique technical skills. According to Hamlin, "architecture, if it means anything as a creative art, must be based on the essential qualities of space-composition and arrangement, of balancing the big against the little, of creating out of a complex nexus of varied needs a whole which is unified and beautiful. What more inspiring subject for such composition than an entire designed community?—and that is what in its essence each large-scale housing group must be, whether of individual houses or of apartments." While certain iconic examples from Europe were included at the 1932 International Exhibition, the low-cost, large-scale housing projects Stein and Wright had developed as complete communities were not. One year later, the AIA Committee on Housing Exhibition, which included Stein as chairman, Bauer, Mumford, and Kohn, showcased such projects, including examples Bauer and Wright had recently seen in Germany.[10]

Despite the deepening Depression, Stein maintained a luxurious lifestyle. He entertained in his spacious apartment's "Sky Parlor" with its view of Central Park, attended cultural events, and frequented the theater; a dinner party with muralist Diego Rivera and visits to various speakeasies one night in the company of poet and houser Archibald MacLeish were particularly notable. As he continued his advocacy of working-class housing, he acknowledged to MacMahon the awkward sensation of living in different worlds—"I asked for a simple lunch and got—caviar and sherry—celery—a whole lobster—strawberries—coffee—The year of the depression—aren't you ashamed to run such a home?" Yet, with fewer jobs coming in, his concern for his own workers was palpable. In early 1932 he remarked, "I have been home for three days—the office has been closed. If the men don't work too much, their jobs will last longer."[11]

In a metropolis like New York, the impacts of the Depression were visible everywhere. The view from Stein's apartment, though, was particularly wrenching as he reported to MacMahon the misery he saw daily among his fellow New Yorkers who, evicted and often unemployed, sought shelter in a massive Hooverville that had formed in Central Park. He commiserated with, and occasionally supported, his less fortunate friends. With several of his colleagues, he raised funds and lent professional support to a group of unemployed draftsmen, many of them young men with families. As Nazism gained strength in Germany, Stein also raised money at dinners he threw in the Sky Parlor to support the efforts of Jennie Baerwald, a friend of his sister Lillie's, to get Jewish professionals who were already being persecuted out of that country and also, along with Whitaker and Mumford, sponsored the architect Walter Curt Behrendt in his relocation to the United States and a teaching position at Dartmouth College.[12]

As these personal and professional networks were thriving and deepening, one of his most important collaborative partnerships was under considerable strain. With their drastically different socioeconomic circumstances and work philosophies, Stein and Wright's practically ten-year architectural partnership came to a close. During the summer of 1932, Wright started a school for architects on his farm. "He has no work—but thinks this is the great time to do things. Not only is most of the family on his hands—or rather his farm—but he has one of the unemployed draftsmen—and now he wants a crew of them—to remodel a part of the old mill as drafting room and dormitory—So they can study and work with him." By August the school was thriving, and later that year, Stein and Kohn helped fund a research trip Wright took to Europe to examine innovations in international housing.[13]

As Wright continued to experience significant economic distress, with no upcoming projects, a seriously ill wife, and children to support, he became incensed when he discovered Stein in the early planning stages for Hillside Homes. Wright had not played a role at Phipps Garden Apartments. Given previous frustrations with Wright, the CHC was able to convince Stein not to bring Wright in as a partner on the project. Further, though initially engaged in discussions with Wright and Charles Lewis to continue the collaboration on the second phase at Chatham Village, Stein was not included in that project. An observation Stein made during this time to his wife reflected the growing rift in their partnership, "Henry Wright in town—one of his temperamental days. So I listened patiently while he expanded in regard to the fact that I was not making him partner or associate in all housing jobs—and he didn't have his private office and so on."[14]

The formation of the Housing Study Guild in 1933 by Wright, Mumford, and Albert Mayer reinforced this split, although Stein was listed as one of the nine directors. Wright believed a coalition of prominent architects was better positioned to secure government housing support. Stein had no desire to work as part of such a group—"the Chicago Fair and Radio City had taught me all I wanted about architecture born from the group mind." Given that Stein appeared to thrive in collaborative work environments, particularly those under his leadership, conflicts between Stein's pragmatic can-do approach and Wright's introspective desire to question and bring a proposal through multiple iterations probably more likely resulted in the two parting ways. These characteristics certainly did not recommend Wright among the CHC board members. In fact, according to Stein, the CHC had never "directly employed" Wright:

> Though his compensation was agreed upon between H. W. [Henry Wright] and A.M. B. [Alexander M. Bing] it was paid through me, as part of my office expenses. Henry used my men to assist in his studies. I remember being asked to be present without H. W. at a meeting of the C. H. C. Board (or Planning Com.) [to] discuss highway layout [at Radburn]. This had been Henry's work. But A.M. said he irritated the practical members of the Board. Henry was naturally mad.[15]

By 1933, Stein acknowledged that Wright was moving in a new direction, becoming "more of a teacher and a theorist." A talk between the two architects in late June 1933—specifically addressing the Hillside Homes project—provides the clearest documentation of the dissolution of their partnership:

> Henry and I had a talk yesterday as to our future relations—I am glad it was his suggestion. It has been growing more and more apparent that the relation of partners in any of these jobs was difficult. I have got to have the right of final and definite decision in conferring with such people as Eken. In fact in any housing problem or where there are so many possible solutions and so many factors to be considered, a time comes when some one must decide on the road to take—and then stick to it—unless reasons of the greatest weight for change come along. Henry as you know is not one to cooperate on final decisions or to take the responsibility of action—On the other hand he is an inspiring (if sometime annoying) critic. Here after he is to be consultant on my work—as on that of other architects—That will be better don't you think?"

Even in the area of town planning, which Stein acknowledged he had previously left to Wright's expertise, Stein had come to "enjoy being on my own." In early August, Wright wrote Stein that "after a very long struggle [he had] come to the conclusion that it would be wiser for me to withdraw from the association of the past 10 years."[16]

The "complete neighborhood community" continued to revolve around the touchstone of Radburn, but even here, Stein and Wright's visions began to diverge. Wright adapted the Radburn Idea, creating an urban application consisting of modified grids, superblocks, and apartments of up to sixteen stories.[17] A flexible interpretation of the Radburn Idea offered the potential for more effective integration of affordable units. For his part, Stein continued to reproduce lower-density designs. As Wright immersed himself in the Housing Study Guild's focus on theory, technical research, and education, Stein embarked on one of the earliest limited dividend projects funded under the New Deal housing program, Hillside Homes.

## Hillside Homes

Stein's efforts to get Hillside Homes built provide insight into the development industry in New York City and the challenges and opportunities associated with emerging federal programs. In 1932, Stein began actively seeking a developable site near transit, financial partners, and a construction company to undertake a new project. He envisioned what became Hillside Homes as a means to take advantage of the New York State tax incentives he had helped draft to encourage low-cost housing development and to further advance design and construction innovations introduced in the first phase of Phipps Garden Apartments, but at a significantly reduced rental rate. The search for the site and efforts to get approval for the limited dividend corporation and the project from the State Housing Board, various city departments, and ultimately the federal government for purposes of receiving a low-cost loan delayed the project for months, allowing time to consider innovations in design that translated into cost savings. "The Phipps rents for an average of about $16.85 a room. Can we design an attractive livable apartment with great gardens to rent for $10 or $11?—It is true building costs are cheaper—Nonetheless we have a lot of simplification to do—or we have to find quite new methods of building. We go through one of these after another—and each time come on a catch—unions-laws-safety-costs.—It is not as easy as it sounds." A critical step in realizing that goal was securing the vacant twenty-six-acre site on the Boston Post and Eastchester roads in a recently developing area in the Bronx for only seventy cents per square foot. Nathan Straus owned the property and served as director of the limited dividend corporation formed to develop the project.[18]

Certainly Stein had no patience for the political maneuvering that ensued during late 1932 and early 1933 to gain approval for the project from the State Housing Board over the objections of private developers who argued that it unfairly competed with their developments. After several months of trying to get the approval, which would allow them to secure a loan from the RFC and gain tax exemption status from the state, he observed: "The Reconstruction Finance Corporation has decided to lend money to the big housing development on which I have been working. None the less, our troubles are not all over as most of the real estate men in the Bronx are attacking us and are trying to induce the Acting Mayor to take away the right of tax exemption which has been given us by the Housing Board."[19]

In fact, as the RFC was poised to sign the required paperwork, the chairman of the state's Housing Board contacted the RFC requesting that Fred French's Lower East Side project—Knickerbocker Village—be the first to receive a loan from the RFC. Stein resented the support this project received, particularly because it involved slum clearance, resulting in much more expensive land costs than his proposal. Slum clearance in New York City, he argued, could never deliver decent housing at adequate rents to rehouse the populations that were living in these areas. Further, increasing density to lower costs robbed the children of a connection between their home and play areas outside.[20]

In early 1933, the fight continued as Kohn, who was on the board, felt he had to recuse himself from supporting his colleague's project and as Stein learned that "social organizations are half hearted in backing us because we haven't promised them low enough rents." In response Stein argued that he would not compromise a certain "standard of living" to arrive at a sufficiently "cheap rent."[21] After all, he thought, the job of the government was to provide funding to address the gap between what low-income households could afford and what decent housing cost.

During this hard fought effort to secure a loan through the RFC, Stein was closely monitoring Washington in anticipation of a more favorable program. As part of his first one hundred days, Roosevelt proposed and Congress passed the National Industrial Recovery Act (IRA), a whole series of emergency programs to get the country working again. With passage of the IRA in June 1933, support for limited dividend projects came under the umbrella of the Public Works Administration (PWA) Housing Division; the PWA Housing Division could also support public sector housing through a combination of grants and low-interest loans to local housing authorities or directly develop these as a federal entity. These approaches later diverged—support for limited dividend projects into the mortgage insurance program through the establishment of the FHA in 1934 and direct public sector engagement through local housing authorities into USHA's permanent public housing program in 1937. They reflect the two enduring approaches to developing federally supported housing.[22]

The RPAA certainly approved of such a multipronged approach. In June 1933, just as the IRA was passed, the RPAA published its call for a "Housing Policy for the Government." In their last major initiative before the group disbanded for more than a decade, members acknowledged the significance of the new program to boost employment while promoting a "sound neighborhood environment." They advocated for deeper subsidies to house the lowest income; supported reduced speculation through the purchase of excess land for recreation and open space; argued for mixed income housing with "class segregation avoided in ... the design and layout of the new buildings"; promoted design based on the "neighborhood community," "scientific standards of orientation and spacing" to optimize light and air, integration of open spaces, and insulation from through traffic. In addition, attending to the cost of land, addressing financing, the rate of amortization, and maintenance costs all were essential components of establishing and sustaining low-cost housing. These cost savings could then be passed along to the consumer in the form of reduced rents or selling prices. Finally, housing should be proximate to existing and prospective employment centers located through scientific surveys, not related to slum clearance initiatives.[23]

Using his title "Former Chairman, Commission of Housing and Regional Planning, New York," Stein published a companion piece also in *The Octagon* addressing "the opportunity [created by the IRA] to start at once to build new communities and replace obsolete blighted areas." Stein believed architects were in a unique position to apply their design expertise to take advantage of the fundamental changes ushered in by the Depression to "build homes, communities, cities for this new age."[24]

In June 1933, when the president signed the IRA establishing the new PWA and its housing programs, Stein was ready. He withdrew the Hillside Homes application from the RFC and submitted it to the new PWA. He also had ready a number of additional proposed projects. Employing research assistants, such as Bauer and Frank Vitolo of his office, he evaluated five sites, one each in New York (Valley Stream); Secaucus, New Jersey; Pittsburgh; San Francisco (Alameda); and Milwaukee.[25] Groundbreaking in their comprehensiveness, these housing studies assessed the extent of need in the community, the relation of the proposed site to public transit and employment centers, and the cost associated with developing and maintaining each project.

The most ambitious among these was Valley Stream—envisioned as a "complete integrated community for approximately 18,000 residents." Stein considered it significant enough to include in the book that documented his life's work, *Toward New Towns for America*. It was one of only two unbuilt projects featured in the book—the other one being the Greenbelt Town of Greenbrook, New Jersey, designed by Wright and Allan F. Kamstra. Modeled on Radburn, Valley Stream would be entirely owned and managed by the limited dividend developer. Monthly rents for the single family, two-family, and apartment units averaged $9.50 per room, including 50 cents per room for management of community facilities. Further, the profits secured from commercial establishments—two markets, a theater, two garages, and a social hall, all contained in a cluster of six remodeled airport hangars—would be used to reduce the rental rates on the homes and apartments.[26] Stein maintained that the cost and other studies done for this community informed his recommendations to the Resettlement Administration regarding the new town program a few years later. In addition to these projects, Radburn Terrace Apartments, Inc., a development corporation consisting of Bing as president, Herbert Emmerich as vice president, John O. Walker as secretary, and Stein and Butler as architects, proposed an apartment development of the same name at the New Jersey project.

While none of these other projects were funded, Hillside Homes, which was already well along in the review process for an RFC loan, qualified under the new PWA program. Thus Stein felt thwarted when program implementation was initially delayed.

This housing with governmental assistance is like a dream where you struggle up a great stairway only to find that the stair has reversed and what seemed the top is really the bottom of a much longer flight. When I was in Washington … it looked as though one of my projects would be first in line for action. The President signed the Bill and left on a three weeks vacation—but he did not appoint the group that R.D.K. [Robert D. Kohn] and the others had so carefully organized during the past weeks [to oversee the program]—in fact as far as they can find out he forgot all about them—So there they are—and there I am—all in a heap at the bottom of the stairs.

In early July, word officially broke that Robert Kohn had been named director of the Housing Division of the PWA. Kohn excitedly shared with Stein and Butler details of the approval of his position by the cabinet, noting that when they asked him what policy he planned to pursue, he outlined "something much like the proposals of the Regional Planning Association." Finally, Stein thought, their ideas had an advocate in a prominent position.[27]

Clearly, Stein saw this new formal connection to Washington, DC, as an opportunity to continue his efforts at informal policy making. In July 1933, at a lunch with George Gove, then a member of the New York State Housing Board, Gove acknowledged to Stein that the members had warmed to the idea of a "Housing Authority which would actually build houses." Immediately upon returning to his office Stein called Kohn in Washington asking that Kohn contact New York's governor to urge him to propose legislation during the upcoming special session enabling the establishment of local authorities. Stein acknowledged to MacKaye that Kohn would likely "surround himself" with other members of the RPAA while in Washington, including Black, Wood, and Wright; meanwhile Stein wanted to take the opportunity to "get some of the houses built." In fact, by the end of the month, Klaber had been named chief technician and Black, Wright, Ackerman, and Wood had all been retained as consultants. Kohn again though showed his reluctance at having his support of Stein's projects misconstrued as favoritism.[28]

In September 1933, the PWA Housing Division prepared a contract outlining a loan for Hillside Homes equal to 85 percent of the projected costs based on a site plan Stein had developed for four- and six-story fireproof buildings. According to the loan documents, the project's "general plan has been so arranged that it will be possible to walk from any apartment to it [the playground] without crossing a vehicular road. This will give the development the safety feature that has made the town of Radburn, New Jersey, famous throughout the world." Further, an underpass was proposed to connect the project to the new grade school across a major thoroughfare directly to the north. The city's engineering office refused to approve the project with the closed streets, and the underpass was never constructed. "If the Borough Engineer of the Bronx had not stubbornly prevented the closing of a short portion of three streets: The final plan of September 1933, which had been approved by the Federal [government] would have been carried out. Hillside Homes would have been a safer place, and even more tranquil."[29]

Throughout the fall of 1933 and early 1934, the review process for Stein's proposed PWA housing projects continued. Without certainty regarding funding, it was difficult for the architect to keep his office open and draftsmen consistently employed. The contract was not fully executed until spring of the following year. In early June 1934, Kohn was forced to step down. Further, practically everyone that Kohn had brought to Washington was fired shortly thereafter.[30]

Hillside was the largest of the PWA limited dividend projects, at 1,416 apartments, and the second largest, after Williamsburg in New York City, of the fifty-one public projects developed under the PWA housing programs (see table 4.1). The $5,636,316 project earned Stein $149,156 in architect's fees.[31]

Using a survey method to identify desired amenities, Stein included various community facilities at Hillside—a central playground, wading pool, a sheltered seating area for outdoor events, community rooms, a nursery school, and a meeting hall. This combination of community services prompted Straus and Wegg to attribute to the project "a life appreciably richer than that which any resident might find if he were to fashion it himself without aid or cooperation." At Hillside, Stein also began a collaboration with Louise Blackham who helped structure, manage, and monitor the community facilities and activities. At the dedication on June 29, 1935, Stein stated, "Hillside will never be blighted. It was planned, built and will be operated as a complete integrated neighborhood. It will control its own environment. It will be managed by a company that knows that its success depends on the preservation of its unique features. Above all, the people who will live here will preserve and develop the gardens and recreation spaces that offer an opportunity for a finer and more abundant community life."[32]

Within a few months after its opening, Hillside's occupancy rate had soared to 98 percent, a level maintained for the remainder of the decade. Though the

TABLE 4.1 Comparison of housing costs and rents for selected federally
assisted housing projects

| Project name | Year completed | Location | Agency | Program type | # of units | Cost per unit | Rent per month |
|---|---|---|---|---|---|---|---|
| Hillside Homes | 1935 | Bronx, NY | PWA | limited dividend | 1,415 | $4,038 | $41.39 |
| Carl Mackley Homes | 1935 | Philadelphia, PA | PWA | limited dividend | 284 | $3,957 | $38.95 |
| Williamsburg* | 1937 | NYC | PWA | public housing | 1,622 | $8,298 | $29.51 |
| Queensbridge | 1940 | NYC | USHA | public housing | 3,149 | $4,888 | $22.04 |
| Baldwin Hills Village | 1942 | Los Angeles | FHA | limited dividend | 627 | $4,911 | $52.00 |
| Harbor Hills | 1942 | Los Angeles Co. | USHA | public housing | 300 | $4,206 | $25.00 |

Sources: Catherine Bauer, "Description and Appraisal ... Baldwin Hills Village," Pencil Points 1944 (September): 46–60; United States Housing Authority, Annual Report of the United States Housing Authority for the Fiscal Year 1939 (Washington, DC: Government Printing Office, 1940); Clarence S. Stein, "Harbor Hills Housing," Pencil Points November (1941): 677–683; Michael W. Straus and Talbot Wegg, Housing Comes of Age (New York: Oxford University Press, 1938).

*The cost per unit for Williamsburg is based on the best information available—allotting the $13,459,000 provided by the PWA as reported by Straus and Wegg after completion of the project.

Note: Cost per unit for all projects except Williamsburg, as noted above, reflect the actual costs incurred including land and construction costs and demolition, if applicable. Williamsburg and Queensbridge are the only projects that required demolition. Rent per month includes utilities.

rents at Hillside were comparable to similar limited dividend projects assisted through the PWA's Housing Division, they were criticized for being significantly higher than the public projects that were transferred to the successor agency, the USHA (see figure 4.1). In discussing the "inadequacy of limited-dividend and co-operative housing," the Federal Writers' Project noted in its companion guide to New York City, "The lowest possible monthly room rental that private enterprise is able to offer is $11. Limited-dividend developments such as Knickerbocker Village, the Hillside project in the Bronx, and other similar projects, average $11.30. ... But the unescapable fact is that $6 a room is the highest monthly rent that one-third of the population now living in the city's unregenerate fire-traps can pay."[33]

Despite this criticism, the amenities and design of Hillside were universally praised. Shortly before its opening in the summer of 1935, Henry Saylor, writing for Architecture observed,

FIGURE 4.1 Hillside Homes, early aerial photo dated December 8, 1934. McLaughlin Aerial Surveys, 29 West 57th St., New York City, Box 38, CSP/CUL.

Hillside is not the result of this age-old impulse to make a given piece of land yield a profit, either in money or in satisfaction. Hillside started rather as an abstract idea, having no intimate connection with land or building materials or profit. The idea was this: Would it be possible to create a complete and integrated community within the larger framework of a city—a community in which families of limited income might find the setting for what President Roosevelt has called "a more abundant life"?

In 1935, Wright touted Hillside Homes in his seminal book, *Rehousing Urban America*, as the culmination of "a new type of planning" to inform the design and amenities of large-scale housing projects "fostered by a continually enlarging concept of the importance of low-cost housing and the participation of government in its provision." Though they had taken different paths, Wright had moved on sufficiently to rightfully praise the advances in design that Stein made at Hillside.[34]

## The Greenbelt Towns and
## Public Housing

In April 1935, Congress provided the funds and established the authority for the president to create the Resettlement Administration (RA). Rexford Tugwell, then undersecretary of Agriculture, was appointed the administrator of the agency and charged in part with the authority to resettle "destitute or low-income families from rural and urban areas, including the establishment, maintenance, and operation in such connection, of communities in rural and suburban areas."[35] The RA consolidated several disparate agencies that had been established in 1933 through the IRA. These agencies had initially focused on assisting farmers in foreclosure or with resettling to more viable farming sites, but by 1935 the decision was made to expand the program to assist city residents in distressed housing to resettle in new communities.

Within the RA, John Lansill oversaw the Suburban Resettlement Division, which administered the Greenbelt Town program. The program targeted increased employment through construction jobs, design improvements, and community amenities made possible through cooperative initiatives. The appropriate mix of land uses and the population required to bring into balance the economic and social conditions of the community were critical concerns of the agency. Though the program ambitiously began by surveying a hundred urban areas to determine their potential as sites for new town development, only four areas were chosen and ultimately only three were developed.

Stein enthusiastically welcomed the new program. He had untiringly promoted his proposed new town of Valley Stream for two years in Washington as a candidate for federal housing assistance and considered the Greenbelt Towns a means to finally see his project realized. On May 23, 1935, Stein presented the "Valley Stream scheme" to "the Tugwell branch of the government," enthusing to his wife that they "wanted to do nothing but whole towns all at one time." Yet for Stein, who focused so much on details and workmanship, concerns remained about cost and quality issues associated with the program strictly adhering to local materials and relief labor and burdensome rules and review processes.[36]

Still the opportunity to participate in the program seemed imminent when he was called back to Washington at the end of May to discuss "the terms on which I would design a complete town." Then Tugwell invited Stein to participate in a conference from June 30 to July 3 regarding the structure and management of the program. According to Stein, at the meeting Tugwell publicly stated his intent for Stein "to design one of our towns." By the end of the summer though, Valley Stream was quietly dropped from consideration. Stein's desire to do the work of programming and designing a new town with his colleagues in New York City and his disdain for working with a group selected for him by the government, resulted in him not being considered for the job. As he described in a letter to MacMahon from Washington toward the end of September:

> I didn't succeed in showing the Tugwell crowd that they would do much better to give me one of their towns to take back with me to New York. They are all set on building a departmentalized organization here to turn out the three or four towns. City planning, site planning, architecture, engineering, building, community organization—each in a separate compartment but all working together—that's their idea—My claim is that they all must be one—or rather not only all under one head but also an organization that is accustomed to work together as a single unit—It takes a long time to develop a group that can take the problem of lay[ing] out a town—and making it work—we have the nucleus of such a group in the office. … Well, what's the difference? They didn't see it—Perhaps I am a poor salesman, when I seem to be selling myself—It embarrasses me to seem only to be trying to get something for myself when I am trying to get the thing done in the best way.

In fact, it is likely that government regulations prevented Tugwell and Lansill from allowing the work to be awarded to private consulting firms.[37]

Despite this setback, the agency's leadership asked Stein to provide his technical expertise. Given his role as one of the principal architects on Radburn, touted by the RA as "America's first scientifically planned garden town" and his recent experience on a major large-scale housing project at Hillside Homes, Stein was among the best qualified for the job. Lansill charged him with the responsibility to "set up the community requirements for their towns …—What can a poor community afford in community facilities—how to plan them and make them pay their way." The architect acknowledged that this assignment "is really the essence—the heart of the whole problem of building new communities." While he provided cost studies and recommendations regarding the mix of land uses, Stein also traveled to Washington, DC, almost weekly for the next two months to review the designs of the towns, particularly Greenbelt, Maryland, which was the furthest along. Many of the architects had little or no experience designing low-cost communities and housing. As Stein remarked in a letter to MacMahon, "My job was to keep them tied up to reality—and gather the essentials first—so that we will know something about what it is going to cost to run our towns before we have them built and it is too late to modify the design to meet the income of those who are to live in them." Throughout his career, Stein continued to evaluate the projects on which he worked, with a specific focus on operating and maintenance costs. Stein also conducted general design studies for the Greenbelt Towns to examine issues such as "the comparative efficiency of various methods of grouping houses as affecting street, yard, and park improvement costs."[38]

Previous members of the RPAA and other associates of the community architect were well represented in the new program. As chief of planning, Frederick Bigger provided ongoing oversight of the design teams. A city planner for Pittsburgh, he had conducted preliminary studies on Chatham Village, participated in the RPAA, and partnered with Stein, Wright, and others in their circle on AIA committees. He and John Nolen were responsible for choosing the general advisors to the program as well as the design and planning teams for each of the towns. Trained as a landscape architect, Nolen was a nationally recognized planning consultant who worked in the federal World War I housing program and who designed the new town of Mariemont, Ohio, among other projects. In addition to Stein, five other experts served as general advisors on the Greenbelt Towns: Bauer, Black, Tracy Augur, Earle Draper, and J. Andre Fouilhoux. Augur and Draper were both educated as landscape architects and practiced as planners. Shortly after earning his graduate degree from Harvard, Augur worked in New York City as a planning consultant in 1922 and 1923. While Stein may have met him at this time, he definitely became familiar with Augur during his tenure with the Tennessee Valley Authority (TVA) from 1933 to 1948. After Draper earned his degree in 1915, he went on to work in Nolen's office. He is best known as the planner for Kingsport, Tennessee, while in Nolen's office and as the planner for Norris, Tennessee, while planning director for the TVA from 1933 to 1939. Fouilhoux was a key architect on Rockefeller Center and on the Trylon and Perisphere at the World's Fair of 1939. These general advisors to the Greenbelt Town program assessed design and development proposals with a focus on issues such as construction costs and long-term management needs to ensure ongoing solvency of the towns. The team for one of the four proposed towns, Greenbrook, New Jersey, consisted almost entirely of current and former associates of Stein in his architectural firm: Henry Wright and Allan F. Kamstra, town planners; Albert Mayer and Henry S. Churchill, principal architects; and Ralph Eberlin, engineer.[39]

As the Greenbelt Town program was getting underway during the summer of 1935, Stein was also working, among other projects; on the second phase of Phipps Garden Apartments; preliminary designs for Red Hook Houses—the New York City Housing Authority's (NYCHA) first project; another project for the Phipps Foundation; and an FHA job consisting of two hundred moderate rental units at the Palos Verdes Estate in California. While the latter two jobs did not make it past preliminary discussions, Stein did in fact devote considerable effort to Red Hook Houses. He was excited about the opportunity, especially "if I am really given complete charge of planning." Such enthusiasm was misplaced since this group project was to be undertaken by a total of nine architects. Stein acknowledged his fears of "endless talking and squabbling and compromising." Still he had a great deal of respect for one of the lead architects on the project, Alfred Poor, with whom he later designed the Temple of Religion for the World's Fair of 1939.[40]

He moved quickly to persuasively share his vision for the Red Hook project, bringing the other eight architects out to Hillside to impress on them the scale and pattern of open spaces and then introducing plans he and Mayer had prepared at the office. As at Hillside and Phipps and Sunnyside before it, the courts were to be particularly significant in creating community while also offering more intimate spaces. Following arguments from his colleagues that his proposal might be inconsistent with the NYCHA's vision, a disappointed Stein acknowledged that the project did not enhance his reputation or provide significant funds nor would it be designed by his draftsmen at the office. Why do it? Though Ackerman as technical advisor to the NYCHA still supported lower-density garden apartment design, the costs of slum clearance and the resulting desire to intensify residential use on the site meant that the agency had already committed to changing policy direction. The garden apartment was not a model for the slum clearance public housing projects in the heart of the city. And Stein ultimately was not involved with this project.[41]

Thus though 1935 was a busy year, it was also a year of profound disappointments—Valley Stream, the lost bid to design a new town for the Greenbelt Town program, the confirmation that the Pasadena Art Institute would go to another architect, the evaporation of a proposed redevelopment job for the Phipps Foundation and of the Princeton Museum, even the loss of a moderate income rental housing project in California, all weighed on the architect. When he learned that the FHA would not likely support a loan on the latter project, he dejectedly observed, "It was a blow—I had been going full steam—and here was a rock on the track." But given that the Greenbelt Town program epitomized, at least on paper, so much of what he and his colleagues had worked for through the RPAA, Sunnyside, and Radburn, his friends acknowledged that this loss probably hurt the worst. In a letter to his wife in early October about a trip to Washington to report on his cost studies, Stein acknowledged, "It is an interesting job—but why I should be doing this instead of designing one of their towns—it's absurd." Mumford agreed, "Clarence, though doing some of the preliminary work has not, I regret to say, been given one of them [the Greenbelt Towns] to do." In addition, by the end of the summer, two major projects—Hillside Homes and the Wichita Art Institute—were practically complete.[42]

MacMahon was also struggling with several significant challenges to her career, particularly an ongoing dispute regarding her contract so that she could have the freedom to choose more diverse and better parts. Most upsetting was being turned down for the starring role in *The Good Earth*. For months, both MacMahon and Stein had been discussing a trip to East Asia. In anticipation of that trip, Stein trimmed down his office staff that fall, practically shutting it down. Toward the end of 1935, they departed on a trip to China, Japan, and Bali that stretched well into the spring of 1936. As they had in their earlier trip to India, they took their time getting to their destinations, and once there spent considerable time getting to know each place. They spent a month in Peking, choosing to live in "a little Chinese house at the end of [a] lane," and while there visited with Liang Sicheng, already a preeminent architect and historian, who earned his bachelor's and master's degrees in architecture from the University of Pennsylvania between 1924 and 1927 with subsequent training at Harvard.[43]

With no other projects on the boards upon his return in the spring of 1936, Stein faced a lull in his practice. A major blow came in July 1936, when Henry Wright died unexpectedly after a brief illness. Stein lamented the loss to the profession, especially given his friend and colleague's recent award of a sizable Carnegie Foundation grant for a period of four years to teach at Columbia and conduct research. In a remembrance of Wright published the following month, Stein explained what he admired most in (and probably at times frustrated him most about) his colleague, "His was an unusually active mind—an inquisitive, analytical mind—that constantly drove him on from one problem to another, and from one solution to a still better solution of a problem. His ingenuity forced him to follow his reasoning to its ultimate conclusion and to fight for that conclusion. No matter what sacrifice was needed, financial or otherwise, he made them for his beliefs."[44]

Stein missed Wright's energy for innovative solutions and felt disconnected from the profession. The jobs simply did not return, nor did he seek them out. Instead, he relied on family and friends to sustain his engagement with the profession. During this time, he designed his sister Gertrude's house, discussed with close friend Aline Bernstein her dream of establishing a costume museum, and made preliminary studies for a movie house commissioned by his brother-in-law Arthur Mayer. In fall 1936, the architect had no paying job. More significantly, he was disappointed with the work he was doing, especially critiquing his housing designs.[45]

At this time, he participated in early planning meetings regarding the World's Fair of 1939. Officially a "collaborator," or consultant, to the Board of Design, on which Kohn was a member, Stein found this committee work frustrating—in a letter to his wife, he complained, "The Fair seems so futile. I get up at meetings once a week—and find fault with the plan."[46] With the CHC facing imminent ruin and the Greenbelt Town program shutting down, it seemed that much of what Stein and Wright had worked together to create was in jeopardy.

By early 1937, Stein's emotional and mental health was compromised enough that MacMahon remained in New York City to provide support rather than returning to Hollywood. On February 21, Stein admitted to his friend MacKaye, he was suffering from "nerves" and "under Doctor's orders" to stay at home "for the time being. As a result I have been staying away from work for some time." His illness was serious enough for him to be admitted to Silver Hill, a sanitarium in New Canaan, Connecticut, in early April. In later years he would return and undergo electroshock therapy as treatment when he suffered similar symptoms. In mid-May, Stein updated his friend, that he was at Silver Hill "taking a rest— and trying to find my old self." He did not return to work until late August 1937, when he notified Mumford, "at last I am getting busy again, architecturally."[47]

Certainly, Stein's friends and colleagues were not standing still. Mumford had shared a draft of his landmark *The Culture of Cities* with Stein, which the architect generally enjoyed. Bauer was also finally realizing a significant goal. Practically since the adoption of the temporary public housing program in 1933, she had promoted passage of a permanent program that located housing near jobs and facilitated development of the complete community. Her significant advocacy and policymaking skills led to passage of the 1937 Wagner-Steagall Housing Act that August. The act connected slum clearance with new development, provided low interest loans for up to 90 percent of project cost amortized over a sixty-year period, offered capital and operating grants to maintain low rents, and set cost limitations for projects.[48]

## Consulting on Baldwin Hills Village and Government Housing

Many progressive housers applauded government intervention despite the compromises made to secure approval of the public housing program. Stein certainly was among them, stating in an October lecture at the Massachusetts Institute of Technology, "The work of the semi-philanthropic companies, the so-called limited dividend corporations, has been invaluable in developing new techniques, not only in design but in management. But they did comparatively little building and none for the very poor." Thus, he concluded, direct government support for housing became essential. Congress "[has] taken the step that makes governmental housing on a colossal scale inevitable. We can no longer turn back." At the same time, Stein expressed concerns that centralized authority equated with lack of sufficient flexibility to meet local needs. "What will prevent them from refusing loans unless the Architect copies specifications prepared in Washington and accepts their canned plans?" Despite these apprehensions, he had faith that with the right combination of federal oversight, local responsibility, and flexibility—both for the local authority and the architect who worked with that agency—the program would be a success.[49]

Thus, by the fall of 1937, there were two permanent programs through the federal government for large-scale rental housing; the other had been established earlier under the FHA. The National Housing Act of June 1934 created the FHA, which under Section 207 of Title II enabled the lending industry to provide backing from the government to insure mortgages or private- or government-issued bonds for low-cost rental projects targeting moderate-income households. The PWA staff pointed out that "projects constructed under this system approximate in type and rentals those that were privately constructed under the limited-dividend policy of the Public Works Administration." But there was a fundamental difference. Under the Large-Scale Housing Division established in January 1935, later called the Rental Housing Division (RHD), the program targeted limited dividend corporations—in fact purposely moved to support such corporations—not as philanthropic enterprises but as sound real estate initiatives by developers who wanted to take advantage of this FHA program. According to a monthly newsletter of current projects and jobs printed in the architectural journal *Pencil Points*, FHA was more likely to consider them favorably due to their financial record and because "exploitation of real estate values was not the first consideration, planning and construction have been sound and social and economic considerations have had weight." From the beginning, limited dividend projects had higher rents than units constructed under the temporary public housing program. The average cost per unit of an FHA project stood around $5,000 in 1939 while the average cost for a public housing unit (excluding site clearance costs) was almost $1,000 lower at $4,068.[50]

After three years, only limited dividend corporations had secured mortgage insurance through FHA, and the program was still getting off the ground. As director of architecture in the RHD, Stein's old friend and colleague Henry Klaber was in a position to advocate for Stein and Wright's distinctive garden apartment design concepts. In fact, the design and community building innovations Stein and Wright applied at Sunnyside and Chatham Village were reforms duplicated in this FHA program. Architectural historians Laura Bobeczko and Richard Longstreth maintain that the agency "became the catalyst for a new form of garden apartment complex, spurring the construction of nearly 300 such 'communities' across the nation in just seven years." Further, while Stein, Wright, and their colleagues promoted these concepts among architects and planners, developers and contractors who embraced the program in its early days did much to popularize these ideas for a broader audience in the real estate industry.[51]

In 1938, Stein tapped the FHA mortgage insurance program for large-scale rental housing and the new public housing program to contribute to the designs of three projects on the West Coast, one of which he considered the most significant of his career. That spring, Stein entered into a contract to consult on a project he believed epitomized the attributes of large-scale housing—Baldwin Hills Village (BHV) in Los Angeles. As an FHA-insured mortgage rental project, it also marked Stein's return to limited dividend housing. Stein acknowledged that such housing targeted an income group that neither the public housing program nor the for-profit market could reach. He maintained, "There will remain those who, although they do not require large subsidies, cannot pay enough to tempt business investment. Their homes can be financed by the use of money at the very low interest rates at which the government alone can afford to lend." Limited dividend housing financed with an FHA-insured mortgage (or "investment housing," as Stein called it) also "differs fundamentally from speculative housing because it is planned, built, and operated so as to establish and maintain the security of its investment."[52]

Originally called Thousand Gardens, BHV was designed by Associated Architects—Reginald D. Johnson and the firm of Wilson, Merrill and Alexander—with Stein as consulting architect. In 1935, Johnson, formerly a designer of luxury homes, had traveled east to Washington, DC, to learn more about large-scale housing programs and to meet with Stein and visit Chatham Village, Sunnyside Gardens, and Radburn as he and his colleagues, Lewis Wilson, Edwin Merrill, and Robert Alexander, began to envision a superblock development on the Baldwin estate southwest of Los Angeles. As Miles Colean, technical director of the FHA, noted, "The privately financed field of large-scale housing opens a new career for architects." Initially proposed as a much larger phased residential project, activity on BHV intensified in 1938 when the Associated Architects contracted with Stein to work as a consultant. According to his contract, Stein's responsibilities with BHV included drafting and critiquing the site plans and "financial setups" and "when requested act[ing] as our eastern representative in connection with conferences with the FHA regarding this project." Clearly Stein's prominence, personal connections to the architects, and experience with large-scale housing recommended him for this collaboration as did his friendship with Klaber, then in a leading role at the FHA.[53]

Despite this advantageous positioning, the project was delayed, not due to lag time in implementing a new program or resistance at the local level but to difficulty in securing financing. Initially, banks were quite unwilling, in part due to lack of experience, to provide the sizable loans necessary for these low-cost housing projects. In 1941, the RFC finally stepped in to provide the mortgage. Stein's frustration was still palpable in 1957 when he noted, "Too much of these three years was spent in securing approval, loans and mortgage insurance from cautious government officials." Though Stein certainly experienced his frustrations with this project, he also considered it the fullest realization of investment housing and the Radburn Idea.[54]

Bauer found much to praise in the project's design, but she also severely criticized the management practices that ensured an all-white tenancy and the careful selection process focused on families with incomes too high to be accommodated in public housing and too low for the typical market rate housing development. She argued, "Another, much larger question, in which I am probably even more alone, is this matter of 'careful selection' of tenants. I have a strong chemical reaction against everything this phrase implies: racial discrimination, and the conscious effort to create a one-class community of nice, conforming, socially acceptable people."[55]

Clearly the well-documented institutional racism evident in the discriminatory practices of the FHA, as well as the public housing program, fostered such conditions. Still Stein, unlike some of his colleagues, was quiet on one of the most critical social issues of the twentieth century. While he mixed housing sizes, types, and tenures to accommodate a range of income groups and advocated housing assistance for the working-class and middle-income households as part of his social progressive agenda, the architect did not explicitly address racial discrimination in any of his published or unpublished writings nor did he do so in his personal communications. Unlike other societal challenges, he seemed to accept segregation as a fixed condition that he could not change. When arguing for local autonomy in the implementation of federal housing programs, he noted, "The requirements of living in different cities differ for a great variety of reasons: climate, racial inheritance, habits and way of living, the use of different materials in building and what not."[56] While an acknowledgement of racial differences, the statement did nothing to acknowledge institutional segregation and the role government, private developers, architects, and others in the housing industry could play to challenge and reverse it.

While Stein collaborated with his California colleagues on BHV, he also began work on some of the earliest public housing projects in California for the Los Angeles County Housing Authority (see figure 4.2). In fact, it was Stein's

FIGURE 4.2 Stein drawing, on the patio of Aline's home in Brentwood, California, circa 1938 possibly during a visit to work on Baldwin Hills Village, Carmelitos, and/or Harbor Hills. Box 43, CSP/CUL.

reputation and his connections to Washington, DC, that recommended him for these projects. In bidding for one of these projects, Reginald Johnson initially used Stein's name to gain a competitive edge, writing to him in June 1938: "Remembering what you said to me in New York about a Slum Clearance project in Los Angeles, I have assumed it was all right to include you as Consulting Architect in our group [Johnson and the firm of Wilson, Merrill and Alexander]. This work, of course, would be handled through the local Authority and Washington, but as the local Authority has had no experience whatsoever, I feel that unquestionably a good deal of responsibility would come upon your shoulders and the whole deal would require much more of your time and effort than an F.H.A. project."[57] Though he already had a working relationship with this same group of architects on BHV, Stein was naturally mad when he learned in September that design work on the public housing project was moving forward without his input. The community architect stated that he wanted his name removed from the project unless his colleagues funded a trip to California to see the site and learn more about the project.

Ultimately, Johnson agreed to Stein's request. In fact, Johnson knew that another group of architects had approached Stein to work on a different Los Angeles County Housing Authority project and warned Stein against acting as consultant, suggesting it would weaken Johnson and his colleague's proposal if Stein appeared as consultant on a competing application. In mid-September, Stein traveled to Los Angeles. He met with Johnson, Wilson, Merrill, and Alexander on what became Harbor Hills, located on a ninety-five-acre tract donated to the housing authority by the Palos Verdes Corporation and consulted with them on BHV. In addition, he met with his colleagues Cecil Schilling and Kenneth Wing on what became the Carmelitos public housing project, located on a site just outside of Long Beach. Contrary to Johnson's fears, the commissioners of the housing authority made it quite clear to Stein that his work was welcome on both projects: "The head of the housing authority ... wants very much that I act as advisor of both county developments. It seems when my name was mentioned Straus spoke well of me—strange things happen!" On September 21, when the two projects were formally presented to the LA County Housing Authority, the commissioners invited Stein to join them first for an informal session and then asked that he remain sitting with them as the two projects were presented by his colleagues.[58]

FIGURE 4.3 Stein with his colleagues on the roof of the offices of Associated Housing Architects (Schilling and Wing) working on the model for Carmelitos in Los Angeles. Box 2, CSP/CUL.

Stein began immediately working on the design of both public housing projects. He was particularly enthusiastic about the possibilities offered by Carmelitos, the first public housing project for the authority (see figure 4.3). "I am just hoping that the jobs we are doing may be a new beginning—The one at Long Beach has a large enough spread of land, so that we may be able at least to point the way. The architects seem delighted to co-operate in going the next step beyond Radburn. I may be able to go even further with them than with Reg Johnson's crowd—[They] are not the stars of their profession but I think they are able enough." Upon returning to the East Coast, Stein initially reported favorably to Melville Dozier, executive director of the authority, on progress in Washington with the two projects:

In general the conferences were very satisfactory. Mr. Straus seemed very much interested in what you are doing and very anxious that you go ahead just as soon as the drawings go through the regular routine at Washington. I found the attitude of those with whom I conferred very broad minded. They did not want, any more than necessary, to tell us what to do. They simply wanted to give us whatever suggestions they could and emphasized the need of economy, particularly economy of maintenance.[59]

Yet, later letters reflected Stein's frustration with implementing the program as numerous cost constraints barred him from providing the quality design, materials, and amenities he thought necessary to ensure the long-term viability of the projects. This was particularly true of the Carmelitos project. In early 1939, Stein reported to Dozier that the technical staff at the USHA found the cost estimates "substantially higher than they are willing to allow." In response, Stein angrily noted: "It is not up to the Washington group to design projects, though they may suggest means of decreasing costs (original and maintenance) and improving living conditions. By suggest I do not mean command."[60]

Schilling, Stein's main contact on Carmelitos, responded by complaining that the architect's inability to secure approvals in Washington for the earlier plans required the California architects to redesign the site entirely, costing them significantly on the project. Stein clearly resented Schilling's remarks that he had not delivered on his connections in Washington, implying that Stein's value lay in his networking capabilities, not in his architecture skills. These demands came at a particularly difficult time due to the death of his father, who had been such a vibrant part of his daily life. In a telling reply, Stein fumed, "I refuse to consider having my fee reduced on the basis of failure to render service neither called for in my contract nor promised at any time, nor one that honestly could have been offered to you by anyone." He demanded that his colleagues withdraw the criticism and the letter, agreeing to an almost 30 percent reduction in his fee for services if they indeed did so.[61]

Despite these frustrations, Stein decided to do another public housing project. In 1940, he worked collaboratively with his colleagues Butler, Churchill, Kohn, and Eberlin to design a phase of the Fort Greene public housing project in Brooklyn. With a total of nine firms involved, the massive 3,501-unit development was designed and constructed in phases, with Stein and his colleagues doing the third phase of six- and eleven-story buildings containing a total of

866 units. Though New York state sponsorship—it was the first public housing project to have such support—allowed more flexibility in income targets and design guidelines, including larger unit sizes, than the federal program, Stein was highly disappointed with the outcome. Of the "largest housing development in the country" at its groundbreaking on May 6, 1941, Stein dryly observed, "I never had less enthusiasm about any housing job on which I have worked—Too many cooks—no leadership—no sense in the location or the scheme as part of the future city or as a community in itself."[62]

As Stein worked on Fort Greene, he was also increasingly focused on the country's impending entrance into the war overseas and the opportunities to showcase his regional planning, new town design, and housing ideas. "In the present emergency all idea of speculation and private monetary gain must be put aside if we are to succeed.... The government can now determine on the location of new industries and on the form of residential communities as it is financing both of them. With single control it is possible to really plan in a big way and to immediately carry out big plans." Enacted in October 1940, the Lanham Act outlined a government role through the Federal Works Agency (FWA) for the production of war worker housing. John Carmody, administrator of the FWA, regarded the Lanham Act "as an opportunity to design and build communities that would 'set a pattern for the future development of housing in America.'" Given Carmody's broader social agenda for the defense housing program, it is no surprise that within a few months Stein visited his office hoping to secure such an opportunity.[63]

On January 14, 1941, both Stein and his old colleague Hardie Phillip arrived in the nation's capital seeking support for a defense housing project in Honolulu first with the navy and then the army. Stein had much better luck when he met the following day with Clark Foreman, housing assistant to Carmody. Stein critiqued the work underway on site planning at the Public Buildings Administration (PBA), like the USHA, an agency under the umbrella of the FWA. The PBA was responsible for "direct construction in conjunction with the defense program" from design specifications to acquiring property and completing the buildings, whether warehouses or residences. Stein's friend, Kline Fulmer, who had worked as an associate architect on Greenbelt, joined him. As the assistant resident manager at Greenbelt, Fulmer oversaw the development of one thousand units of defense housing in the community later that year. Regarding the work they witnessed underway at the "architectural factory," Stein wasted no time informing Foreman that "the principal difficulty with their [the government architects'] work—in addition to the fact that they needed site—city planners— was the fact that they had no program." In addition, Carmody considered these projects as complete communities while W. E. Reynolds, the head of the PBA, appeared to be focused on the disposition of the buildings after the war individually. Stein reminded Carmody that Reynolds worked for him "and that it was his business to go give the architect—Reynolds his program. A clear statement on a few sheets of paper would save lots of time and talk." During this early period, the legislation gave Carmody the flexibility to seek out and encourage architects and builders who applied innovative techniques in design and construction. Not surprisingly, Stein was asked to write the program, which he did that afternoon with the assistance of Fulmer and Bauer.[64]

Upon seeing Stein's work the next morning, Carmody tapped him to develop a site plan for a model demountable defense housing project proposed nearby in Maryland. In early February, Stein presented his alternative site plan for Indian Head to Carmody, who compared it with the "the endless rows of similar lots" proposed by the PBA in-house architects. The FWA administrator favored Stein's work, prompting the architect to exclaim, "This should mean the acceptance of the idea of community planning in place of the old type lot subdivision not only for Indian Head but as a dominating policy for the future." Carmody then appeared personally before the PBA advisory committee to endorse Stein's site plan for Indian Head, which appeared, Stein reported, "much the same as Radburn—but adjusted to the beautiful site above the Potomac River."[65]

Stein knew that work on the Indian Head site plan could not sustain his office and hoped to continue exploring his housing and site design ideas through the defense housing program with the goal of securing prominent jobs. In May 1941, after several months of seeking further opportunities, Stein was offered what he considered two minor projects north of Pittsburgh in Shaler and Stowe townships (see figure 4.4). Congress had just endorsed an additional appropriation of $150 million for defense housing, and the city and county housing authorities were planning to develop approximately five thousand units in the Pittsburgh area. By the war's end, Pennsylvania ranked among the top states in the number of defense housing units with the Pittsburgh area leading all other cities in the state.[66]

At roughly 250 units each, the two projects actually approached the national average of 270 units each at defense projects developed during this period. Stein

FIGURE 4.4 Defense housing, Stowe Township, Pittsburgh, Pennsylvania. Image from promotional brochure with the housing toward the center rear on the higher piece of land, photo dated October 8, 1941. States in part on front, "Stowe Township, Pa., Defense Housing, Federal Works Agency, Project No. 36,171x, Mellon-Stuart Company, General Contractors, Clarence Stein, Arch." Photo by F. C. Viets, Pittsburgh, PA, Box 2, CSP/CUL.

decided to make the most of the opportunity, acknowledging that "the larger developments have already been promised to local architects—which is natural." Even though the local representative of the FWA, Bryn Hovde, the director of the Pittsburgh Housing Authority, had established a policy that no one architect should receive more than one defense project in the Pittsburgh area, he and his colleague, Frank Palmer, director of the Allegheny County Housing Authority, recognized Stein's proficiency with hillside design—the premiere example being Chatham Village—and agreed to award Stein both projects.[67]

While Stein clearly loved what he was doing—creating something new and learning from it—his letters occasionally took on an almost frantic tone given the quick turnaround demanded for delivery of the drawings. As he finished Stowe in mid-June and turned his attention fully on Shaler, he observed to his wife, "Meanwhile it is grind—grind, grind—time is short—time is flying—Decisions must be made immediately—the work of the various technicians must be co-ordinated—the form and plan of the house and the site work—the sewers—the water lines, the gas lines—and the electric poles—the roads and paths and steps—every step just where it belongs—and a place for the garbage can—and then the landscape work—each shrub and tree in place—And each engineer must know what the other is doing."[68]

Following the frantic pace of his defense housing work that summer, Stein took a break by visiting his and MacMahon's country retreat in Westchester County. Called A Thousand Years, their farmhouse was located near property owned by Robert Kohn and Gerard Swope, president of General Electric (see figure 4.5). While they initially intended to build a new home on the property, Stein instead designed a small redwood house on a hill above the farmhouse. Echoing the design of a Japanese teahouse, the modernist structure featured broad windows that allowed sweeping views of the property. He then had improvements made to the farmhouse, adding heat, sewer, and hot water in the fall of 1939 so that he and MacMahon could comfortably visit the property year-round. They entertained their friends frequently at A Thousand Years, though Stein also visited alone to rest and reflect (see figure 4.6).[69]

Still, these quiet moments were not enough to ease the strain Stein felt from supervising so many at his office, working under such tight deadlines, and maintaining such a busy travel schedule. By the end of summer 1941, the Honolulu project had fallen through and a third defense housing project in Pittsburgh—the Clariton project—was in question with no further work from Washington imminent. Earlier that year Stein had prophetically commented to MacMahon on his earlier "dark period" in 1936–1937. Comparing his efforts to get a Greenbelt Town to design in 1935 with his current efforts to get defense housing work in Washington, he observed, "How things repeat. Tugwell promising me a town to do—All those hopes—And then that dark period when I suffered so—But there was little sign of it in the letters. I kept it pretty well hidden—Only there was that house of Gertrude's—always wrong—I don't think it will happen again. I must steel myself to hear that I am not getting any of the housing jobs—not even Honolulu—That will be hard."[70]

FIGURE 4.5 Drawing by Stein featuring his three homes: at upper left, A Thousand Years in Westchester County, New York; at upper right, MacMahon's home in Brentwood, California; and at the bottom, the apartment at West Central Park in New York City; dated February 22, 1941. Box 36, CSP/CUL.

FIGURE 4.6 Stein standing in the drive to 1000 Years with his home in the background circa 1952. Box 43, CSP/CUL.

By the fall, he was ill again. In a mid-January 1942 letter to his old friend MacKaye, Stein revealed just how ill he had been, including a drawing of himself as a frail stooped man with MacMahon helping him along. He began, "Above is pictured my first venture out of doors. Yesterday I was guided from bench to bench [by Aline] ... and we covered two blocks going and coming!"[71] He continued his recuperation that winter in Tucson, Arizona, at the Double U Ranch, a dude ranch frequented by affluent Jews—Stein referred to it as a "Jewish colony." As he recuperated, he began looking again for work in Washington even before his return to the east coast in mid-March 1942. By that time, much had changed in the defense housing program.

On February 24, 1942, Roosevelt issued an executive order consolidating sixteen housing agencies into the new National Housing Agency (NHA), under which the Federal Public Housing Authority (FPHA) now oversaw all publicly financed defense housing programs. Carmody had already stepped down from his position at the FWA due to health reasons and with him had gone the New Deal emphasis on the potential for social reform realized through innovations in the economics, design, and construction of housing. While acknowledging "the valiant and patient work by a small group of reformers" who established the nation's permanent public housing program, the editors of *Architectural Forum* noted that with the war on, the defense housing program was no place "for social experiments, intramural contests, administrative setting up exercises and mass production of red tape." With this reorganization, the country's defense housing policy focus was indeed also changing.[72]

Herbert Emmerich, who as general manager of the CHC had overseen much of the administrative work at Radburn and most recently served on the War Production Board, had been appointed commissioner of the FPHA. Stein applauded the decision, writing to Bauer, "Herbert is the best man who could be chosen for the job." Yet Emmerich supported the shift in policy to "encourage private builders to participate in the war housing program [through Title VI of the FHA] and grant them war priorities in a time of great shortage of building materials and labor" while the FPHA focused on building temporary housing as efficiently as possible. He noted, the adoption of standardized types "streamlined the production schedule" while still demanding "certain minimum standards of health and decency and of simple community facilities."[73]

In late April 1942, he called on Stein to act as consultant for the government "to make a survey with recommendations of the standards that should govern the provision of various community facilities in the war projects we have under contemplation." Critical considerations in the programming and design of these places were the shortage of construction materials, accommodations for women in defense industries, the potential isolation of these places and limits of transportation, and the need to enhance morale and create community among strangers who had been thrown together to work long hours. Stein interviewed experts on infirmaries, day care, stores, recreation, and education to develop standards and began working on diagrams of prototype multipurpose centers. By early June, Stein had prepared some initial specifications and floor layouts of community buildings clustered around an internal courtyard with parking on the outlying edges and separate pedestrian ways connecting to the residential areas of the community.[74]

Stein also resumed his extremely busy social schedule, attending a dinner featuring the writer Richard Wright, a presentation by Hugh Ferris and Roland Wank to the Architectural League focusing on designs for the TVA, openings at the Museum of Modern Art and the Metropolitan Museum, plus frequent dinners at his home with visiting architects and old friends. This intensive period came to an abrupt end as Stein again became incapacitated by illness. He wrote to his friend Henry Klaber, "Things move too quickly—Too many things happening at one time.—If one could only concentrate on one of these interesting problems." By June 15, Kohn was interceding for Stein, writing a letter to Emmerich asking that Stein be given a few weeks off "so as to get a complete rest. He will be getting himself in a bad condition if he does not quit, and I understand that the various things he was to study are not in such a rush after all." At the end of June, Stein submitted his resignation letter. By that fall, he had returned to Silver Hill. In 1943, he continued his recuperation in the company of his sister Lillie and a nurse at the Double U Ranch in Tucson where he had spent the winter of 1942.[75]

## Advocacy of Investment Housing

By May 1943, Stein was healthy enough to resume his architectural practice, partnering on a series of large-scale projects with John W. Harris, an architect who headed a major construction management company, John W. Harris

Associates, Inc. (Harris Associates). Harris had already constructed several nota-ble buildings, including the RCA and Associated Press Buildings at Rockefeller Center, and Stein considered him a critical partner as he sought to establish a network of professionals to design, develop, and manage complete commu-nities of investment housing for the postwar era. With Harris on board, Stein began exploring the potential of partnering with private insurance companies as investors in limited dividend housing developments at a grand scale. In early 1944, he coordinated with Louis Pink, at the time head of New York's Insurance Department and former director of the State Housing Board and City Housing Authority, to convene a meeting of representatives from banks and insurance companies. He updated Frank Palmer, director of the Allegheny County Housing Authority, "A few weeks ago I felt that the next thing to do in New York housing was to develop a large run-down area for the use of the middle class as well as poor. As an example of how New York should be re-built, we needed at least one complete community with adequate recreation, shopping centers, apartments of different types and heights, planned for safety and peaceful living, close to working places, and yet with convenient means of getting to open country." Stein had already gotten a favorable review from the FHA of the preliminary site design, and Mayor LaGuardia sent Robert Moses to the meeting as his representative. While nothing further came of these proposals, Stein's efforts did get the attention of the New York Life Insurance Company, with whom he and Harris partnered on an investment housing proposal at Fresh Meadows in Flushing, Queens.[76]

The 202-acre site, primarily a golf course, consisted of rolling land with some concentrations of wooded areas bounded by a park and single family homes and major roads on the north and south sides and with row houses and garden apart-ments nearby. A subway extension was proposed proximate to the site. Harris As-sociates dubbed it "one of the most desirable vacant sites for a large scale housing development remaining in New York City." The construction company proposed investment housing in partnership with an insurance company or other major equity investor, a diversity of housing types and sizes, integrated open spaces with as much as possible of the site's natural attributes retained, and education, com-munity, and commercial uses. The initial assessment prepared by Harris's in-house architect, Lathrop Douglass, included a mixture of two- and three-story garden apartments with the potential for "a few" six-story elevator apartment buildings grouped together on the highest elevation on the site. The average density was projected to be nine units per acre, and the residences rented at approximately eighteen dollars per room. For his part, Stein drafted unit layouts and a site plan of the community consisting of 1,500 apartments in three- and four-story walk-up buildings clustered at approximately 30 units per acre, 1,000 row houses at approximately 7.5 units per acre, a school site of 5.5 acres, parks and playgrounds on a total of 10 acres, and a store center including parking on 9 acres. A more diverse selection of housing could accommodate singles and families at different stages of life, Stein argued, resulting in a more stable project.[77]

Stein promoted the moderately sized project on cheap land in Queens as an initial means for the New York Life Insurance Company to get involved with investment housing—in a financially feasible project without requiring local tax exemptions. Doing so also avoided compliance with any obligation for racial integration.[78] The company's vice president, George S. Van Schaick asked Stein to meet with New York Life's architect, Harmon Gurney, to begin discussing specifics regarding the project. Over the remainder of the summer of 1944, Stein held a series of meetings with the insurance company's architect as he designed the unit layouts and site plan for the project. As Stein produced the designs, Gurney critiqued the cost of the units, arguing that a price closer to fourteen dollars per room as opposed to eighteen dollars per room as originally projected, was more consistent with the company's desire to do a less expensive project to start. In particular, Gurney was concerned about greater plumbing costs associated with kitchens being separate from bathrooms and the small number of units accessible from each landing area in the apartment buildings. While Stein argued that these features made the apartments more appealing in design and function and were in fact modeled on the Phipps Garden Apartments, he did agree with the proposal to consider relocating the stores from their central site to the edge of the project to attract shoppers from outside the development.

Although Douglass, Harris's own architect, had initially proposed the eighteen dollars per room rental level, Harris joined the criticisms regarding the development cost, noting that Phipps Garden Apartments was too pricey a model, that the densities for Fresh Meadows were too low, and that the proportion of "no-bedroom" apartments was too high. Further Harris became concerned that Stein's community plan used the entire 202-acre site rather than focusing on the 140-acre golf course property with potential expansion onto the additional 62 acres should the insurance company be able to acquire it. He also felt the plans were too detailed—an insurance executive at New York Life had indicated to Harris that once the company decided on the property and the project, they would "tell us what to build." The contractor, who was currently working on several projects, including the Standard Oil Building at Rockefeller Center, continued, "It is to be regretted that so much time has been spent studying a scheme which though obviously desirable from an aesthetic and social point of view does not solve the unavoidable economic problems and criteria established."[79]

When the property was finally sold to the insurance giant in April 1946, Harris was shocked to hear that Van Schaick did not know Harris Associates had initially brought the property to the attention of New York Life. Harris had been confident in securing the project and now had to scramble for it. A representative of his firm quickly brought to the insurance company's attention Harris Associates' considerable efforts to undertake cost studies and draft plans for the project in 1944. To Harris's dismay, company executives responded by hiring another architecture firm, Vorhees, Walker, Foley & Smith, and a competing contractor, George A. Fuller, which had constructed the Carmelitos project. A partner in one of the largest architectural firms at the time, Ralph Walker was a good friend of Stein's; he had made a name for himself with his art deco skyscraper designs beginning with the Barclay-Vesey Telephone Building in New York City and his entries in the 1933 Chicago Fair and the 1939 New York World Fair. The frustrated Harris discovered that Gurney had discussed with Stein at the outset his inability to commit on behalf of the company to a particular architect. Further, Harris learned Gurney had harbored significant unease about working with Stein on the project due to the small size of his office and concerns about his health. In early 1947, Harris initiated a lawsuit against New York Life in hopes of collecting the costs incurred for working on the project. Stein refused to participate either as a complainant in the lawsuit or as a witness for Harris's firm, arguing that no formal agreement for work existed, that any similarity in the two plans reflected the current trends in middle-income residential design of this type, and that he would not participate in a suit against his friend Walker.[80]

Under construction from July 1946 to October 1949, the project ultimately included 3,000 apartments with 600 total in two thirteen-story buildings located on the highest elevation on the property and the remaining 1,400 units in 138 two- and three-story apartment buildings scattered throughout the site.[81] The lowest priced units were projected at $21.44 per room, certainly more than Stein proposed.

Clearly, Stein's efforts to contribute to the design and development of investment housing on the East Coast, a complement to his successful West Coast project at Baldwin Hills Village, failed. Although delays with program implementation at Hillside and BHV had indeed irritated Stein, his greater concern was with Washington's cost restrictions and limiting "guidelines" for public housing projects. This resulted not only in compromises to design and materials but also elimination of amenities and facilities that the architect considered essential to create the complete community. The defense housing projects in Pittsburgh were Stein's last realized government housing jobs. As he explained to Ralph Eberlin in 1944, "The truth is I have made very little effort to get any Government Housing work. It is all cut and dried now. All the drawings for buildings are canned and sent out from Washington. In most cases the architect merely crosses out certain things in the drawings." In contrast, the more flexible limited dividend and FHA large-scale rental programs afforded him significant opportunities to promote his progressive housing ideas. These are the projects where he advanced innovative site design to create enhanced and integrated spaces intended to foster community—a key component of the Radburn Idea.[82]

# 5

## THE RADBURN IDEA

The Radburn Idea reflected more than the strategic siting of streets and parks, the clustering of homes, and the integration of diverse uses and housing types; the socioeconomic and administrative concepts were just as essential. Nor, as Stein noted, were these ideas anything new. What then differed? One answer is found in the way these ideas redefined the Garden City of Victorian England for an America of the automobile age. Because the site design concepts were a primary consideration, which Stein also applied to a range of other projects, including museum designs, and because they were and are so readily misconstrued, a closer examination of their component parts in evolution and application provides a fuller understanding of the innovative contribution at the heart of this idea.

Consistent with social reformer and educator John Dewey's philosophy, Stein indeed was an experiential learner. He discerned more about site layout and the use of open space from the intimate and grander parks of Paris and his European travels from 1905 to 1911 while he trained at the École than in the institution's ateliers. Later, at Raymond Unwin and Barry Parker's Hampstead Garden Suburb, he saw superblocks infused with communal greens much as he and Wright applied to Radburn. In fact, Unwin's *Town Planning in Practice*, published in 1909, extolled the "site planner" of small houses to "secure for as many as possible of these houses some extent of outlook by arranging breaks in the street line, by setting the houses back round greens, by planning his roads so that they may command some distant view or may lead on to some open space; and wherever a specially fine view is obtainable, by grouping as many of the houses as possible so that they may enjoy it." Stein considered Hampstead Garden Suburb Unwin's "greatest work in site planning," returning to the late Unwin's home there when he was writing his seminal book *Toward New Towns for America*.[1]

When he went to work for Bertram Goodhue, an architect who valued regional traditions and materials in his projects, Stein already had an eye for these features. While with Goodhue, he honed his site design skills especially relating more formal and more intimate community spaces, introducing cost savings without compromising critical elements, and seeking a balance between circulation and open space. As he grew to become what he termed a "community architect," he engaged his site design skills more readily. These ideas were applied in a range of projects and promoted in numerous architectural publications and lectures. After World War II, clustered housing, hierarchical circulation systems, and innovative open space design concepts were translated abroad in new town designs, and more episodically emulated in the United States.

## Emerging Expertise in Design

Early work through Architects Associated included new permanent structures for the Ethical Culture Society's Hudson Guild Farm camp in Hopatcong, New Jersey, which led to subsequent projects in the early 1920s for nearby affluent clients.[2] In the Dining Hall and Rose Walter Cottage at the Ethical Culture Society retreat and the housing for city youths at Camp Aladdin, Stein extensively used local fieldstone and exposed beams to create a rustic sensibility consistent with the use and setting of these country refuges. Based on the designs of these modest buildings, Stein secured contracts for three homes in 1922—the redesign of a barn into a home for William Pollak and the Paul Rie and Edwin Wasser houses, all of which adopted a rustic Arts and Crafts style similar to that applied in the camp buildings. The largest of the three, the Wasser house, was particularly distinguished for the way in which Stein connected interior and exterior spaces. The restrained appearance of the fieldstone façade facing the entry drive contrasts significantly with that along the rear of the house, which though of the same material incorporates much larger windows that link the adjacent interior rooms—all family gathering spaces—with the rear yard. A verandah runs the entire length and features French doors that provide access. A low wall defines the more formal area of the rear yard nearer the house with the outlying area characterized by strewn boulders.

Stein's early large-scale unbuilt projects demonstrate his emerging talent in site design—at Sunnyside Park in Shelton, Connecticut, with Kohn in 1920; Fort Sheridan Gardens with Ernest Gruensfeldt; and the Spuyten Duyvil Housing Development in the northwest Bronx in 1923. At both Sunnyside Park and Fort Sheridan Gardens, the architects clustered attached and detached homes around loop roads, devoting the remainder of the site to a park, school, and other community spaces. As sole architect, Stein designed the higher density, upscale Spuyten Duyvil apartments for the Dunnock Realty Company at the busy corner of the Spuyten Duyvil Parkway in Riverdale, a historically wealthy section of the Bronx that was experiencing an infusion of apartment development. Here, on the site's highest elevation, the seven four-story apartment buildings enclose a formal terrace with a central reflecting pool (see figure 5.1). This community space, intended for residents alone, steps down to a more organically arranged landscape with meandering pathways leading into an adjacent public park. The floor plans for each unit reflect Stein's intent that the apartments turn inward toward the terrace, with numerous windows and French doors providing visual and physical access to the shared community space. As at the other projects he was working on at this time, his application of regional fieldstone on the first two stories and along a wall that connects the individual buildings draws attention to and thematically links the buildings (see figure 5.2). What distinguishes the detailed drawings of the unbuilt project is Stein's use of enclosure to create a haven from the busy parkway and sophisticated articulation of linkage between private and public realms.

Just four years earlier, he had also designed, as part of a statewide competition sponsored by New York State's 1919 Reconstruction Commission, another garden apartment project in Riverdale on West 239th Street. The July 1920 issue of the Architectural Record featured this project as "Garden Apartments in Cities" along with designs by noted architects such as Andrew Thomas. Despite a density of over thirty units per acre on the three-acre site, Stein maintained individual entries to foster "the old American small town ideal of individuality and privacy."[3] By alternating buildings, a perimeter arrangement was realized with the shared interior space at the center accommodating three formal gardens and

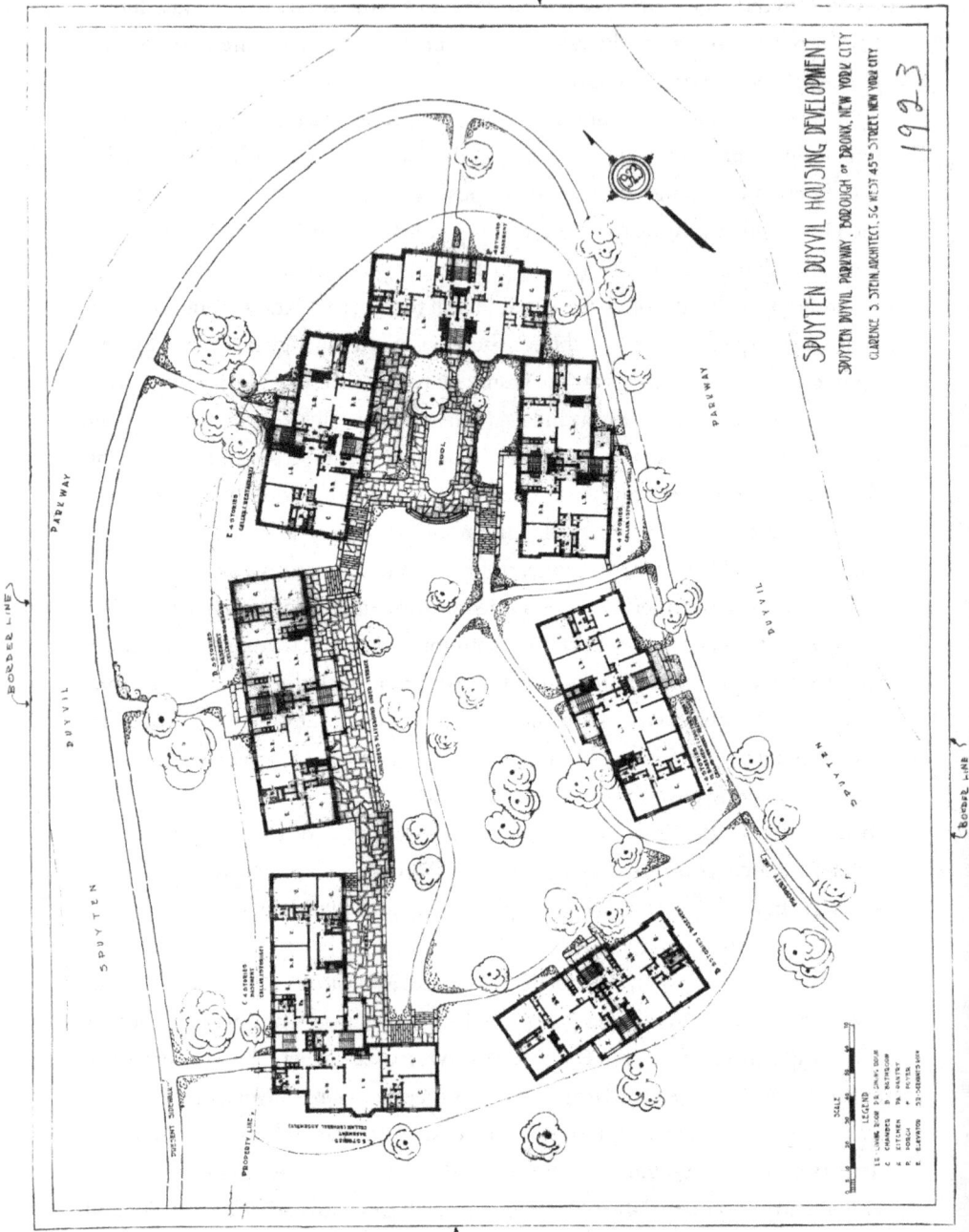

FIGURE 5.1 Site plan of Spuyten Duyvil Housing, C. S. Stein, architect, 1923. Box 1, CSP/CUL.

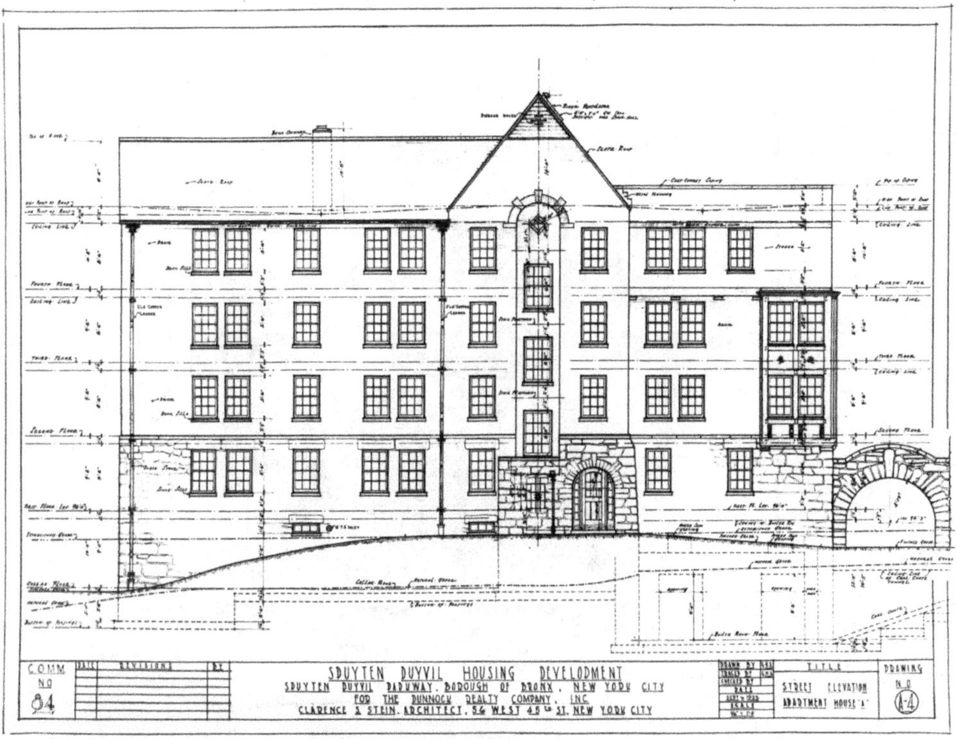

FIGURE 5.2 Elevation of Spuyten Duyvil Housing, C. S. Stein, architect, September 6, 1923. Box 1, CSP/CUL.

two larger playgrounds. Even with one two-story building of six units (see figure 5.3), this design more effectively and efficiently housed families on a sixty-five-foot-wide lot as opposed to traditional detached single family homes, with the goal of allowing middle-class families access to housing with community amenities they could not otherwise afford. Certain aspects of this design, particularly the alternating types of housing and centralized space, though not the I- and U-shaped building configurations, were adapted to the Sunnyside Gardens site.

The heyday of the garden apartment, with these centralized green spaces, began in the early 1920s, with the growing middle class in New York City seeking less expensive and less crowded options in the recently opened outlying boroughs now accessible by subway. Lessons about large-scale, low-cost housing had already been learned via the World War I government housing programs for

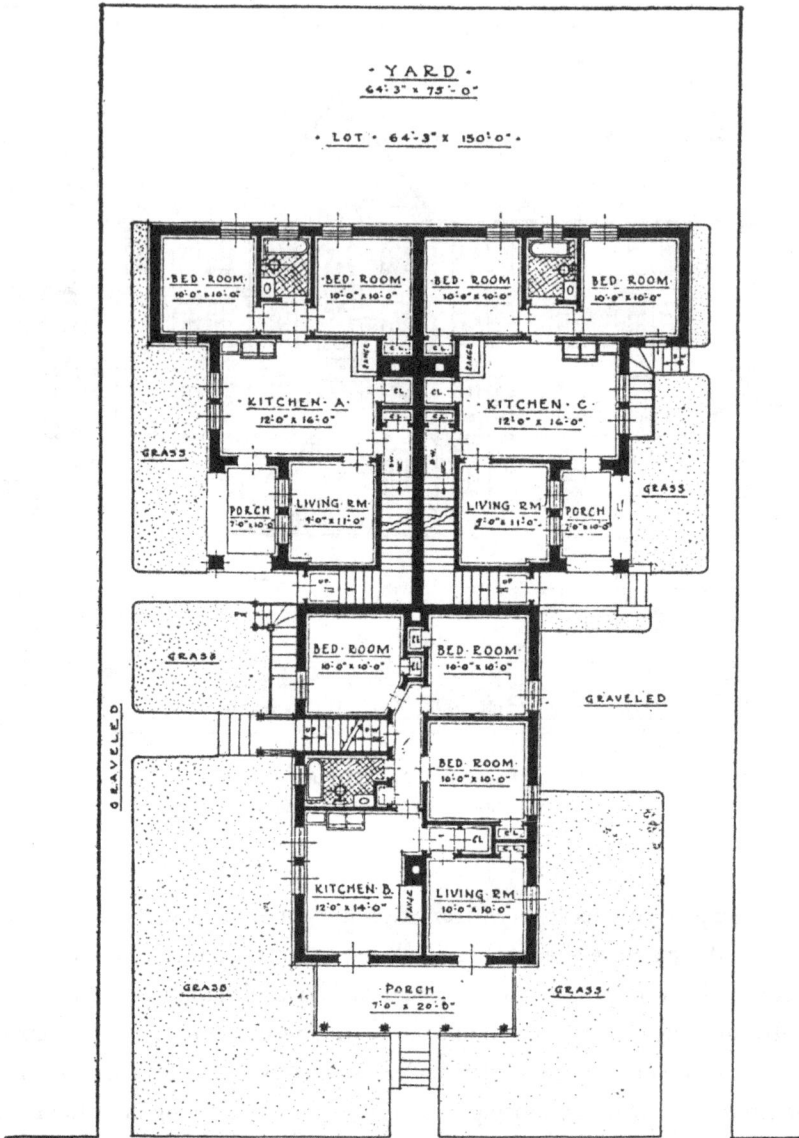

FIGURE 5.3 Detail, garden apartments in Bronx Borough, New York City, Clarence S. Stein, architect, 1920. John T. Boyd Jr., "Garden Apartments in Cities," *Architectural Record* 48 (July 1920): 53-74, 69.

war workers, in which architects such as Kohn, Wright, and Ackerman had participated. Examples from Germany and England had also made an impression. Further, architects such as Thomas had combined properties to design perimeter structures at the city block level, much of it philanthropic and limited dividend housing offering increased light and ventilation as an alternative to the crowded tenements. Other influences, such as Raymond Unwin's *Nothing Gained by Overcrowding* published in 1912 had done much to promote this design, especially at the lower density of two- and three-story buildings. Unwin argued that the advantages of cooperation were fostered by spaces designed to encourage social interaction. He also advocated for more responsive design of local roadways based on traffic levels as a means to further decrease development costs without sacrificing any community benefits. This combining of smaller city lots to more flexibly design the site appealed to Stein who understood the benefits of reduced lot coverage while maintaining or perhaps even increasing the number of units to ensure an adequate profit and creating a community amenity in the centralized open space. As his colleague Walter Behrendt observed, the economic and social innovations introduced by this new housing type were compelling:

> The obsolete scheme of subdividing the block in individual plots, characteristic of the old tenement house system, was entirely abandoned, and replaced by a system adapted to the principles of large scale construction, connecting in one homogenous plan the area not only of a single block, but of entire city districts. With the whole block as a unit, only its borders are built upon, and with the structures no more than two rooms deep. Rear buildings and courtyards are thereby eliminated, and replaced by large open spaces in the interior of the block, developed into common gardens and playgrounds for children.[4]

Later, Stein and his colleagues applied clustering and roadway designs based on anticipated capacity as further innovations to ensure low-cost housing without compromising their community building ideals.

During the summer of 1924, as the first phase of Sunnyside Gardens was under construction, Stein and Wright traveled to England to participate in the International Town Planning Conference. While in England, the two architects conferred with Unwin and Parker, the architects of Hampstead Garden Suburb and Letchworth, and Ebenezer Howard regarding their work at Sunnyside and plans for their next project. Stein noted what an inspiration Unwin and Howard were, though "I do not think that Henry Wright and I really borrowed form and arrangement, not intentionally so, anyhow." Yet the visit was significant in its timing and in its access to two of the most respected thinkers in Garden City planning:

> We visited Ebenezer Howard in Welwyn and Raymond Unwin at Wyldes. We got acquainted with them, talked things over with them and saw how their ideas were realized. I remember walking about Welwyn with old Ebenezer, and how alive he was to the way his conceptions developed and changed in practice: "Some people like to work in gardens, but others don't. So we have learnt to lay out different types of lots to fit their varied desires." Of Unwin's work we were most impressed by Hampstead Garden Suburb—the wonderful feeling that he and his partner brother-in-law, Barry Parker, had for the relation of buildings to the form of the land, to each other and to the background of foliage. I know nothing finer of that romantic age before life and cities were molded to serve the requirements of speeding autos rather than humans.[5]

At Hampstead Garden Suburb, the size of the property, its irregular topography, the desire to integrate the countryside, maintain views, and introduce a variety of housing types and patterns to accommodate a range of incomes, resulted in a more organic street arrangement with courts and quadrangles characterizing the residential layout. At Sunnyside, the existing gridiron pattern resulted in a more regimented series of perimeter structures, though certainly intended to accommodate a range of residential needs and reflecting a traditional design, here more colonial than medieval, with varying roof lines to create a sense of individuality.

Sunnyside's first phase included eight one-family and forty two-family houses two stories in height and six- and seven-family apartment buildings of three stories. Throughout, the blocks ranged in size from 190 to 200 feet wide and 600 to 900 feet long. The houses and apartments were two rooms deep, leaving an area approximately 120 feet wide between the units, consisting of thirty feet of private garden space on either side and a remaining width of sixty feet of shared community space controlled by a forty-year easement. Roughly 28 percent of the land was built on at a density of twenty-seven units per acre. Individual or paired entryways and porches on the rear characterized the homes with gable and flat roofs further distinguishing the individual units while traditional brick facades reinforced a sense of continuity.

As subsequent blocks at Sunnyside were developed, Stein, Wright, and later Ackerman worked together improving the floor layouts of individual units and the overall perimeter design. Wright explained the intricacies behind the seemingly basic facades, "Although the architectural effect at Sunnyside is on the whole harmonious and apparently homogenous, it represents a continuous evolution of fundamental planning and planning theory." Simple standardized units grouped in varying ways created diversity while ensuring economies of scale, and thus lower project costs. The grouping of garages offsite from the apartment blocks allowed the central areas to be open for recreation and other community building activities. Though as Wright later pointed out, "Merely the reduction of land coverage is not a solution; scattered open space does not accomplish the necessary results. The solution lies rather in concentrated open areas properly related to the rooms within the apartment."[6]

In the second year of development, adjustments were made to the design of these central spaces, creating a series of smaller areas more in scale with the surrounding two- and three-story structures than the continuous open space at the center of the first unit (see figure 5.4). Wright explained one such approach: attached one- and two-family row houses were "terminated by a three-family two-story dwelling set back to cut into the block. This divided these unusually long blocks into three interior courtyards, providing cross-walks at two points, increasing the apparent width of the court, and adding to the architectural interest."[7]

Marjorie Sewell Cautley, the landscape architect who later worked on Radburn, Phipps Garden Apartments, Hillside Homes, and Valley Stream, lent her considerable expertise to the layout and plantings in these critical central places. Cautley was brought into the project based on a series of articles she wrote for *Country Life in America* in 1921 regarding garden designs for modest homes. In making her decisions, she carefully considered the costs associated with long-term maintenance of these spaces. In general, she designed these sites with the existing topography and native plants in mind and used plantings and paving to program and delineate specific types of outdoor spaces. She was also sensitive to the relationship between various private and public realms and the need for mothers to be able to supervise their children, especially their younger children, whether from inside the house or within a nearby park. Reflecting back on her legacy, Stein characterized her landscapes as "rich, varied and imaginative."[8]

By the summer of 1926, a three-acre playground and park had opened at Sunnyside, and the community association was thriving, with among other initiatives "a private nursery school for children from two to six years, conducted by

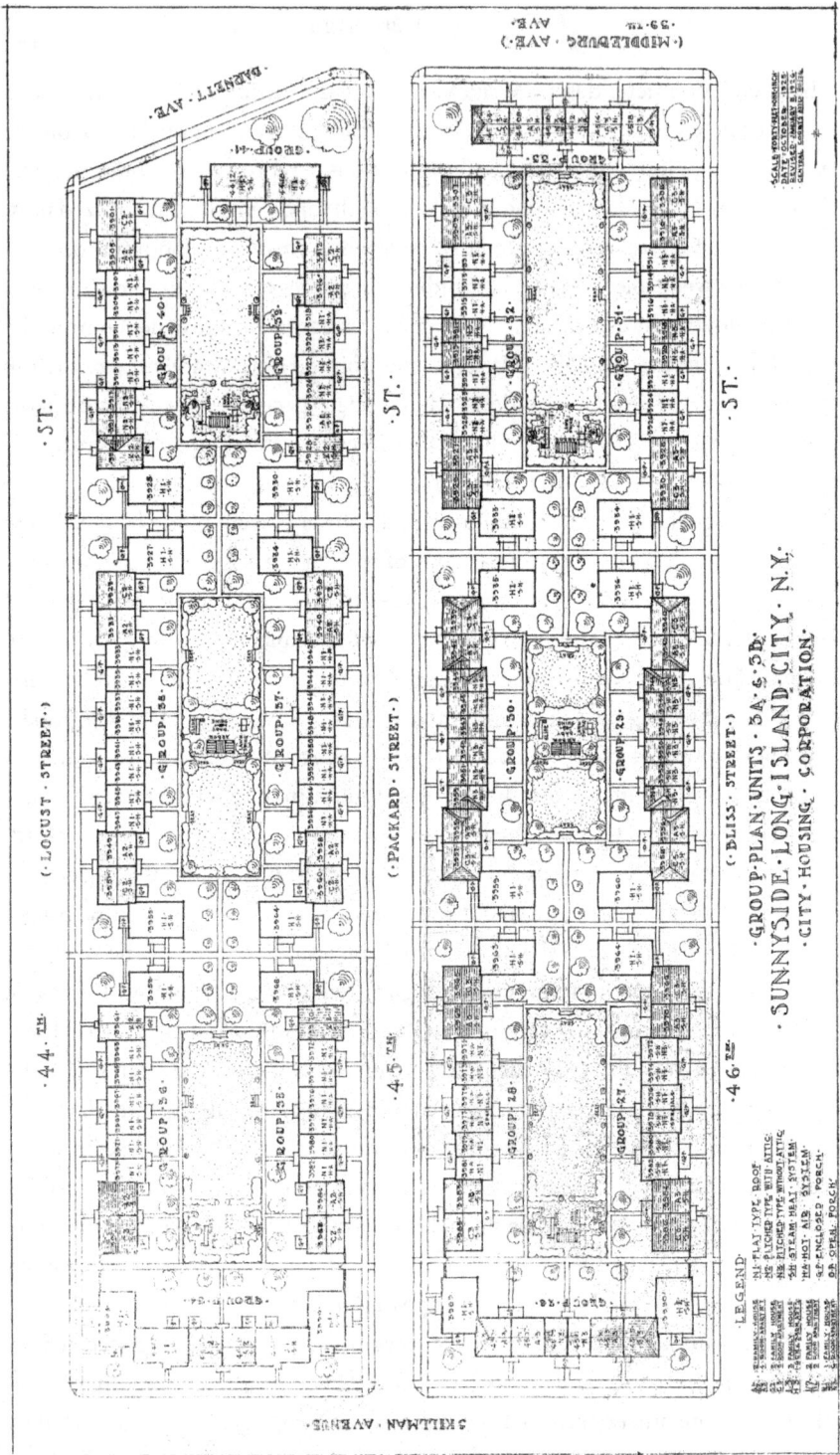

·GROUP·PLAN·UNITS·3A·&·3B·
·SUNNYSIDE·LONG·ISLAND·CITY·N.Y·
·CITY·HOUSING·CORPORATION·

·LEGEND·
·F·FLAT·TYPE·ROOF·
·H·PITCHED·TYPE·WITH·ATTIC·
·HE·PITCHED·TYPE·WITHOUT·ATTIC·
·1H·STEAM·HEAT·SYSTEM·
·HA·HOT·AIR·SYSTEM·
·P·ENCLOSED·PORCH·
·OP·OPEN·PORCH·

154

the Progressive Association" on the property. As Mumford, a resident since 1925, noted, "Sunnyside ... is now big enough and thriving enough to show what a difference there is between a dormitory district merely, and a real community, and how much the second depends upon having at hand the appropriate 'plant.'"[9] When completed in 1928, the 1,202-unit community had conveyed the lessons and resources for the architects to plan their next project—envisioned as a new town for twenty-five thousand families—Radburn.

Yet Sunnyside was not the only project during this time that helped Stein hone his site planning skills. Individual campus, museum, and religious projects brought to Stein through current and previous partners also kept him extremely busy. These projects reveal more about the evolution of his design sensibilities that informed his community designs—particularly connections between spaces as they transitioned from interior to exterior and private to public.

In 1925, work with Hardie Phillip on the Gates Chemistry Annex at the California Institute of Technology campus in Pasadena, California, brought Stein an individual commission with the city for an art museum. During his time at the École, museums had formed a central component of his education. As such, Stein considered himself an expert in their design. Themes that run throughout his writings on museums include that form should follow function; that the designs of rooms, windows, lighting, walls, and floors should be flexible to accommodate evolving and changing exhibits; that natural lighting and connection with the outdoors should be integral aspects of exhibits; and that aesthetics that draw in the casual visitor—the most common visitor—should be as true as possible to the objects on display. Perhaps influenced by his friend Lee Simonson or by his fiancé, then wife, Aline MacMahon, he thought of museum design theatrically, as a stage set to provide appropriate background for the exhibits. In 1927, he described his strategy for his first museum design, the unbuilt Pasadena Art Institute, which certainly took advantage of a dramatic site in the Carmelita Gardens:

> In every sense the museum will be part of the Gardens. Its long, low masses of concrete walls will be spread over undulating ground in a picturesque manner, so that they will from the beginning seem to belong to the place. The fine old trees

Figure 5.4 Blueprint showing two blocks at Sunnyside Gardens, dated October 1925 and January 8, 1926. Box 17, CSP/CUL.

are to be preserved and related to the building so as to increase its picturesque qualities. In turn, the simple wall surfaces of the building will form a background for the trees and shrubs. . . .

Even after the visitor has passed into the large rotunda under the tower, he will still feel that he is in the Gardens. Directly in front of him he will see a long green court terminated at its northern end by a view, through an arcade, of the mountains beyond. Through the entire length of this court will run a small stream of water with planting on either side.[10]

The romantic description of the museum was matched by renderings that showed a central tower, evocative of Goodhue's signature design for the Nebraska state capitol, dramatically rising above relatively low-lying wings nestled into the California landscape. The red clay roof tiles and flattened ornamentation, designed to draw the eye to the main door and past the cornice lines up the tower, reflected the Art Deco style of the period. Each exhibit area had an underlying theme to a period and place with the intent to make them more accessible to a larger public and to enhance their beauty (see figure 5.5). Stein explained, "The Spanish exhibit will surround a court such as that in the house of El Greco in Toledo or the smaller courts of the Alhambra in Granada. Likewise, the atmosphere most favorable for viewing the Japanese and Chinese collections will be secured by relating them to a court Asiatic in character." The Roman court would be "decorated in brilliant Pompeian painting" and would include an outdoor lecture room that would also double, "with its background of the mountains, as an excellent place for pageants and small dramatic entertainments."[11] This sense of drama, thematic connections, and linkages between the interior and exterior spaces also informed his housing projects and community designs.

Just as Stein's continuing ties with his old firm had offered the opportunity to work again in California, so too did the Ethical Culture Society bring him and Kohn, a close friend of Adler, the commission for developing a school campus for the institution in the Riverdale section of the West Bronx. Earlier in the decade, Stein had designed the camp buildings at the institution's Hudson Guild Farm, and Kohn was the architect of the Ethical Culture Society's main building in Central Park West completed in 1910. Funded in part by John D. Rockefeller,[12] the Fieldston School commission offered the architects an opportunity to design a campus worthy of ideals they strongly supported on a somewhat challenging, but desirable, site.

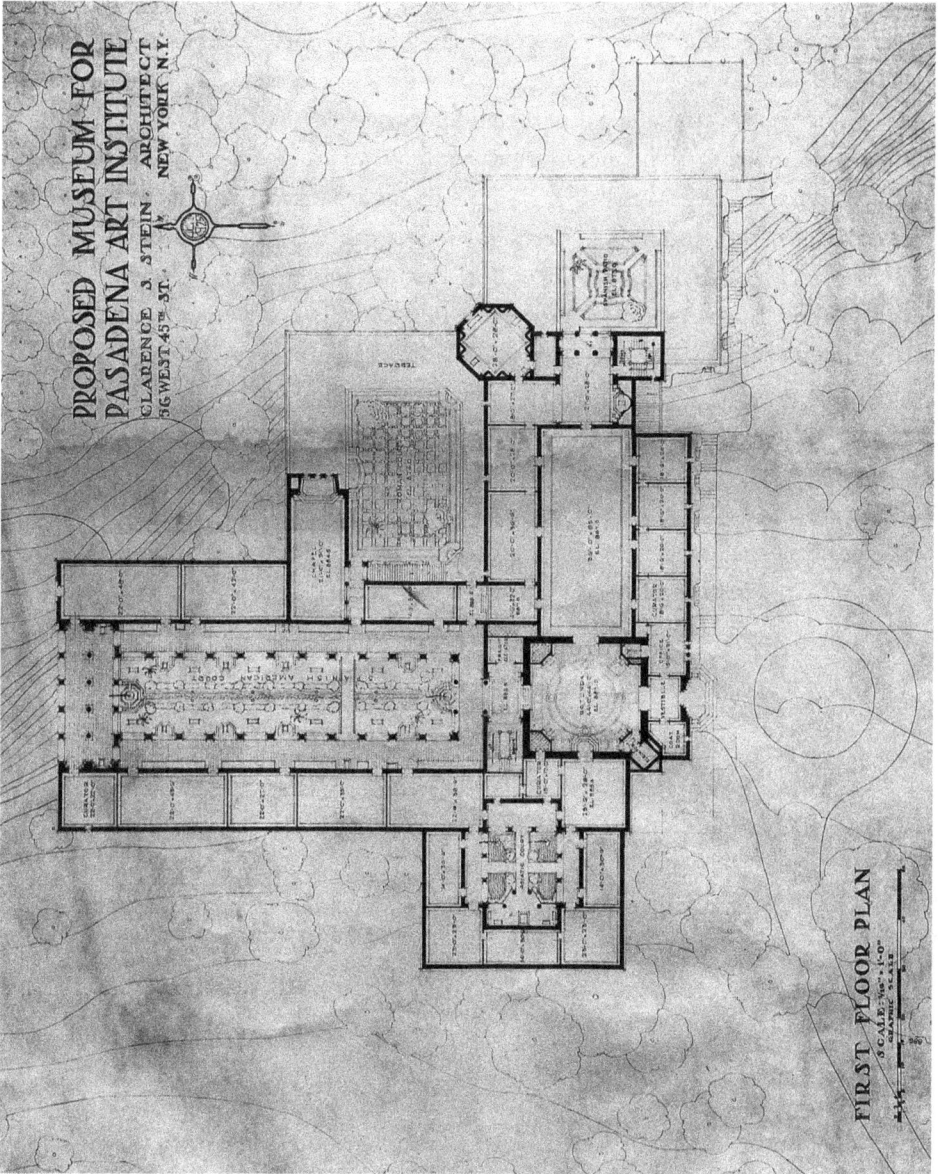

FIGURE 5.5 Pasadena Art Museum showing floor layout for the first floor and in lighter ink the exterior courtyards in relation to the interior rooms. Box 38, CSP/CUL.

While an early plan dated February 12, 1926, shows a much more formal symmetrical arrangement of the central campus with an outside amphitheater as a critical focal point opposite the semicircular drive, a later isometric view depicts a more organic arrangement of the buildings nestled into the hilly landscape, though elements of the more formal symmetrical arrangement remained. As opposed to the initial collegiate Gothic design, a later drawing featuring the elevation of the Arts and Administration Buildings connected by the Bell Tower, a key organizing feature, reveals a more rustic design that integrates the local fieldstone. This first phase of the campus, the high school, was completed in 1928 with Kohn and Stein also working on the lower school in 1931 and 1932. Stein praised the sense of enclosure and connection among the buildings to create an interrelated whole while also offering opportunities for the institution to grow—"a setting in which modern education will not be cramped down—but can grow and relate itself to the life—the best of life."[13]

Another commission during this period was also related to Stein and his colleagues' ties to the progressive Jewish community in New York City. In December 1925, Kohn, Stein, and Associated Architects colleague Butler were chosen to design the Temple Emanu-El. One of the largest synagogues in the world when completed in 1929, the temple was to be home to the oldest Jewish congregation in New York City.[14] With consulting architects Goodhue Associates, the firm behind many prominent religious structures, including St. Bartholomew's, the architects began the process of designing the building in 1926. Their challenge was to lay out essentially a group of three buildings—the temple (with twenty-five hundred seats), chapel, and community house—on the constrained L-shaped lot fronting on the northeast corner of Fifth Avenue (150 feet) and Sixty-Fifth Street (253 feet).

Butler's 1930 article for *Architectural Forum* describes the design of the building and the rich marble, granite, and walnut interiors and brass fixtures in significant detail, but it is Stein's article, which follows, that provides fascinating insight on the design process. The three main architects devoted the first six months of work on the building focusing on the parti—the floor plan and interior arrangement of the three buildings. Initially working individually on the design, Stein noted that all the architects came to the same solution that the main temple—the main mass of the building complex—would be most impressive on the corner. Then Kohn, Butler, and Stein and their compatriots at Goodhue

Associates began to consider the main elevations, specifically the style in which to design the buildings. The architects decided on the basilica plan for the temple and a Byzantine two-domed arrangement for the chapel with an overall character reminiscent of the early Romanesque (see figure 5.6). The temple's main facade on Fifth Avenue features a "great recessed arch … enclosing three entrance doors and the rose window with its supporting lancets."[15]

A critical feat in the design was the use of a structural steel frame to allow the interior space of the temple to be spanned without creating interference with the sight lines toward the Ark at the front of the main structure. In fact, the architects managed to convince "the building committee to permit us to change the usual arrangement of Jewish temples by placing two pulpits, one on each side of the sanctuary, instead of a single reading desk directly in front of the Ark" to allow the Ark to be the "center of decorative interest."[16] The chapel essentially consisted of a second, more modest synagogue set back from the Fifth Avenue building line of the temple. This setback of twenty feet created the only open space on the site, with Cautley in charge of the landscape design. The community house that rose eight stories toward the rear of the structure anchors the building on the eastern side of the property without overwhelming the primary temple structure.

Not only is the resulting building complex considered a dignified, aesthetically pleasing, and functional solution, the collaborative design process was also quite successful. The sheer number of consultants on the project, from an expert in acoustical tile to a structural engineer to artists skilled in stained glass, mosaic, and wrought iron was quite impressive. As Kohn extolled on completion of the project:

> It would be impossible today for any one of the three architects to say who is mainly responsible for the designing of this group. Each had a hand in it, each fought and bled and almost died in opposition to, or in favor of, each step in the procedure. But they tell us now that the building has a feeling of unity throughout. We three are still fast friends and are friendly with the various consultants. That is surely an unusual and enviable record breaker in modern architectural practice!

Thus Stein was engaged with no less than seven major projects on two opposite coasts when he turned his attention to developing a new town to demonstrate the benefits of communitarian regionalism as envisioned by him and his colleagues in the RPAA.[17]

Inside the images, the following handwritten text appears:

TEMPLE EMANU-EL 65ᵗʰ Sᵗ @ 5ᵗʰ Aᵥₑ N.Y.C. ROBERT D. KOHN CHARLES BUTLER CLARENCE S STEIN ARCHTS ASSOC.

. DETAIL . OF . CHAPEL .       DETAIL . OF . ARK .

INTERIOR . OF . CHAPEL .       . INTERIOR . OF . TEMPLE .

PART OF EXAMINATION EXHIBIT OF CLARENCE S. STEIN

FIGURE 5.6 Photos of Temple Emanu-El–"Part of the Examination Exhibit of Clarence S. Stein," circa 1927. Box 1, CSP/CUL.

## Radburn and Chatham Village

At Radburn, Stein and Wright had greater freedom and flexibility to adapt Unwin's concepts that they so admired at Hampstead Garden Suburb. This included designing interiors with attentiveness to the view outside and using open space to connect and create a sense of community. Still, the densities at Radburn, with single family detached and duplex units in addition to attached townhomes and apartments, and the broader scale of interconnected open spaces distinguished it from the consistently denser Hampstead Garden Suburb (see figure 5.7). The initial size of the British forebear at 243 acres was also significantly smaller than the site planned for Radburn. Further, the accommodation of the automobile and sophisticated street system distinguished it from Unwin and Parker's design. The intent at Radburn too, despite discussions to the contrary, was to introduce enough supporting commercial uses and amenities to create a complete community, even if many residents found themselves commuting to New York City for jobs.

Totaling 1,250 acres, or two-square miles, this "complete town" for twenty-five thousand would include "all the other facilities and conveniences which go to make for comfortable, pleasant living." They designed the shopping in close proximity to the residential development for easy accessibility on foot. With the shop fronts oriented to the adjacent streets, "the core of the block will be used for parking or garage space, bringing motor parking close to the commercial buildings." Individual storefronts along the first floor faced Plaza Road and included a barber and beauty shop, cleaners, stationary store, grocery, and meat market; the second and third floors accommodated community and social functions, including a theater and library, and the offices of the Radburn Association. The project provided amenities and accommodated leisure activities previously common only in upscale neighborhoods. Perhaps one of the most interesting proposals involved the brief consideration of incorporating a golf course in the project adjoining the east property line along the Saddle River. As Stein proclaimed, "Recreation instead of highways [would form] the backbone of our city plan."[18]

Stein, Wright, and their colleagues conceived Radburn as three neighborhoods based on Clarence Perry's neighborhood unit concept, with a school at the center of each and the boundaries based on a one-half mile radius distance from that center. Design and location of housing was sensitive to the existing

FIGURE 5.7 Diagram of Section 1 and Vicinity of Radburn dated March 15, 1929, Clarence S. Stein and Henry Wright, architects. Note the relationship between private parks, residences, and streets and the shopping center on block 3 to the plaza and train station. Box 1, CSP/CUL.

topography and retained significant trees and other landscaping when possible. In addition to mixing housing types—from apartments to single family detached to row house and duplex homes, the developers proclaimed "each house is charmingly individual and at the same time all blend harmoniously in their grouping to make up unusually attractive streets." As Wright maintained, "All the houses would be substantially built and architecturally designed; the difference between one income group and another would not be a matter of outward appearance so much as of commodiousness and elaboration of appliances." Further, "two widely separated kinds of dwelling" should probably not be "on the same block; but there would be no objection from any point of view in having them on adjacent blocks." Doing so "would produce a more interesting and varied result, both architecturally and socially."[19]

Clustering the homes along cul-de-sacs resulted in reduced costs for infrastructure improvements, including roadways. Buying materials wholesale and creating an efficient construction process also resulted in reduced costs, as did modifications to the floor plan to eliminate wasted space and "useless hallways" thus ensuring "maximum convenience." One significant improvement, widely touted at the time, was the use of attached garages to save on development and electricity costs.[20]

For his part, Mumford expressed concern that the project would simply become another Forest Hills Gardens with detached homes and too much vacant space. Interestingly, he directed his criticism toward Bing—"He [Bing] is not ready to go the whole hog; and unless he is willing to make the houses as modern and efficient as the street layout, it will turn out that the street layout isn't efficient either."[21] In fact, the street layout garnered the most attention in 1928 as construction began, and continues to do so. Yet the true contribution at Radburn was the design and integration of open spaces. The design of the streets and the superblocks made this possible, thus Stein's argument that the Radburn Idea, which embraced all these principles, was the key.

Interestingly, Stein consistently credits Olmsted and Vaux's Central Park as the inspiration for these design innovations at Radburn. The separation of the street circulation system of a major metropolis from the varied open spaces that comprised the vast park and the interconnectedness of these open space systems clearly inspired Stein, whose home offered him a stunning view of the park. As he later acknowledged to Mumford, "Pop Stein and I used to walk downtown through the park during much of the period I was working on Radburn. It was a long time before I noted that what we considered was original at Radburn had been done with so much skill in the Park." Wright and he designed Radburn to accommodate the automobile and as a respite from the automobile. As Stein commented in the final pages of *Toward New Towns for America*, "Going places and enjoying the use of places"—these are "quite distinct and different

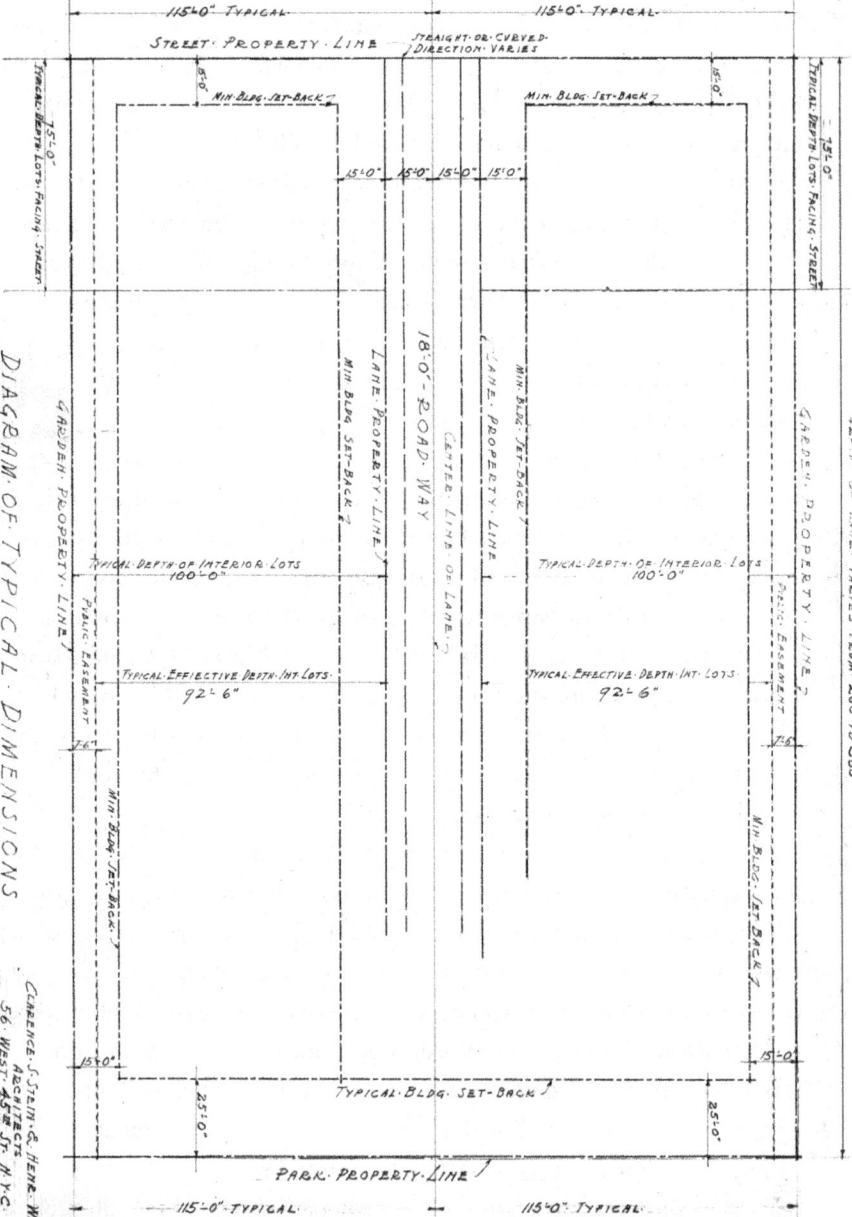

STREET

DIAGRAM·OF·TYPICAL·DIMENSIONS·
OF·LANES·IN·FIRST·VNIT·OF·RADBVRN·
RADBVRN·N·J·

CLARENCE·S·STEIN·&·HENRY·WRIGHT
ARCHITECTS
56·WEST·45TH·ST·N·Y·C·
SCALE 1/16"=1'-0"

NOTE This plan is subject to modification and must not be taken as final except.

April 24/24.

PARK·

164

functions.... Although they complement each other, they require different locations and forms, diametrically contrary in use. To coordinate these two is a basic problem of contemporary planned city development. That is the purpose of the Radburn type of plan."[22]

Another distinctive feature at Radburn that emphasized the significance of the parks as a means to find respite and create community was the house turned around. The service side truly faced the street—with the attached garage and kitchen in this sector. The family and living rooms faced the park with the private yard connected to, but distinguished from, the community park so that the resident could enter through a hierarchy of private, semiprivate, and public spaces designed to be distinctive but still visually connected and also controlled through the association with easements to legally establish the use and responsibility for these spaces. Along a typical eighteen-foot-wide paved lane, the single family and duplex homes sat on lots one hundred feet deep with fifteen-foot building setbacks and an easement accommodating a footpath to the park (see figure 5.8). On the park side, a twenty-five-foot setback accommodated a private yard with Cautley's planting of trees and low hedges defining this space directly adjacent to the winding neighborhood parks that served as the connective tissue for the community (see figure 5.9). Further, Cautley designed each block to have a distinctive landscape:

> To obtain interest and variety, a different foliage scheme was planned for each garden group and for each motor street. Not only may a householder choose between brick and clapboard, six rooms or eight, but he may also select an orchard garden such as Arlington with round-leaved snowberry hedges, and round leaved honeysuckle vines and bushes, or he may prefer to live in Bancroft in the shade of honeylocusts, mountain-ash, rose vines, and hedges of Vanhoutte spirea.[23]

She used local trees and plants, but also nonnative species to create cost efficient community spaces with an organic and informal appearance that melded into the domestic landscapes of the private gardens. The Radburn Association played an essential role in managing and maintaining these parks and easements.

---

FIGURE 5.8 Diagram showing typical dimensions of street and lots at Radburn with minimum building setbacks, Stein and Wright, architects, dated April 26, 1928. Box 1, CSP/CUL.

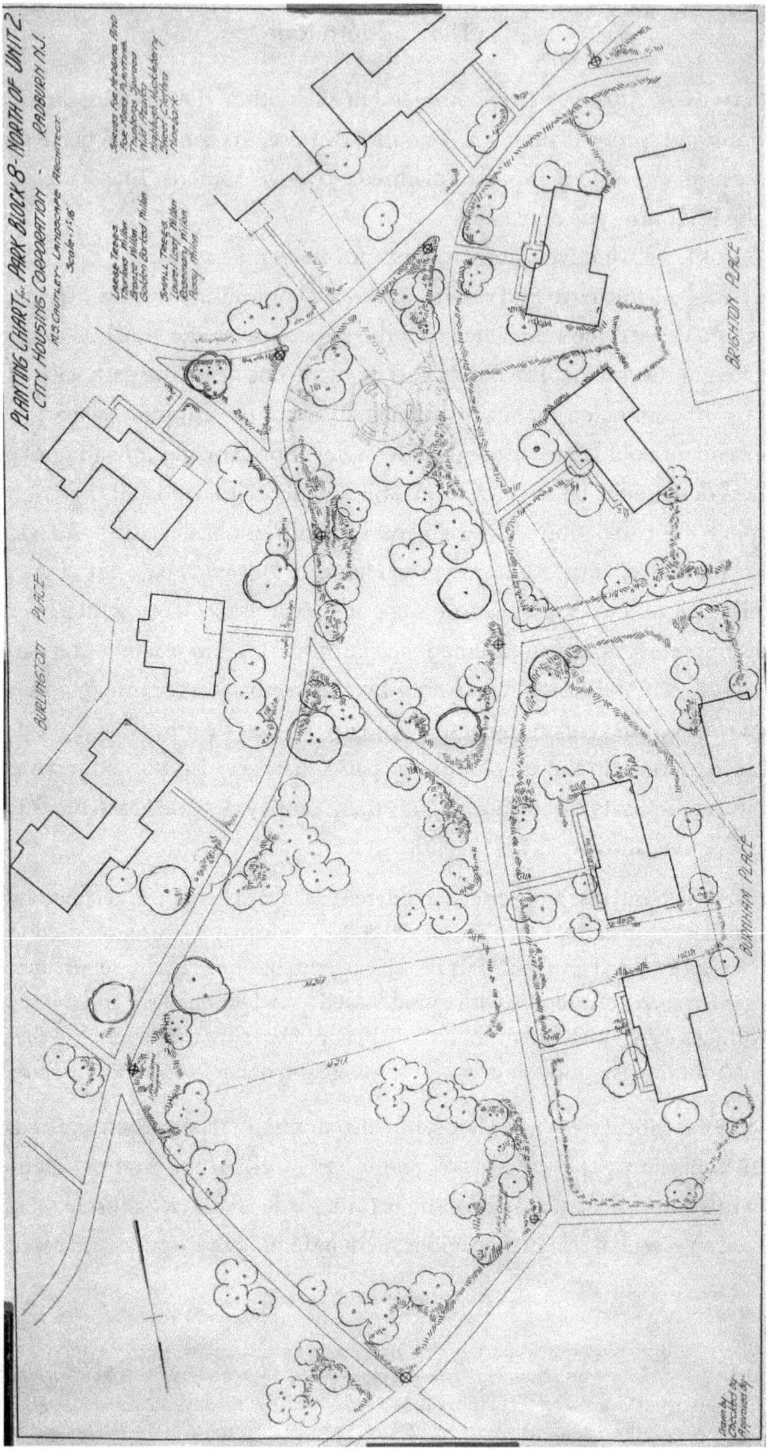
PLANTING CHART for PARK BLOCK 8 - NORTH OF UNIT 2.
CITY HOUSING CORPORATION - RADBURN N.J.
M.S. CAUTLEY - LANDSCAPE ARCHITECT
Scale - 1" = 16'
LARGE TREES
Thurlows Willow
Bronze Willow
Golden Barked Willow
SMALL TREES
Laurel Leaf Willow
Rosemary Willow
Pussy Willow
SHRUBS FOR HEDGING AND FOR MASS PLANTING
Thunbergs Spiraea
Wild Azalea
Highbush Huckleberry
Sweet Clethra
Ninebark
BURLINGTON PLACE
BURNHAM PLACE
BRIGHTON PLACE
VIEW
Drawn by
Checked by
Approved by

In a 1937 lecture at the Massachusetts Institute of Technology (MIT), Stein reflected on the significance of Radburn's key elements working in harmony: "There will be adequate parks and open places located where they are most needed—every house will look out on broad and beautiful vistas. The road system will be an integrated part of the plan for living." The vision and design did not cater to the individual but to the community: "At Radburn every house was built as an integrated and related part of the plan of the whole town, of the neighborhood community, of the groups of houses. Thus, every house gains from its relation to the houses around it." Only the neighborhood unit north of Fairlawn Avenue was completely realized with a small portion of the second neighborhood completed south of the main thoroughfare. Still, with Ackerman's design of Abbott Apartments providing the gateway to the northern section and the commercial district across Fairlawn to the south facing the park and then the train station, the major elements had been established by the time the Great Depression shut down further development.[24]

Innovations in row housing, introduced admittedly late at Radburn due to concerns about the marketability of this housing type in suburbia, allowed Stein and Wright to more effectively plan Chatham Village in Pittsburgh. The two architects, along with longtime colleague and friend Frederick Bigger, were hired in 1930 by the limited dividend Buhl Foundation to design a low-cost project targeting downtown office workers who were solidly middle class.[25] Located two miles from downtown in the city's Mount Washington neighborhood, the forty-five-acre site looked down on a public park, its topography having relegated it to accommodating one nineteenth-century estate and nothing more in the rapidly developing neighborhood. Bigger prepared an initial study of the site—a rectilinear plan that introduced many of the later elements, including a greenbelt and housing facing interior parks with traffic circulation primarily at the perimeter.

Though the concept originally was to sell free-standing homes, Stein and Wright's community of row housing, projected to cost two thousand dollars less per unit in construction, offered a more appropriate alternative. With the modified unit as a cost-effective model for group housing and the charge to

FIGURE 5.9 Detail of Radburn landscape by Marjorie Sewell Cautley—showing views toward the community park. Cautley landscape for Radburn City Housing Corp. A10.8–9, Avery Architectural and Fine Arts Library, Columbia University.

consider not only construction but operating costs for the rental development, the architects were ready to introduce further innovations in design to take advantage of the hillside site. Wright explained,

> On a hillside it was found that a somewhat greater intensiveness of coverage can be secured without impairing openness and view.... It was shown that grouped row houses could be fitted to hillsides with actually less expense than detached houses. One reason was the reduction in the number of terrace and step adjustments in spaces between dwellings. Another reason was the fact that the foundation wall of the row house formed a satisfactory retaining wall at much less expense than an independent wall.[26]

Local architects Charles Ingham and William Boyd, and landscape architect Ralph E. Griswold all contributed their expertise to the project. The brick exteriors, hipped and gabled slate roofs, and limestone trim, most prominent around the entryways, lent a pleasing homogeneity to the neo-Georgian exteriors while the topography allowed Wright and Stein to vary the building siting and create visual interest. Further, the local architects referenced regional colonial history and the recently opened Colonial Williamsburg, to introduce some distinctive decorative features that further emphasized a sense of place.[27]

Stein attributed the innovations in site design at Chatham Village to the genius of his partner Henry Wright. Wright integrated the Radburn Idea, including the perimeter roads, superblock configurations, and orientation to inner greens (see figure 5.10). The terraced curvilinear superblocks with row houses variously arranged into buildings of from two to seven units skillfully addressed the site's topography and safeguarded numerous established trees. Further, the staggered terracing allowed many in the two-story units an unimpeded view. As at Radburn, the area directly adjacent to each row house entrance, though here more modest in size, functioned as a private garden, connecting via a walkway to the community park at the center of each block (see figure 5.11). A sidewalk delineated the edges of this community park, which was further distinguished from the private realm by an allée of trees along the inner green and modest hedges framing the individual gardens. For those without hillside units, which easily accommodated a recessed garage on the basement floor, three garage courts were located at the edges of the development, two hidden from the view of the adjacent inner green, accessible down a flight of stairs. The initial phase, completed in May 1932, consisted of 129 homes.

FIGURE 5.10 Aerial photo of Chatham Village, First Unit, by Aerial Surveys of Pittsburgh, Inc., No. 2045, no date, circa 1932. Box 1, CSP/CUL.

When a second phase was completed in 1936, increasing the number of units to 197, the forty-five-acre site consisted of sixteen acres of housing, four stores located on the busiest street corner, four acres of playgrounds, and twenty-five acres of wooded parkland with two miles of pathways. The existing manor became the community house, and the parkland, adjacent to three sides, functioned as a greenbelt. As Stein remarked, "A greenbelt, even one as small as that of Chatham, insulates a community from neighborhood depreciation and external annoyance."[28] Thus Chatham Village functioned as an oasis among the modest single family homes along gridded streets that characterized the Mount Washington neighborhood, offering residents in the Buhl Foundation

FIGURE 5.11 Early photo of Chatham Village showing the use of grade, walkways, and landscaping to distinguish the public from the private realms. Box 1, CSP/CUL.

community amenities and open space due to the superblock design that the adjacent single family neighbors did not have.

As Stein and Wright collaborated on Chatham Village, they revisited their work on Radburn, preparing an exhibition of drawings, at significant expense to Stein, for the 1931 International Housing and Town Planning Federation Congress in Berlin. Stein considered it an opportunity for the architectural team to further clarify their master plan for Radburn, despite the stalled housing market. "We are making some show drawings of Radburn—which means working out at least in tentative form—many parts of the plans about which we have merely theorized in the past."[29] Stein next focused on incorporating the Radburn Idea into a variety of garden apartment designs stretching from New York to California.

## Garden Apartments in New York City

As at Sunnyside Gardens and Chatham Village, the design of Phipps Garden Apartments—the relationship between the landscaped courts and housing units—with a focus on serving working-class and middle-income households, reflected a key factor of the garden apartment concept. Architectural historian Richard Plunz praised this residential type:

> Fundamental to the success of the garden apartment was the balance between building mass and open space so that a level of proximity was maintained which involved a strict definition of the public realm to be shared by neighbors. Important to this neighboring was a sense of theater, which required use of architectural language bordering on the scenographic. The language of the "garden" of the garden apartment, together with its enclosing facades, was critical to the transformation of housing from a consequence of economic formulas to a unique environment.[30]

At Phipps Garden Apartments, different unit plans formed various configurations of perimeter layouts, allowing Stein to further experiment with site design.[31] In addition, the depth of the two-unit deep apartments was also increased to create greater efficiencies in the floor layout, and unit entries were clustered around the access hallways in the elevator buildings with a goal of reducing unnecessary space and limiting the number of units on each hallway to enhance privacy and diminish noise.

Stein combined sixteen four-story, walk-up "I" buildings with six six-story, elevator accessible "T" buildings without sacrificing the proportional scale between the great court (as the resulting open space was called) and the buildings. As Isadore Rosenfield of Stein's office explained, "Obviously, a simple perimeter for so large a plot would have created a rather monotonous inner court. Thanks to the projections of the 'T' stems, the court assumes a great deal of interest, and at the same time the effectiveness of the perspective of distances is not destroyed." Wright agreed. Further, establishing buildings at two different heights created "the very great advantage of relieving the group of the ponderous institutional aspect which has marred the effect of many large projects grouped around a single large interior court." The dramatic central six-story entry building features a tunnel that provides access to the central green, lending a real sense of arrival to the community's premiere open space.[32]

In addition to the visual interest created by the integration of the "T" and "I" buildings and their alternating heights, Stein decided to make the fire escapes a decorative rather than a simply utilitarian feature. Thus, though the Art Deco ornamentation was modest, the masterful variation in brick patterns, which created a linear affect particularly around the entry features; the "ingenious method of combining the necessary fire escape with the highly desirable balcony"; and the striking pergola that capped the roof of the central six-story building, culminated in a distinctively pleasing design.[33]

As at Stein's other projects, exterior spaces were carefully arranged with Cautley once again lending her expertise to the landscape design (see figure 5.12). The proximity of the Sunnyside Gardens playground meant that the open spaces at Phipps could be more passive, though they were used in a variety of ways. For instance, a play area for younger children directly adjoined the nursery school located on the ground floor of one of the buildings. In addition, many of the ground floor apartments had direct access to small private gardens. Cautley's delineation of intimate spaces in the public realm and use of plantings, including the installation of mature trees, created the illusion of a more spacious area that enhanced Stein's vision for the community.[34]

The 1933 AIA Committee on Housing Exhibition, with Stein as chairman and Bauer, Mumford, Kohn, Butler, Ralph Walker, and William Lamb as members, urged this holistic approach to developing residential projects. "It is a demonstration of the possibilities of modern housing when the community rather than the individual dwelling is taken as the unit of design." The committee specifically advocated "integrated neighborhood communities," superblocks, grouped housing, and large-scale development. Their traveling exhibit, first shown at the annual Architectural Exhibition in New York City, highlighted perimeter design in the United States and England, and other European examples, including the German Zeilenbau. Sunnyside, Radburn, Phipps, and Hillside, were all featured, as were Klaber and Grunsfeldt's Michigan Boulevard Apartments in Chicago, Thomas's Paul Lawrence (Laurence) Dunbar Apartments in New York, and Kastner and Stonorov's Carl Mackley Houses in Philadelphia. Stein and his colleagues intended their exhibit to showcase "the basic standards that must be embodied in new designs, while the financial mechanism for national aid to housing is already in existence in the Reconstruction Finance Corporation."[35]

As the public housing program got underway, massive projects such as Wil-

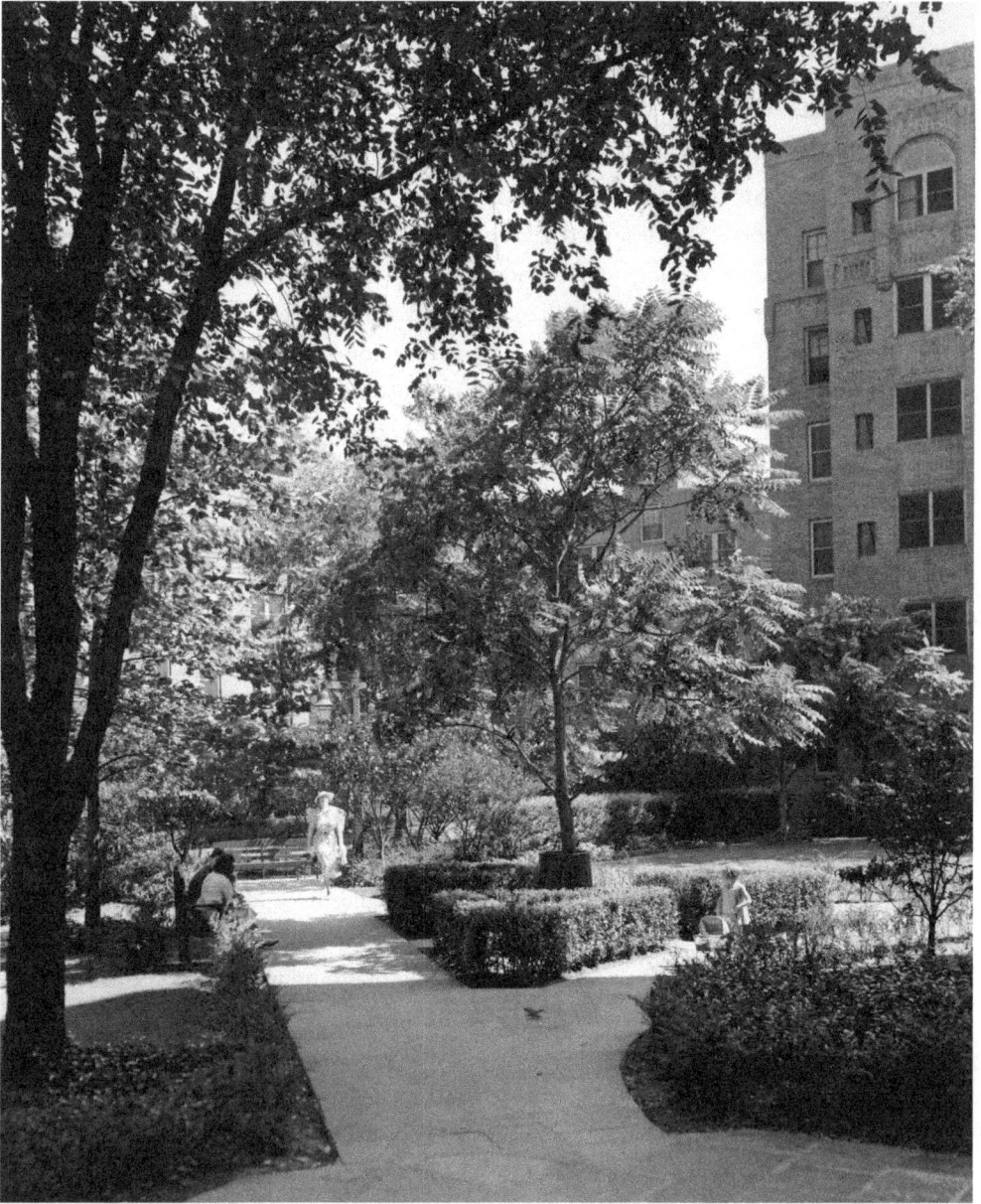

FIGURE 5.12 Interior courtyard of Phipps Garden Apartments circa 1936 highlighting the artful use of open space mitigating the impact of the six-story structures, photograph by Wurts Bros., General Photographers, 15 East 40th St., New York City. Box 17, CSP/CUL.

liamsburg Houses in New York City reflected the differences between Stein's application of the superblock—the low-rise garden apartment perimeter design—and the clumsy application of international design sensibilities in an urban template resulting in a disconnect within the community and with the adjacent neighborhoods. Particularly in the design of hierarchical open spaces in his projects, Stein continued to balance an intimacy and respect for privacy and personalization with a desire to build community through public spaces without ignoring the surrounding neighborhood (see figure 5.13). With one exception— his collaborative work in 1940 and 1941 on a phase of the Fort Greene Houses in New York City—Stein remained squarely on the side of lower-density perimeter design in philanthropic and government supported housing.

Despite delays, Stein had an unprecedented opportunity to innovate at Hillside Homes in the Bronx, in design, construction techniques, materials, and community services offered. Only later, in spring 1935, after frustration with local architects not proficient in designing large-scale projects, did the PWA Housing Division issue its first book of "Sample Plans" not to "impose standardization" but to offer "suggestions" to expedite the development process. Operating prior to the adoption of these guidelines, Stein instituted advances at Hillside Homes beyond the recently developed Phipps Garden Apartments, Phase I. These included reinforced concrete fireproof construction, basement apartments on the sloped site, a simplified grouping in the walk-up buildings to realize greater efficiency and livability, and a revised interior layout to improve circulation patterns within the unit.[36]

The final configuration consisted of nine smaller irregularly shaped landscaped courts formed by a perimeter garden apartment design of six- and four-story buildings. Using models to experiment with grouping various unit plans, Stein revised his design from one consisting primarily of "T" units to one that used a combination of "I" units for the four-story walk-ups and "T" units for the six-story elevator buildings. While Wright lauded the "T" as the "simplest type to provide an increased number of suites to carry the cost of an elevator," he, like Stein, favored the "I" for walk-up units. Further, Stein arranged the "I" units in a "T" form to accommodate more apartments than a simple "I" design. This evolution of the site design reflected "large-scale planning which has been fostered by a continually enlarging concept of the importance of low-cost housing and the participation of the government in its provision."[37]

FIGURE 5.13 Early garden scene at Hillside Homes, showing use of open space. Box 38, CSP/CUL.

With Andrew Eken of Starrett Brothers and Eken as building contractor and vice president of the limited dividend corporation, innovation in construction techniques and materials was also possible. Yet Stein still had to maintain vigilance to ensure the realization of his vision. When Eken and his partners asked Stein to "simplify the exterior of the building" by reducing the "bands" of brick ornamentation, Stein had ready within hours a new design that concentrated the decorative brickwork around the doors and windows. When they promoted white brick because it was cheaper, Stein found a suitably priced red brick alternative of an acceptable quality, going through multiple samples to do so. To ensure that the detailed drawings of the brick design were closely followed, Stein visited the site regularly while the brick was being laid, inspecting the work of the master bricklayers.[38]

Stein also focused on broader issues such as the appropriate mix of community facilities and shops. As he and Bauer explained in an article they coauthored during this time, "The economic success of a neighborhood community and the well-being of its inhabitants depend to a great extent on the planning of the neighborhood shopping center." Scientific analysis of census and other data informed size, location, number, and types of stores, but concerns about pedestrian safety required a design to accommodate the drive-in traffic while also allowing access for those on foot, preferably through an adjacent park. They clarified, "When the neighborhood store group has turned its face toward the life of the park rather than the haste and danger of the traffic road it will become a real center of the community." Thus, while Stein appreciated the decreased land costs realized when Straus retained a 100-foot strip along the main thoroughfare for commercial development, he lamented the lost opportunity to integrate these uses into the community. Throughout, his intent was to design Hillside, spatially and functionally, "as a separate integrated community within the larger pattern of the bigger city." This sensitivity to broader site design issues and adjacencies as well as attention to detail, as evident in the brickwork at Hillside Homes, continued to define Stein's approach as he next applied his design philosophy to a range of projects well beyond the confines of New York City.[39]

## The Wichita Museum and the Radburn Idea Informs Garden Apartment Design

Stein's focus on community building reflected his commitment to environmental humanism,[40] ranging from the experience of the individual museum visitor to the quality of life for his community residents. And always, the relation between the introspective or more private interior spaces and the broader more public exterior spaces informed his design with the goal of improving the human condition. This approach informed his only realized museum design as well as garden apartment communities from Greenbelt to Los Angeles to Pittsburgh.

Not only was Hillside dedicated and opened in 1935, but the Wichita Art Institute, a project on which Stein had devoted over seven years, was also completed at that time. Like his proposed Art Institute in Pasadena, the Wichita Art Institute exemplified several core principles that Stein continued to promote in museum design: relying on windows to allow natural light to showcase the art and to create a connection between the interior and exterior; differentiating spaces based on the user—student, general public, artisan, art lover; integrating local materials into the building and regional themes into its design; and coordinating the design of the building and the landscape to enhance the aesthetic experience for the visitor. As he explained his vision to the Board of Park Commissioners for Wichita, Kansas, "The primary purpose of this Institute is that of developing an appreciation of the beautiful. Not only the contents of the museum but the building itself as well as its surroundings must serve this purpose. Every detail in the decoration of the structure should be by a master artist or artisan.... The gardens should not only be examples of beautiful landscape design but should serve as delightful settings for exhibitions of sculpture."[41]

Although the proposed three-story building was reduced to two stories and only the central building was constructed, its scaled-back design was still striking, more Art Moderne than originally envisioned with the elimination of the highly decorated third floor (see figure 5.14). The more austere cast concrete structure emulated the flat surfaces of Pueblo structures with bold sculptures around the main entrance inspired by the Mayans and Aztecs and designed by Lee Lawrie. These regional influences, also evident at the Pasadena Museum, reflected the legacy of Stein's years with Goodhue, leading Walter A. Vincent,

FIGURE 5.14 Rendering of the Wichita Art Museum as designed by Stein. Rendering by J. Floyd Yewell, photographed by Palmer Shannon of New York City, no date, circa 1930. The wings were not completed, but the central section minus the top floor was. Box 38, CSP/CUL.

chair of the Wichita Park Commission, to pronounce the design "a triumph of the symbolic representation of Spanish-Aztec influences on Southwestern art."[42]

Though the Wichita Art Institute was the only one of Stein's museum designs to be constructed, the community architect continued to work on a variety of proposed museum projects and to write and lecture considerably on this subject during this period. For Stein, flexibility was a critical characteristic of design—form needed to follow function to be responsive to current needs and trends. Further, like theaters, he considered museums an essential part of his Regional City concept, with specific types at the neighborhood, town, and regional levels.[43]

His efforts to integrate community amenities and facilities was of particular significance during his tenure with the Resettlement Administration as technical consultant to the Greenbelt Town program. He maintained that three guiding principles informed their development: "the Garden City, the Radburn Idea, and the Neighborhood Unit." The Radburn Idea was the most clearly articulated guiding principle, though each of the three towns established under the program also bore the distinctive stamp of the prominent architectural team charged with its design. In fact, a 1936 Resettlement Administration publication promoting the towns touted the Radburn Idea, including superblocks bounded by streets and housing clustered around a series of parks that safely accommodated pedestrians and provided access to nearby shopping, community, and education centers.[44]

Among the three towns, Stein clearly favored Greenbelt, Maryland, as the best articulation of the Radburn Idea. A plateau in the shape of a crescent suggested the overall site plan with two parallel roads and a series of cross streets giving shape to the six original superblocks each about fourteen acres in size (see figure 5.15). Most of the units were attached (306 in three-story apartments, 574 in row houses, and 5 in single family homes), and rather than a cul-de-sac, a service court provided auto access to the rear or service side of the homes. With 885 units available, approximately 9,000 applications were submitted upon the project's opening. The town's residents were carefully screened with the average rent in 1939 set at thirty-one dollars per unit, clearly affordable to a middle-income rather than a lower-income demographic.[45]

Private gardens adjacent to community open spaces with walkways, the concept of the house turned around and the park as backbone defined Greenbelt. As Stein's colleague Mayer noted just over thirty years later upon passage of the Housing Act of 1968, which included incentives for new town development, Greenbelt "might be called the most nearly 'authentic Radburn,' with dividing hedges around and between private gardens, with footpaths or bicycle paths into the interior park or play area and, past them, under surrounding roads, directly to the shopping center." Stein was especially proud of the separation between the auto and pedestrian in this commercial center. Through an underpass at Crescent Road, the pedestrian accessed the town center of stores, a grocery, theater, post office, and bank arranged around a central community square with parking adjacent to the sides and the rear of these buildings (see figure 5.16). Bounded by these structures on two sides with a formalized landscape that further defined and unified the site, the square led to a wooded area through which residents could reach a variety of recreational facilities, including a pool, and the nearby community building/school. The design concepts here were consistent with ideas Stein was simultaneously presenting before the New York World's Fair Board of Design in 1936, when he proposed integrated hierarchical open spaces through the creation of "enclosed courts and gardens" connected to the larger

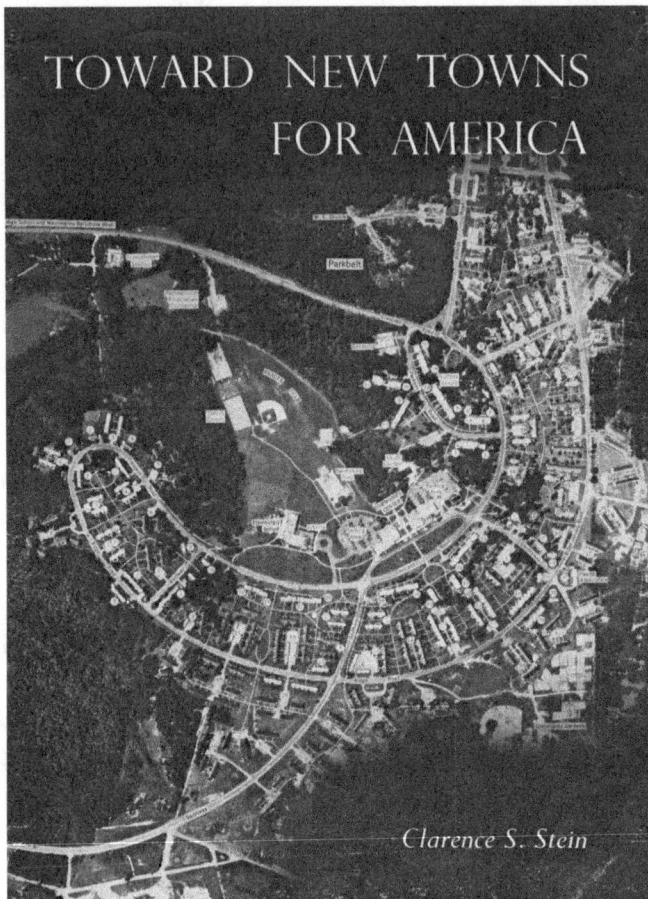

TOWARD NEW TOWNS
FOR AMERICA

Parkbelt

*Clarence S. Stein*

FIGURE 5.15 Greenbelt featured as a proposed front cover for *Toward New Towns for America.* Box 17, CSP/CUL.

FIGURE 5.16 Greenbelt shopping center (foreground) and school (background), photo by O. Kline Fulmer, received by Stein on November 10, 1939. Box 17, CSP/CUL.

public spaces. Stein returned to the central square as a unifying space as part of a pedestrian oriented shopping district with peripheral parking in his commercial centers—in 1943 for the new town of Maplewood, Louisiana; in 1950 for the new town of Stevenage, just outside of London, England; and in 1952 for the new town of Kitimat in Canada.[46]

Large-scale, low-cost housing made it possible to create such community spaces and design them as amenities available to an income group that previously had not been able to afford them. Published in 1935 just as the FHA rental housing program was getting underway, Wright's seminal *Rehousing Urban America* showcased these residential designs, including the work he and Stein had completed in partnership and individually. He began, "The idea of this book has been to provide a general and comprehensive digest of the elements of good community planning and housing technique related to a hypothesis of future large-scale city rehabilitation which calls for a fairly compact and carefully related community organization rather than the loosely organized sprawling suburban expansion of the last few decades." Garden apartments offered one solution. "Because we have had longer experience in a wider field of application in large-scale planning, the development of the garden apartment has been carried further toward a satisfactory technique than have other forms of dwelling design."[47]

The FHA Large-Scale Housing Division agreed. A May 1940 *Architectural Forum* article documented the popular appeal of and market for garden apartments. They "offer renters the nearest thing to 'home' that can be found in apartment buildings, ... [and] an attractive development from the builder's point of view; it is the most economical rental project for a site of low or moderate value." They house "about 50 per cent of all U.S. renters. In both quality and quantity this market is under-supplied." Within its first six years, the FHA program supported approximately 240 projects of which 200 were considered garden apartments.[48]

One of these projects, BHV, Stein maintained, was the fullest realization of the Radburn ideal. The low-density, 627-unit project (roughly 7.3 units per acre) resembled Sunnyside Gardens more than it did a strict garden apartment design in that the two-room deep buildings combined flats (356) and row houses (216) in two-story buildings bracketed by one-story bungalow homes (55). The California modern style of these attached units was accentuated by second floor balconies, low hipped and gabled roofs with deep eaves, and eyebrow roofs that extended in some cases beyond the first floor entries to cover the windows as

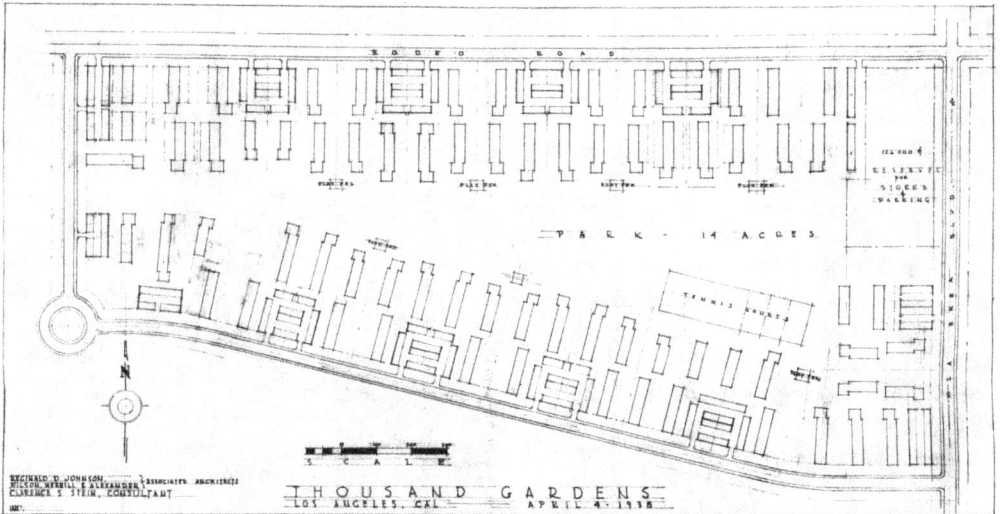

FIGURE 5.17 Early site plan of Thousand Gardens (Baldwin Hills Village), dated April 4, 1938. Box 2, CSP/CUL.

well, reinforcing the horizontal plane. No streets crossed through the 1,100-foot by 2,750-foot site. Further, unlike Sunnyside, the large superblock accommodated a much larger central green—most of the twenty acres of open space on the eighty-acre site were devoted to the centralized Village Green (see figures 5.17 and 5.18). A formal axial arrangement was limited to the main entrance, where the club house and administration buildings faced each other across a formal terrace. At three of the superblock's four corners and adjacent to the formal entrance at the center, the units angled away from the busier public roads and intersections and inward toward the Village Green. As at Greenbelt, local traffic was channeled into a limited number of service courts on the property, here with garages, so that vehicles and pedestrians were separated.

A well-defined though complex series of open spaces distinguished the project. Enclosed patios and balconies offered access to the service side of the unit adjacent to the garage courts while the garden entrance, as at Radburn, provided access to the living room (see figure 5.19). These private entryways resembled the residential garden courts Stein had visited in his 1935 trip to China and featured in his 1938 article, particularly the pavements used in the Gardens of

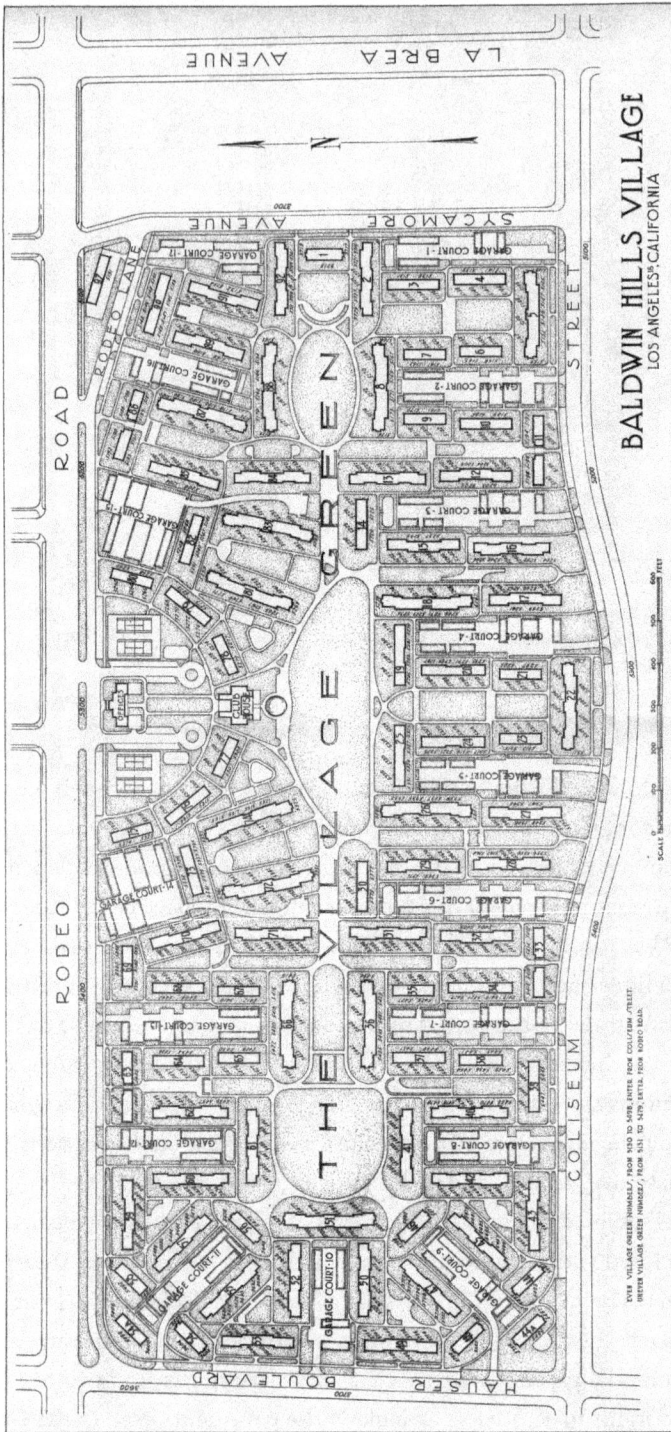

BALDWIN HILLS VILLAGE
LOS ANGELES¹⁶·CALIFORNIA

184

Soochow. He lyrically described the synergy between materials, courtyards, and residences—how they came together almost organically to create a distinctive place. "Separated from the narrow, crowded roads of Soochow by the blank walls that encircle all Chinese homes, the wealthy merchants and princes attempted in their gardens to simulate the countryside. They sought free, natural beauty and the problem of tying in this irregularity with architectural forms was solved by the design of the pavements, which are at once geometric in form and natural in material." The majority of homes at BHV (450 out of 627) had private patios, most enclosed by six-foot walls and with carefully designed and laid pavers that distinguished these refuges and essentially added an outdoor room to these dwellings.[49]

A hierarchy of open spaces led from the ivy-covered areas that defined the more private areas directly adjacent to the buildings to an inner park, or "garden court," and then into a series of large central parks collectively called the Village Green. An earlier more simplified plan showed a massive unbroken green (see figure 5.17). The three large connected central parks that comprised the Village Green ensured a scale more consistent with the low-density project (see figure 5.18). Across the Village Green from the community buildings, the residential units bounded an allée defined by a row of trees on either side and through an opening in the building that faced Coliseum Road provided an unobstructed visual connection to the hills to the south that gave the project its name. This design, described Bauer in her appraisal of BHV, "emphasizes the feeling of entering a protected retreat" much like the entry into the much more urban Phipps Garden Apartments.[50]

The landscape played a key role in defining and reinforcing these integrated outdoor spaces. Reginald Johnson tended to work with noted Los Angeles landscape architect Katherine Bashford on his projects, and Fred Barlow, a junior partner in her firm, is credited with the planting design for the community.[51] Barlow used plantings to give each of the smaller courtyard spaces a distinctive feel and color, designed to enhance the pastel color palette chosen for the buildings that defined each of these areas. Architectonic elements such as shade trees defined the circulation system at the edge of the central Village Green

---

FIGURE 5.18 Final site plan of Baldwin Hills Village. Box 17, CSP/CUL.

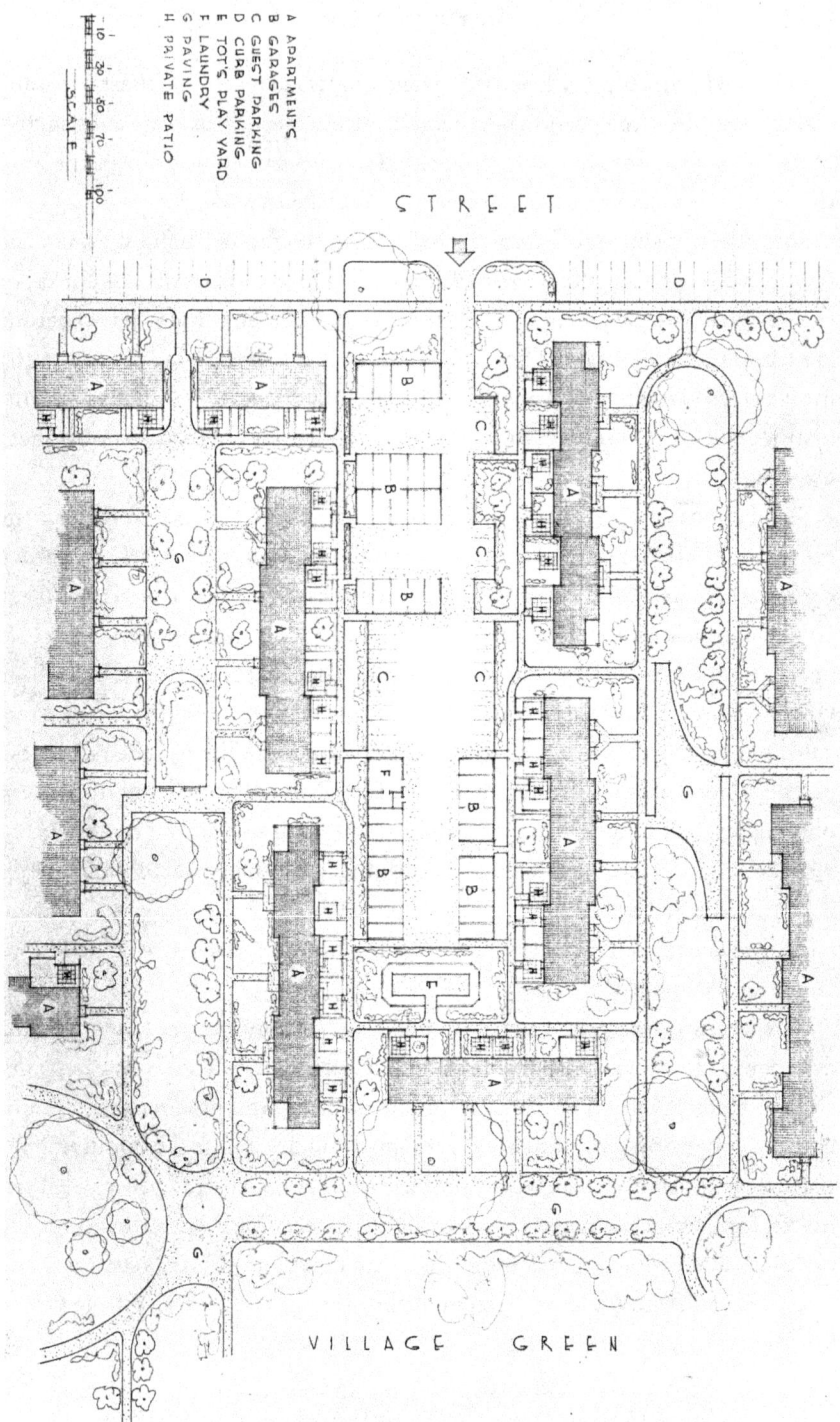

STREET

VILLAGE GREEN

SCALE
10 20 30 40 50 60 70 80 90 100

A APARTMENTS
B GARAGES
C GUEST PARKING
D CURB PARKING
E TOT'S PLAY YARD
F LAUNDRY
G PAVING
H PRIVATE PATIO

and the courtyards in the smaller spaces between the buildings; hedges further delineated these spaces.

Support facilities included meeting rooms, a child care center, and tennis courts on site with, as at Hillside, a school directly to the north of the project. Renting at roughly $12.27 per room per month or approximately $52 per month, the project reached the solidly middle class. The size of the units, on average 1,080 square feet, with ample storage space, oak floors, and many with fireplaces, reflected this target market.

Just two years after its completion, BHV earned recognition at the Museum of Modern Art's "America Builds" exhibition for its distinctive improvements over public housing design. "The major differences between this [BHV] and the rather less costly public projects are increased spaciousness, inside and out, more extensive landscaping, individual garages, and private patios." Bauer agreed, noting that "a lot of the attractiveness of the Village derives from standards of space, facilities, and equipment measurably higher than those in other large-scale housing, public or private." Stein's concurrent experiences with public housing highlight his increasing frustration with the restrictions and cost cutting already associated with that program.[52]

In fact, his California colleagues, Cecil Schilling and Kenneth Wing, practically redesigned Carmelitos, and not for the better, in response to criticisms from Washington. Stein directly addressed his displeasure with the outcome to Schilling, "It seems to me that in making the changes many of the most important features of the town plan that would have served for good living have been sacrificed." These included separation of pedestrian and road ways—in fact Stein felt that the site suffered from too many roads, which required residents to cross at dangerous curves in order to access community facilities (see figure 5.20). In addition to hazardous street conditions near the community building, the project lacked open areas near the park to buffer adjacent residences from noise and to accommodate sufficient recreational space and lacked integrated open areas throughout with placement of units much too close to the adjacent rail line.[53]

While awarded to a nationally prominent contractor—the George A. Fuller

FIGURE 5.19 Baldwin Hills Village, detail from site plan showing relationship between buildings, parking, more intimate and more public open spaces (the Village Green). Box 17, CSP/CUL.

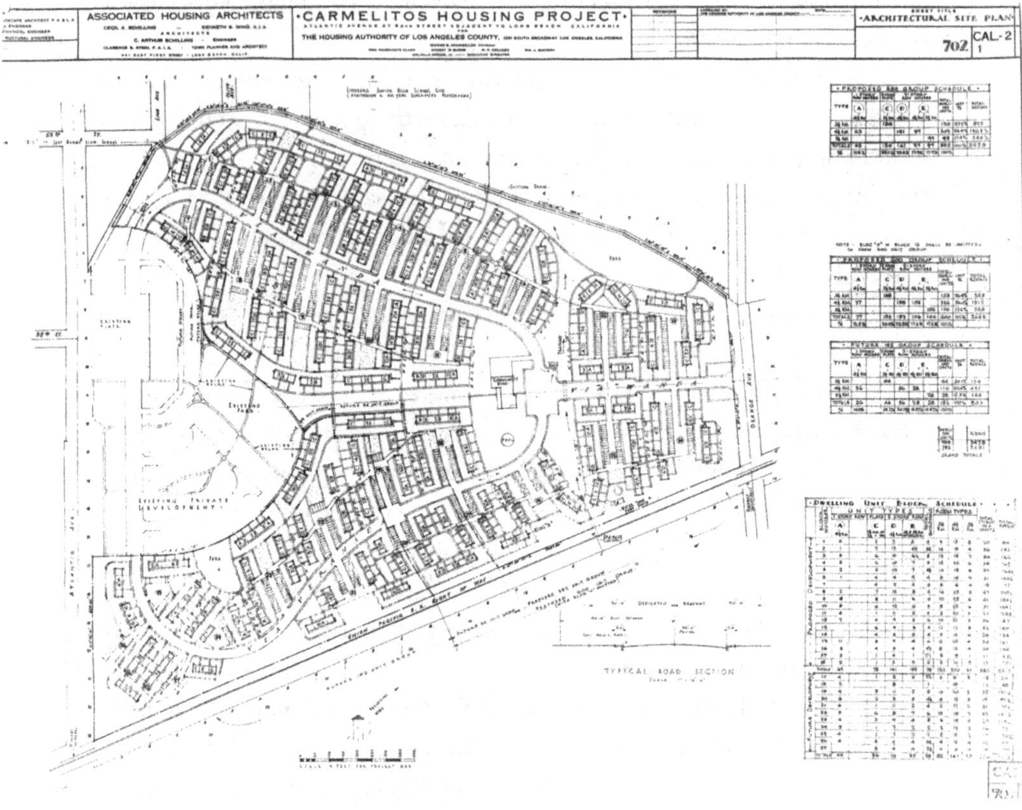

Figure 5.20 Carmelitos, site plan for the project, no date, circa 1939. Box 38, CSP/CUL.

Company—the resulting project, constructed of reinforced concrete with red tile roofs—indeed had a disappointing site plan. The attached units were arranged in monotonous rows—with 180 more added to the site to achieve even greater cost savings per unit. Stein's criticisms were accurate—streets and parking lots disrupted any opportunity for integrated open spaces in the project, and the community building was cut off from much of the housing by a formal street plan intended to focus attention on that structure.[54]

In contrast, Harbor Hills did not disappoint, but Stein warned colleagues Johnson and Wilson that the cost cutting necessary at Carmelitos might also be visited on the other Los Angeles County public housing project. After they

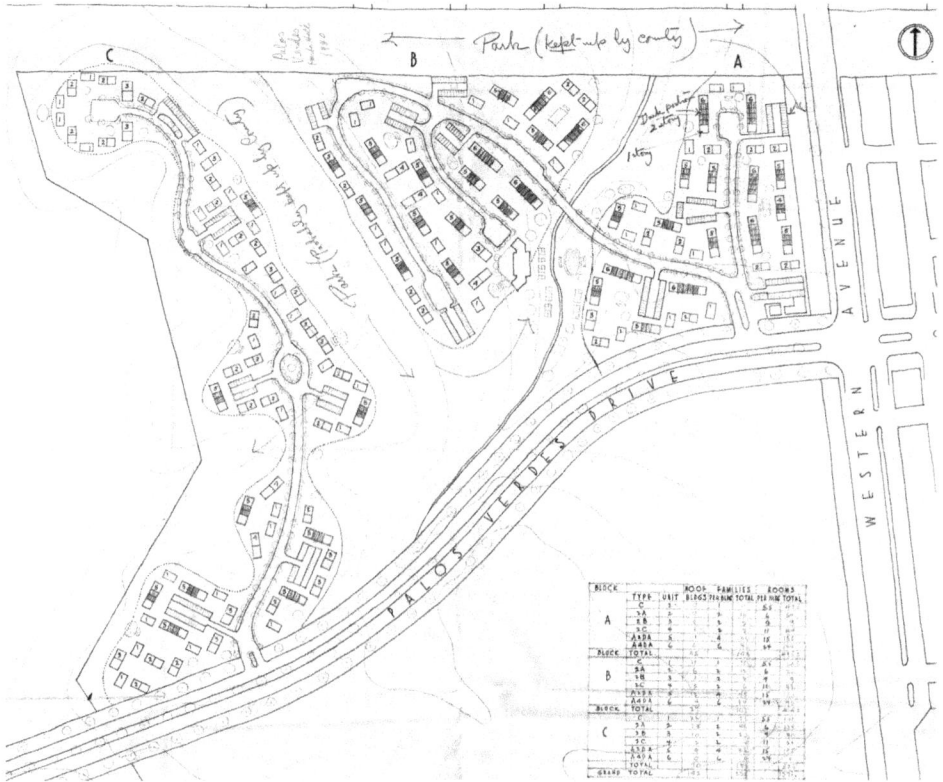

FIGURE 5.21 Early working drawing by Stein of Harbor Hills, dated September 14, 1938. In this plan, Stein accommodates all the units on only one side of Palos Verdes Drive (North Drive). Box 2, CSP/CUL.

received criticisms from Washington, Stein replied, "Fundamentally, the scheme and the unit plans [of Harbor Hills] are fine. I think it is foolish after all this work to be stampeded into a more commonplace design."[55] Unlike Schilling's team on Carmelitos, Johnson's team did not struggle at Harbor Hills to incorporate cost reductions while meeting state and local code requirements. Certainly, their recent experience designing (and redesigning) another large-scale housing project—BHV—did not hurt. Possibly, they made better use of Stein's site planning and unit layout skills, recognizing that he was unfamiliar with state and local code requirements.

Ultimately, the final design of Harbor Hills, perhaps because of the more

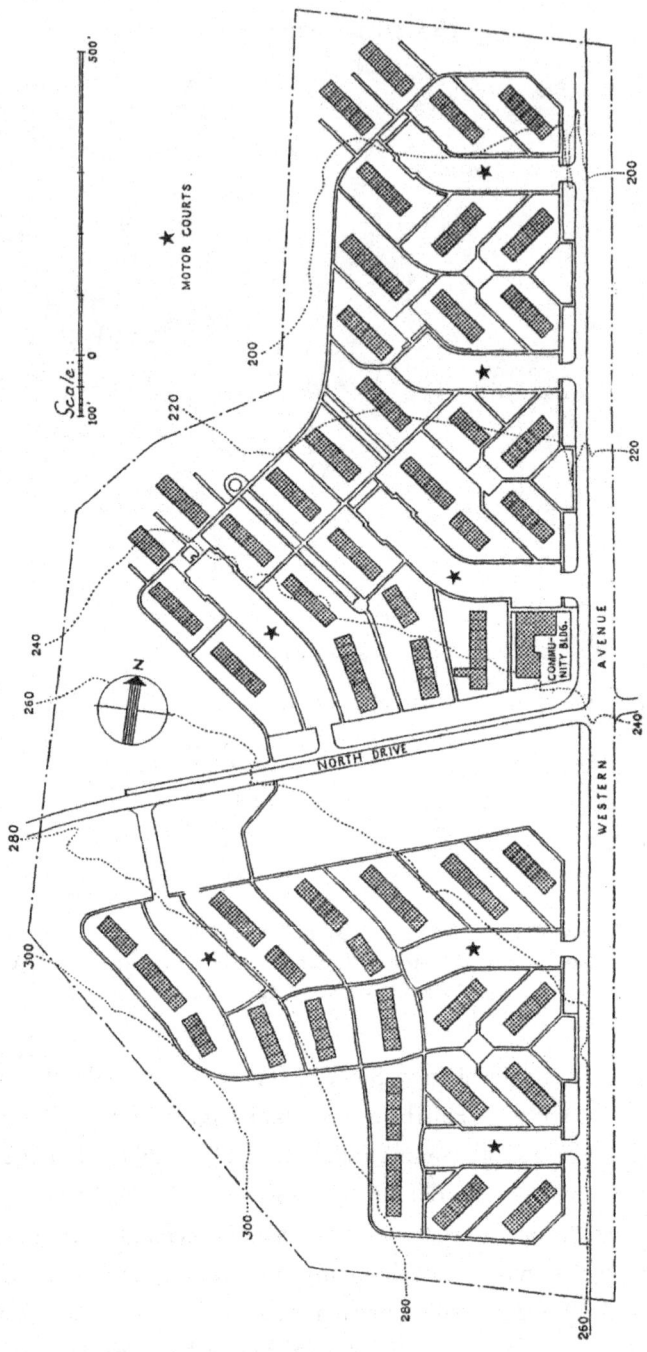

FIGURE 5.22 Site plan of Harbor Hills as built. C. S. Stein, "Harbor Hills Housing," *Pencil Points* 22 (November 1941): 677–683, 679.

topographically interesting site, pleased Stein to a much greater degree than Carmelitos (see figures 5.21 and 5.22). He was particularly pleased that the chevron plan was maintained—"Following the contours, the architects evolved a varied arrangement of the buildings in a chevron pattern, thus making the project a relief from the endless repetition of parallel rows of similar buildings that one has come to think of as 'public housing.'"[56] The use of rough brickwork introduced texture along the otherwise smooth surface of the exterior walls and connected the band of windows, and the choice to cantilever the floors to create balconies and hoods over the front doors emphasized the horizontal appearance of the buildings. Diversity was also maintained due to the color palette of distinctive earth tones chosen for the buildings.

Similar to BHV, a number of two-story buildings had one-story end units. Though the service sides of the buildings were clustered around parking areas as at BHV, the Harbor Hills project lacked the intimate and connected series of open spaces that grace the FHA-insured project. Further hampering connections between the residences, a two-lane road, North Drive, cut through the site, essentially dividing it in half. The community spaces were cramped, and the community building was located on the corner of North Drive and Western Avenue, a major roadway that bounded the site on the east.[57] Despite the delays in gaining approvals in Washington and the war in Europe, Carmelitos and Harbor Hills were completed, respectively, in 1940 and 1941 slightly before BHV.

Just as these projects were being completed, Stein began work on a series of defense housing projects, the first designed to be a demonstration of demountable structures that could be assembled quickly in wartime. Given the standardization of the housing units, Stein was hired to introduce some diversity and thus interest in the site layout. In 1941 at Indian Head, Maryland, site of a major naval arsenal on the banks of the Potomac, ten prefabricated housing companies participated in the 650-unit defense housing project. Engaged by John Carmody to prepare the site design, Stein expressed early concerns that with its "knock-down houses," it might "look like the devil." Even prior to its completion, Indian Head was widely considered a "complete flop as a demonstration" that "did not prove much to Government that was not already known or could not have been discovered more quickly and economically in other ways." Noted another critic, "the entire effect of scores of identical units with minimum standards is generally depressing." In comparison Stein's site design was praised as being "considerably more attractive than [the] houses." Similar to the earlier plan for Harbor Hills, most of the housing units clustered around cul-de-sacs and loop roads. These backed up to an open area that included recreational space and room for commercial and community buildings. Regrettably, a road on the eastern edge of the community cut off some of the residences from this shared space. Calling it "an intensive application of the cul-de-sac principle," Frederick Gutheim, a young planner who had met Stein in 1933 when he was drafting policy for the new TVA, acknowledged that the effect of "prefabricated housing en masse . . . is mitigated somewhat by ingenious site planning."[58]

Next Stein designed two defense housing projects on the outskirts of Pittsburgh in part on the strength of the work he and Wright had done years earlier at Chatham Village. One called Stowe Township was located northwest of downtown overlooking the Ohio River, the other, Shaler Village, was located almost directly north of downtown near the Allegheny River. Despite their proximity to heavy industry and the role Pittsburgh played as the villain in the documentary *The City*, where Stein and his colleagues promoted their new town ideals just two years earlier, the community architect was immediately taken with both sites when he visited them in early May 1941. "I have been walking up and down the hills of Pittsburgh—looking at sites. The second one [in Stowe] is splendid. A great plateau with distant views. I can do something good with that one. The other [in Shaler], which is all hillside is much more difficult—but it will be exciting." He had only until July 2 to complete designs for both projects. During the summer of 1941 he made frequent trips from New York City to Washington and Pittsburgh as he completed work on both projects and sought out a third.[59]

Later called Ohio View Acres, Stowe consisted of one long entry road with two cul-de-sac streets at right angles providing access to the residences. A community building with a parking area stood as a gateway to the development. Stein considered this the easier of the two projects, though the relatively flat topography did fall away on the edges of the site, with the hillside buildings featuring efficiency apartments on the bottom floor. The architect skillfully arranged the open spaces to connect visually to the river below. *Architectural Forum* called the resulting design "a really excellent site plan," clarifying that it exemplified "a simple, economical and informal arrangement of the streets and buildings carefully adjusted to the contours and worked out to make the most of views in all directions."[60] The sixty-eight buildings were unadorned, gable roofed, which together with the regular repetitive pattern of windows, emulated an economical Colonial Revival style. The exterior treatment of the mostly two-story buildings varied with either brick or clapboard siding, and the clustering of the buildings around the pocket parking areas interspersed along the roads and at the cul-de-sacs also succeeded in creating a more diverse and appealing project.

The rather hilly site at Shaler (later called Shalercrest) presented some challenging opportunities. With multiple hills, the structures varied more across the site, ranging from one to two and a half stories in height with basement units in the hillside homes equaling roughly half the floor area as that in the story above. Here the roads were more organic, designed in a serpentine pattern connecting the hilltops on the site where the housing was clustered (see figure 5.23). As at the Stowe project, this clustering accommodated more economical layout of utilities and infrastructure, which allowed the remaining open spaces on the thirty-eight-acre site to function as smaller connected garden courts among the buildings on the more level parts of the site and larger recreational areas on the lower elevations of the property. The project also featured a community building, an administration building, and a small store centrally located and oriented toward the larger recreational area. Like Stowe, the fifty-nine buildings at Shaler featured an unadorned Colonial Revival style with either brick veneer or clapboard siding. Ralph Griswold, who had designed the distinctive open spaces at Chatham Village several years earlier, lent his landscape architecture skills to both of these projects. As Stein watched the two projects under development, he acknowledged the excellence of the site design: "They have a freedom of design and a variety of pattern—It is going to be good to live in these houses—And such views!"[61]

While Stein secured a third defense housing project in Pittsburgh by mid-July, the project, southeast of downtown Pittsburgh in Clariton on the Reed-Wylie farm site, ultimately was not developed. Designed in collaboration with local architects Charles and Edward Stotz, it was to include 499 units on an eighty-five-acre site. The site design reflected many features that Stein had incorporated at Shaler, Stowe, and Indian Head, with the loop roads establishing two distinctive and separate open spaces around which the housing clustered. By the end of July with the design work well underway, Stein remarked, "We [the draftsmen and architects in his office] are building on our experience with the two last projects. The individual houses will not be very different than those I have used before—but the form of the land leads to different groupings—As a

DEFENSE HOUSING PROJECT
SHALER TOWNSHIP, PA.
FEDERAL WORKS AGENCY
JOHN M. CARMODY, FEDERAL WORKS ADMINISTRATOR.    B.J. HOVDE, DIRECTOR, PITTSBURGH DEFENSE HOUSING
ALLEGHENY COUNTY HOUSING AUTHORITY
EDWARD J. J.CSNARD, CHAIRMAN    FRANK L.PALMER, EXECUTIVE DIRECTOR
CLARENCE S. STEIN, ARCHITECT

194

whole I think it will be the best of the three." Thus, with each project, regardless of cost and time constraints, Stein incorporated the clustered housing, integrated open space, roadway and pedestrian way designs associated with the Radburn Idea while making adjustments for site constraints and pushing himself to learn something new regarding the adaptability of these linked design concepts.[62]

As he became more adept at the layout of these projects, the government issued increasingly restrictive site design guidelines, making it more difficult to incorporate the size and complexity of Stein's open spaces much less the mixture of community uses and amenities he envisioned. Stein increasingly chafed under federal cost-saving requirements, particularly those associated with the public housing program, such as prescriptions on overall unit size, storage space, building materials, open spaces, and landscaping. Thus the community architect welcomed the opportunity to innovate as consultant to the nationally recognized firm of Harris and Associates with their large-scale project in Maplewood, Louisiana, just two years later.

## A Partnership with John W. Harris

Harris had first tried to get in touch with Stein to work on the new town of Maplewood near Lake Charles, Louisiana, in January 1943, when the community architect was recuperating at the Double U Ranch in Tucson. In May 1943, Harris secured Stein's services to review site and housing plans that had already been prepared for the project, at the time called Pine Gardens, and to "study and work up the scheme for the town center, consisting of stores and other community buildings." Located in a major industrial region, the 295-acre property had been purchased by Harris Associates from an oil company that had a refinery nearby. Touted as a "completely self-sufficient town," Maplewood intrigued Stein as a chance to participate in designing a Regional City owned and managed by one entity, Harris Associates.[63]

Stein devoted three hundred hours to the Maplewood project in 1943 during the months of May, June, and July. The site plan dated April 9, 1943, shows a typical subdivision of single family homes on a modified grid. A town center and

FIGURE 5.23 Shaler—rendering of site plan for the project, circa 1941. Box 2, CSP/CUL.

a school sit on the southern edge of the project with apartments directly adjacent to the north and then single family homes. The community also had three small parks. Stein's recommendations included establishing more cul-de-sacs, eliminating the connection between Center Boulevard and Highway 90 so that this street running through the center of the community ceased to function as a major thoroughfare, making the lots smaller, widening the local streets to twenty-four feet to accommodate on-street parking, reducing the size of Center Circle—the street that bounded the shops and community buildings, and introducing more interior parks by turning some streets along with the adjacent houses into park areas (see figure 5.24). He also provided detailed comments on each house plan, from the floor layout to its orientation on the lot. Stein met in Washington with Seward Mott, director of the Land Planning Division at FHA, and Gabriel Harmon, the land planning consultant to the FHA regional office in Dallas, to review the project. Mott agreed with some of Stein's recommendations, particularly the redesign of the floor layouts and a minor reduction in some lot widths.[64]

A critical disagreement with the FHA regarding the single family homes involved the location of the garages. As he had in Radburn, Stein strongly urged locating the garages "mostly nearer the street." When Harmon argued that this proposal created an "improper relation between the garage and dwelling," Stein replied, "[The] garage should not be in the quiet garden space behind the house."[65] Still, Stein appeared to be restraining himself from making recommendations for the residential areas that were too revolutionary. Certainly his proposals only mildly adopted the Radburn Idea as they did not include superblocks, clustered housing, or an integrated park system.

As opposed to the residential sections, the town center was to be his to design. Stein energetically began his analysis to determine the appropriate mix of community and commercial uses, floor layouts, and site configuration of the town center. In order to determine the proper mix of uses for a town the size of Maplewood—a total of 1,065 units for 3,500 people—he wrote letters to contacts with knowledge of theaters, stores, offices, education, and recreation and revisited the design of previous centers, particularly Greenbelt, Maryland.[66] His proposed site layout emulated a Beaux Arts design with a strong axial focus centered on a series of open spaces beginning with the site entrance through the "Great Porch" to the north then walking south into a garden with a fountain (see figure 5.25). This garden space narrowed before opening onto a larger area

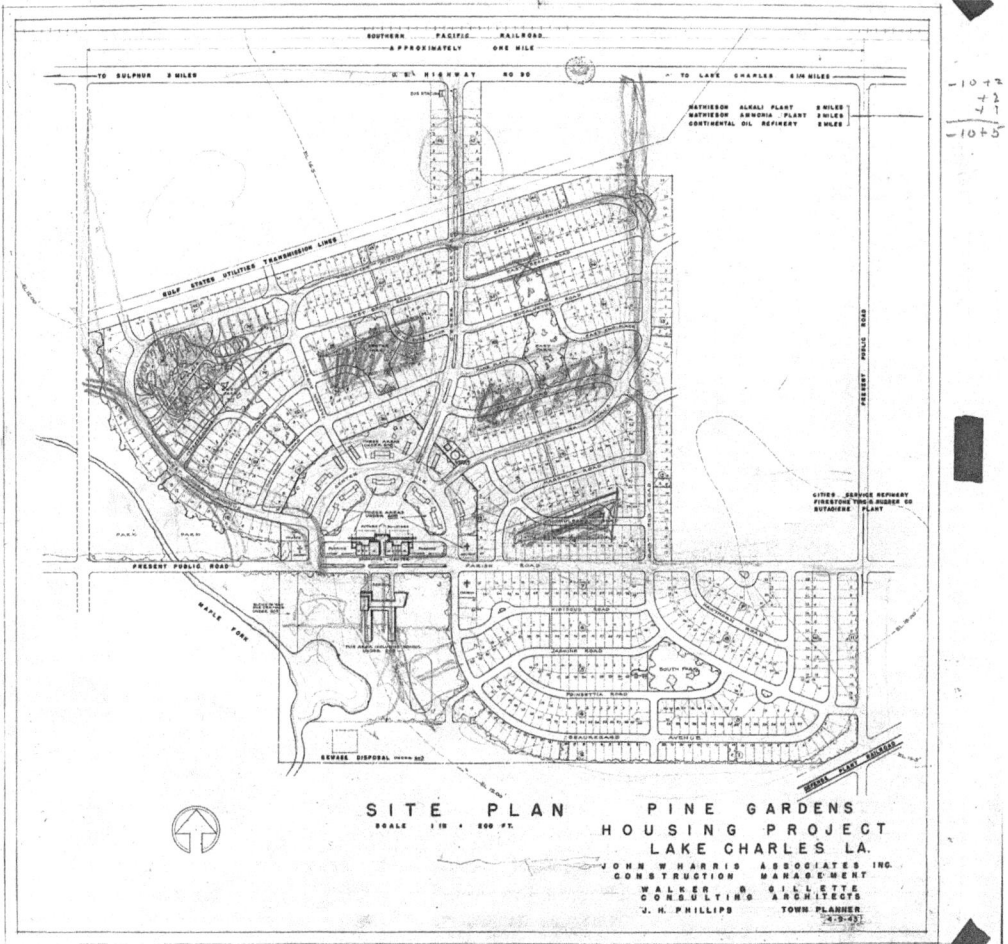

FIGURE 5.24 Marked-up site plan for Pine Gardens (Maplewood), Louisiana, showing Stein's recommendations for revisions to create centralized parks for each block, dated April 9, 1943. Box 4, CSP/CUL.

centered on a park across Parish Road in front of the community school. The structures in the town center shaped these series of unifying spaces and helped create the forced perspective through the site. To the north along the semi-circular drive—Center Circle—were located two structures—the community building and administrative building, which included a health center. The Great

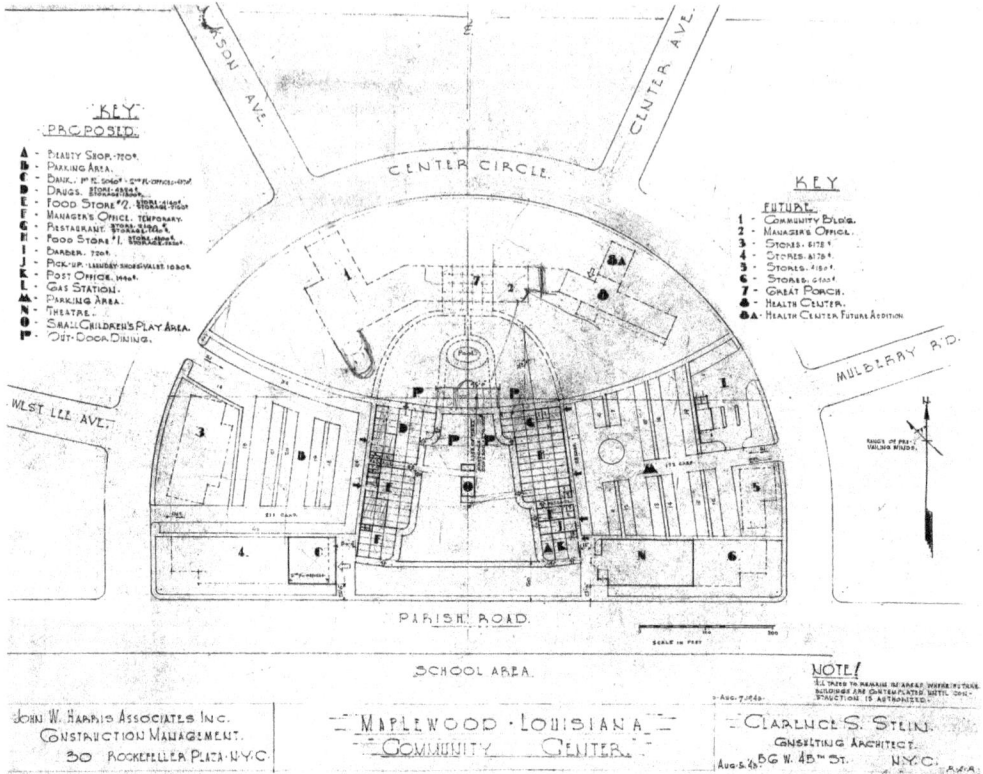

FIGURE 5.25 Maplewood shopping and community center, sketch, Clarence S. Stein, consulting architect, dated August 5, 1943. The community center is the lighter series of structures on the upper (north) part of the site and the shopping area is an inverted V oriented toward the school on the south part of the site. Box 4, CSP/CUL.

Porch connected the two. The shops to the south of these buildings were arranged in the form of an inverted "V" with the central space between the shops oriented toward the fountain in the smaller garden and the Great Porch on the north and the school, across Parish Road, to the south. This open space in the commercial section allowed access to the shops from the interior of the project while also accommodating outdoor dining and a play area for younger children. Some parking was located in front of the community and administrative buildings with the majority on the eastern and western edges of the property, so that the emphasis was placed on pedestrian access through the central sections of the town center. A separate bank and a theater building were located toward the rear of the site adjacent to the parking areas. Community facilities included a 730-seat hall with a stage, a nursery school with play yard, a workshop, a health room, club rooms, a library, and exhibit space. In addition to the bank and movie theater, the shopping center included a grocery, drugstore, post office, laundry service, gas station, and restaurant.

Stein and Harris met in Washington with Mott, who had visited the site, and other agency representatives to discuss the design of the shopping center and community buildings. Mott offered a few criticisms, but overall he approved of the scheme. Upon reviewing more detailed site drawings shortly thereafter, Harmon did not. He wrote the chief underwriter in New Orleans that he had some major concerns regarding the town center design. Gingerly approaching the subject, Harmon noted, "His [Stein's] plan is so much in conflict with what we have seen done elsewhere, however, that we hesitate to criticize it too severely for fear of criticism that we oppose new trends in business center planning." He then warmed to the subject, listing concerns he considered particularly significant, especially given that the plans were fairly detailed and Harris was pushing for early approval. These concerns included—that the commercial structures were "buried" as they were located away from the surrounding streets; that the amount of parking was inadequate and that Stein had "perhaps, unconsciously subjugated this primary requirement in an effort to produce a park-like character in his scheme"; and that the community buildings appeared to be more accessible than the commercial structures. Harris Associates responded that Harmon's criticism seemed to be "based on shopping from the seat of an automobile" rather than conventional window shopping, and the firm stood by Stein's design. Though the town center ultimately did include the arrangement of shops that Stein recommended, the lack of the community and administration buildings on the northern part of the site and the lack of outdoor dining areas diminished the overall effect of an enclosed, pedestrian-oriented town center (see figure 5.26). In fact, because the development was initially concentrated along the Parish Road to the south of the site, the shopping center had more of an auto-oriented design, though Harris Associates did not locate parking in the central open space as the FHA had recommended.[67]

Clearly open space design was a key feature of Stein's projects—built and unbuilt, residential and nonresidential. Connectivities, scale, and type (intimate

FIGURE 5.26 Maplewood aerial showing the shopping area (center) and school (lower right) circa 1944. Photo by Elwood M. Payne, Houston, 1468-21. Box 4, CSP/CUL.

and private to active and communal) distinguished their form and function, together with the enclosing structures, mixture of uses, and street systems that bounded and characterized them. Stein considered all of these model projects— models for what could be possible in community design once the proper programs were in place. These programs included sufficient government funding for working-class housing to accommodate an acceptable standard of design from the unit to the entire community, and concepts of planning and community ownership to allow the entire site to be addressed as one cohesive property—to allow an appropriate mix of uses, residences, parks, and street layouts as well as efficient long-term project management. As he looked forward to the end of World War II, Stein reflected, "The elements of new form and new procedure have been gradually evolving during the past ten to twenty years. New street patterns and grouping of houses at Radburn, Greenbelt, in public and defense

FIGURE 5.27 Federal Housing Administration guidelines for subdivision design. The description states in part, "The Radburn type plan showing a series of culs-de-sac grouped in a super-block around a central park." FHA, "Planning Neighborhoods for Small Houses," Technical Bulletin No. 5 (1936; rev. ed., Washington, DC: Government Printing Office, 1938), 24.

housing, at Chatham Village and in other investment housing projects; new conceptions of community living; a completely new procedure of production and operation—management as different from the old speculative method as light from dark—all have been taking form."[68]

Interestingly, the publication in 1938 of a single image in a widely distributed FHA pamphlet of design guidelines may have had a greater impact on postwar residential design than Stein's "model" projects, whether limited dividend, public, FHA-insured, or defense housing. Featuring the "Radburn type plan," FHA's "Planning Neighborhoods for Small Houses" promoted the concept of the cul-de-sac with the integrated park system as a recommended approach to subdivision design (see figure 5.27). Unfortunately, while the image of the cul-de-sac was repeated throughout the publication, the integrated park system was not. Irwin Chanin's design of Green Acres in 1936, which was built on the site of

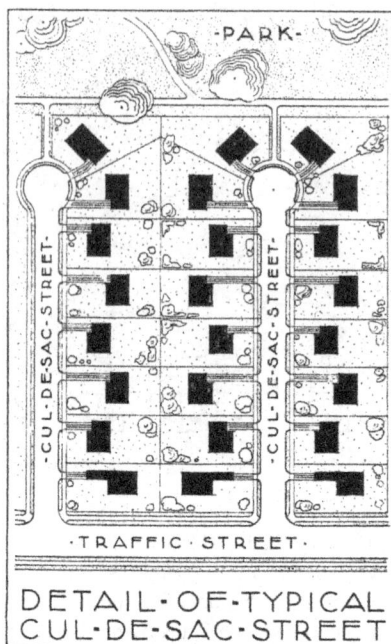

DETAIL·OF·TYPICAL
CUL·DE·SAC·STREET

FIGURE 5.28 Irwin Chanin's design for
Green Acres touting its similarity to the
Radburn plan. "Green Acres, A Resi-
dential Park Community," *Architectural
Record* 80 (October 1936): 285–286, 286.

Stein's proposed Valley Stream project, provides an early example of a project
promoted on the Radburn principles that failed to apply them comprehensively,
instead focusing primarily on the cul-de-sac. A brief article in the *Architectural
Record* lauding the project as "A Community for the Motor Age" directly referenced two significant characteristics of the Radburn Idea—"the principle of
traffic separation and the use of a park system, to deliver the future residents of
this project from the menace of the automobile." Yet unlike Radburn, the houses
were not clustered nor "turned around" to face private backyards directly adjacent to public garden ways. Instead, sidewalks along the community's eighty-five
local streets culminated at the head of each cul-de-sac in an access point to the
linear park system (see figure 5.28). The direct connection between the private

yard behind each home and a hierarchical system of more modest garden ways and then more generous community parks and recreation areas was lost as was the complete separation of pedestrian and automobile.[69]

Stein viewed the postwar era as an opportunity to promote the Regional City afresh, translating the Radburn Idea for an audience eager to leave the aging industrial cities, with pent-up expectations, wealth, and government support to do so. While Green Acres, not Radburn, became the predominant model of postwar suburban residential development, the community architect's Regional City and town planning principles manifested in a range of postwar initiatives that informed regional planning in salient ways during and beyond this period.

# 6

---

# THE REGIONAL CITY AND

# TOWN PLANNING

Stein and his colleagues began to regularly use the term *Regional City* in 1927. In a letter to MacKaye, Stein noted, "We are at last starting actively to campaign for the Regional City. It is astonishing how easily this new name for garden city has gone over." Their early conception envisioned an amalgam of the romanticized medieval village with connections to the land combined with all the conveniences offered through new technologies to enhance modern lifestyles in distinctive, relatively small towns. Mumford described their vision in an early address before the American Institute of Architects:

> We may be able by one means or another to recover ... the point of view which created the well-rounded and well-balanced agricultural village of the seventeenth century and translate that into twentieth century terms, and in this case city planning would not be merely a matter of dealing with physical apparatus, it would also be a matter of dealing with the social city: it would be city planning in a complete sense, and for the sake of definition we call that community planning nowadays.[1]

Following news of Roosevelt's election, Stein, MacKaye, and Mumford discussed advocating for regional, even national, planning based on the ideas the RPAA had already promoted, including regional river basin planning, the townless highway, and state planning. By February 1933, RPAA members learned Roosevelt was already exploring regional initiatives in the Tennessee River Valley. Stein reflected, "Our suggestion for regional planning sounded merely like an echo of his ideas—Guess we will have to be a little more radical—anyhow in words—to keep ahead of the President." The TVA, formed as part of Roosevelt's first One Hundred Days from March to June 1933, focused on a watershed that covered forty-one thousand square miles and seven states and addressed a range of initiatives from improving navigation to rural electrification via the development of dams and from armament production to regional planning and new town development. Of course, the latter was of particular interest to the RPAA, and connections were quickly made to key contacts in the new TVA. In July 1933, Stein and Herbert Emmerich showed Earle Draper, who had just been appointed to head up planning for the agency, around Radburn, showcasing their design and town planning ideas. The combination of technical achievement and appeal to Arcadian roots through the formation of Regional Cities in this major rural river basin appealed especially to MacKaye, who took a job with the agency in spring 1934. In just over two years, MacKaye stepped down from his position. He described the situation to Stuart Chase, "The power program got into good hands—Lillienthal's. But the planning program—thereby hangs a tale." While he praised his direct supervisor Draper, he faulted the program for not allowing land planning to lead and coordinate the work of the other divisions.[2]

At the same time, the RPAA members' housing and new town ideas seemed to find some traction in the new public housing program initially headed by Kohn and in the Greenbelt Towns. Despite these strong connections to policy and policymakers and despite Stein's engagement in these new programs, they remained demonstrations rather than developing as the norm. Stein's response was to target the general public at the 1939 World's Fair by showcasing the superiority of new town and community design in *The City*. Following the war, Stein increasingly focused on advocacy and education, fighting to safeguard the Greenbelt Towns and defense housing by maintaining them under single ownership through cooperative housing ventures, making numerous visits to Washington, DC, to advocate for this approach. He formed the Regional Development Council of America (RDCA) to promote regionalism for a postwar era, continued his lecturing and teaching at various universities, and consulted on degree programs to educate the next generation of housers, regionalists, and community architects.

## Chapter 6

# *The City* and Preparations
# for a Postwar Era

Stein's primary interest in the fall of 1937 as he began to get back to work after his long illness turned to community building and advocacy for regionalism and new towns. Energized by the opening of the Henry Wright Library of the Housing Study Guild at the Federation Technical School, Stein began teaching a weekly lecture series there entitled "City Planning and Housing." In addition to understanding "spatial requirements" and design, Stein maintained the student architect needed to anticipate "human requirements" in terms of "changing habits, requirements, and inventions." In his course outline, which he shared with MacKaye, Stein also contrasted the rampant metropolitanism of New York City with the small town, the countryside, and the Regional City.[3]

As Stein again actively engaged with regional planning and community building concepts, he expanded his lecturing to New York University and MIT and tried to revive the RPAA. "Very little," he explained to MacKaye, "has been added during the last 35 years to the fundamental ideas that were laid down by our old friend Ebenezer Howard in his book Garden Cities of Tomorrow. As I wrote Lewis today, it is about time we did something about it."[4] Though he hosted a dinner in February 1938 that included many previous members of the group—MacKaye, Mumford, Black, Ackerman, as well as Unwin—to formulate recommendations for the design of new towns, they did not meet again on a regular basis until late in the next decade.

For Stein, housing and regionalism remained synonymous. Local government officials could use the new public housing program and recognize the realities of land valuation and taxation in applying economic development tools to do no less than rebuild cities and establish new towns. These new initiatives created burgeoning opportunities for architects "to build ... a richer and finer environment." By making these connections and presenting them in lectures to student architects, Stein saw himself as continuing to adapt and promote Howard's ideas for the modern age. In fact, the new housing program offered a means for "American architects [to be] drawn into community development" and thus community planning. Unlike city planning, which Stein maintained forced development into "a preconceived physical framework," community planning "molds the forms of buildings around these requirements for individual and community living.

It ties them together, spaces them, and arranges them in relation to each other and to open spaces in such a way as to make living and working more effective and more pleasant."[5]

In the fall of 1937, he devoted much of a lecture at MIT to arguing why decent housing should be a local concern and responsibility and emphasizing the critical role that the local government should play from an economic development perspective in attracting industries that pay a living wage. Citing studies conducted in Cleveland (1934) and Boston (1935), Stein maintained that most residents do not pay sufficient property taxes to cover infrastructure costs and that like education, housing is a local governmental responsibility. Further, cities should "beware of the character of their growth." Specifically, "any municipality should think twice before it invites any industry to settle within its border that does not pay a substantial wage to its workers."[6] Local officials must, through economic development initiatives, attract those businesses that pay adequately.

In 1937, he also anticipated the urban renewal program when discussing the reaction of the real estate industry to remaking cities. "In spite of the natural opposition of the real estate interests to any governmental interference or competition, it is easy to see how the idea of a large program of national financing could be sold to those who had any financial interest in the blighted areas. It was somewhat more difficult to prove the economic advantages to the municipalities unless the national government could be induced to buy up all the property that was not paying taxes and put it in such condition that it would again pay its share of municipal costs (taxes)."[7] Eventually, through local redevelopment authorities, the 1949 Housing Act targeted federal funds at blighted areas with the goal of increasing their value. While Stein was lecturing on these topics, he was also getting back to work "architecturally."

With BHV, Carmelitos, and Harbor Hills underway in 1938, Stein sought another way to demonstrate his and his colleagues' town building ideas. He turned his attention to a film for the World's Fair that he had been discussing with Robert Kohn and his brother-in-law, Arthur Mayer. He had recently seen Pare Lorentz's movie *The River* (1937) and was impressed by the way documentary films could address critical social topics, such as, in this case, the significance of the TVA's flood control programs. With assurances of a grant from the Carnegie Corporation of New York to fund the film, Civic Films, Inc., was established as a nonprofit corporation on June 10, 1938, with Stein as its president.[8] The goal was to produce a film that reflected the RPAA's Regional City philosophy emphasizing the opportunities afforded by new towns for working, leisure, and living as contrasted with the congested metropolises and smoke-belching industrial centers. Entitled *The City*, the film was sponsored by the American Institute of Planners (AIP), which established a committee to oversee its development consisting primarily of the directors of Civic Films, Inc. In addition to Stein, the directors were Tracy Augur, who was president of the AIP; Russell Van Nest Black, a former AIP president; Harold Buttenheim, editor of *The American City*, an influential magazine that addressed planning, finance, and infrastructure issues of interest to local officials; Robert Kohn; Frederick Ackerman; and Lawrence Orton, commissioner of the New York City Planning Commission.

Of Lorentz, who had already made a name for himself in the new field of documentary films, Stein remarked to Mumford, who was coordinating with the filmmaker on the script, "He has unquestionable ability and his name is going to help." Still, the filmmaker chafed at the sheer volume of material the AIP Committee and Civic Films expected him to review to prepare the script outline. The film opened in MacKaye's hometown of Shirley, Massachusetts. "The purpose of it," Stein explained to MacKaye, "is to show that towns did exist, and if you will, still exist, with all the essential characteristics of the garden city. It should show the close relation of countryside and town, the simple and wholesome idea of community, and all that you have suggested in the very simple description of the New England village in your book." Still, in working with the cinematographers, Stein cautioned MacKaye to assist Willard Van Dyke, photographer and codirector with Ralph Steiner, in getting the iconic New England town filmed so that the scenes showed the community without "a whole lot of automobiles in the foreground."[9]

The theme for the two-square mile fair in Queens just south of Flushing Bay was "Building the World of Tomorrow." With an investment of more than $155 million, Park Commissioner Robert Moses and Grover A. Whalen, president of the New York World's Fair 1939 Incorporated, oversaw development of the former dump site at Flushing Meadow into government, transportation, communications, production and distribution, community interests, food, and amusement zones. Among the most influential exhibits were Democracity, located in the Perisphere, and General Motor's Futurama designed by Norman Bel Geddes. Democracity, designed by Henry Dreyfus, offered an image of a "futuristic metropolis ... of a million people with a working population of 250,000, whose homes are located beyond the city proper, in five satellite towns" with the highways providing the connection between these and "the city's heart." Distinct residential and industrial satellite towns provided housing in a gardenlike atmosphere. The overall message of the exhibit was unity with the show culminating in a diverse array of workers representing "modern society" marching together symbolizing hope for the future. Futurama, a fair favorite with its massive highways and decentralized suburbs, offered a fairly prescient vision of the country in 1960. Featuring a downtown of skyscrapers set in parks, the thoroughfares, parkways, and highways dominated, allowing speeding cars to make their unimpeded escape to the suburbs.[10]

While different visions of the future, both of these major exhibits were certainly consistent with the fair's theme—to "show the most promising developments of production, service and social factors of the present day in relation to their bearing on the life of the great mass of the people. The plain American citizen will be able to see here what he could attain for his community and for himself by intelligent co-ordinated effort and will be made to realize the interdependence of every contributing form of life and work." Stein and his colleagues also considered this theme consistent with their vision. *The City* opened on May 26, 1939, with an invitation-only showing under the auspices of the AIP. Certainly influential beyond the confines of the fair, the film advocated the RPAA's, particularly Stein and Mumford's, vision of new towns created through "unified planning" framed by green belts with "green nature" integrated throughout so that "the houses blend into the green landscape." The metropolis was absent from their vision, except as the villain in the story, and highways, the automobile, and other recent technological innovations were essential, yet here they did not take center stage. They did not intrude on the community, though they made this new way of life possible.[11]

Pittsburgh and New York City provided the dramatic contrast of the Industrial City and the Metropolis, respectively, with Radburn and Greenbelt showcasing the attributes of "The Green City—the New City that foresight makes possible." As Stein noted earlier that spring at the national planning conference, new towns offered an alternative to the dinosaur or speculative city—a fresh start. "In existing cities, although we see the disadvantage of the old forms, we are not free to use the new patterns because of the investment in the old and the high cost of government.... The important thing at present is that we do not waste time, energy, and money in building communities as part of the obsolete and of the past. Rather let us relate them to the life of the present and the future. To do so we must make a fresh start." Yet it was this abandonment of the "old city," at least for the immediate future, that garnered Stein some criticism from fellow planners. Nationally recognized planning consultant Harland Bartholomew responded, "We must think in terms of the whole urban community, and not certain parts. ... Decentralization of the large urban community into isolated sectors is a theoretical ideal but a practical impossibility. It would not work either from the standpoint of living or from the standpoint of economics." Bartholomew argued that people would continue to rely on nearby cities for work, social reasons, and cultural events and thus tax municipal resources. Looking at new communities in isolation did not inform planning practice.[12]

In fact, the sheer chaos, congestion, drama, and energy of the Metropolis shown in the film made for an appealing contrast with the sedate Radburn and Greenbelt. While acknowledging *The City*'s "immense success at the World's Fair," a critic maintained

> The new city [which] is laid before our admiring eyes, has about it the coldness of a utopia just delivered by mail. ... Only the children seem really to be having a good time. ... The old city is not a child's world; the new city is. So far, so good. But it is going to take a truer and more penetrating documentary than The City, fine as it is in technique, structure and dramatic effect, to explain why the old city is not a place for the adult to live in either, and to give that same adult a more mature reason for wanting to will the new city into being than a game of bridge while the washing machine is in operation.[13]

In fact, it was the film's focus on community—on families, particularly children—and the benefits they realized from this new form of living that leaves a lasting impression. The World's Fair allowed the opportunity to expose even more people to the concept of complete communities—communities designed to accommodate living, working, and leisure with integrated open spaces to create social and physical connections and hierarchical street systems to safely contain the automobile. Shown over a four-month period at the fair, *The City* continued to be leased, through an exclusive agreement with the Museum of Modern Art, for almost two decades. With their vision outlined to a broader audience, Stein and his colleagues looked forward to a new era of regionalism, town building, and redevelopment.[14]

Stein had never relinquished the goal of a statewide plan for New York. As he completed the majority of his work on Maplewood in August 1943, Stein traveled with his wife to California for a short vacation before MacMahon began filming *Dragon Seed*, which earned her an Academy Award nomination. While there, Stein began work on a report detailing the establishment and functions of a statewide planning agency for New York. Harold Buttenheim, in his capacity as president of the Citizen's Housing Council of New York, had been asked by Governor Dewey to prepare the report. Since Wright, MacKaye, and Stein's recommendation for statewide planning practically eighteen years earlier, Stein maintained that New York continued to rely on a weak system of agencies, which faced similar problems as in 1926. "If we're going to get real results in state redevelopment we need a single commissioner and he will have to have standing and power.... He'll have to know the state and enough about regional planning to know where he's going. Besides he'll have to combine Bob Moses' ability at getting things done with Benton's understanding of what should be done." That December Stein presented the report in his capacity as chairman of the subcommittee of the Citizen's Housing Council proposing a "Division of Planned Development in the Executive Department" to coordinate all planning, redevelopment, and housing initiatives in the state. Stein heard back from Governor Dewey shortly after presenting the proposal to him. According to Stein, while the governor acknowledged his interest, he admitted, "[The] memo has been read by several people, however, and the disagreement is so widespread and for so many different reasons that it seems impossible to follow through on it at this moment."[15]

Certainly, he admitted to Bauer, little planning appeared to be occurring in anticipation of the war's end, "The more I look around, the more I feel that after the war we are going to have a repetition of the crazy, purposeless growth of the Twenties. Even where there are pretenses of broad postwar planning, the habits of the past and the force of those who have property interests promises to be too strong for any common sense reasoning." To proactively address the situation, Stein decided to form an organization that would pursue jobs focused on "comprehensive technical service in creating new towns and neighborhoods, from preliminary studies to completely constructed communities, equipped and organized with government and management as well as buildings." They could include neighborhood redevelopment "but only on the basis of being clear cut jobs without crippling compromise."[16]

Proposed services included "explorative" surveys, design, engineering, construction, organization of government, and housing management. "The idea is to get together a small but experienced group that can do a complete job in the creation of new towns and neighborhoods, or the rebuilding of existing cities or neighborhoods." In making this proposal, Stein faced two challenges he already had experienced—devoting too much time to "chasing jobs" or perhaps even compromising ideals in order to maintain solvency and ensuring each member of the team remained available, in effect placing them on-call. Stein addressed these issues by proposing that the team "create the client," initiating desirable jobs much as he had done with Hillside Homes and that until steady work became available, the team members could continue their regular employment lending their expertise to the organization only as needed. As much as possible, Stein intended the team to function in an advisory capacity to local professionals, turning the project over to them to implement and manage. In this way, those more sensitive to local conditions, aesthetics, and needs would be in charge of executing the project. Of course, this approach was predicated on local expertise being available.[17]

Stein prepared a document entitled, "Prospectus of Clarence S. Stein and Associates New Towns and Neighborhoods," outlining his proposal and circulated it among his colleagues. As carefully as he outlined the expertise of the organization's team, Stein also specified the potential clients: "Services Are Offered To Industries, Labor Organizations, Large Scale Investment Organizations, Governmental Authorities and Agencies." While large employers—"Industries"—could be a client, he warned against partnering with any single company for fear of the boss also being the landlord and having too much control over the workers' lives. Rather, groups of industries should be approached to participate cooperatively. Given this target clientele, Roland Wank, chief architect for the TVA and principal architect of Greenhills, expressed some legitimate concerns regarding the proposal: "Will there be operations enough carried out by other than speculative builders or operators to warrant their exclusion as clients?" Stein was convinced that the previous success of the small number of limited dividend projects and the public's growing awareness of an alternative way of living, through means such as the film *The City*, would result in sufficient demand for these new towns and neighborhoods. Throughout 1944, he contacted Bauer; MacKaye; Eberlin; Wank; Frank Palmer of the Allegheny County Housing Authority; Major John O. Walker, the first manager at Radburn; and other colleagues to promote this idea.[18]

The opportunity to partner with a housing authority and a major employer ("Industry") became a possibility in spring 1944 as Stein discussed with Palmer first the option of working out a project with Carnegie-Illinois Steel Corporation (Carnegie-Illinois) in Pittsburgh and then in Gary, Indiana. While no documentation remains regarding the Pittsburgh project, both Palmer and Stein contacted E. D. Hollinshead, manager of Real Estate for Carnegie-Illinois, regarding approximately 1,525 acres the company owned in Gary, Indiana. Hollinshead put Stein and Palmer in touch with S. H. Cohn, president of the Gary Land Company, a major land owner and real estate firm in the city since 1906. Cohn showed Carnegie-Illinois' properties to them. For Stein, Gary represented a city well suited to take advantage of new economic development opportunities after the war. It had a significant amount of subdivided and unsubdivided vacant land in its downtown area, a number of manufacturing concerns, and provided it planned well, the potential to attract diverse new industries following the war that would employ workers at wages sufficient to establish a solid tax base to build and maintain a desirable community. As Stein discussed the project with John Harris, he proposed that he and Harris form the Harris-Gary Corporation to provide general management with Stein conducting planning and architectural services; Harris Associates undertaking the construction work; Hollinshead overseeing the sale, rental, and operation of the industrial properties; and Palmer conducting research, sales, and leasing of the housing as well as related community and commercial facilities. Yet Harris's response to this opportunity was not satisfactory to Stein. Rather than submitting a proposal to Carnegie-Illinois that reflected the partnership Stein proposed, Harris Associates outlined an arrangement in which Stein's office would be part of the construction company and that Harris Associates, not Stein, would conduct the planning work Stein proposed to do. It is not clear what led to this proposal being dropped—whether it was the business arrangement outlined by Harris, which was clearly unacceptable to Stein, or the lack of vision and understanding on the part of Carnegie-Illinois regarding the "broad planning services" Harris, Stein, and the rest of the team would provide in the disposition of the company's land. No further correspondence occurred after July 1944 regarding this partnership, which so closely paralleled the collaborative team Stein hoped to assemble for a new type of planning, design, and development in the postwar era.[19]

Stein's argument for what amounted to public-private partnerships to create cost efficient complete communities was a powerful one. In this new era, he maintained, government officials, enlightened businessmen, and skilled professionals needed to come together more effectively to address housing needs.

> So far government has attempted to attack the Herculean task of replacing the slums with decent communities singlehanded. When one considers the extent of blight in most of our cities, it is apparent that the job of replacing those areas is beyond the capacity or means of government or any single agency. Nor is it desirable to centralize all experimentation in the development of new forms and technique. Here is a task that requires the coordinated efforts of government, sound business, and far-seeing technical skill, and vision.

Recently adopted policy and program tools facilitated "large-scale integrated community building with a public purpose." The community architect recognized these opportunities and stood ready to collaboratively design, develop, and manage the Regional City for a postwar era.[20]

## Postwar Advocacy of Communitarian Regionalism

Stein first formally introduced his complement to the Radburn Idea in a 1942 article in *Pencil Points*. The Regional City provided a means to further explore the concepts—both design and functional—associated with his completed projects. He further formulated these ideas in the final chapter of his seminal book—*Toward New Towns for America*. While the rest of the book described in detail the design, development, and early history of some of his most significant housing projects, "Indications of the Form of the Future" addressed what the lessons learned from these projects meant for town planning and building. Mumford advised his friend that the concepts outlined here were inconsistent with the rest of the book and in fact were not ready for publication: "I have gone over this chapter carefully; and on thinking it over again this morning I have come to the conclusion that it would be better to leave it out. This question is a very complicated one: it involves, who is to take the initiative in conceiving and planning new towns; who is to organize and carry out the work of building, and who is to supply the money; and I don't think that what you say here is sufficiently conclusive, or that all the aspects of new town building have been fully explored." Stein intended his next book, *Cities to Come*, to do just that. An unfinished manuscript on the Regional City, it complemented *Toward New Towns for America* by presenting the theory behind his community designs. In it he planned to include a table outlining the types of facilities and amenities required to maintain a desired quality of life from the group to the town level, relating their scale to the population size (see table 6.1). This communitarian regionalism continued to define his advocacy of the Regional City throughout this period.[21]

The Greenbelt Towns epitomized the realization of Stein's Regional City and the government's role in new town design, development, and management. Though initially disappointed when he learned in the summer of 1946 that the federal government intended to dispose of the Greenbelt Towns, Stein maintained they could be safeguarded and enhanced as models of community building if their disposition was handled properly. He wrote Mumford:

> The greenbelt towns were the most important step in the direction of Garden Cities that has been made in America—in spite of the lack of industry—Otherwise all the elements were there. As [an] experiment in economic as well as social and physical planning they are important—and that value will in great part be lost—if the towns get in the wrong hands—or are sold off in lots. You remember I laid out the budget for operation of the towns. Since then I have followed their development (particularly Greenbelt) and checked actual costs of various government functions against original estimates. This should be continued—we are going to need all their experience badly when the attempt to build up the old cities from within breaks down.[22]

In 1947, the American Institute of Planners established a committee to make recommendations regarding disposition of the towns from the FPHA, later PHA, to private ownership. In addition to Walter Blucher, executive director of the American Society of Planning Officials, and Paul Oppermann representing the FWA, the members included many who had been involved with the design, development, and/or management of the towns—Stein, Tracy Augur, Frederick Bigger, Jacob Crane, Justin Hartzog, Hale Walker, and Sherwood Reeder. Issued on December 26, 1947, their report established the significance of the towns as complex experiments and models in community building and design.[23]

In making the transition to private ownership, two essential features had to be acknowledged and maintained—the towns as complete satellite communities and the greenbelts as a buffer to ensure unity of the towns and protection from sprawling adjacent developments. To secure these goals, the committee mem-

TABLE 6.1. Stein's Regional City table dated January 1954

| Level and population<br><br>Types of centers | FACILITIES BY FUNCTIONAL CLASSIFICATIONS | | | Leisure time activities | | | |
| --- | --- | --- | --- | --- | --- | --- | --- |
| | Commerce | Education | Health | Physical recreation | Cultural | Government | Industry |
| Group—up to 3,500 (sub-neighborhood)<br><br>*School center* | "Convenience store" | Nursery school, K-3 or K-6 school | School medical room | Play lot— for small children | Work shop, meeting rooms | | |
| Neighborhood— 5,000 to 7,000<br><br>*Neighborhood center* | Shopping and services for daily requirements | Community school (K-6 school with community facilities) | Health clinic | Playground, gym, and other school facilities; swim pool | Club rooms, craft shops, Branch library, little theater, churches | Public gathering, election day, post office | |
| District— 10,000 to 25,000<br>*High school center* | *Town center* Shopping for durable goods, clothes, specialties | Junior high (1 per 15,000 or less pop.), Senior high (1 per 25,000 or less pop.) | | Playing fields, gym & other high school facilities, arena, | Theater and auditorium of high school | Police station, fire station | Light manu-facturing for local use |
| Town 25,000 to 100,000<br>*Town center*<br>*Service center* | *Service center* Auto sales and service, whole-saling, service industries | Town center SHS has town level community facilities | Hospital & health center, including doctors' offices | golf, skating | Library, museum, studios, theatres, meeting halls, entertain-ment | Legislative and administrative center, magistrates court, municipal garage | Large industrial plants and groups of small related industries |
| Regional City— Approx. 1 million<br>*Regional centers for various functions* | *Regional shop centers* for all kinds of commerce | University technical college | General hospital and medical school | Regional parks— all open country activities | Central library, museums, convention hall, theaters for music and ballet | Regional center administrative offices and courts | Adminis-trative and policy making offices |

*Source:* Box 9, CSP/CUA. This table previously appeared in Larsen, "Cities to Come," 41.

bers recommended that each town, including all developed and undeveloped lands, be conveyed in its entirety to a single large investor at a price "written down to a point where such investment and continued development will be practicable." Independently, Stein expressed to the commissioner of the PHA that the towns be owned cooperatively by the residents or that a local authority, modeled on the TVA, own the town, though he acknowledged that these approaches probably were not practical. In an effort to "preserve the desirable qualities," he acknowledged the best solution was to sell them in their entirety to a large insurance company, such as New York Life, which could maintain them over the long term as they had done with large-scale housing projects in New York City. Over the next few years as the details of the disposition of the Greenbelt Towns were instituted, advocates continued to support sale of the complete towns at a negotiated price established to attract a large investor or to accommodate cooperative ownership.[24]

Stein felt personally responsible for the towns, particularly Greenbelt, because he had "been more intimately in touch with its development." In addition to corresponding with current and former town managers, Stein made frequent trips to Washington, meeting with key officials, including PHA commissioner John Taylor Egan and Senator Robert A. Taft, in an effort to influence the legislation so that the towns would not be sold piecemeal to the highest bidder. In a June 1948 letter to his wife, Stein noted, "I am on the way to save the Greenbelt Towns— ... 'seeing folks' just scouting until I know who's on our side and how impregnable is the Enemy. I enjoy the game." By 1949, legislation was before Congress regarding their disposition, and Stein, who was writing about them for Gordon Stephenson's *Town Planning Review*, described his strategy. "What I am fighting for now is to prevent their getting in the speculative market. The special legislation that is proposed would limit their sales to cooperatives or limited dividend corporations. I am trying to get a clause into the law that will preserve the character of the towns in their future growth, and above all prevent housing being built on the green belts. Before my article is completed a decision will probably have been reached."[25]

On May 19, 1949, Public Law 65, allowing the PHA commissioner to convey the towns via negotiated sales, was signed by President Truman. Stein and other advocates succeeded in securing first right of refusal and negotiated sales to such groups defined as "mutual ownership or cooperative housing associations or limited dividend corporations." Within days of passage of the legislation, Stein in partnership with architects Albert Mayer and Julian Whittlesey proposed to do an extensive study to help guide disposition of Greenbelt. Stein and his colleagues' concerns about the leader of the tenant's group that proposed to purchase Greenbelt and about the location of a proposed superhighway testified to the need for "an imaginative type of study and planning that goes far beyond an appraisal." Appealing to that section of the law that addressed the public interest, they emphasized that such a study would help preserve the town's character, accommodate residents with limited income, and ensure the town remained a model of community building and "economical planning."[26]

Though their proposal to conduct such a study was not accepted, Stein continued to vigorously follow disposition efforts for the next two years. Concerned that the intent of the legislation, particularly as it pertained to the public interest, was not being followed, Stein visited Washington, DC, in early October, including the offices of Egan; Housing and Home Finance Agency (HHFA) director Raymond Foley's attorney, who had drafted a version of the legislation that Stein particularly liked; and Senator Douglas, who wrote the report accompanying the legislation and supported many of the elements that Stein favored. Despite these efforts, only Greenbelt's reorganized nonprofit established by World War II veterans ultimately secured any housing over the long term. Communitarian regionalism continued to guide Stein and his friends and colleagues in a range of postwar initiatives that opened their network to a broader group of established and emerging planners across the country.[27]

## The Regional Development Council of America

With the federal government moving toward disposition of the Greenbelt Towns, the first significant changes proposed to federal housing legislation since its passage in 1937, and threats of atomic war calling for dispersal of industry, Stein considered it even more critical to promote the idea of new towns in America and began pressing his colleagues in 1946 to revive the RPAA. Mumford was convinced that the group's best days had passed, and during its dormancy, it had been all but forgotten.

We affected, for a brief while, such a partnership of theory and practice, of ideals and experiments, as is rare at any time, for both sides of our life and our thought were in organic balance. If there had been greater vision in Washington in the thirties, we all would have been used more effectively than we were. That is a great pity, for it might have prevented the housing movement and the planning movement from getting lost in a bog of compromises and retreats. But in our best days we lifted the banner high, and it is there for any one to see and to seize and to carry forward. ... In this respect, [Frederic] Osborn has been more fortunate than we were; for his long, steady, relentless pushing of the Garden City idea in the days when it seemed lost and apparently discredited, has now gained, and almost overnight, an almost universal acceptance.

Frederic J. Osborn—writer, new town advocate, former manager of Welwyn, and protégée of Ebenezer Howard—was extensively involved in postwar town building in Great Britain. On December 13, 1947, Stein used the occasion of Osborne's visit to New York City to engage previous RPAA members, such as Bauer, Mumford, and MacKaye, and potential new members such as Hugh Pomeroy, the director of Westchester's Planning Board, and architect Ralph Walker to consider forming a national organization "to start a campaign for the building of new towns in America." With parallels to Osborn's Town and Country Planning Association, which advocated new town laws in Great Britain, this revitalized RPAA would take advantage of its U.S. base. Structured similarly as the well-financed and politically connected Regional Plan of New York, it would engage the interest of progressive industrialists moving to outlying areas of cities as well as the FHA and developers familiar with investment housing, such as the Metropolitan Life Insurance Company, to get new towns built. From the beginning, the strategy was to adopt the approach taken in Great Britain with the resources and corporate culture of the United States.[28]

Thus Stein wanted to marry ideas with action, establishing a nationwide membership of experts to advocate and even sponsor the development and dispersal of new towns while also addressing critical current issues in regionalism by lobbying in Washington and by educating the public nationwide. In some ways, this proposed RPAA New Town initiative mirrored his proposal in 1944 to form a loosely affiliated consultancy team of professionals to do planning and community design work. His draft program for the organization included "assistance in production of New Towns" most likely involving the membership "in large part on paid consultation basis."[29] In March 1948, some who had been present at the December meeting with Osborn joined Stein in a series of meetings in Washington, DC, to discuss highway planning, suburbanization and dispersal of industry, impending urban redevelopment legislation, and the Greenbelt Towns as models. Meeting with key representatives of the FWA, PHA, FHA, HHFA, and Council of Economic Advisors, Stein integrated these ideas to advocate for new towns as part of national policy.

Yet some of his most trusted critics considered the role of the revived RPAA to be too broad in activities and membership. Bauer most clearly articulated the need to focus on research, advocacy, and the region. Rather than another demonstration (and the necessary financial support to make it happen), Bauer recommended establishing "real philosophic social-economic groundwork." Mayer agreed that the group needed to be more focused on critical regional issues, while Kohn questioned whether a need existed "for a Regional Planning Association as separate from [an already established] National Planning Association." In response, Stein proposed a New Towns Committee affiliated but separate from the RPAA. This committee would advocate for legislation, survey demographic changes, promote new towns to potential investors and the general public, identify development sites, and coordinate with developers to design and build the towns.[30]

On April 22, 1948, with the support of previous members Mumford, Bauer, Bruere, MacKaye, Ackerman, Chase, Klaber, and Kohn, the group unanimously agreed to "continue and revitalize" the RPAA. To ensure that representatives from around the country could attend, the inaugural meeting occurred on October 10, 1948, the day before the American Society of Planning Officials conference in New York City. A critical goal was to establish principles and means for implementation—Stein meant to settle the degree to which the group was willing to undertake political action and practical experiment. Opinions varied from focusing exclusively on research and self-education to establishment of branches for direct local action. No specific decision was made at the five-hour meeting. Following the business meeting, old and new members celebrated the fiftieth anniversary of the publication of Howard's book *Garden Cities of Tomorrow* and the twenty-fifth anniversary of the first meeting of the RPAA.[31]

Rechristened shortly thereafter the Regional Development Council of America (RDCA), the membership included practicing planners and educators from around the country. In addition to former RPAA members Mumford,

MacKaye, Bing, Bauer, Chase, Klaber, Kohn, and Ackerman, this national network of planning experts and "leaders in regionalism" included Augur, Mayer,
Churchill, Bigger, Buttenheim, Wank, Pomeroy, Gutheim, Odum, Paul Oppermann, Matthew Nowicki, Carl Feiss, T. J. Kent, Elisabeth Coit, Eric Carlson,
Chloethiel Woodard Smith, and Roger Willcox.[32]

The core membership did not view direct development of model communities as a realistic activity for the organization. Still, the RDCA clearly continued
to support new towns as a solution to postwar growth with no more ardent
advocate than Stein himself. Before the end of 1948, the RDCA had identified
its first critical action areas—to advise the Hoover Commission regarding reorganization efficiencies in the executive branch of the federal government and
housers involved with drafting the housing bill that established the federal urban
redevelopment program.

The membership approached the opportunity to influence Herbert Hoover's
commission, which was presenting its report and recommendations to the Congress in spring 1949, by asking, "How should the Federal Government be organized to further regional planning and development?" Their answer mirrored
Stein's earlier proposal on behalf of the Citizen's Housing Council for a similar
position in the governor's offices in New York State to coordinate all planning
activities. Individual projects and programs from public works to those involving
natural resources would be more effectively structured and implemented if key
personnel better understood how they fit into broader plans both within and
across relevant agencies and departments. As Gutheim clarified, "A measure of
coordination, properly in the Executive Office of the President, is needed to
insure the coordination of public works and development projects, and their
integration into wider and more long-range plans." The RDCA members maintained that the failure of the National Resources Planning Board (1933–1943) to
achieve its goals due to lack of political and financial support reflected the need
for authority at the highest level. Established by Roosevelt during the depths
of the Depression to facilitate nationwide and statewide planning, the National
Resources Planning Board was relegated to conducting research and serving as
an advocacy organization.[33]

During this period of focus on federal initiatives, RDCA members also maintained the necessity of a state and local role. Stein asserted, "State as well as
federal legislation is essential to make possible building [of] the badly needed

new communities. The States should permit setting up of local or regional governmental agencies to supervise such activities; the states also should give such agencies power of taking land by eminent domain. However, the federal government should take the lead by giving the development of new communities on open land equal opportunities for loans and other financial assistance, with redevelopment or slum clearance." In fact, the RDCA addressed New York State legislation to establish a Division of Planned Development in the Executive Department that had been introduced in 1948 and was still "open for revision" in early 1949. The following year, legislation was indeed passed and the division created to guide urban renewal and other planning activities. Yet it did not have the authority or comprehensive role the organization's membership advocated.[34]

Ongoing efforts to establish an authority in the Columbia River Valley region similar to the TVA, attested to the need for more coordination through regional agencies. As an attorney based in the Pacific Northwest, RDCA member Ben Kizer reported that earlier initiatives among federal agencies in the region had ended in failure due to the lack of such an authority. In fact, regional councils could be established across the country, Gutheim recommended in a 1948 report to the RDCA, to "help overcome the pressures of existing functional or local interests and strike for a broader, long-range program." By fall 1950, the proposed regional structure had become more formalized, with Mumford presenting the "Regional Redistribution of Federal Government Functions." While a strong central government would remain in place, Stein maintained in a follow-up to the RDCA membership, "a dozen or more subcenters of Federal administration—subcapitals in a sense" would be established. Each of them would "carry out and coordinate all local and regional functions of the Federal government." In subsequent years, Stein and his colleagues returned to this call for a coordinating planning agency at the regional level.[35]

The federal program that appeared to have promise though was urban renewal. As proposed, it presented a means to establish a town building program to potentially rival the work underway in Great Britain. The RDCA membership's unease about the connection between slum clearance and new housing development was heightened by the postwar housing crisis. In response to this crisis, they called for a new town provision in what would become the Housing Act of 1949. In December 1948, the RDCA presented their position to Edward Weinfeld, president of the National Public Housing Conference (NPHC):

The development of urban communities that will assure at the same time the most desirable living conditions and the maximum security requires both (a) the comprehensive redevelopment of existing blighted and outmoded urban areas at densities that are socially and economically sound, and (b) the development of properly designed, balanced communities in new urbanization. (New urbanization either in the enlargement of existing small urban centers or in the establishment of new communities.)

Yet the group struggled with how to structure "an effective New Towns movement in this country." Particularly troublesome were the issues associated with taking and holding sufficient amounts of land, assuming the significant up-front costs of public works and community facilities, and coordinating location of workplaces and residences.[36]

Notwithstanding this discussion of how to structure the New Towns movement, Stein closely monitored the housing legislation to ensure development of new towns would be an eligible activity. In a letter to Lee Johnson, executive vice president of the NPHC, Stein wondered aloud whether language including support for development on "large open areas of land" was sufficient to realize the RDCA's goals. Slum clearance was a popular component of the bill, so much so that President Truman issued a letter on June 17, 1949, as debate was about to begin in the House, outlining the wide-ranging support for the bill and reassuring the powerful real estate lobby that the Housing Act indeed included slum clearance as a focal activity. In fact, an informational handbook on the 1949 Housing Act issued by HHFA shortly after Truman signed it into law on July 15, 1949, noted, "Throughout the Housing Act of 1949, and particularly in title I, continual strong emphasis is placed on the elimination of unsafe, insanitary, and inadequate existing housing and stimulation of provision of decent, safe, and sanitary new housing." Thus, even though title I included among the eligible projects those on "any open land—land inside or outside the corporate limits," the amount of funding available for this type of project, and the requirement that the land be predominantly residential either prior to or after redevelopment/development, resulted in no new towns being created as a result of the 1949 Housing Act.[37]

At the invitation of Nathaniel S. Keith, director of Slum Clearance and Urban Redevelopment for the HHFA, Stein briefly served as consultant working directly with Carl Feiss, then chief of the Community Planning and Development Branch of HHFA, to set standards for local program implementation. In early 1950, as he reflected back on the legislation, Stein noted, "Thus far, the American public has only been aware of two key facts regarding housing: (a) the tremendous shortage of homes for lower and middle income groups and (b) the need for wiping out slums. Somehow a third and equally important key factor needs to be brought into popular focus: (c) the necessity for properly guided development of new communities on vacant land."[38]

Other opportunities to promote new towns as a superlative development pattern emerged shortly thereafter in Washington, DC, in response to the need for dispersed industrial sites due to concerns about vulnerability to atomic attack and to military buildup for the Korean War. In his capacity as a principal planner for the U.S. National Security Resources Board, Augur reported to Stein in November 1950 on the current thinking regarding dispersal in Washington. According to Augur, while President Truman wanted to begin modestly by developing "four office centers at points outside the city," the General Services Administration (GSA) was also moving forward with an assessment of "plans for the dispersal of federal activities in the Washington area." As with the Housing Act of 1949, RDCA members wanted to recalibrate and broaden federal action, in this case to adopt a comprehensive new town program to meet dispersal and defense emergency goals. As Stein outlined in an RDCA memo for Mumford's review, "Whether private industrial builders or State or local government carry out the work rather than the Federal Government, the financing as well as the determining of policy—including that of the form and manner of decentralization and dispersal—must come from the Federal Government. It must select location and determine plans, whether or not it builds." Ultimately, the RDCA's ambitious goal was "an increase in the pace of new urban building, in order to rehouse between thirty and fifty million people during the next ten years in self-contained communities."[39]

Owing to his familiarity with the topic and the ease with which he negotiated his way through relevant federal agencies, Stein was asked in November 1950 by Augur, then urban planning officer with the GSA, whether he was interested in joining a consulting panel assessing dispersal of federal buildings with the goal of providing direction on dispersal plans. Prior to the confirmation of his appointment in late December 1950, Stein, as president of the RDCA, testified at a Senate hearing that dispersal planning in the nation's capital would provide a model for the rest of the country. Stein asserted, "To break up the present pattern of continuous sprawling growth, which is both costly in terms of the economic burdens of congestion and insecure against aerial attack, the Federal Government must assume the responsibility for leadership in planning and decentralized organization. The pattern you work out here in Washington can in large degree be applied to other centers." The structure and means were in place to make this possible through local housing authorities and redevelopment agencies. Yet as reported out of a congressional committee on April 11, 1951, the legislation focused specifically on dispersal of the necessary additional office space and demolition of the temporary structures functioning as office space in downtown Washington. The possibility of new town development was summarily dismissed. The Committee on Public Works of the U.S. Senate observed, "With respect to possible community development around the dispersal sites, the two adjoining States and their respective counties involved in this area apparently prefer that they be allowed exclusive jurisdiction of whatever communities may grow near the sites."[40]

In early 1951, Stein also appeared before the Senate to advocate for complete communities as a key component of the Defense Housing Act (S. 349). As in the proposed dispersal bill, new communities were not part of defense mobilization for the Korean War. As director of HHFA, Foley's response to Stein, who as president of the RDCA wrote key government officials about these matters, is telling. While acknowledging his appreciation of the RDCA proposal, Foley stated that "a major part of the defense production effort will be met through the conversion and expansion of existing production facilities, and I know that an effort will be made to locate much defense activity in such a way as to minimize the need for large-scale labor immigration and provision of additional housing and community facilities." Shortly thereafter, Mayer, writing an editorial for the *Journal of the American Institute of Planners*, also expressed reservations about the idea of new towns being "inevitable"—"there is a tremendous force of inertia and of civic and private vested interest which prefers continuing sprawl in bigger and bigger cities, and will strongly fight creative decentralization."[41]

In order to facilitate new town planning and development around the country, Stein and his colleagues recognized that another front needed to be engaged—planning education. As Stein reported to the director of Planning and Housing Division at Columbia University, "There should be a broadening of the program.... So few of them [recently graduated planning and architecture students] are relating their individual work to the conception of a new type of community. I think that in our schools of design work should be coordinated with the problems of community development." With urban renewal, rapidly expanding metropolitan areas, and highway development, planning and related professions were experiencing unprecedented growth. Between 1940 and 1952, college programs in planning increased from four to twenty-one with demand for more across the country. Thus there were opportunities to influence the next generation of architects and planners and provide input on the burgeoning civic design and planning schools that were being established. Given their expertise, connections to colleagues at various universities through the RDCA, and experience in the classroom, Stein, Mumford, Mayer, Feiss, and others in the group were consulted during this period on new programs and curriculum.[42]

In 1950 alone, Stein made recommendations to the University of Pennsylvania on a new undergraduate degree and graduate degree in planning and to the University of North Carolina on a graduate program in "Regional Development and Planning." These recommendations offer insight on what the community architect considered essential skills in order to properly plan. At Pennsylvania, Stein, Mumford, and Mayer consulted, with Stein recommending the new head of planning, G. Holmes Perkins, establish a program in civic design to train specialists in three dimensional thinking—"we must have three dimensional design in which buildings are built as a unified whole in relation to each other, to streets, playgrounds, and other open spaces." At the University of North Carolina, his proposal was broader. With the goal of "a more habitable globe," students would specialize in physical, social, or economic planning while having enough training in all three to understand the relation between their specialization and the others at the global, regional, and local levels. By the end of the year, Turpin C. Bannister, head of the Department of Architecture at the University of Illinois in Urbana offered Stein an appointment to teach in the graduate program in the field of housing during the spring of 1951. Stein's response declining the offer was emblematic of the skills he believed were needed. "I am immensely interested in helping you to work out a course that prepares men in the architectural profession for the big job that I think is ahead of us. This, however, is not mass housing. It is, in my opinion the building of new communities.... We must have planners who understand all the elements of the physical makeup of a community and how to put them together."[43]

By the mid-1950s, Stein was convinced that planning was being taught in two ways, with a focus on administrative and regulatory activities—the primary approach in the United States—and community building in three dimensions—a design-based approach more common abroad. As part of a team, that included Feiss and T. J. Kent, Stein assessed the MIT planning program at the invitation of the university's president in October 1955. At the time, the school had one of the largest and oldest planning programs. Stein made his position clear in a memorandum he issued to other committee members and colleagues, such as Bauer and Mumford, in November 1955. "The preparation and administration of restrictions and other limitations of use, height and bulk is an important part of the city planners' activities. Although this type of work is at present an essential requirement, it is quite different from designing a city or any other community that is to be predetermined in form and mass as well as in plan: that is, to be molded in three dimensions, with all its elements related to each other as designed." What he proposed was a new School of Community Architecture, affiliated with the architecture program, but separate from it. He recommended that students of architecture be trained quite differently. However, "if, from the beginning, he [the architecture student] thinks of every building he designs as an essential related part of a community, functionally and visually; he will be prepared to continue his studies and experience in the broadening fields of city and regional planned development."[44]

Stein formulated this community architecture professional broadly. Essentially he was promoting a hybrid—a professional with the skills necessary to plan and design new towns. Yet the two fields had been growing apart since Stein and his colleagues moved effortlessly between them in the 1920s when the first planning program was established at Harvard. With the two fields taking on distinctive differences, others, like Bauer, became concerned about affiliating too strongly with architecture. In response to his proposal, she wrote, "As for putting the training of professional planners back inside an architectural school, I am sure this is wrong. Architectural schools should do a much stronger job of training civic designers, site-planners, and the like. But they are not, and never will be, equipped to handle the public policy and public administration aspects that are so fundamental to city planning." She continued, "All planners need to be trained for 'three-dimensional thinking'—i.e. the ability to relate social, economic, technological, political and aesthetic factors together in terms of human activities and environment in a given area. And architectural training is one good way to get a start on this. But once you get to the scale of the district, the city and the region, it just isn't any longer in the realm of architecture." The committee reviewing the program at MIT agreed. "A major responsibility placed upon professional schools of planning, then, is the training of potential planners who are broadly equipped for leadership in this 'generalist' profession, rather than for specialists in any of the many related fields of activity whose contribution is also essential. Traffic engineering specialists may better be trained in engineering schools; civic designers, in schools of architecture." Among architects though, Stein was not alone in his reasoning. A 1962 meeting of international architects agreed, referencing the AIA's Urban Design Committee's principle objective to "bring architectural and town planning work into more effective relationships." The community architect continued to advocate for town planning from university campuses to redevelopment projects. His last opportunity to apply his collaborative regionalist and town planning ideals in a concrete project occurred at Kitimat in Canada.[45]

## New Town, Planning, and Renewal Proposals

With the GI Bill, many universities experienced unprecedented growth. In 1947, Stein and Hardie Phillip, who had both worked on the California Institute of Technology while they were in Goodhue's office, revisited Goodhue's proposals as they pursued a job to create a site plan outlining opportunities for the campus' long-term growth. Stein very much considered campus planning equivalent with new town planning, and while they did not secure this job, Stein worked a few years later on a much more ambitious proposal at another California university.[46]

Stanford University wanted to develop some of its excess lands as a means to fund its operating budget and invited Mumford in 1947 to provide some feedback on these plans. Mumford recommended continued ownership of university land through ninety-nine-year leaseholds with new development concentrated in neighborhood units separated by greenbelts and a redesigned transportation system to avoid through traffic on the campus core and to more efficiently serve the campus overall. By April 1950, the Board of Trustees had requested "a specific proposal for a comprehensive professional study of the utilization of all

University-owned lands surrounding the campus and for a development of a master plan for these properties." Stein and Paul Oppermann, director of planning for the City and County of San Francisco, visited Alf Brandin, Stanford's business manager, in April 1951 to discuss the possibility of doing the job. In a proposal to Brandin, Stein noted, "The size of the property, of some eleven square miles, undeveloped and in a single ownership, permits the creation of a truly contemporary, open green city of some 50,000 population. Its success, both as an investment and in terms of good living, demands [a] fundamentally different procedure in planning, building and operation than that by which our existing cities have come into being." He recommended a master plan outlining land uses and design standards for a new town to attract insurance companies, foundations, limited dividend companies, and cooperatives to develop investment housing. The university would retain ownership of the land to ensure proper development of "complete neighborhoods" and safeguarding of the greenbelt.[47]

That August, Stein and Oppermann secured a meeting with Wallace Sterling, president of Stanford University. Sterling informed Stein that he had carefully read the proposal and wanted it to be developed further, including a budget for services. Stein agreed to meet with Sterling again in New York City in October. While Sterling made several attempts to meet with Stein that fall and in the early winter of 1952, Stein, busy with planning the new town of Kitimat in Canada, could not find time for the meeting, though he did contact various members of the Board of Trustees during this period to advocate for his proposal. In January 1952, the Advisory Committee on Land and Building Development adopted an initial survey and preliminary land use plan prepared by a local engineer. Noting that it lacked detailed planning information, they "strongly recommended, therefore, a recognized planner of the caliber of Mr. Clarence Stein, Mr. Paul Oppermann, or Mr. Walter H. Blucher be retained to undertake the necessary studies and present a community plan for Stanford lands."[48]

Stein responded to Sterling's renewed efforts to get a more specific proposal by acknowledging just how busy he had been over the past four months on the plan for Kitimat while expressing his enthusiasm for the Stanford project calling it "one of the great opportunities for leadership in the development of the technique of building cities in America." Finally in mid-April, Stein submitted his detailed proposal, indicating that for a total of thirty thousand dollars he would prepare "a sound and related program for comprehensive planning, development and operation of the Stanford property" that would establish a framework for future improvements. In delaying his response to the university president's request, Stein clearly missed his opportunity to promote his town building ideas to a receptive audience. Brandin began promoting the firm of Skidmore, Owings, and Merrill (SOM) to the President's Office, noting, "This is a firm whose work would be comparable to that of Clarence S. Stein." At an April 16, 1953, meeting, the Board of Trustees approved the recommendation to hire SOM at a cost of no more than fifty-two thousand dollars to draft the master plan for developing the property. By the end of the month, Brandin had issued an official letter to Stein summarily telling him that SOM had won the bid for the project. During the course of his efforts to secure the Stanford project, Stein was focusing on his last major consulting job.[49]

With Kitimat, the new town for the Aluminum Company of Canada (Alcan), Stein saw an unprecedented opportunity to demonstrate the significant integrated components of the Regional City. While he consulted on Kitimat, Stein further refined the functional and physical aspects of the Regional City he was exploring in his manuscript *Cities to Come*. He examined the type, size, configuration, and integration of uses that formed the interlocking groups, superblocks, districts, and towns. Rather than beginning with the street and then lot layout and hastily concluding with community facilities, operation, and government, Stein argued that "the customary process of creating towns should be reversed."[50] Learning about future residents and their needs represented the first step, which then determined the type of facilities and their financing and management. Only then could the physical characteristics take form.

In July 1951, Stein received a letter from Eric West of Alcan inviting the architect to submit a proposal to act as consultant on the master plan for the new town. Stein replied by asking West to join him on a tour of Radburn. By the end of the month West confirmed receipt of Stein's proposal, noting "seeing that town [Radburn] has brought out all the more clearly to me the importance of the selection we are to make in choosing the consultant for Kitimat." During the tour of Radburn, the community architect explained his desire to reverse the planning process and to establish a functional plan to inform the physical plan. Initially, West expressed some concerns, though Stein reassured him, "I can very well understand your original difficulty in comprehending the somewhat different approach that I desire to make to the study of the requirements of the new town. I admit that it is an unusual approach, but to my mind it is the only one that has any commonsense and has the possibility of leading to success from the beginning." West secured a meeting between Stein and the Alcan company president, R. E. Powell, and by early September Stein was appointed coordinator and director of planning for Kitimat with the understanding that he would recommend the remaining members of the planning team. In less than one week, Mayer and Whittlesey were also retained to complete the lead team on the project.[51]

"Single enterprise communities" such as Kitimat were more common in Canada due to the vast land area and the desire of the government, corporations, and large land owners to develop complete communities, often quite remote from the nearest sizable settlement. With Kitimat, Alcan wanted to do more though than simply lay out infrastructure, subdivide lots, and develop a mix of industrial, commercial, office, civic, and residential land uses. As Stein recommended, the company wanted functional or operational plans consistent with the social and economic needs of the community in addition to a physical plan. Stein, Mayer, and Whittelsey clarified, "[For] example, the functional plan for education is expressed in terms of school administration, composition of schools, optimum size and number of classes per grade, students per grade. This is translated into a physical plan showing the number, location and size of school sites relating these to parks, transportation, health clinics." They considered the functional and physical interdependent components of the overall community master plan.[52]

Alcan deemed the site, four hundred miles northwest of Vancouver, a prime location due to the water power available and the nearby protected ice-free harbor that allowed the raw alumina to be shipped in and the finished ingot to be shipped out. The ambition of the massive industrial undertaking exceeded that of the new town. The "daring scheme" to establish and run the industrial site involved "damming up the roaring Nechako River with the great Kenney Dam (third largest rock-filled dam in the world) to the east, drilling a 10-mi. tunnel through the mile-high western mountains to their western face, there letting the water of the great new storage basin drop 16 times as far as Niagara Falls to a powerhouse at sea level at Kemano, then carrying the power over mountains and glaciers 50 mi. to Kitimat, where the Kitimat River flows into the Kitimat Inlet." The company planned to build the world's largest aluminum smelter with the town site to the east separated from the industrial area by the river system and flood plain—overall an area of 66 square miles. Intended for 50,000 people once the smelter was fully functioning, the population was roughly 12,250 five years after its incorporation in March 1953.[53]

With a budget of close to $100,000 for research alone, Mayer, Whittlesey, and Stein along with associates Milton Glass and Roger Willcox began work on the project in September 1951. Educated as an architect at Columbia University, New York University, and the Beaux Arts Institute of Design, Glass had worked in several offices, first as draftsman then architect, before joining Whittlesey and Mayer's firm as architect and office manager in 1940. Willcox earned his undergraduate degree from Harvard (1941) and his graduate planning degree from the Massachusetts Institute of Technology (1947). Within a year of graduation, he was representing the RPAA (shortly thereafter RDCA) at the national planning conference with a discussion of current growth trends in New York State decrying the sprawling development underway and introducing a discussion on new towns in the metropolitan region as the solution. Given the years of friendship between Willcox's family and Stein and given his enthusiastic support of the RDCA vision, it is no surprise that Stein trusted him with these responsibilities.[54]

The substantial budget for research allowed the architects to assemble a team of top experts in their respective professions to inform the community's function and shape. Among those who lent their expertise to the project were Dan Kiley, landscape architect; George Butler, director of research, National Recreation Association; Kenneth Ross, Federal Power Commission; Larry Smith, nationally recognized consultant on commercial development; James Buckley, transportation engineer, formerly director of airport development for the Port Authority of New York and New Jersey; and Dr. Margaret Witter Barnard, associate professor at Columbia University School of Public Health. Former colleagues Ralph Eberlin, Charles Ascher, and Benton MacKaye joined the team as did Walter Kroening, community manager at Greendale, and Lawrence Tucker, manager of the Cincinnati Community Development Corporation, formerly community manager at Greenhills. Stein entrusted his old friend and colleague MacKaye to assess the Kitimat region, particularly the area along the river. Along with Ross, a hydroelectric engineer who had worked with the TVA, MacKaye prepared a report that began, "The town plan is not sufficient to fulfill the requirement for river control." A regional plan was essential "to prevent ill conceived development." Ross and MacKaye outlined the primary elements in the plan: "The preservation of the upland forest; the careful use of the main valley land; and the establishment of communities so as not to cause trouble downstream; are essential to maintain a regulated quantity and quality of water for industrial and municipal supply, for fish and wild life, for agriculture and recreation and for scenic purposes." They went on to state that Canada had a structure in place to facilitate regional planning oversight (see figure 6.1).[55]

In addition to collaboration among professionals involved in the project, town planning and building also forged public-private partnerships. The municipal incorporation allowed the town to assume public debt to fund infrastructure, school, and hospital construction and adopt a council-manager form of government, consistent with the recommendations of the master plan. For its part, Alcan enforced the master plan—via its own planning staff—and private developers constructed the homes and businesses.[56]

In addition to addressing regional issues regarding the river basin and the location of the greenbelt and government structure and property management, Stein consulted with Mayer and Whittlesey on neighborhood and community center planning. Three types of arrangements existed between the house groups and interior parks, echoing aspects of the Radburn Idea. These included the larger superblock consisting of houses on cul-de-sacs arranged around a sizable central park, "self-contained" smaller subneighborhoods on smaller superblocks of approximately one hundred families with more "intimate central community green areas," and "local house groupings" accommodating twelve to sixteen families on local lane access courts. Nechako, the first neighborhood, incorporated all three types of residential configurations. Whittlesey and Mayer observed that a diversity of residential options from apartment to row and free-standing houses, with the opportunity for home owners to self-build, introduced "a satisfying range of living possibilities and inter-relationships" so that "no sharp distinction between different social and economic levels" existed.[57]

As he had done with Maplewood's town center, Stein assembled shopping and community facilities in Nechako around a pedestrian mall with parking on the periphery and a school acting as a focal point with a park just beyond the school property. The neighborhood center facilitated community building, maintained Stein and Willcox, by being "the focus of community life, a symbol of neighborhood unity." The architect-planners knew that they were designing

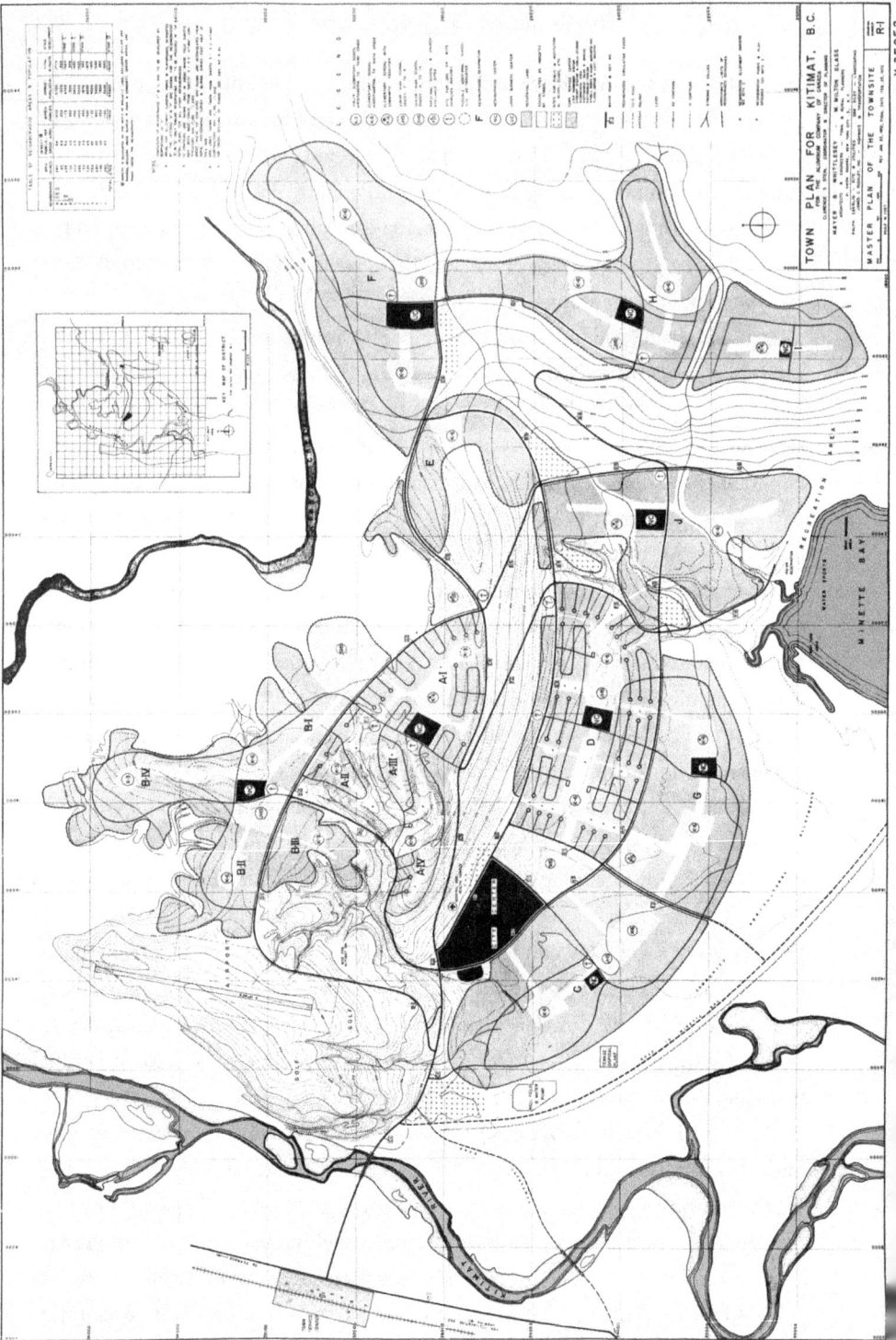

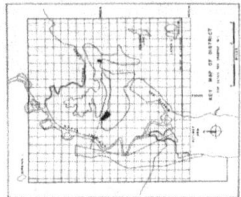

TOWN PLAN FOR KITIMAT, B.C.

MASTER PLAN OF THE TOWNSITE

X-35052

R1

a town to be built in phases but that still needed to function satisfactorily at each phase.[58]

The design of the City Center mimicked the smaller neighborhood centers (see figure 6.2), but the more extensive commercial, civic, and cultural facilities located at "the point of maximum economic potential" along the highway to and from the plant was intended to serve the entire community. As Stein explained, "Pedestrians will be completely separated from automobiles here—as in the residential areas. Pleasant verdant parks with garden promenades will replace the typical congested 'main street' as the central features around which building[s] are grouped—shops, theatres, office buildings will open directly on covered ways surrounding the greens." Meanwhile, a service center was located at more of a distance at the intersection of two major roads—one connecting the nearby town of Terrace to the plant site and the other going to Kitimat. It accommodated light industry and warehousing proximate to the rail line. The proposed center emulated the British Industrial Estate with single ownership and land leases intended to consolidate and coordinate transit, storage, and distribution activities while ensuring sufficient flexibility for expansion and growth.[59]

Stein worked intensively on the project until he fell ill again in 1953. But, by that time he had already contributed significantly to the plan. In their 1956 article, Peter and Cornelia Oberlander cite Stein's contributions, "Kitimat's just claim to fame rests with the fact that, for the first time, a complete planning program was developed by Clarence Stein in which the total organization as well as physical needs of the new community were anticipated, not just a layout plan of streets and building lots."[60]

Unfortunately, neighborhood building was rushed to keep pace with plant development, making it difficult to realize the Radburn Idea. In fact, within the first few years, town officials acknowledged, "sub-neighborhoods were being

---

FIGURE 6.1 Kitimat, British Columbia, Master Plan of the Townsite dated February 25, 1952. The darker lines depict the major roads that delineate the neighborhoods. The residential areas are light grey with the integrated and interconnected white areas indicating the neighborhood open space. The smaller dark areas designated "NC" are neighborhood centers with the larger dark area at the center left the City Center. Recreational, forest, and floodplain areas surround the town with a golf course designated to the northwest of town and a recreational area to the southwest and south. Box 39, CSP/CUL.

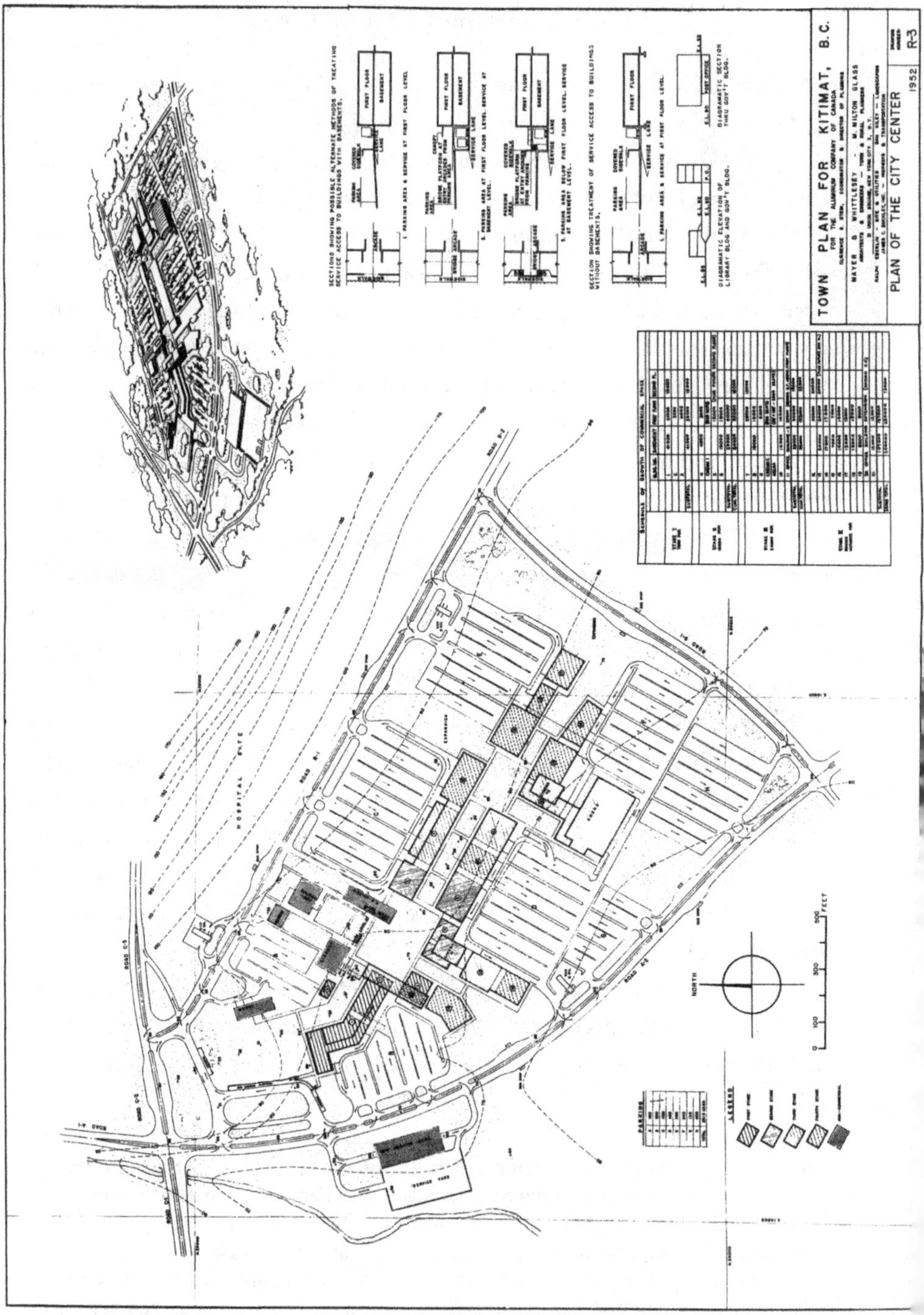

FIGURE 6.2 Kitimat—City Center site plan dated 1952. Box 39, CSP/CUL.

built on by the two major housing contractors and private builders at a speed sometimes ahead of the installation of services. People had to be accommodated, needs had to be met, and a continuous stream of requests for special use permits, exceptions from Municipal regulations faced the Council at almost every meeting." Further, the architects admitted they were dealing with a difficult site featuring steep slopes and flat areas cut through with gullies, which created "a complex of irregular buildable areas and not that blank piece of paper or virgin land of which planners dream."[61]

While Kitimat may have been a new town, Stein did not consider it a Regional City, explaining, "A broader pattern of interrelation between a group of such towns within a region of which they form an associated part" in fact defined a Regional City. Despite significant flexibility and support from Alcan, at least initially, Stein ultimately did not realize his goal. As he noted in one of his last reports for the town site plan, "Realization cannot be left to chance. It cannot be based on unrelated decisions, and hasty improvisations and opportunism.... Realization requires a type of preparation, programming and scheduling all its own. This must be comprehensive, adequate, economical, and above all flexible and dynamic."[62]

An example of regional planning he particularly admired had been underway in Southern California for close to a decade. In 1945, Charles Bennett, director of planning, and Milton Breivogel, principal planner for Los Angeles County, proposed a comprehensive zoning ordinance with a "flexible zoning scheme" to accommodate a "gradual and orderly expansion" of the San Fernando Valley through the year 2000. At the time, the area was still largely undeveloped but experiencing significant growth pressures due to its proximity to the city. A 1945 article by the planners in *Pencil Points* elaborated the outcome as the "the regional city" resulting in "a number of well-planned and moderately sized communities of reasonable density, separated by agricultural areas, the whole bounded together by a well developed system of parkways and highways for various types of traffic."[63]

While Stein admired the Los Angeles County plan and regulatory controls, particularly "the most farsighted attempt at constructive use of zoning in the U.S.A.," he observed that in December 1950, some of the land in the San Fernando Valley agricultural zones had already been redesignated for residential development. Though a minor amount of land, Stein sensed that this "small leak" would become a "flood," highlighting the "weakness of zoning as an instrument of constructive planning or rather community building."[64]

As in the rest of the country, the predominant development pattern in Southern California was disheartening. During a 1955 visit with Breivogel and Bauer, Stein observed, "As there is one class of house all at the same price—so there is one economic and one social class seemingly in each development. Racial discrimination makes it practically impossible for Negroes to get in any new development. There are no balanced communities—such as the new towns in England—with varied income levels and occupations—and with a balance of home and working places.... It generally requires a goodly automobile trip to get to work, to go shopping also."[65]

Stein continued to seek planning models, especially among experienced, progressive planners working in the public sector, to realize balanced communities within the region. Strengthened rural-urban relations seemed particularly important. He became involved with another California county experiencing the growth pressures of a metropolitan region—Santa Clara near San Francisco. The 1954 Generalized Development Plan for Santa Clara County reflected the "combined recommendation of local planning officials" including among its basic objectives "protection of open space," "development of new towns," "containment of urban sprawl," and "decentralization of industry." In the summer of 1956, while MacMahon was artist-in-residence at Stanford and both she and Stein were living on the Stanford campus, Stein engaged in discussions with local officials and residents, advocating a regional approach to protect farmland with legislation allowing the state and local governments to purchase development rights to ensure permanent preservation. He advocated for a strong regional government to foster balanced development and community building and to conserve and safeguard resources. His experience at Kitimat had reemphasized the significance of river basins as a means to define regions, and the water-shed district as a tool to protect open spaces "without [requiring] public ownership of farm areas as well as parks." Stein considered the Regional City and the water-shed district as "parallel conceptions.... [They] must be consolidated and unified if we are to limit wasteful dangerous flow and flood not only of water and soil but of humans, and if we are to find and hold desirable or practical patterns of urban-rural relations." A regional authority could also coordinate the efforts of the growing number of special districts and specialized agencies active in the area. According to Stein, the public sector remained uniquely qualified to shape regional development using proactive planning rather than regulatory tools.[66]

Stein also maintained his connection with major planning proposals in New York City during the late 1950s and early 1960s, as in California promoting the application of integrated open spaces, though here as part of urban renewal and public housing projects. During 1958 work was underway on an urban renewal study of the West Side between Eighty-Seventh and Ninety-Second streets from Central Park West to Amsterdam Avenue. This area—half a mile long and one-quarter mile wide—included Columbus Circle and was near enough to Stein's home at 1 West Sixty-Fourth Street to be of particular interest. Stein communicated with Sam Ratensky, who oversaw preparations of the West Side Renewal study as part of his responsibilities with the city's Urban Renewal Board, and James Felt, chairman of the City Planning Commission and also a member of the Urban Renewal Board. Stein, Mayer, and Chloethiel Woodard Smith recommended that the city use the project as an opportunity to close certain underutilized east-west streets and increase capacity on the remaining streets, thus creating superblocks that could accommodate interior parks, playgrounds, and pathways to more safely and efficiently serve residents. They stated,

> For this age of ever-increasing leisure, one of our greatest needs is small green places, attractive for peaceful, quiet, leisurely loafing in the sun or under a great tree. These parks should be placed where they can be reached without crossing dangerous roads. The closing of two out of three streets gives such an opportunity in the center of the resulting superblocks without use of a great deal of land. A moderate sized, carefully designed area can give a sense of spaciousness and beauty and varied charm, and a setting of green to contrast with the dead monotony of the house-lined streets.

Community building could also be achieved by rehabilitating the brownstones for families rather than cutting them into small apartments for singles. Their recommendation specified, "This proposed pattern of superblocks with parks and play spaces in the center joined to enclosed courts of houses by paths completely separated from vehicular traffic would give an ideal setting for urban life with children.... The remodeling of the brownstone houses with their rear yards offers an unusual opportunity to develop apartments for families with children that will harmonize with this setting."[67]

In early 1959, Stein and Mayer presented their recommendations, including a report with supporting conceptual drawings, to the Urban Renewal Board, but these ideas were not implemented. Given the concerns documented with major street congestion as the City Planning Commission and Department of City Planning initiated several studies in preparation for revisions to the city's comprehensive zoning code, this proposal for redevelopment and street closures may have been too radical. Despite this setback, Stein continued to promote adoption of a city policy "that for every redevelopment or renewal project an adequate park be created."[68]

Later that year, Stein and Mayer undertook a general study for the NYCHA assessing design and utilization of open space at the authority's projects. In June 1959, they toured several projects with Alexander Bing and Ira Robbins, vice chairman of the NYCHA, noting the "wasted and inadequately used" outdoor space at these projects. At Robbins's request for "preliminary recommendations ... regard[ing] how this important problem might most effectively be investigated and solved," Stein and Mayer proposed the engagement of the "ablest landscape architects and architects" to design "attractive settings appropriate to the buildings and pleasant outdoor community life."[69]

They also promoted, through their participation on the Lavanburg Foundation Board, a cooperative venture in which the nonprofit foundation could partner with the NYCHA to fund a more intensive study and demonstration project. Stein and Mayer explained, "It is a thesis of this proposal that many or possibly most of the shortcomings of large-scale housing projects are due to reasons quite different than their size; and that vast improvements can be made in design and arrangements, in family and social living conditions and relations." Their site design studies arrived at a more effective way to use the open space at housing projects, thus creating more livable communities—in essence taking a new town approach to address the "monotony and institutionalism" they encountered at these projects. "Projects are small towns in population, but are not and should not be institutions. Let us try out within the individual project itself, differential spacings between buildings, more drastic differences in height and in ways of living—very much as in a small town of 5,000 people." While "the Foundation unanimously approved the importance of a study of this kind" in December 1959, they "side-tracked" support of Stein and Mayer's proposal in meeting after meeting, finally arguing in March 1960 that the architects' work in fact "duplicate[d] and was derive[d] from" an earlier study conducted for the foundation. These actions resulted in Mayer's resignation in 1959 and Stein's in 1961.[70]

Aware of the architects' efforts, Marie MacGuire, commissioner of the Public Housing Administration, encouraged Stein and Mayer to submit an open space proposal, given her interest "in getting as many actual demonstrations of good planning underway as possible." In 1961, the NYCHA approved their study-design demonstration, but the agency could not finance it. Further, while the 1961 Housing Act included "grants for public open space projects," a request to support research had been denied by Congress. At a meeting in 1962 with representatives of the Housing and Home Finance Agency, which oversaw the Public Housing Administration, the architects were told that only research that yielded an actual demonstration project could be considered for funding. Robbins decided on a strategy to directly link the research Stein and Mayer advocated with a demonstration project focused on open space. The NYCHA executed a grant application in June 1963 that incorporated Stein and Mayer's proposal. Although a number of high-profile landscape revitalization projects were implemented during the 1960s, Stein and Mayer's proposal did not get funded. During this period, Stein continued participating on other prominent committees and foundation boards, such as the Citizen's Housing and Planning Council of New York and the Foundation for Cooperative Housing (FCH).[71]

This postwar period produced its own set of challenges for the community architect as he used his growing network of planning connections across the country to effect change and support for the Regional City as an alternative to the homogenous, sprawling suburbs. In *Toward New Towns for America*, he energetically argued, "Solutions are to be found not only in terms of individual Garden Cities but also in regional constellations of varied types of New Towns set in a broad background of agricultural land and regional parks."[72] From the federal and local levels and at prestigious universities, he promoted a proactive vision of community building through the engagement of knowledgeable public and private sector partners. Publication of his seminal book in 1951 not only documented the implementation of his ideas through large-scale community design, it solidified his appeal at the international level as bold new conceptions of town planning were taking hold.

# 7

## INTERNATIONAL INITIATIVES AND
## BUILDING A LEGACY

As one of the most prosperous periods in American history unfolded in the years after World War II, Stein found himself turning his attention toward international translations of his new town ideas. Communications with international architects, housers, and planners characterized this period, with a focus on specific projects, such as the new towns of Chandigarh in India and Stevenage in Great Britain, and broader community building concepts with housing and planning experts in places as diverse as Sweden and Israel. While recuperating from a particularly serious bout of illness in the summer of 1945, Stein anxiously anticipated a postwar boom.[1]

He closely followed planning efforts in Great Britain. There, postwar rebuilding studies paid tribute to Geddes's survey before planning and Howard's Garden City while also incorporating the neighborhood unit and other community building concepts that Stein favored or had integrated into his large-scale designs. Unwin had contributed to an important interwar report that advocated satellite communities located outside a greenbelt around London. But it was Patrick Abercrombie's County of London Plan (1943) and more notably Greater London Plan (1944) that set the stage for British postwar new town development. While Stein considered the County of London Plan for reconstruction of that city as "limited" due to its "scheme for rebuilding within the framework of the old structure so as to make it workable under modern conditions," he praised its coordinated approach. He specifically appreciated the adoption of the neighborhood unit, integration of open spaces, and the "specialized" and "comprehensive" highway system. Still, the minimal acreage recommended for parks, potential for roadway and parking congestion, and high densities resulted in his conclusion that the plan "did not go far enough."[2]

The Greater London Plan was another story. New development would be tightly controlled with a greenbelt surrounding the city to prohibit sprawl and the overflow of population and industry to be directed to eight new towns located beyond the greenbelt. Osborn noted that here was the realization of Howard's ideals. "I rank the Greater London Plan 1944 with Howard's book and the Barlow Report as the third in the classic canon of planning. It is the first fully-worked-out 'garden city' plan for a great Metropolis." The New Towns Act of 1946 established the structure for creating new towns. The minister of town and country planning had the authority to designate the sites and appoint development corporations, which would then acquire the land, plan, and build the town. The 1947 Town and Country Planning Act granted the funding for land acquisition.[3]

Stein certainly was excited about the prospects for new towns in Great Britain, especially in comparison to the United States. Shortly after the war his observations of sprawling development in California and lack of real progress in addressing housing needs in New York City attested to his concerns. As he continued his recuperation in southern California during the spring of 1946, he observed "they are building more and more of worse and worse"—"The speculative builder is setting the pattern [in Los Angeles] within the restrictions of obsolete street plans, absurd zoning laws, [and] building regulations of an inexperienced small town." Back on the East Coast, Robert Moses, "Housing Dictator" as Stein characterized him, was not meeting his promises of providing 127,000 units of permanent housing in New York City. In a way, Stein was relieved that the number of poorly planned and constructed temporary units and rehabilitated "old law housing" had fallen behind. The NYCHA still managed to construct some new permanent units of housing. Institutional investors, those that Stein had relied on to partner with the government, were not doing much, and even the Citizen's Housing Council, which issued a vision to address housing needs well into the future, offered nothing regarding new town proposals. Stein complained to Mumford, "Worst of all no big plan or prospect of it nearby."[4]

In May 1947, Stein returned to a New York City energized by plans underway for the United Nations (UN) headquarters—to be located on a seventeen-acre site consisting of slaughterhouses along the East River. The international team of ten architects on the UN Board of Design Consultants included Liang Sicheng of China, Matthew Nowicki of Poland, and Sven Markelius of Sweden. Stein was delighted to see Sicheng again. The architect and historian had recently been named chair of the new Department of Architectural Engineering at Tsing Hua University in Peking. The university had sent Sicheng to the United States in the fall of 1946 to learn more about its notable architecture programs. As head of the Society for Research in Chinese Architecture, Sicheng had also gained prominence as the leading expert on historic Chinese structures, and both Yale and Princeton had invited him to come to the United States, to respectively teach a course and participate as a keynote speaker at an international conference. In this very busy period that stretched from November 1946 to July 1947, Sicheng also worked on his groundbreaking *Pictorial History of Chinese Architecture*. While in New York City contributing to the design of the UN headquarters, Sicheng stayed with Stein. Wilma Fairbanks, the celebrated biographer of Sicheng and editorial collaborator on the English version of his book, credits Stein for Sicheng's emerging interest in planning. "From Stein he learned first hand about the possibilities and difficulties involved in urban planning. This guidance was to prove invaluable to him when, on his return to Peking, he added a concentration on urban planning to the curriculum of the Tsinghua department."[5]

Stein enjoyed the sharing of ideas among the international architects and entertained them quite lavishly in his home, throwing numerous parties in his "Sky Parlor" and at 1000 Years. During this time, he also got to know and admire the young Polish architect Matthew Nowicki. He attended a meeting of the Architectural League in mid-October where Nowicki presented the plans for rebuilding Warsaw with Osborn participating as part of his American tour. Stein appreciated Nowicki's design skills, working with him on a proposed shopping center in southern California in 1948 and Columbus Circle in New York City in 1949. In both, the Polish architect complemented Stein's sensitivity to open space and relation of uses to that space with his modern design aesthetic.[6]

As to Markelius, it appears that Stein's wife might have had the first opportunity to meet the architect, planning director of Stockholm, and designer of the new town of Vallingby. During the summer of 1947, Aline MacMahon traveled to

Switzerland and Germany to film *The Search* about camps for displaced persons following the war. She left with a letter of introduction from Bauer to Markelius as the actress and her mother decided to stop in Sweden first. MacMahon fell in love with Stockholm, and given the exciting work underway there in town planning, with Markelius in the lead, Stein vowed to visit the city soon. He would indeed do so as part of travels in Europe to new towns as he completed documentation of his own visionary work in what would become *Toward New Towns for America*.

## New Towns in Europe and Toward New Towns for America

In this early postwar period, Stein entered a world more receptive to his regional and town planning ideas, particularly in Great Britain and Sweden. In April 1946, he looked forward to hearing news of Mumford's trip to Great Britain and new town activities there. Stein remarked to his friend, "I hope you will return with good news that plans are going to be realized and improved. I hope that some of Osborn's Garden City will be realized."[7] In fact, Stein took an active part in designing the town center of the first postwar new town in that country.

Stevenage was the first satellite community to be designated under the New Towns Act. Gordon Stephenson, an architect who contributed to the Greater London Plan and drafted the 1946 master plan for Stevenage while he worked for the Ministry of Town and Country Planning, invited Stein to consult with him on the community's town center. Stephenson remained quite impressed with Radburn, which he visited when it was under construction in 1929. A conceptual drawing Stephenson prepared of "A New Town" in 1942 to promote the work of the ministry through British secondary schools included a passage that could have come straight from Stein: "The neighbourhood unit, the superblock, and footpath/cycleways separate from the roads and integrated with the park system."[8]

According to Stephenson, he finally met Stein in 1948. As the new head of the Department of Civic Design at Liverpool University, Stephenson sought to "reorganize the department and revive the Town Planning Review" an influential British planning journal.[9] He traveled to the United States that summer to assess graduate planning programs in preparation for establishing the first such program in Great Britain and to attend the American Society of Planning Officials' annual conference in New York City. Stein and MacMahon invited Stephenson and his wife to a party they were throwing for young planners at their home. Stein's discussion of Radburn, including criticisms of its design, intrigued Stephenson, who began considering the possibility of publishing articles on the community architect's large-scale projects.

Upon returning home, he wrote Stein, "One of the ideas in my head when I returned was that somebody ought to persuade you to write a critical appraisal of all the housing and planning projects with which you have been associated.... It would be marvelous if you could write as the architect responsible for so many of the projects which have influenced both thought and practice." In fact, Stein had already begun working on a draft manuscript about his large-scale developments, showcasing the Radburn Idea by recounting his site design and community building philosophies as realized at each residential project. Motivated by Osborn's *Green Belt Cities* (1946), Osborn's visit to the United States in 1947, where Stein engaged him in discussions regarding new towns, and Mumford's support, Stein began work on *Garden Cities in America* in the summer of 1947. In a letter to MacMahon, he updated her on his progress:

> I have been reading F. L. Osborn's Green Belt Cities to-day. He tells of the experience building and operating old Ebenezer's two Garden Cities—Letchworth & Welwyn. It occurred to me that there was no similar analysis of our attempts— Radburn and the Greenbelt Towns. Why were they such partial successes? With all our good intentions and hard work why haven't these towns been all they should have been—all that Howard visualized?—Don't take this as a regret—I know only too well the importance of these towns—And I recognize that the bridge between the past and the future can't be planned and built without many trials.—To move on we need not only experience—but understanding of our past work. So I spent the day outlining a study of what was intended and accomplished at R[adburn] and the Greenbelts. Such an analysis will be of value to F. J. Osborn when he comes here to us.

Two summers later in 1949, Stein traveled to Europe, stopping first to see regional planning underway in Denmark, before heading to Sweden to take in the town building there, and finally to Great Britain where he refined the articles that ultimately became his book.[10]

While in Denmark, Stein visited the architect Steen Eiler Rasmussen, a proponent of British town planning who had recently developed a "finger plan" for Greater Copenhagen with Peter Bredsdorff. It endorsed development along major transportation routes with the areas between left open as a means to ease congestion. Though renowned, Copenhagen's finger plan was not as fully realized as the new town initiatives underway in Sweden.[11]

As he continued his trip, Stein met with Markelius, director of Stockholm's Town Planning Office; Goran Sidenbladh, Markelius's chief assistant; J. H. Martin, in the city's Real Estate Department; Yngve Larsson, former director of Stockholm's Town Planning Department; and Tage William-Olsson, formerly with Stockholm and at the time town plan director for the City of Goteborg. While a great opportunity for Stein to learn more directly about new town planning progress in Sweden, these prominent planners also recognized the significance of meeting with Stein and exchanging ideas. During the visit, Stein saw plans for Vallingby—a new town designed for sixty thousand people in the greater Stockholm area. More a suburb due to residents' reliance on employment in and proximity to the city center, Vallingby represented to Stein planning on par with that underway in Great Britain. He later reflected, "As I look back over the summer, it seems to me that the strongest impression of progressive movement in planning was that which I got in the short time that I was in Sweden.... A tremendously valuable contribution is being made, not only in the orderly manner in which the remainder of Stockholm is being planned and built as a single process, but also in the design of the neighborhoods as units related both to the requirements of living and the form of the land."[12]

Designed by Markelius to accommodate the growth of Sweden's largest city via planned clustered neighborhoods arranged around commercial centers located at two light rail stops, Vallingby reflected many key characteristics embodied in the Radburn Idea. Among these were the centralized parks in superblocks, houses clustered and oriented toward the parks, and the hierarchical street system. "Each neighborhood is planned and built as a unified, related entity." As William-Olsson mentioned in a letter following Stein's trip, the Radburn Idea had been promoted in Sweden since the early 1930s. "But naturally there was to begin with very little appreciation of such ideas. They have slowly won ground and as you could see for yourself when you were here, are working largely on your lines." The significant amount of control the municipal government wielded through land ownership and the development process with financial support from the national government and participation of the private sector intrigued Stein as a model, though he acknowledged Americans would not allow it.[13]

Stein's next stop during his summer trip in 1949 was Hampstead Garden Sub-urb, where he spent almost two months at the invitation of Stephenson in the late Sir Raymond Unwin's Hampstead Gardens house Wyldes, writing, editing, and finalizing the articles that later became *Toward New Towns for America*. It was a truly inspirational environment in which to recount his seminal projects. "These are happy days," he remarked to MacKaye, "I am writing this in the room where Raymond Unwin studied and designed & wrote. In the early morning... I reread his book—Then later in the day I ramble around [Hampstead] Garden Suburb.... It is Unwin's greatest work in site planning—planning building[s] in relation to each other and to the lay of the land—No one that I know surpassed him." While his article (later chapter) on Radburn acknowledges Unwin and his partner Barry Parker's use of the superblock as a "precedent," Stein maintained, "If the superblock had not existed logic would have forced us to invent it." The first set of articles appeared in the October 1949 edition of *Town Planning Review*. Stephenson introduced the series, characterizing Stein and his long-time collaborator Wright as "humanists who were both skilled and practical. Their fundamental contribution is the 'Radburn Idea.'"[14]

Shortly thereafter, Stephenson embarked on a 1,200-unit residential develop-ment in Wrexham, Wales, in which he introduced lower-cost housing designs and attempted to demonstrate the applicability of this practical idea on Brit-ish soil. From the beginning, Stephenson referred to the design as a "modified Radburn layout" in part due to its more compact form. Similar to Radburn, the cul-de-sac roads provided access to the kitchen side of the houses and "a separate and continuous footpath system [led] to the front doors, playgrounds and open spaces." Yet, the topography, specifically a creek running through the site, did not allow Stephenson to form superblocks and the generous, continuous internal park system that characterized the New Jersey development.[15]

As Stephenson began design work on Wrexham, the chief planning officer at the Ministry of Town and Country Planning asked him to prepare Stevenage's town center plan. In the 1946 Stevenage master plan, Stephenson had "suggested" a pedestrian oriented shopping street with an internal ring road surrounding it as part of the main commercial, cultural, civic, and educational center for the town. By 1950, after further consideration and an exploration with Stein of the Kalverstraat in Amsterdam, "Europe's first pedestrian shopping mall," while in the city at the International Federation of Housing and Town Planning conference, Stephenson "was convinced that Stevenage town center could be planned with an internal pedestrian system separate from an external road system." Due to postwar economic hardships and shortages, the controversy over the designation of the town, and continuing issues with the location and design of the town center itself, construction on Stevenage had been delayed. Given these issues and the recent recognition that Stein had received with the publication of the articles in *Town Planning Review*, Stephenson knew Stein would make an excellent "second consultant." Thinking back to that time, he clarified, "Having worked closely with him during the previous summer, I knew that it would be a congruous relationship and his experience, keen mind and calm voice of authority would be invaluable in discussions with the ministry and corporation."[16]

Though significantly larger and urban, Stevenage allowed Stein to achieve what he had attempted at Maplewood—a pedestrian shopping district, including offices and community services compactly arranged on a superblock. Transportation routes and parking defined the outer edges. In early August 1950, Stein and MacMahon stayed at the historic Cromwell Inn in old Stevenage, just north of the proposed town center site, while Stephenson was the guest of Clifford Holliday, Stevenage's chief architect and planner, at his home in nearby Langley.[17] The three architects spent the next several days working on a sketch plan and drafting a preliminary three-page report outlining the design, function, and uses at the one-hundred-acre site (see figure 7.1). Before he returned to the United States in early September, Stein met with Holliday, Stephenson, and the corporation members to finalize the plan and the preliminary report.

In the report, Stein addressed critical features that defined the center.[18] Since the center was intended to draw patrons from the community and the region, accommodations were made for drivers, bicyclists, and pedestrians. Service roads bounded the outer edges of the pedestrian oriented town center, providing access to parking behind the shops and access to a bus and a railway station. Shops and office spaces were compactly arranged around garden promenades opening to ample plazas to accommodate entertainment spaces and outdoor seating near cafes. These buildings were to be unified with covered arcades to provide protection from the elements. Occasional passageways between the buildings would provide access to the parking areas. The cultural center to the south of the shopping district would be affiliated with the local college and

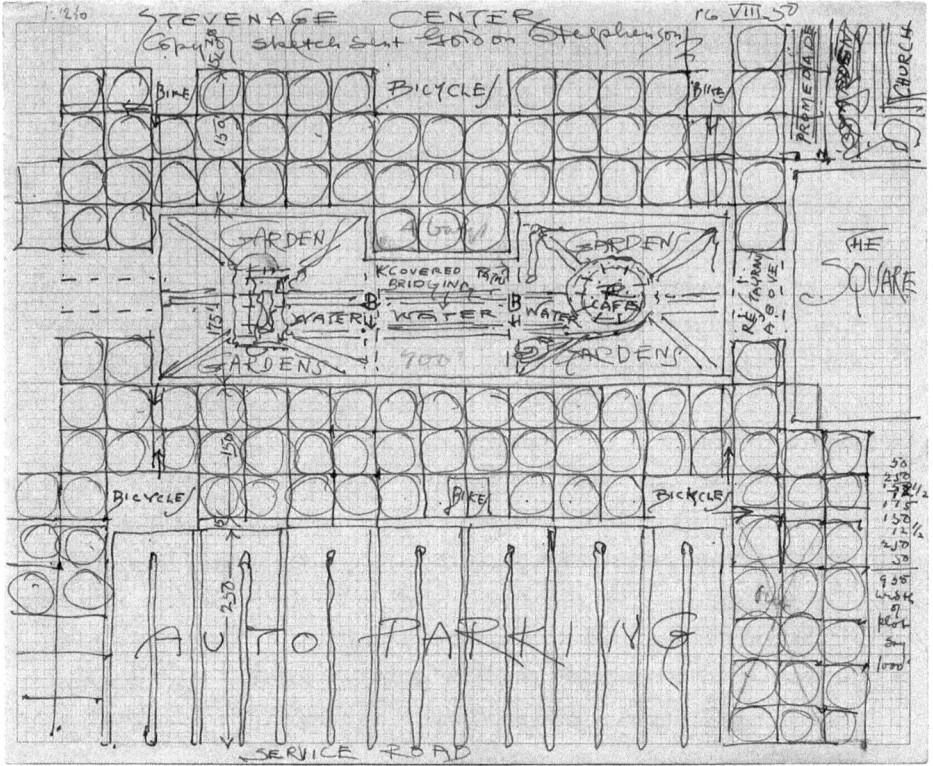

FIGURE 7.1 Stevenage Town Centre—rough sketch of central pedestrian area by Stein dated August 16, 1950. Box 2, CSP/CUL.

physically incorporated into the town center so that certain facilities such as an auditorium, library, meeting spaces, and recreation areas could be available to the entire community. To the north, the civic center buildings were arranged around the civic square. A recreational area to the east would include an artificial lake and more restaurants. Stein's conceptual drawing that accompanied his report focused on the central shopping district arranged around these garden and plaza areas with connecting walkways. Holliday, Stephenson, and Stein's design retained these features, particularly the strong north-south axis of the pedestrian district, which opened up to plazas on the north around the civic center and south around the cultural center. Their proposed site diagram included the surrounding area, showing parking and service roads, the railway station to the west and recreational area to the east (see figure 7.2).

Stephenson and Holliday presented the report as drafted by Stein largely unchanged. There were three areas of criticism from the officers of the Stevenage Development Corporation: limiting commercial structures to one-story, not allowing residences above the shops, and restricting the central area to pedestrians only. While the corporation officers approved the preliminary town center report and diagram, and planners at the ministry supported the proposal, as at Maplewood, business interests and some officers expressed concerns that commercial activity would suffer due to the lack of auto access. They continued to argue for a road through the town center and blocked the design for a period of years, well after Stephenson left Great Britain to consult on the plan for Perth in Western Australia and then moved to Toronto for an academic position there.[19]

As Stevenage grew, residents advocated for the pedestrian shopping area. In April 1954, the new architect and planner to the corporation at the direction of the corporation and the ministry submitted a revised plan that retained the central pedestrian-only shopping district, though further revisions by the end of the year resulted in a significantly narrower pedestrian way. Unfortunately, the college and related cultural structures were now separated from the town center by a major road running on the south side of the shopping, office, and service district. Further, a major bus station was located adjacent to the center of the pedestrian shopping district. Still, Stein's pedestrian core remained, and Stevenage was especially praised for its town center. Shortly after the opening of the central forty-acre shopping district in the summer of 1958, *Town and Country Planning* observed, "The new all-pedestrian town centre of Stevenage is one of the boldest planning and architectural experiments of recent years. It is indeed already more than an experiment; it is an achievement.... A triumph not only for modern planning but also for local opinion ... over the more cautious advocates of the orthodox traffic-traversed shopping centre." Osborn and Whittick observed about Stevenage, "If there is one regret about so excellent a centre it is that the town square is not more spacious.... Still it is good to see the idea of the pedestrian precinct so completely realized in face of much opposition." Once again, thoughtfully designed interconnected open spaces heralded a key feature of Stein's community design, a community design recognized well beyond the parameters of Western Europe.[20]

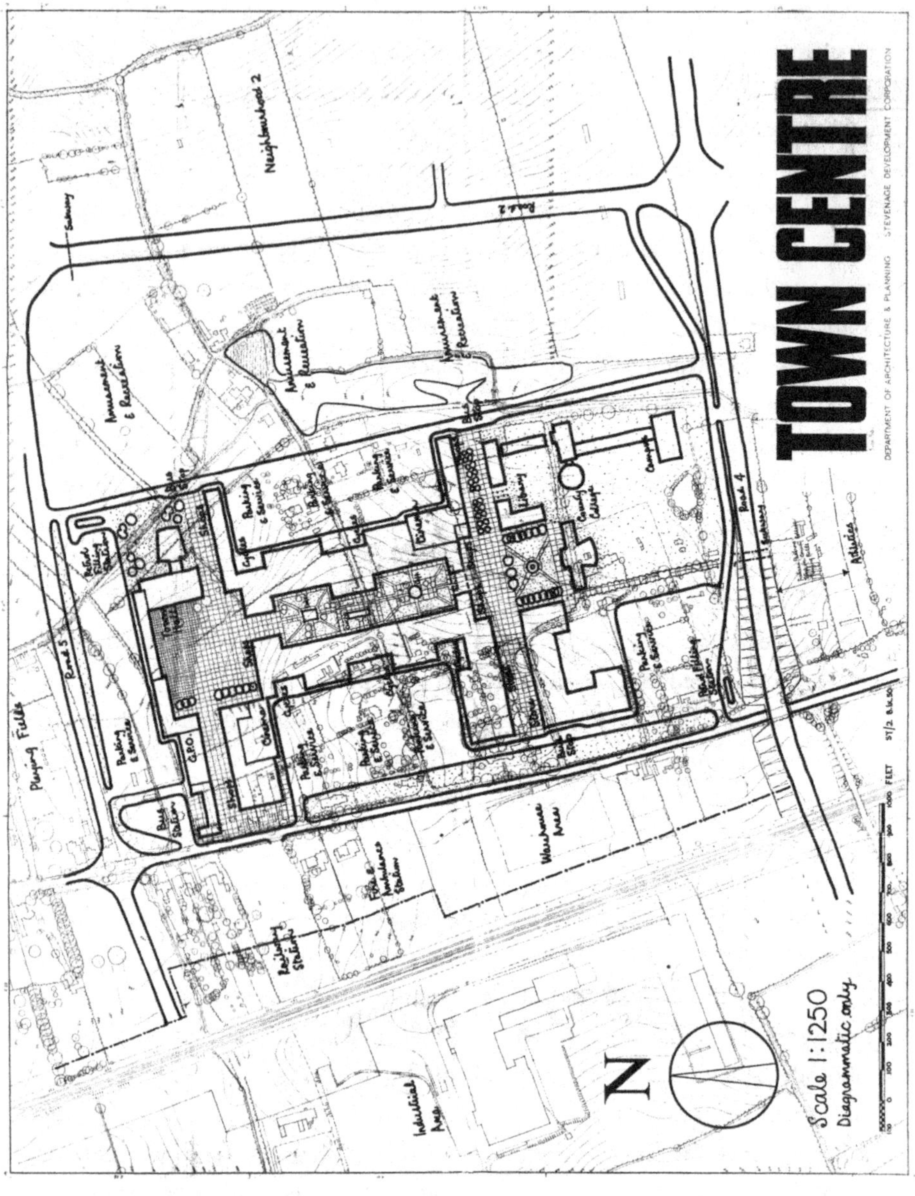

FIGURE 7.2 Stevenage Town Centre—marked up site plan by Stein dated October 1950, showing the collaborative process between Stein and Stephenson. Box 2, CSP/CUL.

## Town Building in India
## and Israel

As Stein consulted on the town center at Stevenage, his colleagues Mayer and Nowicki were intensively working on the Chandigarh master plan and architectural design guidelines respectively for the new capital of 150,000 in the East Punjab province of India. Mayer had served in India as a lieutenant colonel in the U.S. Army Corps of Engineers during World War II. Given the regard Prime Minister Jawaharlal Nehru had for his planning expertise, Mayer was appointed in various capacities as planning consultant to the Indian government, participating in several major planning and town building projects from 1946 to 1958.[21]

With Chandigarh, Mayer believed he had "a unique opportunity, the opportunity of a lifetime … being in many of the customary ways unhampered, it casts basic light on what we seek to accomplish in planning anywhere." In early 1950, Mayer sought Stein's advice, in addition to others, as he embarked on the project, hiring Stein to review concepts, plans, and drawings and to examine issues relevant to the plan. From the beginning, he acknowledged his debt to Stein, "We are drawing on the principles and experience of Baldwin Hills, Radburn, the Greenbelt towns, adapting and fusing them into the Indian scene, to their habits and problems of living and working and traffic."[22]

Stein concurred, providing frequent feedback during that winter and spring on the adaptation of the Radburn Idea to the project, including separation of pedestrians, cyclists, and autos with major roads delineating the edges of the superblock and the houses oriented toward a centralized park system. He also conducted a study of the Los Angeles farmer's market, noting the adaptability of its flexible, inexpensive, and compact plan to the neighborhood, and potentially central shopping districts in Chandigarh. In regards to the public buildings in the new capital, he promoted the use of park and mall spaces to create vistas highlighting significant structures, arguing that the only acceptable way to view them was on foot. In reviewing the preliminary general plans that March, Stein maintained that greenways should be designed to make the government buildings "the dominating focus of the plan." He specified, "The greenways require much more emphasis. In fact, they should be the paramount framework around which the important structures should be planned."[23]

Mayer's master plan was based on the neighborhood unit—essentially the

Radburn superblock—informed by the cooperative village unit in India. He adapted the segregated circulation plan and individual superblock, for approximately 3,500 families (roughly 18,000 people), with a neighborhood-serving school, cultural center, shopping district, and small workshops to the Indian village familiar to so many. In late March, Mayer sent Shri Varma, the chief engineer for the development, a model district plan, consisting of three superblocks, and a neighborhood or superblock plan predominantly for low-income households. Mayer called the district plan, "the microcosm of the city." Norma Evenson, who wrote an early history of Chandigarh that details Mayer and Nowicki's contributions before Le Corbusier took over, describes Mayer's master plan as follows:

> A fan-shaped outline, spreading gently to fill the site between the two river beds. The provincial government buildings are located beyond the upper edge of the city within a fork in one of the rivers, while the central business district occupies an area near the center. A curving network of main roads surrounds the residential superblocks, each of which contains a central area of parkland. Two larger parks may be seen stretching through the city, and to the east is an area set aside for industry. The initial development of the city was to take place in the northerly portion of the site, with possible expansion projected toward the south.[24]

When Nowicki and Mayer traveled to India in the summer of 1950 to see progress on the development of the town plan details, they were surprised to learn that Varma was leaving his position, and no local architects had been hired to begin the more detailed designs and working drawings of the structures. At this point, Mayer and Nowicki decided that Nowicki would stay and design a complete superblock. On June 21, Whittlesey wrote Stein that the plan had been approved by the Cabinet "in all major respects."[25] Though Nowicki was frustrated with the minimal assistance, extensive administrative requirements, and alternating slow and frenzied pace of his work, he was excited at the opportunity to have an office on site to oversee the detailed town design efforts.

On his way to India that summer, Nowicki had visited with Stein, who was contemplating an article on old town design and was focusing on Paris. Anticipating his return to his family and friends in the United States at the end of the summer, Nowicki wrote Stein, "Our two days in Paris are a wonderful memory. ... I am looking very much forward to our meeting and to long conversations and sharing of our experiences of this summer." Unfortunately, the talented young architect's life was tragically cut short several days later when the plane he was on crashed. With the loss of Nowicki as designer, though the Indian government had approved Mayer's master plan, officials quickly turned to Le Corbusier to complete designs for the town. While Mayer's master plan was supposed to endure, Le Corbusier ultimately revised it. Their visions were quite different, with Le Corbusier's international design replacing Mayer's lower density urban villages informed by the Radburn Idea. The French architect organized the town on a massive gridiron with streets cutting into the shopping district and superblocks, but adhering to the separation of auto and pedestrian and also retaining large superblocks or "sectors" oriented internally toward centralized open spaces.[26]

In addition to India, some of the most exciting town building initiatives were occurring in the new country of Israel. In 1951, Stein met and began an ongoing correspondence with Artur Glikson, an architect then in charge of regional planning and the supervision of new town design for the national government and later chief architect in the Planning Department of the Housing Division. Over the next decade, Stein closely followed town planning in that country, corresponding with other nationally and internationally recognized architect/planners such as Arieh Sharon, director of Israel's Planning Department (1948–1952). New towns represented a critical component of the National Plan with neighborhood units forming the building blocks of these towns. Stein acknowledged that the relatively small amount of arable land, rapid population growth, military threats from nearby countries, and significant amount of publicly controlled land put Israel in a unique position to plan at an unprecedented level. "I know of no other nation that is actually being developed so thoroughly according to a comprehensive, interrelated National Plan for the use and development of its land, water and other natural resources, for the distribution of population in rural, service and urban centers, for the limitation of the growth of these, for the location of agriculture and reforestation." At the same time, he and his closest colleagues had made quite the impression on planners in that country. Glikson particularly noted MacKaye's concept of geotechnics, which Glikson applied in 1952–1953 when he was locating new towns in the northern part of the country, assessing the regional geography and topography to determine likely locations for infrastructure and from that a hierarchy of new towns. "The planner should direct his best efforts towards the construction of a living bridge between nature, whose optimum potentialities should be developed according to its inherent law—and between the emerging human society."[27]

The Radburn Idea also was evident in some of the new town designs. As Glikson informed Stein about his plan for a neighborhood in the new town of Beersheba, "I hope you will be glad to find in it another practical application of the Radburn principle, though reduced to the scale of sub-units of a neighbourhood, and with special emphasis on space enclosure, without deviating too much from the climatically conditioned North-South exposition of buildings." Stein responded, "It is good to see that the new version of the Radburn Superblock is being experimented with in Israel." Stein appreciated that subcenters, including kindergartens, small shops, a clinic, and small synagogue, served sections of the superblock often with centralized parks around which the housing was oriented though these areas were divided by minor roads. In fact, the density rather than the street design seemed a primary concern. He continued "This layout is unusually economical, as far as roads, paths, and utilities go. However, I am sorry that conditions have apparently forced the designers to put so many families on the site." Glikson later clarified in a paper on housing and new towns that the application of the neighborhood unit worked due to practical considerations—it "facilitates the increased efficiency of commercial, social and cultural services ... offers an optimal solution for transport services ... [allows] uninterrupted stretches of public gardens ... enables the most effective utilisation of topographical factors ... develop[s] a growing town in stages and in immediately equipping the first settlers with public institutions and services near their homes." Stein traveled to Israel again in 1959 to meet with architects and see for himself the new town initiatives underway. Reflecting on his trip, Stein noted how impressed he was with the sheer scale and implementation of Israel's National Plan, the adherence to protections for agricultural areas, and the siting and design of new towns and neighborhoods, though the speed of development due to population pressures was a concern.[28]

Although Stein's personal wealth supported his career success, illness dogged him, reducing his productivity as the years passed. Nevertheless, his affluence allowed him to travel extensively and personally witness international trends in urban and rural development; the connections he forged created a worldwide network of leading planning and design experts. Further, it allowed him to work on projects that his fellow professionals did not have the flexibility or resources to choose. Periods of serious illness removed him from practice for many months, and his disappointments over the lack of full adoption of his ideas and incomplete or unrealized projects also took a toll. Yet he remains a major figure in modernizing and disseminating the Garden City movement. His unwavering dedication to new towns, which he called the Regional City, generated interest and implementation, especially abroad.

Toward the end of his career, he received accolades for his significant contributions to architecture and planning. In 1955, the American Society of Planning Officials recognized him for "pioneering toward New Towns for America." That was followed the next year by the Gold Medal of Honor from the AIA, that professional association's highest honor, and then the Distinguished Service Award from the American Institute of Planners in 1958 for his "outstanding services to the planning profession." The citation for the latter award noted in part: "Pioneer in the movement for publicly aided housing; co-architect and planner of Sunnyside Gardens, co-creator of the Radburn plan, the most important contribution to twentieth century city design. No other man in our time has had a more effective influence in furthering regional and city planning worthy of a human, enlightened community. With a generosity of spirit that sets a high example to his peers and successors, his talents as both organizer and designer of new communities evoke our admiration and gratitude." Perhaps the most important award—the capstone of his career—was the Sir Ebenezer Howard Memorial Medal presented by the Town and Country Planning Association in 1960 for his "sincere and consistent [support] of the Garden City movement . . . contribut[ing] in a notable way to its advancement and practical application." With the help of Mayer, Stein continued to promote his ideal of communitarian regionalism, in the guise of the Regional City, well into the 1960s. In fact, Mayer went so far as to attribute the concept of the Regional City to Stein in his 1967 book, *The Urgent Future*.[29]

Mayer took the opportunity in 1964, in consultation with Stein, to draft a series of articles for the *Architectural Record* examining the theme of town building in America. At the time, President Johnson was proposing a new town program generated through public-private partnerships. Despite the consistency of the overall concept with their ideas, Mayer and Stein did not support the FHA as the implementing agency, citing their concern with the lack of design, economic, and social diversity fostered by the agency. One year later, the first in a series of new town legislation was adopted with the recently established Department of Housing and Urban Development overseeing the program.[30]

Stein consistently insisted the way forward demanded a collaborative and comprehensive approach. "The New Town planner requires a broad understanding of aims and objectives, and of all the related functions with which he must work to realize them. As his technical work is part of a larger process of creating a community background ... he must work as part of a team. That was one of the great and inspiring features of the work of the City Housing Corporation."[31] The Radburn Idea represented the outcome of his experiment, an evolving approach to community design.

Stein's search for community, economy, and functionalism—what he called livability—resulted in key innovations that anticipated new regionalism, smart growth, sustainability, green infrastructure, new urbanism, and the largest form of current public investment in low-income housing production. In these ways, his ideas found practical application, not just through a limited list of model communities,[32] but by informing critical movements that energize the planning and design professions today.

## The Legacy of the Community Architect

Stein maintained that the "people," or community, were the starting point for the design and development of the Regional City. The blocks, neighborhoods, districts, and towns that shaped the Regional City were each "an individual community development around its own center of local activity." Form followed function—based on community needs and activities. Further, as Stein, Wright, and MacKaye outlined in their 1926 proposal for a statewide plan in New York, it was the topography, soil, landscape, climate, and transportation networks, among other conditions, which should direct future development.[33]

Stein did more than just facilitate discussion about the region, although this contribution was clearly evident in his input on MacKaye's proposal for the Appalachian Trail, as well as in his advocacy of the regional approach to planning for growth in New York State, and later his participation in the deliberation among the RDCA membership of a regional agency to oversee Washington State's Columbia River Valley.[34] His ongoing commitment to communitarian regionalism with a sensitivity to the environment is also evident in his new town projects; in his hiring of MacKaye and Ross at Kitimat to consider the river, forest, flood plain, and the broader region in the design of the town; and in his activism in California to support regional plans to protect open space and agricultural lands from growth pressures.

This communitarian regionalism was the forerunner to today's smart growth movement and the new regionalism, which integrates a physical, cultural, and environmental sensibility with the economy of place to link fragmented systems. New regionalism thus frames a reaction against the post–World War II regionalism that emphasized quantitative methods and economic development, and ignored spatial dynamics. At the same time, it poses a positive alternative to the homogenous sprawling development that epitomized this period.[35] New regionalism and communitarian regionalism share a similar regard for systems thinking and an activist approach to addressing challenges, not just on the periphery of cities but along river valleys and flood zones and across state lines to accommodate broader needs in physical space. However, equity issues are more centrally integrated into new regionalism, and efforts to coordinate among a wider array of fragmented agencies define it in a way that was never pivotal to communitarian regionalism.

Stein and his RPAA colleagues, particularly MacKaye, Mumford, and Chase, advocated for a holistic approach that integrated layers of government through interstate and federal coordination to engage issues of place, economy, and environment. Throughout they consistently promoted their vision of the Regional City as an antidote to placeless sprawl as much as an escape from the crowded, polluted metropolis. Stein and his colleagues also proposed deconcentration of the population and the introduction of linked green spaces as a means to alleviate these challenging urban conditions.

A desire to understand the natural environment, its networks and functions, to survey and inform site design, including the programming of open space, reflect a keen focus on the ecology of place that anticipated key elements of sustainability and green infrastructure. At its core, sustainability addresses "balanc[ing] local social, economic, and ecological systems." MacKaye and Geddes imparted to Stein and other RPAA members the significance of systems thinking when it came to the landscape and the need to balance natural resources with human needs. MacKaye called this "human ecology," and Stein consistently referred to this balance in his discussions of the region (see figure 7.3). As Stein put it in *Toward New Towns for America*, "Nature will dominate, and all cities

FIGURE 7.3 Picture of Stein (left) and MacKaye (right) at the Cosmos Club, Washington, DC, dated June 1964. Photograph by Kip Ross, Box 43, CSP/CUL.

will be green cities, with parks in the heart of each block and encircling belts of agriculture, natural playgrounds, and wilderness."[36]

At the site level, clustering housing to reduce infrastructure impacts and costs and promoting mixed uses to facilitate a more walkable community certainly resonate as sustainability principles. Developing communities to flexibly respond to evolving needs with design and materials intended to economically endure over the long term further reinforces these principles. In addition, Stein's connected open space systems and his understanding of their significance and function in the community reflect foundational elements of green infrastructure. Consider how John Randolph's 2004 definition of green infrastructure in his influential text on environmental planning compares with the goals outlined by Stein in his communities and more broadly with those of the RPAA: "An interconnected network of green space that conserves natural ecosystem values and functions and provides associated benefits to human populations." In fact, Philip Berke, in his review of prominent historical visionaries and advocates who advanced "the relationship between human settlements and the environment" via "green communities," names the RPAA membership as key contributors over the past century. He clarifies, "when placed beside the extremes of Broadacre City and Radiant City, the Garden City and RPAA polycentric visions seem to hold a realistic yet visionary middle ground that has gained traction in contemporary planning practice and scholarship."[37]

The Radburn Idea provided the direction for new town design—for complete communities more in line with the smart growth and sustainability movements than sprawling suburbs. It offered "efficient planning for use, in place of speculative sale. Large scale building and operation. More efficient government and community organization. ... The related location of homes, community facilities and work places to facilitate safe convenient walking and bicycling. The decrease in the journey to work and other unproductive travel."[38] It also promoted greater densities and mixture of housing types as opposed to the homogenous patterns in the suburbs.

To realize this vision, community planning "with appropriate policy and programmatic support ... was needed, not traditional zoning and planning solutions." As Stein outlined,

[The] present kind of city planning does not deal with substantial realities. ... It is concerned with separate and limited units; lots, individual houses, a single road, not community building. Because city planning outlines and regulates, and does not relate these units in a composed group or neighborhood, it must generalize. This requires stereotyped, conservative, easily classified, standardized objects; these are more easily marketed and regulated.

The present city form is not molded by the planner. It is the random consequence of the separate and unrelated decisions of subdivider, municipal engineer, zoning board, speculative builder, aided and abetted by the FHA and the lending institutions.

Fully adapting his vision would have meant more comprehensive and coordinated planning, including regional and environmental considerations as well as urban and suburban ones.[39]

Some of Stein's contemporaries clearly understood and promoted Stein's community building concepts. Henry Churchill used Radburn as an example of an "investment subdivision" as opposed to a speculative one in his May 1937 article for the *Architectural Record* promoting the constructive application of the FHA guidelines to achieve sound development patterns. In 1942, the renowned architect Richard Neutra called Radburn, "a living example ... to be further developed and elaborated." Stein clearly intended Radburn to be "a living example." In all his efforts, the community architect advocated a spirit of exploration and a dynamic responsiveness in his designs. He maintained,

> A new town must remain contemporary for a very long period. Only thus can we afford it. It must last long enough to allow its original cost to be amortized. That on the face of it may seem impossible, for the main characteristic of the present time is change. ...
>
> New Towns must not only be the flowering of today's life and civilization, but they must have in them the seed of the future—or at least the facility of growing and changing to fit it. They must be dynamic. ... must be flexible. We must plan so as to limit difficulties we now face in the redevelopment of our old cities, which require extravagant destruction and the rebuilding of vast areas.

Later, in a few distinctive examples, such as Columbia, Maryland; Reston, Virginia; and the Woodlands, Texas, Stein's ideas were more holistically applied.[40]

More recently, an appreciation of the skilled coordination of distinctive elements featured in Radburn has emerged. Cynthia Girling and Kenneth Helphand note in their 1994 book that the community, though featuring more expensive housing than many adjacent developments, also offers more in the form of park and other amenities. "Portions of the plan, aspects of the idea, are found in virtually all planned (and unplanned) communities. Unfortunately, they are most often just pieces, segments of the idea: a cul-de-sac, an interior park, a superblock, or a walkway. Rarely do they have the thoughtful, carefully calibrated systemic integration of Radburn, evident in aspects ranging from the scale of rooms and their relationship to the yard and street, to the entire community plan."[41]

Despite some well-documented resistance among the new urbanists, there are also parallels and values shared with Stein, particularly in relation to the Radburn Idea. As they sought a return to traditional development patterns evident in historic neighborhoods with grid-iron streets, alley access, a mixture of housing types and neighborhood services and commercial uses, these architects denigrated the superblock and cul-de-sac elements promoted by Stein, Wright, and Mumford. In his preface to the reissue of Unwin's classic, *Town Planning in Practice*, the renowned new urbanist and a founder of the movement, Andres Duany compares the influence of Radburn and John Nolen's Mariemont, Ohio, the latter a celebrated antecedent to new urbanism. After favorably remarking on Mariemont, Duany disdainfully notes, "The same cannot be said of Radburn, New Jersey, that 'town for the motor age,' which has choked on the three-car family. Indeed, it is the central tragedy of the American planning profession that the influence of Unwin's sophisticated and complex book was overwhelmed by that of Clarence Stein's *Toward New Towns for America*. Its simple-minded slogan, demanding that moving cars be segregated from pedestrians, was the first step toward the segregation of the profession into narrow specialties and toward its collapse."[42] Once again, the transportation network is considered in a vacuum and the coordination of urban form and function is ignored or simply lost.

Yet the values of the complete community in the materials issued by the RPAA (later RDCA) reflect a desire for community that prefigured the new urbanists. As Stein testified regarding the disposition of the Greenbelt Towns, "As neighborhood communities, they preserve the old village character of America that is elsewhere being destroyed by the uncontrolled growth of our monstrous cities.... That these small neighborhoods keep eye-to-eye democracy alive has been well demonstrated in the Greenbelt Towns." Still, the differences in the conception of the street network and open spaces distinguish the Radburn Idea from the new urbanism. For Stein, streets were intended for motorized vehicles and provided access through a network to the service side of the home. However, for the new urbanists, the streets accommodate community and circulation functions, including bicycling and walking. Further, the new urbanists' disconnected plazas and parks that focus predominantly on the civic and aesthetic, lack the hierarchical integration of an open space network that Stein promoted and is rightly perceived as a precursor to green infrastructure. As Jill Grant in her 2006 review of the new urbanism maintains, "Garden city planners," as she calls them, sought the integration of nature into "the managed urban fabric to restore health and happiness." In contrast, the new urbanists saw these two as separate and often antithetical.[43]

The limited dividend model that Stein termed *investment housing* has also resurfaced in current housing initiatives that emphasize private sector partners. The LIHTC, which provides government incentives for private developers to construct or rehabilitate housing at reduced rents for income eligible tenants, has been the biggest producer of low income multifamily housing for more than two decades. The private housing developer, which can include nonprofits, applies competitively for the tax credit through a state agency that has often established additional criteria to incentivize projects that target special populations, include additional tenant amenities, and/or locate in neighborhoods with certain community characteristics. To offset the reduced rents, the LIHTC developer funds construction by selling the tax credit through syndicators, which have formed investor partnerships. With its limited return, focus on working-class populations, reliance on public-private partnerships, and flexible oversight responsive to state and regional needs, the LIHTC program parallels many of the characteristics that Stein valued in the FHA rental housing program, which he more broadly termed investment housing. Still he would not have welcomed the program's complexity, incentives to concentrate such housing in distressed areas, inefficient channeling of federal funds for housing production, and expiration of affordability restrictions.[44]

However, efforts to redevelop severely distressed public housing projects adopt Stein's ideas by emphasizing human-scaled design and community amenities, transforming the international brutalism of high-rise projects into walkable communities. More recently, the 2009 Partnership for Sustainable Communities program integrated the efforts of the Department of Housing and Urban Development, the Department of Transportation, and the Environmental Protection Agency to support projects in distressed communities that promote six livability principles. The focus on facilitating the building of what Stein called complete communities, public-private partnerships, and interagency coordination reflect the types of government housing programs he advocated.[45]

Despite his disappointments and setbacks, which clearly took a personal toll in the multiple and long bouts of severe illness that Stein suffered, his ideas continue to resonate, attesting to their relevance. That his projects still thrive and their distinctiveness is recognized reflects the enduring value of his community building practice. Examining the broad range of his contributions fosters a fuller understanding of planning in the twentieth century and the foundations for current initiatives in this new century.

# ABBREVIATIONS

| | |
|---|---|
| AIA | American Institute of Architects |
| AIP | American Institute of Planners |
| BHV | Baldwin Hills Village |
| BMP/DCL | Benton MacKaye Papers Special Collections, Dartmouth College Library |
| CHC | City Housing Corporation |
| CSP/CUL | Clarence S. Stein Papers, #3600, Division of Rare and Manuscript Collections, Cornell University Library |
| FCH | Foundation for Cooperative Housing |
| FHA | Federal Housing Administration |
| FPHA | Federal Public Housing Authority |
| FWA | Federal Works Agency |
| GSA | General Services Administration |
| HHFA | Housing and Home Finance Agency |
| HOPE VI | Housing Opportunities for People Everywhere |
| HRPC | New York Housing and Regional Planning Commission |
| IRA | National Industrial Recovery Act |
| ITPC | International Town Planning Conference |
| *JAIA* | *Journal of the American Institute of Architects* |
| LIHTC | Low-Income Housing Tax Credit |
| LMP/UPA | Lewis Mumford Papers, Special Collections, Van Pelt Library, University of Pennsylvania |
| MIT | Massachusetts Institute of Technology |
| NETC | New England Trail Conference |

# Abbreviations

| | |
|---|---|
| NHA | National Housing Agency |
| NPHC | National Public Housing Conference |
| NYCHA | New York City Housing Authority |
| PBA | Public Buildings Administration |
| PDR/TA | Phelps-Dodge Records, Tucson, Arizona |
| PHA | Public Housing Administration |
| PWA | Public Works Administration |
| RA | Resettlement Administration |
| RDCA | Regional Development Council of America |
| RFA | Rockefeller Family Archives |
| RFC | Reconstruction Finance Corporation |
| RHD | Rental Housing Division |
| RPAA | Regional Planning Association of America |
| RPNY | Regional Plan of New York and Its Environs |
| SOM | Skidmore, Owings, and Merrill |
| TVA | Tennessee Valley Authority |
| UN | United Nations |
| USHA | United States Housing Authority |

# NOTES

## Preface

1. Kristin Larsen, "Clarence Stein's Formative Experiences and Unbuilt Projects—Transforming Classical Training into Modern Design and Planning Sensibilities," in *Public Versus Private Planning: Themes, Trends, and Tensions* (Chicago: Proceedings of the 2008 International Planning History Society Conference), 1321–1336; Kristin Larsen, "Planning and Public–Private Partnerships: Essential Links in Early Federal Housing Policy," *Journal of Planning History* 15, no. 1 (2016): 68–81; and Kristin Larsen, "Cities to Come—Clarence Stein's Post-War Regionalism," *Journal of Planning History* 4, no. 1 (2005): 33–51.

2. Angelique Bamberg, *Chatham Village: Pittsburgh's Garden City* (Pittsburgh: University of Pittsburgh Press, 2011).

## Introduction

1. Lewis Mumford, "Biographical Sketch of Clarence Stein" (unpublished notes prepared in anticipation of Stein's receipt of the AIA Gold Medal in 1956), Box 189, Lewis Mumford Papers, Special Collections, Van Pelt Library, University of Pennsylvania (LMP/UPA).

2. Wyndham Thomas, Director, Town and Country Planning Association, to Clarence Stein, 5 November 1959, Box 10, Clarence S. Stein Papers, #3600, Division of Rare and Manuscript Collections, Cornell University Library (CSP/CUL).

3. Clarence S. Stein, "Acceptance of Sir Ebenezer Howard Medal" (unpublished notes, March 28, 1960), Box 10, CSP/CUL. The Hudson Guild Farm was the summer camp of the Ethical Culture Society, which played a significant role in Stein's education and later his architectural career. Among the designs he completed for the Ethical Culture Society were two of the camp buildings.

4. Marshall Oliver, "The Way Out," *Architecture* 67, no. 5 (1933): 247–252, 251.

5. Tracy Augur, "Radburn—The Challenge of a New Town," *Michigan Municipal Review* 4 (February and March, 1931); reprint (New York: City Housing Corporation, circa 1931), n.p., Box 1, CSP/CUL.

6. Clarence S. Stein Commemorative Committee, "Clarence S. Stein, F.A.I.A., America's Environmental Architect" (unpublished exhibition brochure circa November 1976). The committee included the architects Chloethiel Woodward Smith, Herbert Epstein, Frederick Gutheim,

Douglas Haskell, and William L. Slayton. Lewis Mumford, introduction to Clarence S. Stein, *Toward New Towns for America* (Cambridge: MIT Press, 1957), 17.

7. See Robert L. McCullough, *A Path for Kindred Spirits: The Friendship of Clarence Stein and Benton MacKaye* (Chicago: Center for American Places at Columbia College Chicago, 2012); and Larry Anderson's more expansive biography of MacKaye, *Benton MacKaye: Conservationist, Planner, and Creator of the Appalachian Trail* (Baltimore: Johns Hopkins University Press, 2002) for more on this remarkable friendship.

8. Clarence S. Stein, *Toward New Towns for America* (Cambridge: MIT Press, 1957), 217.

9. Mumford, introduction to *Toward New Towns*, 13; ibid., 226.

10. In their edited volume on the suburbs, Becky Nicolaides and Andrew Wiese highlight Radburn, and planned suburbs like it, as "models for contemporary reform" of mass suburbia (469). See Becky Nicolaides and Andrew Wiese, eds., *The Suburb Reader* (New York: Routledge, 2006). For more on Radburn as an alternative to mass suburbia, see Dolores Hayden, *Building Suburbia: Green Fields and Urban Growth, 1820–2000* (New York: Vintage Books, 2003). See Michael Southworth and Eran Ben-Joseph's *Streets and the Shaping of Towns and Cities* (Washington, DC: Island Press, 2003) for their characterization of the design innovations that defined Radburn, particularly its hierarchical street system; and Cynthia Girling and Kevin Helphand, *Yard, Street, Park: The Design of Suburban Open Space* (New York: John Wiley and Sons, 1994) who argue that distilling the Radburn Idea down to its individual components negates the very heart of Stein's proposal, the integration of these design characteristics to create this distinctive community. These authors appropriately recognize Stein's ideas as executed at Radburn as the antithesis to mass suburbia.

11. Stein, *Toward New Towns*, 217.

12. Ibid., 226.

13. Lewis Mumford, "A Modest Man's Enduring Contributions to Urban and Regional Planning," *AIA Journal* 65, no. 12 (1976): 19–29, 20.

14. C. S. Stein, "Housing and Common Sense," *The Nation* 134 (May 1932): 541–544, 543.

15. C. S. Stein, "Housing and City Redevelopment during and after the War" (address, Citizens' City Planning and Housing Council, Rochester, NY, November 17, 1941), 4, Box 6, CSP/CUL. C. S. Stein, "Why We Changed Our Name," *Citizen's Housing and Planning Council, Housing News* 6, no. 6 (1948): 1, 4, 1.

16. C. S. Stein, "The City of the Future—A City of Neighborhoods," *American City* 37 (November 1945): 123 and 125, 123. Mumford, introduction to *Toward New Towns*, 14.

17. Stein to Frank Palmer, 27 March 1944, CSP/CUL.

18. Stein, *Toward New Towns*, 225.

19. See FHA, *Planning Neighborhoods for Small Houses*, Technical Bulletin No. 5 (1936; rev. reprint Washington, DC: Government Printing Office, 1938).

20. C. S. Stein, "Recreation and Open Spaces" (lecture, Federation School, January 17, 1938), Box 6, CSP/CUL. C. S. Stein, "Regional Cities for America (Outline: Part II)" (unpublished, June 25, 1961), 2, Box 9, CSP/CUL. Stein, *Toward New Towns*, 225, 219.

21. Stein, notes on letter from Henry Klaber, 28 November 1956, Box 15, CSP/CUL.

22. See Stephen Wheeler, "The New Regionalism: Key Characteristics of an Emerging Movement," *Journal of the American Planning Association* 68, no. 3 (2002): 267–278; William Fulton, "The Garden Suburb and the New Urbanism," in *From Garden City to Green City: The Legacy of Ebenezer Howard*, ed. Kermit C. Parsons and David Schuyler (Baltimore: Johns Hopkins University Press, 2002), 159–170; Robert Fishman, "The Metropolitan Tradition in American Planning," in *The American Planning Tradition: Culture and Policy*, ed. Robert Fishman (Balti-

more: Johns Hopkins University Press, 2000), 64–85; Michael H. Lang, *Designing Utopia: John Ruskin's Urban Vision for Britain and America* (New York: Black Rose Books, 1999); Stanley Buder, *Visionaries and Planners: The Garden City Movement and the Modern Community* (New York: Oxford University Press, 1990).

## 1. The Garden City Idea

1. See especially, C. S. Stein, "City Planning" (unpublished essay, May 13, 1917), Box 11, CSP/ CUL; C. S. Stein, "Housing and Reconstruction," *Journal of the American Institute of Architects* 6 (October 1918): 471; and various lectures during this period before the Women's City Club of New York. This voluntary group established in 1915 by suffragists focused on critical issues for women and children and broader progressive issues such as housing. When Stein delivered several lectures to them in the late teens and early twenties, and they published the work of the Housing Committees, the advocacy group counted several thousand members. See Elizabeth I. Perry, "Women's City Club of New York," in *The Encyclopedia of New York City*, ed. Jackson (New Haven: Yale University Press, 1995), 1269.

2. Ebenezer Howard, *Garden Cities of To-Morrow* (1902; reprint Cambridge, MA: MIT Press, 1965). For those publications that specifically connect Howard to Stein and his colleagues, see Howard Gillette, Jr., *Civitas by Design: Building Better Communities, from the Garden City to the New Urbanism* (Philadelphia: University of Pennsylvania Press, 2010); Buder, *Visionaries and Planners*; Edward K. Spann, *Designing Modern America: The Regional Planning Association of America and Its Members* (Columbus: Ohio State University Press, 1996); Daniel Schaffer, *Garden Cities for America: The Radburn Experience* (Philadelphia: Temple University Press, 1982); Carl Sussman, "Introduction," in *Planning the Fourth Migration: The Neglected Vision of the Regional Planning Association of America*, ed. Sussman (Cambridge, MA: MIT Press, 1976): 1–45; Roy Lubove, *Community Planning in the 1920s: The Contribution of the Regional Planning Association of America* (Pittsburgh: University of Pittsburgh Press, 1963); Kermit C. Parsons, "Collaborative Genius: The Regional Planning Association of America," *Journal of the American Planning Association* 60, no. 4 (1994): 462–482; William Fulton, "The Garden Suburb"; Eugenie Birch, "Radburn and the American Planning Movement: The Persistence of an Idea," *Journal of the American Planning Association* 46, no. 4 (1980): 424–439; John Friedmann and Clyde Weaver, *Territory and Function: The Evolution of Regional Planning* (Berkeley: University of California Press, 1979); Walter Creese, *The Search for Environment: The Garden City Before and After* (1966; reprint Baltimore: Johns Hopkins University Press, 1992); Emily Talen, *New Urbanism and American Planning: The Conflict of Cultures* (New York: Routledge Taylor and Francis Group, 2010).

3. William Alexander Harvey, *The Model Village and Its Cottages: Bournville* (London: B. T. Batsford, 1906), 9. In 1879, the Cadbury brothers had relocated their factory and built a total of twenty-four cottages for workers at what became Bournville. In 1895, George Cadbury began construction of the model village, and five years later, he turned it over to a trust to manage. Harvey was chief architect of Bournville Village from early 1896 until 1904, and even afterward he worked as consultant not just designing the workingman's cottages but also public buildings and planning the site, earning him a reputation as a "pioneer of Garden City architecture." Quote from Michael Harrison, "William Alexander Harvey (1874–1951): Bournville and After," IPHS conference paper, Catalonia, Spain, July 14–17, 2004, 2.

4. Schaffer, *Garden Cities for America*.

5. John L. Recchiuti, *Civic Engagement: Social Science and Progressive-Era Reform in New York City* (Philadelphia: University of Pennsylvania Press, 2007). Walter I. Willis as quoted in Richard

Plunz, *A History of Housing in New York City* (New York: Columbia University Press, 1990), 120. Frederick Law Olmsted Jr. as quoted in Plunz, *A History of Housing*, 118. Perry worked for the Sage Foundation from 1909 to 1937. Perry considered the school a broader civic and recreational center in his 1910 publication *Wider Use of the School Plant* and moved into Forest Hills Gardens afterward in 1912. Still, he attributed his broadening ideas of the neighborhood and its physical manifestation to Olmsted Jr.'s plan for the community. For more on this topic see especially Gillette, *Civitas by Design*; Talen, *New Urbanism and American Planning*; and Schaffer, *Garden Cities for America*.

6. The precursor organization, the City Reform Club of New York, had significant support of wealthy New Yorkers who financed the good government movement to battle Tammany Hall. These included J. P. Morgan, John Jacob Astor, and Cornelius Vanderbilt. By the turn of the century, membership in the successor City Club had reached ten thousand. See Recchiuti, *Civic Engagement*.

7. Raymond Unwin, *Nothing Gained By Overcrowding!* (Letchworth, UK: Garden City Press, 1912).

8. See Mel Scott, *American City Planning Since 1890* (1969; reprint Chicago: American Planning Association, 1995) for more on the RPNY. Norton served as the first chairman of the Committee on the Regional Plan. He was replaced by Frederic A. Delano, a close friend Norton met during his vice chairmanship of the Plan of Chicago. Delano had relocated to New York City and been elected a trustee of the Russell Sage Foundation's board at Norton's urging. See Harvey A. Kantor, "Charles Dyer Norton and the Origins of the Regional Plan of New York," *Journal of the American Institute of Planners* 39, no. 1 (1973): 35–44. Shortly before Norton's death, Unwin visited at Norton's invitation to discuss the establishment of garden cities "similar to Letchworth" in the metropolitan area (Norton as quoted in Scott, *American City Planning Since 1890*, 201). Once begun, the RPNY took a total of eight years and $1.2 million to complete, with the final of ten volumes being issued in 1931.

9. Whitaker served as editor of the journal from its inception in 1913 through 1928.

10. For more on Ackerman see Michael H. Lang, "Town Planning and Radicalism in the Progressive Era: The Legacy of F. L. Ackerman," *Planning Perspectives* 16, no. 2 (2001): 143–167; and Paul Emmons, "Diagrammatic Practices: The Office of Frederick L. Ackerman and 'Architectural Graphic Standards,'" *Journal of the Society of Architectural Historians* 64, no. 1 (2005): 4–21.

11. Benton MacKaye, "Regional Planning and Ecology," *Ecological Monographs* 10, no. 3 (1940): 349–353, 349.

12. Clarence Perry, "The Neighborhood Unit: A Scheme of Arrangement for the Family-Life Community," in *Neighborhood and Community Planning* (New York: Russell Sage Foundation, 1929). Gillette, *Civitas by Design*; Christopher Silver, "Neighborhood Planning in Historical Perspective," *Journal of the American Planning Association* 51, no. 2 (1985): 161–174.

13. Stein served as chair of the Committee on Community Planning of the American Institute of Architects (AIA) beginning in 1921, and as editor of this regular section of the *JAIA* until 1925 when Wright assumed the chairmanship.

14. See Robert Fishman, "The Metropolitan Tradition"; and John L. Thomas, "Holding the Middle Ground," in Fishman, *The American Planning Tradition*, 32–63, for more on the historical aspects of regionalism. C. S. Stein, "AIA Committee on Community Planning Outline 1924" (unpublished manuscript, September 9, 1962), Box 1, CSP/CUL.

15. Commission of Housing and Regional Planning, *Report to Governor Alfred E. Smith* (May 7, 1926). C. S. Stein, "Opening Address" (New York State Conference of Regional and City

Planning, Buffalo, NY, June 9, 1924), Box 1, CSP/CUL. International Federation for Housing and Town Planning Congress, ed., *Planning Problems of Town, City and Region: Papers and Discussions at the International City and Regional Planning Conference Held in New York City, April 20 to 25, 1925* (Baltimore, MD: Norman, Remington, 1925).

16. C. S. Stein, "A Plan for the State of New York," in International Federation ed., *Planning Problems*, 282–286. Thomas Adams, "The New York Regional Plan—The Making of the Plan" in International Federation ed., *Planning Problems*: 212–233, 212.

17. Lewis Mumford, "The Plan of New York," in *Planning the Fourth Migration*, ed. Sussman, 224–259.

18. Lewis Mumford, "Regions to Live In," *Survey Graphic* 54, no. 3 (1925): 151–152, 151. Howard to Stein, 7 May 1925, CSP/CUL.

19. See Friedmann and Weaver, *Territory and Function*, for more on this comparison between the RPAA and the Southern Regionalists. The authors further argue that those in the RPAA tended to have an elitist perspective that failed to fully consider the plight of the poor while this was a central concern of the Southern Regionalists.

20. Lewis Mumford, "Approved Script" (unpublished manuscript, n.d.), 12 and 19, Box 7, CSP/CUL. Howard Gillette, Jr. "Film as Artifact: *The City* (1939)," *American Studies* (fall 1977): 71–85, 80.

21. Kohn to Stein, 23 August 1948, Box 8, CSP/CUL. "RDCA By-Laws," 1 April 1949, adopted 7 April 1949, Box 8, CSP/CUL.

## 2. Early Years and Architectural Training

1. "Leo Stein, 88, Dies," *New York Times*, March 28, 1939. By 1898, the National Casket Company was "the largest concern in the casket-manufacturing business" in the country, having acquired factories in Baltimore, Boston, Philadelphia, and Albany and with offices in most major metropolitan areas ("A Coffin Trust Forming," *New York Times*, September 28, 1898).

2. "Leo Stein, 88, Dies." Adler's family had come to New York City from Germany in 1857. His father, Samuel Adler, became rabbi of Temple Emanu-El and quickly gained a national reputation within the Jewish community. See Marc D. Angel and Jeffrey Gurock, "Jews," in *The Encyclopedia of New York City*, ed. Kenneth Jackson (New Haven: Yale University Press, 1995), 620–623. See Ethical Culture Society, "The Workingman's School and Free Kindergarten" (n.p., 1881). Adler was concerned with more than the instruction of working-class children. Considered among the most progressive leaders of New York City's housing reform movement, Adler applied pressure throughout the late nineteenth and early twentieth centuries to improve housing conditions and ultimately hoped to force the government to intervene in a private market system that he deemed had failed the "laboring classes." Howard B. Radest, *Toward Common Ground: The Story of the Ethical Societies in the United States* (Garden City, NY: Fieldston Press, 1969), 208–209.

3. K. C. Parsons, "Growing Up in New York and Paris: Clarence Stein's Urban Roots and Values," Paper presented at the Eighth Biennial Conference of the Society for American City and Regional Planning History, Washington, DC, November 1–4, 1999.

4. The Workingman's School became the Ethical Culture School in 1895. It moved into a new building at Central Park West in 1904. Clarence and Herbert Stein, "The Dispatch," 1, no. 5 (unpublished manuscript, August 28, 1899), Box 27, CSP/CUL.

5. Samuel Stein died on October 8, 1901. See C. S. Stein, "Family History" (unpublished notes, n.d.), Box 1, CSP/CUL.

6. Though Morris had died in 1896, his influence endured, and the company he founded remained fashionable and profitable until 1914.

7. John Elliott to his mother Betsy, 9 and 15 October 1900, Special Collections, Millbank Memorial Library, Teachers' College, Columbia University. Parsons, "Growing Up."

8. "Leo Stein, 88, Dies," *New York Times*, March 28, 1939. Leo Stein held this position until his retirement in 1937. Of the brothers, Herbert alone stayed with the company, becoming an assistant to the company president in Boston and later first vice president. See C. S. Stein, undated notes, Box 1, CSP/CUL.

9. C. S. Stein, undated notes on 1903 trip to Europe, Box 27, CSP/CUL.

10. "Rules for Government of the Young Men's Municipal Club" (unpublished notes, March 1904), Box 27, CSP/CUL. C. S. Stein, "Suggestions of Subjects to be discussed by the Y.M.M.C," (unpublished notes, April 10, 1905), Box 27, CSP/CUL. See Gregory F. Gilmartin, *Shaping the City: New York and the Municipal Art Society* (New York: Clarkson Potter, 1995) for a detailed history of the society focused especially on its early years.

11. Stein to his mother, 3 July 1904, CSP/CUL.

12. Richard Chafee, "The Teaching of Architecture at the École des Beaux-Arts," in *The Architecture of the École des Beaux-Arts*, ed. Arthur Drexler (New York: The Museum of Modern Art, 1977), 61–109. See also Isabelle Gournay and Elliott Pavlos, "Americans in Paris," *Journal of Architectural Education* 38, no. 4 (1985): 22–26.

13. Portions of this section are adapted from Larsen, "Clarence Stein's Formative Experiences."

14. Stein to his parents, 14 July 1905, Box 29, CSP/CUL.

15. Stein to his parents, 23–25 July 1905, Box 29, CSP/CUL.

16. Anthony Sutcliffe, *Paris: An Architectural History* (New Haven: Yale University Press, 1993).

17. Stein to his parents, 4 July 1905; Stein to his parents, 13 February 1908, Box 29, CSP/CUL.

18. Stein to his father, 5 February 1906, Box 29, CSP/CUL.

19. Robert A. M. Stern, "PSFS: Beaux-Arts Theory and Rational Expressionism," *Journal of the Society of Architectural Historians* 21, no. 2 (1962): 84–102, 85.

20. In addition to "a letter of introduction from a known artist," probably Kohn, Stein also needed certification that he did not exceed the age of thirty years (Chafee, "The Teaching of Architecture," 82). Chafee, "The Teaching of Architecture," 97.

21. Paul Cret refers to the École as primarily "a self-governing body of students," a characteristic he refers to as a "liberalism . . . favorable to the flowering of personalities so necessary in art education." See Paul Cret, "The École des Beaux-Arts and Architectural Education," *Journal of the American Society of Architectural Historians* 1, no. 2 (1941): 3–15, 14.

22. Stein to his parents, 23–25 July 1905; Stein to his father, 4 August 1905, Box 29, CSP/CUL. According to Chafee, "The Teaching of Architecture," most aspirants did not pass the exams on their first try. Stein moved into the hotel shortly after arriving and lived in the apartment from 1906 to 1911. Of his living conditions, he stated, "No water, no gas, but this is not New York. This is Paris. Paris at the Latin Quarter is the place to live if you want to appreciate the conveniences of home." See Stein to his parents, 10 April 1906; Stein to his parents, 17 October 1905, Box 29, CSP/CUL.

23. Stein to his father, 15 December 1905, Box 29, CSP/CUL. Stein's assessment of the school's focus is reinforced by others. As former student Jean Paul Carlhian notes, "The École . . . concerned itself with the shaping and training of minds: it aspired to teach future architects how to think, architecturally; and by introducing them to a carefully devised multiplicity of exercises

exposed them, time and again, to the exercise of judgment." See Jean P. Carlhian, "The École des Beaux-Arts: Modes and Manners," *Journal of Architectural Education* 33, no. 2 (1979): 7–17, 17. Stein to his father, 5 February 1906, Box 29, CSP/CUL.

24. Stein to his parents, 30 January 1906, Box 29, CSP/CUL.

25. Shortly after Klaber's arrival in March 1906, the two friends rented the room at 22 rue Jacob. Klaber worked in New York and occasionally collaborated with Stein on civic projects from 1912 until the late 1920s, after which he joined Ernest Gruensfeldt's architectural firm in Chicago. His book *Housing Design* (1954) reflected several decades of experience in federal housing agencies.

26. Stein to his father, 23 June 1906; Stein to his parents, 8 July 1906; Stein to his parents, 19 September 1906, Box 29, CSP/CUL.

27. Stein to his father, 23 December 1907; Stein to his parents, 12 January 1908 and 16 January 1908, Box 29, CSP/CUL. Only aspirants who passed the competitive architectural exam, the free-hand drawing, and modeling exams could advance to the exams in mathematics and history. The exams began in mid-December, and the 127 who completed them did not hear the final decision until January 5. No foreigner could score lower than any of the 45 Frenchmen that were accepted. Stein scored "just after the twenty-fifth Frenchman."

28. Stein to his parents, 6 January 1908; Rose Stein to C. S. Stein, 27 January 1908; Stein to his brother Herbert, 27 January 1908, Box 29, CSP/CUL.

29. Gournay and Pavlos, "Americans in Paris," 23. Chafee, "The Teaching of Architecture," 96. "Hommage a Laloux," *Pencil Points* 18 (October 1937): 621–630, 623. Laloux became an honorary fellow of the American Institute of Architects in 1903 and was awarded the Institute's Medal of Honor in 1921, reflecting the esteem his American students had for him.

30. Stein to his brother Herbert, 13 August 1908, Box 29, CSP/CUL.

31. Harvey, *The Model Village*, 1.

32. Stein to his parents, 3 October 1907, Box 29, CSP/CUL.

33. Stein to his parents, 13 February 1908, Box 29, CSP/CUL. See also Stein to his parents, 3 March 1908, Box 29, CSP/CUL; Chaffee, "The Teaching of Architecture;" and Gournay and Pavlos "Americans in Paris."

34. Kohn to Stein, 1 December 1908, Box 29, CSP/CUL. In the school year 1909–1910, a design he did of a plan and elevation of Un Abri Pour Les Voyageurs en Algerie "received first mention for Les Concours D'Architecture de L'Annee Scolaire." See Anne Boyer Cotten, "Clarence S. Stein and his Commitment to Beauty: Architect First, Community Planner Second" (Master's thesis, Cornell University, 1987), 55–56. Gournay and Pavlos, "Americans in Paris," note that many Americans did indeed enter the first, or *premier classe*, and devoted an additional two years to earn the *diplôme*. Regardless, after two years in the École, students were considered anciens. See Stein to his parents, 10 March 1908, Box 29, CSP/CUL.

35. Stein to his brother Herbert, 24 February 1906, Box 29, CSP/CUL.

36. While it is not clear where Kahn initially worked on returning to the United States, he, unlike Stein, earned the Architecte Diplome par le Gonvernement Francais and the Prix Labarre in his final year at the École. By 1915, he was a professor of design at Cornell University. He also taught at New York University, and by the 1920s was designing office buildings on Park Avenue and Fifth Avenue in New York City. See Ely Jacques Kahn, *Ely Jacques Kahn* (New York: McGraw-Hill, 1931).

37. Richard Oliver, *Bertram Grosvenor Goodhue* (Cambridge, MA: MIT Press, 1983), 54. The third partner in the firm, the engineer Frank Ferguson, divided his time between Cram's Boston office and Goodhue's New York office. The partnership formally dissolved in 1913. For more on

Ralph Adams Cram, see Douglass Shand-Tucci, especially *Ralph Adams Cram: An Architect's Four Quests—Medieval, Modernist, American, Ecumenical*, the second volume in his two-volume biography on Cram in which he continues the theme of Cram's homosexual relationship with Goodhue, thus adding another layer of understanding to the dissolution of their partnership. Portions of this section are adapted from Larsen, "Clarence Stein's Formative Experiences."

38. Goodhue traveled extensively in Mexico in 1892 and 1899, gaining an appreciation and understanding of Spanish-American architecture that he described in *Mexican Memories*, written on his return from the first trip. In 1902 he published *Spanish Colonial Architecture in Mexico*. For more on the fair, including distinctions between the plans and the political jockeying and decision to award the contract for the fair to Goodhue, see Christine Edstrom O'Hara, "The Panama-California Exposition, San Diego, 1915: The Olmsted Brothers' Ecological Park Typology," *Journal of the Society of Architectural Historians* 70, no. 1 (2011): 64–81. She notes that the Olmsted brothers had not traveled in Spain, so they lacked Goodhue's direct experience with the forms and particularly the ornamentation. Oliver, *Bertram Grosvenor Goodhue*.

39. Goodhue did not necessarily oppose classicism itself, but its strict formulaic application. A 1922 article in *Pencil Points* described his disparaging opinion of the École through his comments about a recent hire. "Mr. —— went to the Beaux-Arts. *I hate to admit it, but he did.* But he didn't *graduate.* I have always maintained that the truants and bad boys of the Beaux-Arts turn out to be the best product of that—so far as I am concerned—lamentable institution." In "Twelfth Night in Mr. Goodhue's Office," *Pencil Points* 3 (January 1922): 21–26, 22.

In 1884, when he was 15 years old, Goodhue began his training in the office of Renwick, Aspinwall & Russell. At the time, James Renwick still ran the firm. Renwick had a strong understanding of historical styles, artfully adapting and applying them in projects such as the Smithsonian Institution (1846–1855) and Grace Church (1843–1846).

40. "Twelfth Night in Mr. Goodhue's Office," 22. Goodhue admitted, "Only occasionally ... has it been possible to put the names of the men actually engaged on a given piece of work thereto" ("Twelfth Night," 22).

41. Stein's work on the California Building is evident in detailed drawings of the Churrigueresque sculptural ornament around the main entrance and the tower windows. Stein also designed the reredos in the adjacent chapel. According to his records, Stein devoted just over two hundred hours to work on the reredos. Upon Goodhue's death in 1924, Hardie Phillip became a partner in the successor firm of Mayers, Murray & Phillip.

42. Oliver, *Bertram Grosvenor Goodhue*. The buildings were all designed in the Spanish Colonial style with pearl gray stucco used consistently on the temporary structures.

43. Bertram Grosvenor Goodhue, "The Architecture and the Gardens," in *The Architecture and the Gardens of the San Diego Exposition*, ed. Carleton Monroe Winslow (San Francisco: Paul Elder, 1916), 3–9, 3. Ibid, 4.

44. C. S. Stein, "A Triumph of the Spanish-Colonial Style" in *The Architecture and the Gardens*, ed. Winslow, 10–18, 11. Carleton Winslow, Goodhue's site architect in charge of the temporary buildings, edited the book and provided the brief descriptions that accompanied the numerous photographs.

45. Oliver, *Bertram Grosvenor Goodhue*. Other projects that preceded or coincided with the design of Tyrone and attested to the variety of applications Goodhue made of the Hispanic-inspired designs included the Dater house in Montecito, California; the George Washington Hotel in Panama; and the Santa Barbara Country Club. Although there is some speculation that Stein may have been involved with these projects (Cotten, "Clarence S. Stein"; and K. C. Parsons, "C. S. Stein's Apprenticeship with Bertram Grosvenor Goodhue: The Mining Town of Tyrone,

New Mexico 1915–1919" (paper presented at the Seventh Biennial Conference of the Society for American City and Regional Planning History, Seattle, WA, October 24, 1997), no evidence exists of his participation beyond the visits he made to the California projects in 1916.

Stein also lists Goodhue's St. Bartholomew Church in New York City on his resume. Goodhue had begun the design in late 1914, just as work on the Panama-California Exposition was being completed and work in Tyrone had commenced. Although there is some conjecture that Stein contributed to St. Bartholomew, there is no proof that he did so in a significant way. These other major projects probably negated him spending any considerable time on the design of the church. During the spring and summer of 1914, Stein also worked on projects for other architects including drawings of two churches in Montreal for two separate firms and drawings of a dormitory at the University of Michigan for the New York City firm of York and Sawyer.

46. Oliver, *Bertram Grosvenor Goodhue*; Margaret Crawford, *Building the Workingman's Paradise, the Design of American Company Towns* (London: Verso, 1995).

47. For more on the establishment of the town, see Sidney Paige, "Early History of Tyrone," (unpublished manuscript, 1922), Phelps-Dodge Company Records of Burro Mountain Copper Company, Main Office: Tucson, Arizona, Phelps-Dodge Records, Tucson, Arizona (PDR/TA); "Start Next Month to Build Railroad," *Silver City Independent*, May 20, 1913; Michael Jenkinson, "Tyrone: The Creation of a Model Ghost Town," *American West* 5, no. 2 (1968): 39–42, 78–79; and Leifur Magnusson, "A Modern Copper Mining Town," *Monthly Labor Review* 7, no. 2 (1918): 278–284. Crawford, *Building the Workingman's Paradise*, provides information on what made New Mexico more attractive to mining companies.

48. Walter Douglas to Dr. James Douglas, 15 July 1915, PDR/TA.

49. Ibid. Goodhue to Mayers, 14 July 1915, PDR/TA. Hardie Phillip also worked on this project.

50. Werner Hegemann and Elbert Peets, *The American Vitruvius: An Architect's Handbook of Civic Art* (1922; reprint New York: Princeton Architectural Press, 1988), 107.

51. Robert B. Riley, "Gone Forever: Goodhue's Beaux Arts Ghost Town," *AIA Journal* 50, no. 2 (1968): 67–70, 69. Magnusson, "A Modern Copper Mining Town," 283.

52. The Douglases expected to make a 10 percent profit on the Mexican and American miners' houses and 15 percent profit in rents of the noncompany commercial buildings. A total of sixteen homes in duplex or single family configurations, each with three rooms, were also built for the Mexican workers. The exterior on the Mexican houses was the original gray stucco color and the floors were concrete rather than wooden. The architects requested more funding to improve the design and enlarge the layout, which the Burro Company denied. In the American workers' housing lived the "technical and office men and foremen." The homes had a variety of floor plans, indoor plumbing, and lighting, unlike the housing for Mexicans. To accommodate the topography, a two-story hillside house was introduced. Hegemann and Peets, *American Vitruvius*, 108.

53. Walter Douglas to F. M. Sawyer, Superintendent, Burro Mountain Copper Company, 21 July 1916; Thomson, Assistant to the President to Sawyer, 13 July 1916, PDR/TA. Oliver, *Bertram Grosvenor Goodhue*, refers to Stein as Goodhue's chief assistant on the project (154). A short, undated article, probably from a local paper, also names Stein the "architect in charge of the construction of the mining camp at Tyrone."

54. While working on Tyrone, Goodhue began redesigning the campus of Throop College of Technology in Pasadena consistent with a more modest adaptation of the San Diego Exposition. Along with Hardie Phillip, Stein probably contributed to the Gates Chemistry Building and the redesign of the campus. In December 1916, Goodhue presented his redesign featuring a central plaza based on universities in Spain. Goodhue's firm also worked with a preexisting design for

the Gates Chemistry Building. The successor firm of Mayers, Murray & Phillip continued work on the campus, and in 1926 Stein contributed to the design of the Chemistry Annex Building.

55. He wrote regularly to Goodhue. A set of five reports about the details of materials, color, and construction written in November 1916 is probably typical of the kind of reports Stein prepared during his site visits.

56. Magnusson, "A Modern Copper Mining Town," 282.

57. The Hudson Guild Settlement House that Elliott ran as part of the Ethical Culture Society, the Workingman's School, and the Stein family's first home when they moved back to New York City during Stein's childhood all were located in Chelsea. C. S. Stein, "City Planning" (unpublished essay, May 13, 1917), Box 11, CSP/CUL. Portions of this section are adapted from Larsen, "Clarence Stein's Formative Experiences."

58. Also sponsored by Tammany Hall, Wagner was first elected in 1905 and became Smith's roommate in Albany. Both junior politicians quickly developed a mutual respect and friendship, supporting "social legislation for the benefit of the common people" consistent with the vote-getting of Tammany but also with their concerns about constituents who faced harsh living conditions. See Matthew and Hannah Josephson, *Al Smith: Hero of the Cities* (Boston: Houghton Mifflin, 1969).

59. C. S. Stein, "A Survey of the Chelsea District," (unpublished report, September 20, 1918), Box 11, CSP/CUL. Two major projects, Pennsylvania Station and Chelsea Park had resulted in the demolition of many residential structures. More than five hundred buildings alone had been cleared to accommodate the construction of Pennsylvania Station, completed in 1910. Initial development of Chelsea Park began in 1910 to provide open space and recreation for the nearby tenement residents.

60. Goodhue obtained the two military base projects from the Bureau of Yards and Docks in 1918, and at the latest, Stein probably left the office in September of that same year. A letter from Goodhue, then in Santa Barbara, to Stein in the New York office, responded to some comments Stein had made regarding design of the air base and noted his disappointment at Stein's imminent departure at such a critical time (Goodhue to Stein, 20 August 1918, CSP/CUL).

61. C. S. Stein Commission Papers, Box 27, CSP/CUL. Stein received his discharge from Major General W. M. Black, Chief of Engineers, on November 29, 1918, Box 27, CSP/CUL.

62. Congress finally appropriated funding on March 1, 1918, to the U.S. Shipping Board's Emergency Fleet Corporation for loans to shipbuilders to construct worker housing consistent with agency standards. Established by the federal government in June, the U.S. Housing Corporation directly designed and built war worker housing. Frederick Law Olmsted Jr. directed this agency. John Nolen and Henry Hubbard were two of the noteworthy architects who designed planned communities for the federal government during the few months that the program was operational. Following the war, the federal government quickly ended the program amid concerns that it should not compete with the private housing market.

63. C. S. Stein, "Transportation or Housing," *Journal of the American Institute of Architects* 6 (July 1918), 363. Stein discussed the inadequacy of the city transit system in getting workers from Chelsea and other nearby areas to their jobs in the New Jersey shipping yards. He acknowledged that extensions of the lines into Chelsea and Greenwich would help, but housing type, condition, and location also had to be addressed before the transit solution could work. C. S. Stein, "Housing and Reconstruction," 471. As chief of Housing and Town Design for the Emergency Fleet Corporation, Ackerman was familiar with the federal program as well as the garden cities of England. Stein to Whitaker, 8 September 1918, Box 30, CSP/CUL.

## 3. A Thinkers' Network and the
## City Housing Corporation

1. According to Stein's AIA records, he considered his six years with Goodhue as "office training." In November 1919, he became a member of the New York Chapter of the American Institute of Architects, and in April 1920 Kohn nominated him for entrance into the American Institute of Architects. He was elected into membership in September 1920 without having to take the written exam under the category of Class A or B. Both classes required graduation from recognized architecture programs, including Columbia (Class A) or the École des Beaux-Arts (Class B). While Stein had attended both, he had not graduated from either.

2. Like Stein, Kohn's active participation in the society shaped his ethics and practice. Following World War I, Kohn capitalized on his leadership role in housing and design to form with Ackerman and Whitaker the Post-War Committee on Architectural Practice. They intended to examine the role between architects and their clients, affiliated professions, and even government agencies with the goal of fostering collaborations to enhance living environments for all. While their initial conference was well attended, their ambitious vision did not prevail. See Steven I. Doctors, "The Collaborative Divide: Crafting Architectural Identity, Authority, and Authorship in the Twentieth Century" (Ph.D. diss., University of California, Berkeley, 2010), https://escholarship.org/uc/item/13t043q2#page-6 for an exploration of Kohn's professional ethics and their relation to the Ethical Culture Society.

3. Portions of this section are adapted from Larsen, "Clarence Stein's Formative Experiences."

4. Matthew and Hannah Josephson, Al Smith, 191–192. Smith, a savvy politician, sought the perspectives of women leaders such as Moskowitz, Mary Kingsbury Simkhovitch, and Frances Perkins, which was particularly effective during the first statewide election where women could vote. Smith also appealed to the large Jewish population in New York City not only because of his racial and religious tolerance, but because of their common origins on the Lower East Side and his significant contributions to the Factory Investigating Commission. Moskowitz continued to advise Smith through his bid for the presidency in 1928. Perkins, a social reformer and expert in labor problems and legislation, was another key contributor to Smith's administration, ultimately rising to chair the state's Industrial Board. Later she served as the first Secretary of Labor in the Roosevelt administration. Previously, Moses worked as an aide for Fusionist New York City Mayor Mitchel. Moses also acted as chief of staff to the Committee on Retrenchment and Reorganization and in this capacity prepared the report for the Reconstruction Commission. See Cleveland Rogers, "Robert Moses, An Atlantic Portrait," Atlantic Monthly 156 (February 1939).

5. Wood had just written the pioneering The Housing of the Unskilled Wage Earner, an extremely influential contribution to housing studies and policy making that used a variety of data to document housing needs in the United States and persuasively argued for government involvement in housing production. C. S. Stein, untitled (unpublished paper, August 1920), Box 11, CSP/CUL. For background on housing issues during this period see Plunz, A History of Housing in New York City; Peter G. Rowe, Modernity and Housing (Cambridge, MA: MIT Press, 1993); Gail Radford, Modern Housing for America: Policy Struggles in the New Deal Era (Chicago: University of Chicago Press, 1996).

6. Emmons, "Diagrammatic Practices." Kristin Larsen, "The Radburn Idea as an Emergent Concept—Henry Wright's Regional City," Planning Perspectives 23, no. 3 (2008): 381–395, 394. See Lubove, Community Planning in the 1920s; Sussman, "Introduction," Planning the Fourth Migration; Plunz, A History of Housing in New York City; Rowe, Modernity and Housing. Frederick

Ackerman, "Where Goes the City-Planning Movement?" *Journal of the American Institute of Architects,* 7 (December 1919): 518–520; C. S. Stein, "The Housing Problem" (unpublished Report of the Housing Committee of the Civic Club of New York, April 15, 1921), 14.

7. Larsen, "Planning and Public-Private Partnerships," 3. The earliest national housing acts in Great Britain date back to 1890. During the first decade of the twentieth century, the country's Garden City and the housing reform movements began coordinating efforts. Great Britain's Garden City Association and the National Housing Reform Council advocated for passage of the Housing and Town Planning Act of 1909, conferring greater autonomy on local housing authorities. Catherine Bauer, *Modern Housing* (Boston: Houghton Mifflin, 1934), 262. Ibid, 283. C. S. Stein, "Amsterdam—Old and New," *Journal of the American Institute of Architects* 20 (October 1922): 310–328, 310–311. In addition, the national government targeted a significant subsidy toward rent deficits.

8. For more on limited dividend housing, see Daphne Spain, "Octavia Hill's Philosophy of Housing Reform: From British Roots to American Soil," *Journal of Planning History* 5, no. 2 (2006): 106–125; Thomas Adam, "Transatlantic Trading: The Transfer of Philanthropic Models between European and North American Cities during the Nineteenth and Early Twentieth Centuries," *Journal of Urban History* 28, no. 3 (2002): 328–351. City and Suburban Homes Company as quoted in "Limited Dividend Roll Call," *Architectural Forum* 62 (January 1935): 98–101, 99. Eugenie L. Birch and Deborah S. Gardner, "The Seven-Percent Solution: A Review of Philanthropic Housing: 1870–1910," *Journal of Urban History* 7, no. 4 (1981): 403–438, 406. These companies both rehabilitated existing housing and built new housing.

9. Edith Elmer Wood, *The Housing of the Unskilled Wage Earner: America's Next Problem* (New York: MacMillan, 1919); "Limited Dividend Roll Call." The company also built 248 houses in Brooklyn from 1898 to 1908 to help further fund its limited dividend projects.

10. *Report of the Housing Committee of the Reconstruction Commission of the State of New York,* 22 March 1920, 15, Box 1, CSP/CUL. The Housing Committee presented its recommendations to the Reconstruction Commission on March 22, 1920. The governor passed along the recommendations to the legislature four days later.

11. Paula Eldst, *Governor Alfred E. Smith: The Politician as Reformer* (New York: Garland, 1983), 160–161, 164–168. When Smith was reelected as governor, he appointed a successor committee to investigate the impact of the tax exemption law. In 1924 that committee issued a report acknowledging that the tax exemption had stimulated housing production. The committee recommended extension of the law only if "the means can be provided to insure that the benefit of tax exemption shall be enjoyed primarily by those families of limited income who are to live in the homes which this subsidy is designed to create." See *State of New York Report of Commission on Housing and Regional Planning to Governor Alfred E. Smith and to the Legislature of the State of New York on Tax Exemption of New Housing,* March 14, 1924, Legislative Document (1924) No. 78, 7.

12. Mary Kingsbury Simkhovitch, Jacob Riis, and Felix Adler founded Greenwich House in 1902. C. S. Stein, "Possibilities: Four Opinions by Housing Experts II," *Women and the City's Work* 6, no. 4 (1920): 4–6, 6. Stein as quoted in Louis Levine, "To Solve the Housing Problem, This Expert Says, the State Should Have Power to Hold Land and Develop It for Homes," *Sunday World,* June 20, 1921.

13. Whitaker had strongly supported the World War I federal housing programs, sending Ackerman to Great Britain in 1917 to assess and report on that country's housing initiatives. He closely followed Stein's work with the New York State Housing Committee and relocated the *JAIA*'s editorial offices from Washington, DC, to New York City in 1920.

14. See Radest, *Toward Common Ground*. The camp was located on Hopatcong Lake. Just forty miles west of New York City, the town of Hopatcong and surrounding areas had served as a resort for wealthy city residents who wished to escape to the nearby countryside.

15. MacKaye began working for the newly created U.S. Forest Service in 1905. His first major assignment was a survey of the White Mountains prior to the federal government's purchase of the property. His next major project involved assessing cut-over timberlands in the Midwest and Northwest for the establishment of colonies—the "Lumberjack Utopias" he referred to. He transferred to the Labor Department in 1917 when the Forest Service could not accommodate his desire to expand his work on the colonies.

16. See Anderson, *Benton MacKaye*, for more on MacKaye's formulation of the Appalachian Trail and his initial meeting with Stein. Benton MacKaye, "An Appalachian Trail: A Project in Regional Planning," *Journal of the American Institute of Architects* 19 (October 1921): 325–330, 327.

17. See K. C. Parsons, "Benton MacKaye's Collaboration with the Regional Planning Association of America: Its Influence on the Appalachian Trail and Regional Planning (1921–1931)" (lecture, One-Day Public Conference on Benton MacKaye and the Appalachian Trail 75th Anniversary Celebration of Vision, Planning, and Grass-Roots Mobilization, in Albany, NY, October 24, 1996), for an examination of MacKaye's work on the Appalachian Trail. MacKaye to Stein, December 1921, Benton MacKaye Papers Special Collections, Dartmouth College Library (BMP/DCL).

18. Lewis Mumford, *Sketches From Life: The Autobiography of Lewis Mumford* (Boston: Beacon Press, 1982). Donald Miller, *Lewis Mumford: A Life* (Pittsburgh: University of Pittsburgh Press, 1989), 53.

19. Gertrude introduced them in 1919 when MacMahon worked for Stein's sister at the Hudson Guild Settlement House. MacMahon came from an upper-middle-income Jewish family very much like the Steins—her father had formerly been a broker and lost a considerable amount of money during the 1907 panic. He managed to fall back on his love of writing, ultimately securing the position of editor-in-chief of *Munsey's Magazine*. Mumford, *Sketches From Life*, 348.

20. Edith Elmer Wood, "The International Conference—London," *Journal of the American Institute of Architects* 20 (May 1922): 165. In her article, Wood also addressed the 1921 amendments to the British Housing Act to permit government loans for developing Garden Cities

21. C. S. Stein, undated handwritten notes circa 1922 on United American Lines, Inc. stationary, Box 1, CSP/CUL.

22. Stein to MacKaye, 2 December 1922, BMP/DCL.

23. Stein maintained the commission's responsibilities included recommendations on housing assistance, policy, public education about these programs, and a plan for state growth. Other members of the commission were State Architect Sullivan W. Jones, Industrial Commissioner Bernard L. Shientage, and Highway Commissioner Arthur Brandt. Lay members included Oliver Cabana Jr. of Buffalo; Peter D. Kiernan of Albany; and Mrs. Sara Conboy of New York who was international secretary-treasurer of the United Textile Workers of America. See K. C. Parsons, "Clarence Stein's 1919–1928 Contributions to New York State and National Housing Reform" (lecture, Annual Conference of the Association of Collegiate Schools of Planning, Pasadena, CA, November 1998). The legal opinion of Julius Cohen to Clarence Stein dated February 18, 1926 (New York State Archives) details the case law in support of the State Housing Bank.

24. C. S. Stein, "Proposed Garden City and Regional Planning Association" (unpublished notes, March 7, 1923), Box 8, CSP/CUL. These notes from the meeting allowed Stein to document and circulate the group's perspective as they were developing the organization's mission.

25. RPAA, Minutes (unpublished, April 18, 1923), Box 8, CSP/CUL. By that summer, the

number of members had increased to sixteen and included Edith Elmer Wood and Robert Bruere, associate editor of *Survey* magazine.

26. Mumford, *Sketches from Life*, 342. Geddes is not listed as an attendee at their first meeting in April. He did attend the subsequent meeting on May 19 at the Hudson Guild Farm. See "Memo from the Program Committee" (unpublished, June 12, 1923), Box 8, CSP/CUL. Stein had previously provided financial support to MacKaye for his work on the Appalachian Trail; the RPAA at their July 13 meeting formalized their support, voting to pay MacKaye a thousand dollars from their small treasury. His book eventually evolved into a much broader study of the relationships between metropolitan growth and wilderness open space. It was not published until 1928. The three RPAA members began to formulate their ideas about developing a Garden City in their "Memo from the Program Committee" (unpublished, June 12, 1923), Box 8, CSP/ CUL; and RPAA, "Notes" (unpublished, September 5, 1923), Box 8, CSP/CUL.

27. Alexander Bing, Henry Wright, and C. S. Stein, "Preliminary Study of a Proposed Garden City in the New York Region" (unpublished manuscript, 1923), 1, 4, Box 5, CSP/CUL. Thomas Adams to Colonel Arthur Woods, 7 June 1924, Box 10, Housing Interest Series, Record Group 2, Rockefeller Family Archives (RFA). K. C. Parsons, "Financing Affordable Housing in the 1990s: Lessons from Alexander Bing's Innovations at Sunnyside and Radburn in the 1920s" (lecture, Annual Conference of the Association of Collegiate Schools of Planning, Phoenix, AZ, November 6, 1994).

28. Bing, Wright, Stein, "Preliminary Study of a Proposed Garden City," 6. Parsons, "Financing Affordable Housing in the 1990s."

29. Herbert Hoover to Col. Arthur Woods, 14 November 1923, RFA. Hoover appointed Bing to the Home Finance Committee in 1932 as part of the President's Conference on Home Building and Home Ownership to offer recommendations on the failing home loan industry during the throes of the Depression. Richard T. Ely to Colonel Arthur Woods, 15 January 1924, RFA. In a subsequent letter later that month, Ely was not so encouraging. The annual report, submitted on May 21, 1925, before Rockefeller's purchase of shares, stated that total investment to date equaled $846,000 with 150 stockholders. Other major investors included Eleanor Roosevelt, Felix Warburg, and Ogden Mills.

30. The Bliss Street Station was located only steps from the southernmost Sunnyside Gardens property. Opened in April 1917, it accommodated three rapid transit lines: the Interboro Subway, B.M.T. Subway, and Second Avenue "L". The subway ride to Times Square at the time took about twenty minutes. New York City Subway, 46th Street/Bliss Street (IRT Flushing Line), http:// www.nycsubway.org/perl/stations?195:271, accessed June 15, 2012. See also "Sunnyside Gardens: A Home Community" (n.p., circa 1928/29), Box 1, CSP/CUL.

31. "First Annual Report to the Stockholders of the City Housing Corporation" (unpublished report, May 21, 1925), Box 10, RFA. As outlined in a community promotional brochure, "To secure capital at minimum rates a limited dividend corporation was formed. No public capital is available, the law having made no provision in this direction. It was desired to make the experiment self-sustaining, so that it might be expanded indefinitely. It was expected to attract the investment from persons interested in good housing, but unwilling or unable to give their capital without hope of return" ("Sunnyside and the Housing Problem," [n.p., circa 1925/26], 6, Box 1, CSP/CUL); "Sunnyside and the Housing Problem," 3.

32. "Sunnyside and the Housing Problem," 20–21. "Sunnyside Development of the City Housing Corporation" (unpublished report, circa February 1928), 10, RFA. The CHC projected that when the project was completed, the total of 1,192 families would consist of 51 percent owners and 49 percent tenants in houses and apartments with some owners of two-family houses renting

out the second unit. According to the CHC, the average wage of a homeowner was just under two hundred per month, but that ranged from as little as $125 up to $800 per month, with the latter likely reflecting multiple wage earners in the household.

33. "First Annual Report to the Stockholders of the City Housing Corporation," n.p. "Sunnyside and the Housing Problem," 7. C. S. Stein, *Toward New Towns*, 28. Parsons, "Financing Affordable Housing in the 1990s," 8. "First Annual Report to the Stockholders of the City Housing Corporation." Though innovative for its time, the resale restriction period lasted only three years with a thousand dollar penalty imposed during this time if the agreement was violated.

34. "First Annual Report to the Stockholders of the City Housing Corporation." In addition to the Board of Directors, CHC had an advisory board of experts, including state architect Sullivan Jones, Ackerman, Adams, Thomas, and Simkhovitch.

35. "Sunnyside Development of the City Housing Corporation," 4; ibid., 5. Kohn and Ackerman both purchased $5,000 of bonds; Hoover $10,000, and the Russell Sage Foundation $100,000. The CHC was also authorized to issue $5,000,000 in stock to finance the project. Among the purchasers were Ackerman and the Ethical Culture Society at $5,000 each; Robert Kohn and Stein's father Leo Stein at $10,000 each; Stein himself at $14,000; John D. Rockefeller Jr. and Leo Bing at $150,000 each; and Alexander Bing at $275,000.

36. Notes on a February 6, 1924 conversation with Alexander Bing, probably written by Colonel Woods, Box 10, RFA.

37. *Message from the Governor Transmitting Report of the Commission of Housing and Regional Planning for Permanent Housing Relief*, No. 66 (1926), 32, Box 1, CSP/CUL. Regarding the powers of the State Housing Bank, see Julius Cohen to C. S. Stein, 18 February 1926; *Report of Commission of Housing and Regional Planning to Governor Alfred E. Smith and the Legislature of the State of New York*, Appendix B (February 18, 1926), Box 1, CSP/CUL. *Message from the Governor Transmitting Report of the Commission of Housing and Regional Planning for Permanent Housing Relief*, No. 66 (1926), 51, Box 1, CSP/CUL.

38. New York State Board of Housing, *Preliminary Report of the State Board of Housing to Governor Alfred E. Smith* (December 15, 1926), Box 5, CSP/CUL. The limited dividend corporations had to cover at least one-third of the project costs by issuing stock and could raise the remaining two-thirds by issuing mortgage bonds. Rent restrictions were also specified. The law required the State Board of Housing to approve the limited dividend corporation, which was required to manage any assisted property for a minimum of fifty years. "Governor Seeks Housing Agreement," *New York Times*, April 2, 1926.

39. Commission of Housing and Regional Planning, *Report to Governor Alfred E. Smith* (May 7, 1926), 12. The letter from Stein conveying the report to Governor Smith specifically lists the contributions of MacKaye in conducting "certain preliminary studies" and of Wright who prepared "all of the charts and diagrams" in his capacity as planning adviser to the HRPC. While Sussman (*Planning the Fourth Migration*) in his introductory notes to the excerpt from the plan in his book mentions Mumford conducting studies for the HRPC, Stein's 1926 letter of conveyance does not mention Mumford.

40. Mumford to MacKaye, 18 December 1924, BMP/DCL.

41. C. S. Stein, "Shall We Scrap the Slums?" (lecture, Community Church, New York City, January 22, 1925), 3, Box 6, CSP/CUL.

42. Shortly thereafter the organization was renamed the International Federation for Housing and Town Planning. In total, the region consisted of 282 cities and 144 unincorporated areas. For a history of the plan see David A. Johnson, *Planning the Great Metropolis: The 1929*

*Regional Plan of New York and Its Environs* (New York: Taylor and Francis, 1996). Adams, "The New York Regional Plan," 215.

43. C. Stein, "A Plan for the State of New York," 286. The National Conference on City Planning was also occurring in New York City at this time. An exhibit at this conference, the subject of a *New York Times* article on April 19, featured Wright, MacKaye, and Stein's proposal for a state plan. Alfred Bettman, "How to Lay Out Regions for Planning," in International Federation ed., *Planning Problems*: 287–301, 293.

44. RPAA, Minutes (unpublished, February 5, 1925), Box 8 CSP/CUL.

45. In 1976 with publication of *Planning the Fourth Migration,* Sussman made these scarce documents available to a wide audience and included, by way of an introduction, an extended evaluation of the nature and significance of the RPAA's work.

46. Mumford to Stein, 18 May 1925, Box 8 CSP/CUL.

47. Ibid. Mumford to MacKaye, 22 December 1926, BMP/DCL.

48. In a "Comparative Balance Sheet" for the office, Stein shows commissions of $11,208, $9,962, and $9,690 for the years 1920, 1921, and 1922 respectively with an increase to $73,336 in 1928 and to $83,046 in 1929. His own salary during these years increased from $4,497 (1920), $4,481 (1921), and $6,256 (1922) to $24,763 (1928) and $28,948 (1929), Box 7, CSP/CUL.

49. C. S. Stein, "Address of Clarence Stein," *American Institute of Architects, Journal of Proceedings* (1925): 30–32, 31, Box 6, CSP/CUL.

50. Stein to MacKaye, 1 February 1926, BMP/DCL.

51. Henry Wright, "Institute Business," *Journal of the American Institute of Architects* 14 (November 1926): 499–500, 500.

52. Stein to MacKaye, 6 May 1927, BMP/DCL; Stein to MacKaye, 3 August 1927, CSP/CUL.

53. Mumford to MacKaye, 12 March 1927, BMP/DCL; Benton MacKaye, *The New Exploration: A Philosophy of Regional Planning* (Harpers Ferry, WV: Appalachian Trail Conference and Urbana-Champaign: The University of Illinois Press, 1928), xxv; MacKaye, *New Exploration*, 30.

54. Mumford to MacKaye, 26 July 1927, BMP/DCL; MacKaye, *New Exploration*, 167; Benton MacKaye, "The RPAA Era, A Reminiscence" (unpublished manuscript, circa 1968), Box 9, CSP/CUL. See also Anderson, *Benton MacKaye,* for more on the development and publication of *New Exploration* as well as MacKaye's conception of the townless highway.

55. Stein to MacKaye, 22 September 1926, BMP/DCL.

56. Schaffer, *Garden Cities for America.* According to the April 13, 1927 minutes of the RPAA, Bing reported that the search was underway (Box 8, CSP/CUL). By January 18, 1928, a tract totaling a thousand acres had been assembled (Bing to Charles Heydt, 18 January 1928, Box 10, Series J, Record Group 2, RFA).

57. Scott, *American City Planning Since 1890;* and K. C. Parsons, ed., *The Writings of Clarence Stein* (Baltimore: Johns Hopkins University Press, 1998). See also Louis Brownlow's autobiography for a discussion of his national prominence in community organization and administration—Louis Brownlow, *A Passion for Anonymity: The Autobiography of Louis Brownlow, Second Half* (Chicago: The University of Chicago Press, 1958).

58. "Summary of Discussions of Problems Connected with a Garden City, at a Series of Conferences of the Regional Planning Association of America at the Hudson Guild Farm, October 8 and 9, 1927" (unpublished minutes, October 8 and 9, 1927), 1, Box 180, LMP/UPA. The experts they consulted included Richard T. Ely, Harold Buttenheim, Flavel Shurtleff, Thomas Adams, Elliott and Adler, Sullivan Jones, Lawson Purdy, John Nolen, Moskowitz, Simkhovitch, and Wood. MacKaye did not attend the meeting, choosing instead to devote time to his book.

59. "Summary of Discussions of Problems Connected with a Garden City," 2–3.

60. Ibid., 6. Schaffer, *Garden Cities for America*, 177. A 1934 survey found a number of Jews living in the community, but no blacks at that time. In fact, many new developments included restrictive covenants dictating that only white Protestants could live in the community until the 1948 Supreme Court decision in *Shelley v. Kraemer* (334 U.S. 1, 68 S. Ct. 836, 92 L. Ed. 1161, 1948) struck them down.

61. See Christopher Silver, "Neighborhood Planning in Historical Perspective," *Journal of the American Planning Association* 51, no. 2 (1985): 161–174.

62. Robert B. Hudson, *Radburn: A Plan of Living* (New York: American Association for Adult Education, 1934), 12. Over thirty years later, this was still the case. "Radburn never acquired factories or the people who work in them, and its original white-collar character has been, if anything, bleached rather than blued by the years" ("Radburn," *New Jersey Builder* 9, no. 7 [November 1965]: 1–6, 4).

63. "Sunnyside Development of the City Housing Corporation." In this report, the CHC maintained that as of January 1, 1928, over 63 percent of the profit on Sunnyside (or $210,107) was due to sale of this surplus land. Later in his *Toward New Towns for America*, Stein documents a profit "of over $646,000" on the 20 ¾ surplus acres at Sunnyside (37). It is possible that additional property was sold at Sunnyside to further finance the project following issue of the 1928 report.

64. Bing to Dr. Beardsley Ruml, 28 February 1929, Box 10, Record Group 2, RFA. As Bing noted in a letter to Rockefeller on July 20, 1928, when the first phase of Radburn was underway, "The support that you have given us during the last four years has been a most important factor in whatever success the company has achieved" (Box 11, J Series, Record Group 2, RFA). In 1925, Rockefeller had made a stock subscription to the company, and in 1927, his subscription supported the issue of the second mortgage bond issue, which allowed the CHC to purchase the property at Radburn. Then in 1928, the financier provided a loan to make it possible for the building program at Radburn to continue moving forward. The amount, $3,420,000, equaled 40 percent of the total projected investment in the project at the time. Still, Rockefeller committed to the loan on the condition that it be provided as a series of payments over the next four years and that each payment be matched by equal subscriptions from others. In May 1932, these amounts equaled 1,500 shares of stock for Sunnyside purchased at $150,000 and an advance to date of $2,250,000 for development at Radburn (C. Heydt to J. D. Rockefeller, Jr., 10 May 1932, Box 11, J Series, Record Group 2, RFA).

65. Bing to Kenneth Chorley, 21 December 1925, Box 10, Record Group 2, RFA. As noted in an article on Radburn published just over a year following the sale of the first homes: "The second mortgages are decidedly an innovation and cannot be compared in any particular with the ordinary second mortgage financing usually offered. There are no heavy rediscounting fees. … They are paid out in installments provided for in monthly charges and the home-owner can have from twelve to sixteen years to complete his payments although he can pay it up sooner if he wishes" (A. G. Hinman and G. C. Woodbury, "Landscape Architecture's Role in Modern Housing Projects," *American Landscape Architect* 1 [October 1929]: 9–15, 14).

66. City Housing Corporation, "Radburn Garden Homes" (unpublished pamphlet, circa 1929), 10, Box 1, CSP/CUL. The interest rate on both mortgages was 6 percent with the first mortgage equal to 50 percent of the selling price of the home. The CHC also offered alternative plans with a larger, or a smaller, down payment. Further, these costs, including mortgage payments, taxes, insurance, and "community expenses," essentially a home owner's association fee, were collected by the CHC in "all-in-one monthly payments." In addition to covering the maintenance costs for the community spaces and facilities, the association fees also provided for

municipal services to ensure a certain quality of life until the local government assumed these responsibilities, and to administer "architectural restrictions."

67. Mumford to MacKaye, 5 November 1927, BMP/DCL.

68. Mumford to MacKaye, 20 January 1928, BMP/DCL. Henry Wright, "The Autobiography of Another Idea," *Western Architect* 39 (September 1930); reprint: New York: Regional Planning Association of America, 1930, n.p., Box 18, CSP/CUL. Stein to MacKaye, 12 September 1928, BMP/DCL.

69. "Summary of Discussions of Problems Connected with a Garden City," 5-6.

70. Charles S. Ascher, "The Extra-Municipal Administration of Radburn: An Experiment in Government by Contract," *National Municipal Review* 18, no. 7 (1929): 442-446, 442. The nearby industrial city was probably Paterson, a few miles to the west of Radburn or Passaic to the south. According to Ascher, Clarence Perry posed the key question: "How can a neighborhood within a municipality 'carry on a more advanced form of living than the municipality as a whole is ready to afford?" (quoted in Ascher, "Administration of Radburn," 443).

71. See Schaffer, *Garden Cities for America*, for more on the opening of the community and the organization and activities of the Radburn Association. "Certificate of Incorporation of the Radburn Association" Filed and Recorded March 22, 1929, Box 1, CSP/CUL; City Housing Corporation, "Radburn: Protective Restrictions and Community Administration," 1929, Box 1, CSP/CUL. "By-Laws of the Radburn Association," adopted April 2, 1929, as amended June 2, 1930, Box 1, CSP/CUL. An early undated booklet promoting the community briefly summarized the architectural restrictions as follows: They are "designed to protect the character and value of the community without causing any hardship to the individual owner. The chief requirement is that no change of use of or exterior change in or addition to the premises shall be made without the approval of the Radburn Association. The existing setback of the house from the lane and walk and the existing free spaces at the sides of the buildings must similarly be maintained. No business or trade of any kind is permitted in any Radburn home." See City Housing Corporation, "Radburn Garden Homes," 22; Ascher, "Administration of Radburn."

72. "A New Lease on Living" (unpublished pamphlet, circa 1930), Box 1, CSP/CUL. No author of this promotional brochure is indicated, but it probably was generated by the CHC.

73. "Summary of Discussions of Problems Connected with a Garden City," 1; City Housing Corporation, "Radburn Garden Homes," 7; Hudson, *Radburn*, 12; C. S. Stein, "The Radburn Plan" (lecture, Tenth Anniversary of Radburn, Meeting of the New Jersey Federation of Official Planning Boards, November 30, 1939), 4, Box 6, CSP/CUL.

74. Stein, *Toward New Towns*, 67.

75. American Institute of Architects, Committee on Community Planning, "Report of the Committee on Community Planning to the Sixty-First Annual Convention" (April 6, 1928): 1-3, 1, Box 5, CSP/CUL. Other members of the Committee included Adams, Rudolph Weaver, and H. D. Walker.

76. Stein and MacMahon made 1 West Sixty-Fourth Street their New York City address for the rest of their lives. C. S. Stein, series of drawings (unpublished, May 3, 1928), CSP/CUL. Her performance in Eugene O'Neill's *Beyond the Horizon* had earned rave reviews from Alexander Woolcott and Noel Coward. Of her, the latter said, "The performance of a comparatively unknown actress, Aline MacMahon, remained in my mind as something astonishing, moving and beautiful" (as quoted in Jeanne Stein, "Aline MacMahon Had the Wit to Sense What Audiences Liked Her to Project," *Films in Review* 16 [December 1965]: 616-632, 619-620).

77. This was the first significant play of Hart's career. He went on to win the Pulitzer Prize. In

addition to receiving financial support from MacMahon's movie career when his architectural jobs waned, Stein also received support from his father, who did not retire from the casket making company where he was vice president until two years before his death in 1939. As a gift for the 1936–1937 holiday season, "Pop" Stein gave each of his five children stocks in the company valued at eight thousand dollars (Stein to MacMahon, 2 January 1937, CSP/CUL).

78. Larsen, "Cities to Come, 35.

79. Stein to Dr. Wallace McLaren, Secretary, Institute of Politics, Williams College, Williamstown, MA, 9 November 1929, BMP/DCL.

80. Mumford to MacKaye, 14 June 1929, BMP/DCL. As tensions mounted between the organizations, Bing pulled out of the RPAA so as not to threaten his association with those engaged with the Regional Plan of New York. See Stein to MacMahon, 22 March 1932, CSP/CUL.

81. Mumford, "The Plan of New York," 259; 258.

82. MacKaye to Stein, 10 October 1929, BMP/DCL. Stein to MacKaye, 21 October 1929, BMP/DCL. Mumford to MacKaye, 22 October 1929, BMP/DCL. Benton MacKaye, "The Townless Highway," *The New Republic*, March 12, 1930: 10–11, 11.

83. "Program of the Regional Planning Conference" (unpublished program, October 18–19, 1930), Box 180, LMP/UPA.

84. Ascher to Mumford, 20 October 1930, Box 8, CSP/CUL.

85. Stein to Harris A. Reynolds, Massachusetts Forestry Association, 11 March 1931, BMP/DCL. Stein to MacKaye, 5 March 1931, BMP/DCL. Stein to MacMahon, 15 and 24 March 1931, CSP/CUL.

86. Benton MacKaye, "Cultural Aspects of Regionalism" (lecture, Conference on Regionalism, University of Virginia, July 9, 1931) CSP/CUL; Benton MacKaye, "The RPAA Era: A Reminiscence" (unpublished notes, circa 1968/69), BMP/DCL.

87. Henry Wright, *Rehousing Urban America* (New York: Columbia University Press, 1935), 46–47. Stein, *Toward New Towns*, 75. Angelique Bamberg, *Chatham Village: Pittsburgh's Garden City* (Pittsburgh, PA: University of Pittsburgh Press, 2011). Portions of this section, specifically concerning the President's Conference on Home Building and Home Ownership and the response of the AIA Committee, are adapted from Larsen, "Planning and Public–Private Partnerships."

88. Stein, *Toward New Towns*, 85. In *Toward New Towns*, Stein notes that the rate of return fell below 4 percent only for one year and that rental rates were reduced during the worst of the Depression from $11.35 to $9.65 per month (80).

89. Isadore Rosenfield, "Phipps Garden Apartments," *Architectural Forum* 56 (February 1932): 110–124, 183–187. Employed in Stein's office, Rosenfield wrote this extensive overview of the Phipps Garden Apartments. He noted that the CHC "was retained as the builder," representing the high regard in which the Society of Phipps Houses held the organization and the nearby project of Sunnyside Gardens. Like the Buhl Foundation, the Society of Phipps Houses was founded by a philanthropist, in this case steel magnate Henry Phipps, to develop limited dividend housing.

90. Henry Wright, "The Apartment House: A Review and a Forecast," *Architectural Record* 69 (March 1931): 187–195, 187. In "Phipps Garden Apartments," Rosenfield notes that 80 percent of the units in the project were under a three-year lease in 1932 and another 10 percent had two-year leases.

91. As quoted in a letter from Stein to Mumford, 16 September 1930, CSP/CUL.

92. John M. Gries and James Ford, eds., *Slums, Large-Scale Housing, and Decentralization*

(Washington, DC: The President's Conference on Home Building and Home Ownership, 1932), 68–69. "Socially integrated communities" referred to the amenities and activities available to residents. Ibid., 85.

93. American Institute of Architects, Committee on Economics of Site-Planning and Housing, "Report of the Committee on Economics of Site-Planning and Housing to the Sixty-Fifth Annual Convention—April 1932": 1–6, 4, Box 5, CSP/CUL. "Report—April 1932," 5, 6. The group also vaguely acknowledged the role that segregation might play in creating these conditions, but went no further in fully characterizing or addressing this significant issue. C. S. Stein, "Review for the Nation" (unpublished draft, August 2, 1932), CSP/CUL.

94. As Bing noted in his June 18, 1935, statement, the CHC had "no control" over the first mortgages and had assigned the second mortgages to a trust company, securing these amounts with bonds. See Alexander Bing, "City Housing Corporation, Statement Issued June 18, 1935," 4, Box 10, Housing Interest Series, Record Group 2, RFA. Schaffer, *Garden Cities for America*, notes that sales in June were higher than in any previous month, earning the CHC praise from *Business Week*. Bing acknowledges that the CHC did not realize the severity of these impacts until 1931 ("City Housing Corporation—Statement").

95. Bing to Colonel Arthur Woods, 9 January 1931, Box 10, Housing Interest Series, Record Group 2, RFA. According to Schaffer, *Garden Cities for America*, ultimately only sixteen units were constructed in 1931, eleven in 1932, and ten in 1933 when building came to a halt. For a thorough examination of the mortgage crises at Sunnyside and Radburn, including how the two communities' responses to the CHC differed and why, see Schaffer, *Garden Cities for America*, 191–209; Parsons, ed., *The Writings of Clarence Stein*, 194.

96. F. O. Billings, chairman, Consolidated Home Owners Mortgage Committee, Sunnyside Gardens Community Association to D. E. McAvoy, Chairman, Long Island Division, The Home Mortgage Advisory Board, Federal Reserve, 24 March 1933 (Franklin D. Roosevelt Library). The Sunnyside Committee effectively used the community association that CHC had initiated at Sunnyside to advocate for changes in their mortgage terms and to denigrate the corporation. "Sunnyside Home Owners versus City Housing Corporation," 6 June 1935, Box 10, Housing Interest Series, Record Group 2, RFA. Bing, "City Housing Corporation—Statement." Bing further argued that the law was enacted while Sunnyside was underway, and at the time of completion, only two developments had taken advantage of the state's limited dividend designation. The CHC had tried to work with home owners at Sunnyside to come to individual agreements regarding fair payment amounts, but by the beginning of 1934, the corporation had exhausted its own finances and could no longer make payments on behalf of delinquent homeowners (Bing, "City Housing Corporation—Statement"). See also C. Heydt, Memorandum (unpublished, February 11, 1935), Box 11, J Series, Record Group 2, RFA.

97. Mumford to Bing, 6 June 1935, LMP/UPA. Years later, Stein identified this decision to take the "legal" rather than the "common sense or humanitarian (moral) side" as a critical misstep of the CHC. See C. S. Stein, "The Nature of Communities" (unpublished essay, October 8, 1943), Box 10, CSP/CUL. In a letter to Mumford dated February 4, 1942, Bing opined, "I was naïve enough to have thought that some of those at Sunnyside who knew me, would have come out publicly to dispute the charges" (Box 180, LMP/UPA).

98. Archibald MacLeish, *Housing America* (New York: Harcourt, Brace, 1932), 131.

## 4. The Architect as Houser

1. See C. S. Stein, "Investment Housing Pays," *Survey Graphic* 29 (February 1940): 75–77, 127.

2. During the 1930s and early 1940s, *Architectural Forum* featured more multifamily projects of Stein's (fourteen) than any other architect designing housing assisted through federal programs. The closest contender, Oskar Stonorov, architect of the Carl Mackley Houses, was featured nine times in the architecture journal. These articles often focused on the innovative design achieved despite the low amount of funding available.

3. For an examination of Straus's rocky tenure as head of the U.S. Housing Authority (USHA) from 1937 to 1942, see Roger Biles, "Nathan Straus and the Failure of U.S. Public Housing, 1937–1942," *The Historian* 53, no. 1 (1990): 33–46. According to Biles, Straus's participation in the Hillside Homes project earned him recognition resulting in Mayor LaGuardia sending him to Europe in the summer of 1935 to learn more about housing. His subsequent report outlining what he learned helped Straus gain a position on the NYCHA. One year later, Bauer urged him to take the job as administrator of the USHA.

4. C. S. Stein, "Housing and Common Sense," *The Nation* 134 (May 1932): 541–544, 543; C. S. Stein, "The City of the Future—A City of Neighborhoods," *American City* 37 (November 1945): 123 and 125, 123. Portions of this section are adapted from Larsen, "Planning and Public–Private Partnerships."

5. *Report of Commission of Housing and Regional Planning to Governor Alfred E. Smith and the Legislature of the State of New York*, February 18, 1926, 51, Box 1, CSP/CUL. New York State Board of Housing, *Preliminary Report of the State Board of Housing to Governor Alfred E. Smith*, December 15, 1926 (Albany: J. B. Lyon, 1926), Box 5, CSP/CUL. Michael W. Straus and Talbot Wegg, *Housing Comes of Age* (New York: Oxford University Press, 1938), 23.

6. C. S. Stein, "Address before Public Housing Conference" (lecture, Greenwich House, New York City, NY, March 22, 1932), 1, Box 6, CSP/CUL. Among the other members were Helen Alfred, Lewis Mumford, Louis Pink, Lillian Wald, Edith Elmer Wood, and Representative Fiorello LaGuardia. La Guardia was elected mayor of New York City in 1933, and the New York City Housing Authority (NYCHA) was established in 1934. The New York Public Housing Conference became the National Public Housing Conference, which played a significant role in advocating passage of the 1937 Housing Act. See Nicholas D. Bloom, *Public Housing that Worked: New York in the Twentieth Century* (Philadelphia: University of Pennsylvania Press, 2008).

7. Stein to MacMahon, 18 May 1932, CSP/CUL. Stein to Bauer, 30 June 1932, CSP/CUL. At the time, Gove served as secretary to the State Housing Board of New York.

8. The act also increased the RFC's lending authority by $2 billion to $3.5 billion. See Nathaniel S. Keith, *Politics and the Housing Crisis since 1930* (New York: Universe Books, 1973). Public Works Administration Housing Division Staff, *Urban Housing: The Story of the PWA Housing Division, 1933–1936* (Washington, DC: Federal Emergency Administration of Public Works, 1936). Later that year, Ohio established such an agency, and twelve other states followed suit in 1933. See Edith Elmer Wood, "The Development of Legislation," in *Public Housing in America*, ed. M. B. Schnapper (New York: H. W. Wilson, 1939): 71–78.

9. C. S. Stein, "An Outline for Community Housing Procedure," *Architectural Forum*, 56 (March, April, May 1932): 221–228, 393–400, 504–514; 221.

10. Henry-Russell Hitchcock and Philip Johnson, *The International Style* (1932; reprint New York: W. W. Norton, 1966), 101. Talbot F. Hamlin, "Housing Is Architecture," *Pencil Points*, 20 (February 1939): 81–97, 81.

11. Stein to MacMahon, 31 and 3 January 1932, CSP/CUL. In April of that year, Stein noted

"I owe Pop $2000 and RDK [Robert D. Kohn] about a thousand back rent—and by May 1st draftsmen and expenses will amount to another thousand or more" (Stein to MacMahon, 10 April 1932, CSP/CUL). By June 1932, MacMahon was sending Stein checks to settle these debts (see letters such as that of 11 June 1932).

12. Stein to MacMahon, 1 June 1932, CSP/CUL. Whitaker obtained a grant from the Rockefeller Foundation to establish an academic position for Behrendt at Dartmouth College so he could stay in the United States permanently. When the college initially refused to accept the grant, Mumford and Whitaker collected a portion of the $1,250 required for the appointment, and Stein proposed to provide up to $700 for the rest. With the academic position, Stein noted, Behrendt could "leave Germany without any red tape and enter the U.S. without worry about the quota" (Stein to MacMahon, 25 August 1934, CSP/CUL). Through Mumford and Stein's efforts, Behrendt did present a series of lectures at Dartmouth College during the winter of 1934–1935, which formed the basis of a book entitled *Modern Building* published in 1937. He also secured a position at the college.

13. Stein to MacMahon, 8 June 1932, 25 August 1932, and 28 November 1932, CSP/CUL.

14. Stein to MacMahon, 16 May 1932, CSP/CUL. In 1932, Stein and Wright actually met onsite with Lewis and Boyd, one of the Pittsburgh architects of Chatham Village, to discuss in some detail preparations for the second phase of the development (Stein to MacMahon, 29 March 1932, CSP/CUL). Wright designed a second phase in 1934 with Ingham and Boyd again the architects and Griswold the landscape architect. Completed in 1936, this second unit of sixty-eight homes was similar in design to the first unit. Stein to MacMahon, 18 August 1932, CSP/CUL.

15. For more on formation of the Housing Study Guild, see letters from Mumford to Lubove dated 18 September 1962, Box 16, CSP/CUL, and from Stein to MacMahon dated 7 August 1933, CSP/CUL. Mayer, trained as a civil engineer with degrees at Columbia and the Massachusetts Institute of Technology. Yet he increasingly became concerned about social issues, particularly housing, and secured his architecture license in 1934. At that time, he began working in Stein's office. During this period, he also conducted a survey for the NYCHA of housing conditions and headed a committee on long-range programs for the authority (see Bloom, *Public Housing that Worked*). Other directors of the Housing Study Guild included Kohn, Henry Churchill, and Samuel Ratensky. The directors met as part of a larger council that included Talbot Hamlin, William Ballard, William Lescaze, Carol Aronovici, Bauer, and Ackerman. Stein to MacMahon, 7 August 1933, CSP/CUL. C. S. Stein, Notes (unpublished, August 16, 1947), Box 1, CSP/CUL. Stein in fact elaborated in these 1947 notes that Wright "lack[ed] respect for authority [of the] C. H. C. board members."

16. Stein to MacMahon, 7 August 1933 and 1 July 1933, CSP/CUL. Stein reflected on the recent letter from Wright in a letter to MacMahon dated 7 August 1933, CSP/CUL.

17. For more on this topic see Larsen, "The Radburn Idea as an Emergent Concept."

18. C. S. Stein, *Toward New Towns*. Stein to MacMahon, 4 June 1932, CSP/CUL. For the first half of 1932, Stein searched for the ideal property in the outer boroughs of the Bronx and Queens—a site near a school and large enough to accommodate residential, recreational, and commercial uses to create a complete community. At the same time, he worked to interest investors in the project. Portions of this section, particularly the discussion of the PWA Housing Division and the RPAA's "Housing Policy for the Government," are adapted from Larsen, "Planning and Public–Private Partnerships."

19. Stein to MacKaye, 12 November 1932, BMP/DC. In notes written on June 4, 1944, Stein brought up the example of Hillside Homes noting that it had indeed received a "partial tax-

exemption by [the] City … [which made it] possible to keep rent down to an average of $11.00 a (rental) room … and pay 6 per cent on invested capital." (CSP/CUL).

20. Stein to MacMahon, 20 November 1932, CSP/CUL. C. S. Stein, "The Price of Slum Clearance," *Architectural Forum* 60 (February 1934): 154–157.

21. Stein to MacMahon, 9 and 14 February 1933, CSP/CUL.

22. By the end of 1933, only two states—Ohio and New Jersey—had enabling legislation to allow establishment of local housing authorities. In January 1934, New York and Michigan joined these states and by the end of April, five more states had such legislation (Straus and Wegg, *Housing Comes of Age*, 52). In addition to the delay in passing enabling legislation, the local authorities then had to be created before they could undertake any projects. Due to the lack of local authorities, the federal government became directly involved in the majority of the assisted projects until the July 1935 Louisville ruling, which found that housing was not a federal purpose, so eminent domain could not be used by the Housing Division. The 1937 Housing Act, which established the permanent public housing program overseen by the USHA, did not include support for limited dividend or cooperative housing. The FHA, by providing mortgage insurance for large-scale rental housing, now offered the federal government's sole support for this "higher-income" housing.

23. Regional Planning Association of America, "A Housing Policy for the Government," Octagon 5 (June 1933): 6–7. The members sent out copies of this article to major news organizations including the Associated Press, *United Press, New York Times, The Survey, Real Estate Record and Builders' Guide*, the *New Republic*, and *The Nation*. The informal group met for the last time on May 17, 1933. During this time Stein noted, "I am finding a growing difference among those to whom I am close recently—Frederick Lee [Ackerman], Lewis [Mumford], Robert [Kohn]—All after the same objective—a saner world—but off on different roads" (Stein to MacMahon, 1 March 1933, CSP/CUL). The successor group—the Regional Development Council of America, which included many of the members of the original RPAA—began meeting on April 22, 1948. Mumford later lamented the disbanding of the RPAA as a missed opportunity to play a bigger role in influencing housing and regional planning policy during Roosevelt's tenure in office. See Mumford to Stein, 5 July 1949, LMP/UPA.

24. C. S. Stein, "Housing and the Depression," *Octagon* 5 (June 1933): 3–5, 4.

25. Bankers, who had foreclosed on airfields "the Curtis people bought in the good old days for landing fields," approached Architects Associated to consider using these sites for housing developments. Stein expressed some concern that these properties be "well related to industrial plants and were suitable in plan and price for workers." Architects Associated had enough interest in this concept, probably due in part to the low price of the land—12.7 cents per square foot at Valley Stream—to investigate these sites further. See Stein to MacMahon, 24 June 1933, Box 32, CSP/CUL.

26. C. S. Stein, C. Butler, F. E. Vitolo, Architects Associated, "Description and Financial Set-Up for Proposed Housing at Valley Stream, New York" (unpublished report, August 2, 1933). The Village of Valley Stream had incorporated in 1925 and had an estimated population in 1933 of fourteen thousand. Thus the architects proposed a new town in the unincorporated section that exceeded the population of the village by almost 30 percent. In September 1936, Green Acres, designed on the same site by Irwin S. Chanin, opened its first group of homes for sale to the public. Touted as "A Residential Park Community," the plan for the eighteen hundred units, primarily detached single family homes for sale, differed significantly from Stein's rental community of attached units and apartments.

27. See C. S. Stein, "Hillside Homes," *American Architect* 148 (February 1936): 16–33; and C. S. Stein, *Toward New Towns*, for an overview of the approval process on Hillside Homes. The interest rate (at 4 percent versus 5 percent) was less and amortization period longer with the PWA loan versus the RFC loan. Stein to MacMahon, 18 June and 10 July 1933, Box 32, CSP/CUL.

28. Stein to MacMahon, 14 July 1933, Box 32, CSP/CUL. Stein to MacKaye, 11 July 1933, BMP/DCL. Stein to MacMahon, 21 and 27 July 1933, Box 32, CSP/CUL. In fact there was controversy concerning the partnership of Kohn and Stein. In late February 1934, a photographer for a local paper snapped a picture of Stein's office door, which included both architects' names (Stein to MacMahon, 1 March 1934, CSP/CUL).

29. "Loan application for Hillside Homes," September 1933, Box 46, CSP/CUL. C. S. Stein, Notes (unpublished, August 29, 1962), Box 11, CSP/CUL. Stein was still pursuing the possibility of street closures at the site after the dedication in the summer and fall of 1935. Directly following the dedication, he and Straus gave Mayor LaGuardia a tour of the project where Stein "dr[o]ve home the need of really getting the streets closed" (Stein to MacMahon, 30 June 1935, CSP/CUL).

30. They could not begin drawing down funds on the project until the property was transferred from Straus to the limited dividend Hillside Corporation. During the interim, Eken covered Stein's payroll. See letters dated 30 and 31 January 1934 (CSP/CUL). Stein to MacMahon, 14 June 1934, CSP/CUL. Months earlier, houser Alfred Stern had told Stein, "the only way the housing situation at Washington could be cleared up—was for R.D.K. to get out. It seems that Ickes and he hate [each] other like poison" (Stein to MacMahon, 30 January 1934, CSP/CUL). Stein to MacMahon, 16 June 1934, CSP/CUL.

31. See C. S. Stein, "Principal Work" (unpublished notes circa 1951), Box 7, CSP/CUL, and "Loan Application for Hillside Homes." The additional cost of the land was $522,439 ("Loan Application for Hillside Homes").

32. Straus and Wegg, *Housing Comes of Age*, 170–171. C. S. Stein, "Dedication of Hillside Homes" (speech, June 29, 1935), Box 2, CSP/CUL.

33. Straus and Wegg, *Housing Comes of Age*; U.S. Housing Authority, *Annual Report of the United States Housing Authority for the Fiscal Year 1939* (Washington, DC: Government Printing Office, 1940). Federal Writers' Project of the Works Progress Administration in New York City, *New York Panorama: A Companion to the WPA Guide to New York City* (1938; reprint New York: Pantheon Books, 1984), 435. Langdon Post in his book *The Challenge of Housing* (New York: Farrar & Rinehart, 1938) also forcefully made this argument, adding that the way the number of rooms were calculated artificially reduced the dollar amount per room—$14 per room represented a more accurate rental rate on these projects. In fact, the "controversial" Knickerbocker Village—the high-density slum clearance project Stein had maligned on the Lower East Side—became the model, not Hillside, Bloom contends, due to cost cutting to address high land prices, resulting in simplified design and increased density. Still, Hillside did provide a model for the lower-density projects developed later on the outer edges of the city. See Bloom, *Public Housing that Worked*.

34. Henry H. Saylor, "The Hillside Housing Development," *Architecture* 71 (May 1935): 245–251, 245. For other sources praising the development, see Straus and Wegg, *Housing Comes of Age*; and Catherine Bauer, "Planned Large-Scale Housing: A Balance Sheet of Progress," *Architectural Record* 89 (May 1941): 89–105. Wright, *Rehousing Urban America*, 82.

35. Executive Order No. 7027. The Emergency Relief Appropriation Act (Public Resolution No. 11) was adopted on April 8, 1935, providing the funding and authority for the president's Executive Order 7027 establishing the Resettlement Administration on April 30, 1935.

36. Stein to MacMahon, 24 May 1935, CSP/CUL. Regarding the reliance on local materials, he noted, "They are trying to solve a national problem—but in each locality see it in its narrow local angle." With labor, the concern was that lower pay would result in lower quality construction—"Relief labor is paid less—but it does much less."

37. Stein to MacMahon, 31 May 1935, CSP/CUL. Stein does not specify with whom he and Frank Vitolo met during their visit, but the implication is that he met with "those in charge of the program." Given that he and Vitolo traveled from New York to Washington to meet for merely 1 ½ hours before heading back signifies the meeting's importance to Stein. Stein to MacMahon, 22 June 1935, CSP/CUL. The meeting was held at a mountain resort in Pennsylvania, and attendees included Eleanor Roosevelt, John Dewey, and Bauer. See Cathy D. Knepper, *Greenbelt, Maryland: A Living Legacy of the New Deal* (Baltimore: Johns Hopkins University Press, 2001). Stein to MacMahon, 4 July 1935, CSP/CUL. On September 21, 1935, Stein heard from Bauer that while Tugwell's department had in fact been funded, Valley Stream did not appear to be a likely candidate for the new town program (Stein to MacMahon, 22 September 1935, CSP/CUL). In a letter to MacMahon dated 27 September 1935 he also acknowledges that some in Washington "don't like my architecture" (CSP/CUL). Stein to MacMahon, 28 September 1935, CSP/CUL.

38. Resettlement Administration, *Greenbelt Towns: A Demonstration in Suburban Planning* September (1936), Box 2, CSP/CUL. Stein to MacMahon, 28 September 1935, CSP/CUL. Among his initial recommendations was single ownership of "the entire community plant" and attention to costs not just in the immediate construction but also with consideration for operation and maintenance of the town (Stein to Warren Jay Vinton, 30 September 1935, CSP/CUL). Stein submitted a final report to Lansill in early December 1935 to help guide the planning and design of the community. Stein to MacMahon, undated probably 6 October 1935, CSP/CUL. In a lecture to the Architectural League on May 3, 1939, Stein noted, "Formerly, the architect had to plan for what would sell best, now he has to plan for what will live best from the viewpoint of occupancy, operation, maintenance, and security of investment" (C. S. Stein, "Planning Housing Developments for Economical Operation and Maintenance" [lecture, Architectural League, May 3, 1939], 1, Box 6, CSP/CUL). At a 1941 planning conference, Stein discussed his Greenbelt Town cost studies as a tool to better understand the role planners might play in designing places to minimize maintenance costs. See C. S. Stein, "The Greenbelt Towns: Studies of Operation and Maintenance Costs as the Basis of Physical Planning" (lecture, American Institute of Planners Conference, Washington, DC, January 26, 1941), Box 6, CSP/CUL. Stein to John S. Lansill, memorandum, 19 November 1935, Box 7, CSP/CUL.

39. At the inception of the program, Mayer and Kamstra were both employed in Stein's office. Mayer had only briefly worked there as an architect, though he clearly provided support on designing Hillside Homes. Meanwhile Kamstra had been with Architect's Associated as a draughtsman since 1930 and assisted with work on Radburn, Chatham Village, Phipps Garden Apartments, and Hillside Homes. He became a member of the AIA in 1935. That same year, both he and Mayer relocated to Washington, DC, to work on Greenbrook. Wright had already left by that time. Churchill, who had earned his graduate degree in architecture at Cornell University in 1916, was the only one who had not worked in Stein's office, but he partnered with Stein and Mayer on the Fort Greene Houses in New York City later in the decade. Along with Wright and Mayer, Churchill was also a key participant in the Housing Study Guild. As chief engineer for the CHC, Eberlin had worked on Sunnyside Gardens, Radburn, and Phipps Garden Apartments. He also was the lead engineer on Hillside Homes and worked with Stein and Mayer on Fort Greene Houses.

40. Stein to MacMahon, 4 July 1935, CSP/CUL. Poor had earned his architecture degree

from the University of Pennsylvania and had gone on to design a number of country homes on Long Island during the 1930s, though his work was predominantly focused on nonresidential structures including government, commercial, and office buildings.

41. Stein to MacMahon, 21 and 28 July 1935, CSP/CUL. "I can begin to see Red Hook come to life—spacious vistas—immense space—but yet moderate size courts to give a feeling of intimacy. The courts facing toward the sun and opening on to the parks—spaces for outdoor music and play—but quiet in the court—... Everything where you can walk to it without crossing traffic—even the stores."

42. While Stein admitted he had not worked on the Pasadena Art Institute for about four years, he became excited when he came across an article in the *New York Times* that discussed a sizable gift for construction of the museum. On June 12, 1935, Stein received word from a new friend he had met in Washington, DC, Reginald Johnson, with whom he worked on Baldwin Hills Village, that Myron Hunt was being tapped for the job (Stein to MacMahon, 13 June 1935, CSP/CUL). Stein to MacMahon, 3 June 1935 and undated but probably 4 October 1935, CSP/CUL. Mumford to MacKaye, 25 October 1935, BMP/DCL.

43. Stein to Mrs. Henry Willcox, 24 January 1949, CSP/CUL. Liang's future wife, Lin Whei-yin, also earned her degree from the University of Pennsylvania in design and studied set design at Yale during the fall of 1927 while Liang conducted research in Asian architecture. Given her expertise, she assisted him in his research and writing on the topic of historic Chinese architecture. During late 1935 and 1936, the Chinese people had won a brief reprieve from internal conflict and threats of Japanese invasion. Stein and MacMahon visited Liang and Lin in Peking during April 1936. Of their meeting, Lin remarked, "We fell in love with them and they with us quite simultaneously" (as quoted in Wilma Fairbank, *Liang and Lin: Partners in Exploring China's Architectural Past* [Philadelphia: University of Pennsylvania Press, 1994], 92).

44. As Stein noted in a letter to Mumford dated 10 July 1936—"We heard last Sunday evening that he was in the hospital at Newton—and that the family had given up hope. It was the first I had heard of his being seriously ill" (CSP/CUL). See Stein to MacMahon, 31 October 1935, CSP/CUL. In fall 1936, Raymond Unwin took over lecturing in Wright's place. C. S. Stein, "Henry Wright, 1878–1936," *American Architect and Architecture* 149 (August 1936): 23–24.

45. Aline Bernstein, a costume and set designer, was a very close friend of Stein and MacMahon's. Bernstein's dream was realized years later with the establishment of the costume museum in the Metropolitan Museum of Art. Stein's brother-in-law, Arthur Mayer, played a significant role in the early years of the film industry in New York City, initially working as an auditor for Samuel B. Goldwyn and serving as director of publicity and advertising for Paramount Pictures from 1930 to 1933. In 1933, he took over Paramount's Rialto Theatre in Times Square, which he ran into the 1950s often featuring B-movies. Mayer updated the movie palace in an Art Moderne style in 1935, and it was on this project that Stein probably did some preliminary designs. Though unrelated to Louis B. Mayer, Arthur also distributed films and produced his own movies. He later taught film and communications at three different universities, including Stanford University. For more on Arthur Mayer, see Richard Maltby, "New Cinema Histories," in *Explorations in New Cinema History: Approaches and Case Studies,* eds. Richard Maltby, Daniel Biltereyst, and Philippe Meers (Malden, MA: Wiley-Blackwell, 2011), 3–40. Stein to MacMahon, 20 October 1936, CSP/CUL.

46. Stein to MacMahon, 31 October 1936, CSP/CUL. While organizing for the fair began in October 1935, work in earnest did not begin until May 1936. The World's Fair Board of Design was responsible for "creat[ing] or approv[ing]" the "general layout, art, and architecture of the Fair" (Federal Writers' Project of the Works Progress Administration in New York City, *The WPA*

*Guide to New York City* [1939; reprint New York: Pantheon Books, 1982], 630). According to the *Official Guide Book, New York World's Fair 1939*, Stein served in this capacity. While he participated in the early meetings of the board, his lengthy illness in 1937 removed him from further discussions about the design of the fair. In addition to Kohn, the members of the board were Stephen F. Voorhees (chairman), Walter Dorwin Teague, Richmond H. Shreve, Jay Downer, William A. Delano, and Gilmore D. Clarke. Kohn also headed the Theme Committee charged with establishing the themes and related zoning for the fair. See *"Building the World of Tomorrow": Official Guide Book, New York World's Fair 1939* (New York: Exposition Publications, 1939).

47. Stein to MacKaye, 21 February and 18 May 1937, BMP/DCL. Silver Hill was founded in 1931 as a residential health facility located in a substantial hillside farmhouse that in its bucolic setting gave it the appearance, as a 1959 *Times* article noted, of a "New England resort hotel." Stein's doctor, Dr. Terhune, was director of Silver Hill from 1934 to 1964. Stein to Mumford, 24 August 1937, CSP/CUL.

48. While she wanted to conduct research on PWA projects to inform the new permanent program, Bauer found herself instead running the successor agency's—the U.S. Housing Authority's (USHA)—Division of Research and Information. For more regarding implementation during the early days of the program, see D. Bradford Hunt, "Was the 1937 U.S. Housing Act a Pyrrhic Victory?" *Journal of Planning History* 4, no. 3 (2005): 195–221.

49. See Bauer, "Planned Large-Scale Housing"; Edith E. Wood, *Slums and Blighted Areas in the United States* (1936; reprint College Park, MD: McGrath, 1969); American Federation of Labor Housing Committee, "Should the Administration's Housing Policy Be Continued? Pro," *The Congressional Digest* 15, no. 4 (1936): 117–118; Charles Abrams, *The Future of Housing* (New York: Harper & Brothers, 1946). For a recent exploration of the dissonance between the program as envisioned and the program as approved, see Alexander von Hoffman, "The End of the Dream: The Political Struggle of America's Public Housers," *Journal of Planning History* 4, no. 3 (2005): 222–253. C. S. Stein, "Housing: The Next Chapter" (lecture, MIT, Boston, MA, October 27, 1937), 1–2, Box 6, CSP/CUL. C. S. Stein, "The Wagner-Steagall Housing Act of 1937," *American Architect and Architecture* 151 (November 1937): 36–37, 36. Ibid, 37. Portions of this section, particularly the FHA's role in rental housing, are adapted from Larsen, "Planning and Public–Private Partnerships."

50. See "The National Housing Act," *Architectural Forum* 60 (June 1934): 468–470; and "The NHA Becomes Law," *Architectural Forum* 61 (July 1934): 66. Public Works Administration Housing Division Staff, *Urban Housing: The Story of the PWA Housing Division, 1933–1936* (Washington, DC: Federal Emergency Administration of Public Works, 1936), 26. See Laura Bobeczko and Richard Longstreth, "Housing Reform Meets the Marketplace" in *Housing Washington*, ed. Richard Longstreth (Chicago: Center for American Places at Columbia College Chicago, 2010): 159–180. Chester M. Wright, "Washington Monthly Newsletter," *Pencil Points* 16 (April 1935): 181–184, 181. Bauer, "Planned Large-Scale Housing," 94.

51. Edward P. Curl, "Private Capital in Large-Scale Housing," in *Housing Officials' Yearbook, 1937*, ed. Coleman Woodbury (Chicago: National Association of Housing Officials, 1937), 110–122. Shortly before his death, Wright began work with Kamstra and Albert Lueders on Buckingham, one of the largest and earliest of these projects, located in Arlington County near Washington, DC. Bobeczko and Longstreth, "Housing Reform," 164.

52. C. S. Stein, "Investment Housing Pays," *Survey Graphic* 29 (February 1940): 75–77, 127, 127; ibid., 75.

53. Robert A. Alexander, "Why L.A.? A Planner's Personal View" (transcript of interview, 1993); Stein to MacMahon, 13 June 1935, Box 2, CSP/CUL. "Does Housing Offer a Career to

Architects? Large-Scale, Privately Financed Housing," *Architectural Record* 83 (April 1938): 81–86, 83. These comments were part of a symposium regarding the opportunities provided to architects by the new public housing program and "liberalization of FHA policies" (81). Contract for Thousand Gardens [Baldwin Hills Village], 5 April 1938 as amended on 21 October 1938, Box 2, CSP/CUL.

54. "A New FHA Low Cost Housing Plan," *Architectural Forum* 63 (November 1935): 520–521, 520. In 1936, the RFC was authorized "to purchase mortgages on low rent housing projects directly from limited dividend corporations" to address lending institutions' concerns about the relatively liberal terms of insured mortgages on such projects. See "Improvements to FHA," *Architectural Forum* 64 (March 1936): 208. Also Catherine Bauer, "Description and Appraisal ... Baldwin Hills Village," *Pencil Points* 25 (September 1944): 46–60; and Stein, *Toward New Towns* for a discussion of the efforts to secure financing. Stein, *Toward New Towns*, 189.

55. Bauer, "Description and Appraisal," 56.

56. Stein, "Housing: The Next Chapter," 19.

57. Johnson to Stein, 22 June 1938, CSP/CUL. At the time, Nathan Straus, who had owned the property at Hillside Homes and headed the limited dividend corporation formed to develop the project, was director of the USHA.

58. Johnson to Stein, 9 September 1938, CSP/CUL. Stein to MacMahon, 21 and 22 September 1938, Box 35, CSP/CUL.

59. He reported in a letter to MacMahon dated September 25, 1938, "The Long Beach architects and I have decided on terms and I drafted a contract yesterday—I am to be paid all expenses—100 dollars a day for my time—plus a fee that should amount to something like five thousand on this part of the job—There probably will be additions later—for which I will also be paid—If the job does not go ahead I am only asking for my expenses. I could have made better terms—they need me—but I did not want to—It is the kind of work one should not make too much profit on—and besides I want to do more of this kind of work" (Box 35, CSP/CUL). Stein to MacMahon, 23 September 1938, Box 35, CSP/CUL. Stein to Dozier, 31 October 1938, Box 2, CSP/CUL. Shortly after returning from California, Stein traveled to Washington to confer with representatives of the USHA on both projects.

60. Stein to Dozier, 16 January 1939, Box 2, CSP/CUL. Carmelitos had been changed to a two-phase project. In reviewing the second phase, the technicians in Washington noted the project was the most expensive the USHA had approved to date, that the costs on the first phase were too high, and that since these costs could not be changed at this late date, the costs of the second phase needed to be reduced in order to average out the costs for the entire project in line with what the agency was willing to loan the local authority for its development (see Stein to Schilling, 14 January 1939 and 31 January 1939, Box 2, CSP/CUL). Stein to Lewis Wilson, 11 February 1939, Box 2, CSP/CUL.

61. Schilling to Stein, 24 March 1939, Box 2, CSP/CUL. Letters dated January 20 and February 4, 1939, from Schilling to Stein outlined some of Schilling's considerable frustrations with meeting federal requirements while at the same time complying with state and county laws regarding minimum road widths, building separation, and room sizes. A particularly vexing issue for the California architect was the requirement to reduce the number of 3 ½ room units and increase the number of 5 ½ room units while at the same time reducing the costs of the project. See Stein to MacMahon, 27 March 1939, Box 35, CSP/CUL; and "Leo Stein, 88, Dies," *New York Times*, March 28, 1939. Stein to Schilling, 3 April 1939, Box 2, CSP/CUL.

62. Stein to MacMahon, 7 May 1941, Box 35, CSP/CUL. For more on Fort Greene, see Plunz, *A History of Housing in New York City*; and Bloom, *Public Housing that Worked*.

63. C. S. Stein, "Housing for Defense," *Common Sense* 10 (April 1941): 106–108, 108. Carmody as quoted in Kristin Szylvian, "The Federal Housing Program during World War II," in *From Tenements to the Taylor Homes: In Search of an Urban Housing Policy in Twentieth-Century America,* ed. John F. Bauman, Roger Biles, and Kristin Szylvian (University Park: Pennsylvania University Press, 2000): 121–138, 125. Established on July 1, 1939, to create greater efficiency in oversight of public works, the FWA was responsible for the Public Buildings Administration, the USHA, Public Roads Administration, Public Works Administration, and Work Projects Administration. The first two were especially critical in rental housing production for war workers. See FWA, *First Annual Report, Federal Works Agency* (Washington, DC: Government Printing Office, 1940) for more on establishment of the agency and the subagencies that operated underneath it. Initially, Congress gave the army and navy $100 million and the FWA $150 million in funding ("The Federal Works Agency," *Architectural Forum* 73 [November 1940]: 14).

64. Stein to MacMahon, 14 January 1941, Box 36, CSP/CUL. While they worked on the project into the summer, it did not secure approval. FWA, *First Annual Report,* 30. Stein to MacMahon, 18 January 1941, Box 36, CSP/CUL. Stein was one of several leading architects asked to provide input on projects and programs in general. Szylvian, "The Federal Housing Program," outlines the conditions that allowed such innovation, particularly in prefabricated housing, to occur during the early stages of the program, which she labels the Defense Phase.

65. Stein to MacMahon, 8 February 1941, Box 36, CSP/CUL.

66. In a letter to his wife dated March 1, 1941, Stein noted, "The office was way in the hole last year—and all in all, including household expenses, I was over ten thousand dollars behind.... So next week at Washington I am going to try to get a job" (CSP/CUL). Stein to MacMahon, 24 April 1941, Box 36, CSP/CUL. *Architectural Forum* touted the formation of the FWA's Defense Housing Division in April 1941 as a significant turning point in the defense housing program. Rather than giving the majority of work to civil service architects, the government now secured the expertise of "independent practicing architects." Within six months, more than one hundred architecture firms had secured work in the program, among them, Clarence Stein's. See "Low Cost Houses," *Architectural Forum* 75 (October 1941): 211–212, 212. On April 29, 1941, Congress appropriated an additional $150 million to the FWA for defense housing (Lanham Act Amendment, Public Law 42-H.R. 3486). For an informative overview of defense housing in the Pittsburgh area, see Kristin Szylvian, "Defense Housing in Greater Pittsburgh: 1945–1955," *Pittsburgh History* (spring 1990): 17–28. According to Szylvian, Pennsylvania ranked five behind California, Washington, Virginia, and Texas.

67. "Low Cost Houses," 211–212. The project in Stowe consisted of 250 units, while that in Shaler was 251 units. Stein to MacMahon, 24 April 1941, Box 36, CSP/CUL. The following from the same letter provides some insight regarding his decision: "If I refuse these little affairs even if there is nothing constructive about them the bigger ones will cease coming." Stein to MacMahon, 8 May 1941, Box 36, CSP/CUL.

68. Stein to MacMahon, 26 June 1941, Box 36, CSP/CUL.

69. The first mention of A Thousand Years appears in a brief postscript to MacMahon in a letter written in late November 1935, but the property is not consistently mentioned in letters until early 1938. Clearly Stein begins visiting the property regularly after his first serious illness in 1937. Swope was president of GE from 1922 to 1939, then served as chairman of the NYCHA until 1942, when he again resumed the presidency of GE until 1944. According to Parsons, ed., *The Writings of Clarence Stein,* the little house, designed in spring 1938, was meant as a birthday gift for MacMahon.

70. By mid-May 1941, he had ten men working on the Pittsburgh defense housing projects.

He wrote to MacMahon on May 20, "I can't stay away from here [his New York City office] for long.—Ten men working on the job now—and I have to keep pouring out ideas and decisions to keep them going" (CSP/CUL). Stein to MacMahon, 17 March 1941, Box 36, CSP/CUL.

71. Stein to MacKaye, 16 January 1941, BMP/DCL.

72. The NHA oversaw the work of three subagencies: the FPHA, the FHA, and the Federal Home Loan Bank Administration. See National Housing Agency, *War Housing in the United States* (Washington, DC: Government Printing Office, 1945). See also Szylvian, "The Federal Housing Program," for a discussion of the "War Phase" of the defense housing program. "Buildings First Year at War," *Architectural Forum* 78 (January 1943): 71, 73.

73. Stein to Bauer, 1 April 1942, Box 36, CSP/CUL. Herbert Emmerich, "World War II Housing," *Journal of Housing* 12 (July 1955): 231–233, 231; Emmerich, "World War II Housing," 233.

74. Emmerich to Stein, 23 April 1942, Box 7, CSP/CUL. Stein to MacMahon, 3 May 1942, and Stein to MacKaye, 25 May 1942, Box 36, CSP/CUL.

75. Stein to Klaber, 5 June 1942, Box 36, CSP/CUL. Kohn to Emmerich, 15 June 1942, Box 7, CSP/CUL. Stein may have also misunderstood his assignment, making it a larger project than it needed to be. See Butler to Stein, 22 June 1942, and from Shire on behalf of Emmerich to Butler, 24 June 1942, Box 7, CSP/CUL. In October, Stein notified MacMahon that his doctor "is convinced that this [Stein's illness] grew out of the Washington experience: that I was not physically 100 percent when I started; that the traveling was a physical strain; that I took on too much of a job or rather went at it too vigorously and that it got hold of me psychologically." See Stein to MacMahon, 27 October 1942, Box 36, CSP/CUL. On January 17, 1943 Stein wrote his wife about their accommodations. There were steak dinners, horseback rides, and painting. See Stein to MacMahon, 17 and 31 January 1943, Box 36, CSP/CUL. Henry Klaber, with expenses covered by Stein's sister Gertrude, came to stay with Clarence once Lillie left in early February. For her part, MacMahon was appearing on Broadway in Maxwell Anderson's *The Eve of St. Mark*.

76. Harris had developed these buildings, as well as the Tribune Building in Chicago, when he was in partnership with John C. Hegeman as part of the Hegeman-Harris Company. Harris formed his company in 1939. Stein to Palmer, 27 March 1944, Box 16, CSP/CUL.

77. Lathrop Douglass, John W. Harris Associates, to J. M. Daiger, Housing Consultant, Project Organization and Financing (representing the owner of the property), 28 September 1944, Box 4, CSP/CUL. The golf course consisted of 140 acres, and ultimately, the insurance company was only able to secure approximately 30 additional adjacent acres. Lathrop Douglass, "Report on Proposed Housing Development for Fresh Meadow Golf Course Area" 15 April 1944, Box 4, CSP/CUL; C. S. Stein, "Overview" (unpublished report, September 21, 1944), Box 4, CSP/CUL; C. S. Stein, "Report on Fresh Meadows" (unpublished, September 27, 1944), Box 4, CSP/CUL.

78. According to Plunz, *The History of Housing in New York City*, the recently developed high-profile Stuyvesant Town project had restricted tenants to white-only, resulting in pressure on the agencies authorizing the tax exemption for Metropolitan Life to require the insurance company to build a project in Harlem for black residents. As Stein noted in his minutes of the meeting with Van Schaick regarding Fresh Meadows, "The law now is that to get tax exemption there must be no restrictions and they must admit blacks as well as whites, in the future." See C. S. Stein, "Report of Interview" (unpublished, July 21, 1944), Box 4, CSP/CUL.

79. Inter-office memo of Harris Associates copied to Stein, 6 October 1944, Box 4, CSP/CUL. Stein devoted 355 hours to this project, from approximately April 15 to September 30, 1944.

80. Harris to Stein, 5 April 1946, Box 4, CSP/CUL. Harris to Stein, 11 May 1946, Box 4, CSP/CUL. Stein had proposed to bring Walker's firm into the project to strengthen the depth of the architecture team. Ironically, Harris mentioned this point to Gurney in 1946 shortly after the

insurance company had secured the property, resulting in Gurney recommending Walker's firm for the project. Harris to Stein, 11 May 1946, Box 4, CSP/CUL. Perhaps because of the intensity with which he undertook the work for Harris, Stein again became quite ill in May 1945. He did not fully recover until early in 1946. See Stein's notes of a phone conversation with Harris dated 1 July 1946 and Memorandum of Interview between Mr. Clarence S. Stein and Mr. Brendan McInerney (attorney for Harris Associates) dated 30 January 1947 (Box 4, CSP/CUL).

81. See New York Life Insurance Company, "Fresh Meadows" (unpublished, September 1947) and "Fresh Meadows" (n.p., n.d. circa 1949), Box 4, CSP/CUL. The residential density averaged seventeen units per acre.

82. Stein to Eberlin, 11 March 1944, Box 36, CSP/CUL. Stein favorably compared these two programs. In a letter to Roland Wank dated 28 June 1944, Stein draws a parallel between limited dividend projects completed under the New York State Housing Law and large-scale housing built under FHA (Box 16, CSP/CUL).

## 5. The Radburn Idea

1. Raymond Unwin, *Town Planning in Practice* (1909; reprint New York: Princeton Architectural Press, 1994), 330. Stein to MacKaye, 2 August 1949, BMP/DCL.

2. In 1921, the Hudson Guild Farm opened its fifth summer with an "outing for disadvantaged youth" followed by a family vacation season. Begun by three graduates of the Ethical Culture School, Camp Aladdin at Hudson Guild Farm opened for the first time in the summer of 1921. See American Ethical Union, "Providing Summer Outings," *The Standard* 8 (July 1921): 29.

3. John T. Boyd Jr., "Garden Apartments in Cities," *Architectural Record* 48 (July 1920): 53–74, 70. Based on photographs in the article and other information, within one year, one building consisting of six units had been constructed at West 239th Street.

4. Unwin, *Nothing Gained*. Walter C. Behrendt, *Modern Building: Its Nature, Problems, and Forms* (New York: Harcourt, Brace, 1937), 202–203. Walter Behrendt was a German architect who in 1920 made several contributions to the *JAIA* regarding European housing. During this time, Stein got to know him, and in 1934, Stein and Mumford sponsored his immigration to the United States.

5. C. S. Stein, "The Influence of Letchworth in America" (unpublished notes, June 22, 1953), Box 10, CSP/CUL.

6. Wright, *Rehousing Urban America*, 40; Stein, *Toward New Towns*; Wright, *Rehousing Urban America*, 69.

7. Wright, *Rehousing Urban America*, 38.

8. The landscape architect's Cornell degree got fellow graduate Ackerman's attention. Cautley had earned her undergraduate degree in Rural Arts there in 1917, a program that later became the university's landscape architecture program. She worked on both major public and private projects and traveled to Europe in 1929 to see housing projects and planned communities. See R. Terry Schnadelbach, "Phipps Apartment Houses, Sunnyside Queens, New York: The Landscape Architecture of Marjorie Sewell-Cautley," lecture, the Beatrix Farrand Conference on Women in Landscape Architecture, University of California, Berkeley, CA, November 8, 2002; Thaisa Way, *Unbounded Practice: Women and Landscape Architecture in the Early Twentieth Century* (Charlottesville: University of Virginia Press, 2009). Stein, *Toward New Towns*, 88.

9. "Sunnyside Gardens: A Home Community" (unpublished brochure, circa 1928/29), Box 1, CSP/CUL. Mumford to MacKaye, 29 November 1927, BMP/DCL.

10. Hardie Phillip had become one of three principals in Goodhue's office upon the architect's death the previous year. One of the first buildings completed by Goodhue when he secured the commission for the campus was the Gates Chemistry Building (1917), which required an annex by the mid-1920s. It was this building that Stein and Goodhue Associates designed. The architects were also retained to design dormitories at the campus, but these were never constructed. C. S. Stein, "The New Museum" (unpublished notes, June 6, 1928), Box 5, CSP/CUL; C. S. Stein, "Proposed Building for the Pasadena Art Institute" (unpublished notes, February 16, 1927), Box 6, CSP/CUL.

11. C. S. Stein, "Proposed Building for the Pasadena Art Institute" (unpublished notes, February 16, 1927), Box 6, CSP/CUL. The functional issues of the museum were also addressed including the necessity to receive, process, and repair works of art. His enthusiasm for this project was obvious as he became a member of the American Association of Museums in 1926 shortly before submitting his proposal (C. S. Stein, Resume, Box 7, CPS/CUL).

12. According to Radest in *Toward Common Ground*, Adler was close to Rockefeller due to their shared social and civic interests and efforts. Rockefeller contributed $250,000 to the project. Stein notes that the cost of constructing the high school came to $1,040,200. The lower school, which he and Kohn also designed, cost a total of $228,500. See C. S. Stein, "Cost of Construction Jobs" (unpublished notes), Box 7, CSP/CUL.

13. Here as at Hillside Homes and the Wichita Art Institute, Stein makes use of an outdoor amphitheater as a central organizing feature in the site plan. Stein to MacMahon, 8 February 1931, CSP/CUL.

14. The congregation had been formed by the consolidation of two Jewish reform congregations—Emanu-El founded in 1845 and Temple Beth-El founded in 1874. Adler's father, Samuel Adler, moved the family to New York City in 1857 to assume the rabbinate of the Temple Emanu-El.

15. Charles Butler, "The Temple Emanu-El, New York," *Architectural Forum* 52 (February 1930): 150–154, 151.

16. C. S. Stein, "The Problem of the Temple and Its Solution," *Architectural Forum* 52 (February 1930): 155–211, 168.

17. Kohn as quoted in Stein, "The Problem of the Temple," 168. These included Sunnyside Gardens, the Chemistry Annex at California Institute of Technology, the Pasadena Art Institute proposal, the Fieldston School, the Temple Emanu-El, the Midtown Hospital, which Stein was designing with Associated Architects colleagues Charles Butler and Frank E. Vitolo, and the Lavanburg Homes with Stein playing the role of consulting architect. W. C. Sommerfield was the primary architect on the latter project located on the Lower East Side. It consisted of six-story walk-up apartments in the shape of an "E" organized around two courtyards. Stein became involved with the project through his committee work with the City Club. The Lavanburg Foundation was founded as a nonprofit to promote the provision of "sanitary housing accommodations at low rentals for persons of small income" and to "engage in research or publication" in furtherance of this goal. See Abraham Goldfeld, *The Diary of a Housing Manager* (Chicago: National Association of Housing Officials, 1938), 3.

18. City Housing Corporation, "Radburn Garden Homes" (n.p., circa 1929), 6, Box 1, CSP/CUL; Louis Brownlow, "Radburn. A New Town Planned for the Motor Age," *International Housing and Town Planning Bulletin* (February 1930): 4–11, 6. The shopping center sits on the northeast corner of Fairlawn Avenue, initially the only existing road through the site, and Plaza Road, which runs parallel to the railroad line. The plan placed the shopping center directly east across Plaza Road from a plaza/park that fronted the railroad station, which Stein also designed.

Schaffer, *Garden Cities for America*, 170; Henry Wright, "Memorandum of Town Planning Site Development and Building Problems," Section #1, 14 August 1928, Box 1, CSP/CUL. Stein to MacKaye, 20 January 1928, BMP/DCL.

19. Henry Wright, "Memorandum of Town Planning Site Development and Building Problems," Section #2, 14 August 1928, Box 1, CSP/CUL; City Housing Corporation, "Radburn Garden Homes," circa 1929, 8; "Summary of Discussions of Problems Connected with a Garden City," 6–7.

20. In a detailed overview of costs associated with individual lot improvements and community amenities, Archibald MacLeish argued the superiority of the Radburn model. In addition to community benefits well beyond those offered in a typical subdivision or "Indian Elms," as he called it, MacLeish demonstrates how Henry Wright's proposed subdivision of a forty-acre tract results in a significantly lower cost per lot due to reduced infrastructure costs associated with clustered development patterns. See Archibald MacLeish, *Housing America* (New York: Harcourt, Brace, 1932), particularly appendix B; City Housing Corporation, "Radburn Garden Homes," 8; "A House for the Motor Age," *Architectural Record* 65 (February 1929): 197.

21. Mumford to MacKaye, 20 December 1928, BMP/DCL.

22. Stein to Mumford, 25 August 1947, Box 16, CSP/CUL; C. S. Stein, *Toward New Towns*, 223.

23. Marjorie Sewell Cautley, "Planting at Radburn," *Landscape Architecture Magazine* 21, no. 1 (1930): 23–29, 26, and 29.

24. C. S. Stein, "Housing: The Next Chapter" (lecture, MIT, Boston, MA, October 27, 1937), 31, Box 6, CSP/CUL; C. S. Stein, "The Radburn Plan" (lecture, Tenth Anniversary of Radburn, Meeting of the New Jersey Federation of Official Planning Boards, November 30, 1939), 9, Box 6, CSP/CUL.

25. See John F. Bauman and Edward K. Muller, "The Planning Technician as Urban Visionary: Frederick Bigger and American Planning, 1881–1963," *Journal of Planning History* 1, no. 2 (2002): 124–153. At the time Bigger was secretary of the Pittsburgh City Planning Commission and directed the city's planning department, reviewing land development proposals for consistency with the city's plan. He became chair of the commission in 1934 and continued serving in that capacity until 1954. He also served on the private sector Citizens Committee on the City Plan with founding members, including Henry Buhl, in the business community. This group was dedicated to establishing a comprehensive plan for the city.

26. Stein, *Toward New Towns*, 75. For a detailed history of Chatham Village, see Angelique Bamberg, *Chatham Village: Pittsburgh's Garden City* (Pittsburgh: University of Pittsburgh Press, 2011); Wright, *Rehousing Urban America*, 50.

27. Ingham and Boyd referenced the site's colonial history with decorative cartouches over the doors representing the coats of arms of William Pitt, the Marquis Duquesne, and George Washington. Griswold already had a significant reputation for his work at Colonial Williamsburg, and the tool sheds that distinguished each of the open spaces at Chatham Village were designed to emulate outbuildings, such as smokehouses, prevalent in that historic community.

28. Stein, *Toward New Towns*, 85.

29. Stein to MacMahon, 14 February 1931, CSP/CUL. In a letter dated the following day, Stein clarified the focus of their efforts—"We are playing around with the general plan—Henry and I—the location of the civic—or rather the cultural and educational center—and its relation to the plan as a whole."

30. Plunz, *A History of Housing in New York City*, 164.

31. Unit plans typically reflect the configuration of the floor layouts for multiple units within a section of an apartment building. Wright's *Rehousing Urban America* analyzes different types

of unit plans including the link or "I" type, the angle or "L" type, the "T" type, the "H" type, the "U" type, and the cross type to determine their strengths and weaknesses as applied to various sites. In *Toward New Towns for America,* Stein also assesses the practicality of the unit types employed in these projects.

32. Rosenfield, "Phipps Garden Apartments," 115. Henry Wright, "The Apartment House: A Review and a Forecast," *Architectural Record* 69 (March 1931): 187–195, 193.

33. Rosenfield, "Phipps Garden Apartments," 116.

34. Schnadelbach, "Phipps Apartment Houses," offers a detailed description of Cautley's landscape design principles as realized in the master plan for the project.

35. Committee on Housing Exhibition, "The Planned Community," *Architectural Forum* 58 (April 1933): 253–274, 253. William F. Lamb was the primary designer of the Empire State Building, among other structures with the firm of Shreve, Lamb, and Harmon Associates, formerly Carrere and Hastings. During the 1920s and 1930s, Germany's innovations in site planning at the forefront of the International Style transitioned from smaller enclosed perimeter blocks to massive superblocks with housing arranged in Zeilenbau. These were "open-ended [parallel] rows, with ample space between to permit of light and air and usable open space, and with only narrow streets within the development" (Bauer, *Modern Housing,* 181). The European examples in the exhibit were attributed to Bauer and Mumford with Rosenfield of Stein's office providing the images of Russian housing. Committee on Housing Exhibition, "The Planned Community," 255.

36. Horatio Hackett, "How the PWA Housing Division Functions," *Architectural Record* 77 (March 1935): 148–152, 152. See "Apartment House Planning Requirements Including Basic Dimensions," *Architectural Record* 77 (March 1935): 169–181, for excerpts from the government guidelines. These early guidelines for publicly assisted housing, also applied to privately developed housing with FHA insured mortgages. Wright, *Rehousing Urban America.*

37. Wright, *Rehousing Urban America,* 72; Ibid, 82.

38. Stein to MacMahon, 6 February 1934, CSP/CUL. At the outset of the bricklaying, Stein noted, "In spite of all the care with which drawings are made it all has to be gone over again at the job with real bricks instead of lines.... It is great fun—Building—really building—Escape from all the theory of housing for a while" (Stein to MacMahon, 23 August 1934, CSP/CUL).

39. C. S. Stein, "Hillside Homes," *American Architect* 148 (February 1936): 16–33. C. S. Stein and Catherine Bauer, "Store Buildings and Neighborhood Shopping Centers," *Architectural Record* 75 (February 1934): 175–187, 175; ibid., 185; Stein, *Toward New Towns.* "The stores and movie theater that fringe Boston Road would, I believe, have served the community better and been more successful financially and as civic design, if they had been unified in a group around a green, as was afterwards done at Greenbelt" (96). Stein, "Hillside Homes," 19.

40. The 1976 exhibit that celebrated his work labeled Stein an environmental architect. More recently, Robert McCullough in his *Path for Kindred Spirits* characterized both Stein and MacKaye as practitioners of "interdisciplinary environmental humanism" (3).

41. Although construction was originally slated to begin in the fall of 1929, the Great Depression significantly delayed the museum's development with the dedication ceremony finally being held on September 22, 1935 ("Wichita's New Art Museum Designed to Symbolize the Southwest," *Art Digest,* October 15, 1935, 14). C. S. Stein, "A Building on the Board," *Pencil Points* 10 (August 1929): 535–544, 581; Stein to the Board of Park Commissioners, City of Wichita, Kansas, 1 February 1929, Box 6, CSP/CUL.

42. Stein met with Lawrie numerous times in New York City, where they both lived, to review models and discuss coloring of the ornamentation. Already a prominent sculptor, Lawrie worked with Goodhue early in his career and ultimately secured more than three hundred commissions.

Noted examples include the frieze at the Nebraska State Capitol and Atlas at Rockefeller Center. "Wichita's New Art Museum Designed to Symbolize the Southwest," *Art Digest*, 15 October 1935, 14. Residents of Wichita considered the city to be the "Gateway to the Southwest."

43. Stein met with the directors of the Boston Museum in May 1932 to discuss ideas for flexible exhibits and new ways to display art while he was designing a proposed museum for Princeton University. Like the Springfield Gray Museum, which Stein worked on in 1931, the Princeton Museum most closely followed the International Style. Thus it was a significant contrast to the eclectic regionalism of the Pasadena and Wichita museums. C. S. Stein, "Form and Function of the Modern Museum," *Museum News*, October 15, 1935, 6–8, 8.

44. Stein, *Toward New Towns*, 122; Resettlement Administration, *Greenbelt Towns: A Demonstration in Suburban Planning* (Washington, DC: Government Printing Office, 1936), Box 2, CSP/CUL.

45. See Stein, *Toward New Towns*. At Greenbelt, Hale Walker served as town planner and Reginald Wadsworth and Douglas Ellington as principal architects. Unlike Greendale in Wisconsin, which featured a significant number of single family homes, Greenhills, Ohio, also featured garden apartments in its design, yet did not have the continuously interconnected park system and distinction between private and public open spaces that Greenbelt did. See Knepper, *Greenbelt, Maryland*, for more on the development and history of the new town. See also Joseph L. Arnold, *The New Deal in the Suburbs* (Columbus: Ohio State University Press, 1971), for a history of the new town program. "A Planned Community Appraised," *Architectural Forum* 72 (January 1940): 62–63, 34. The range in rents was from eighteen dollars for a one-room unit to forty-one dollars for a seven-room unit.

46. Albert Mayer, *Greenbelt Towns Revisited* (Washington, DC: National Association of Housing and Redevelopment Officials, 1968), 16. Mayer worked with Henry Wright and Allan Kamstra, town planners, and Henry Churchill, architect, on the design of Greenbrook, New Jersey, which was never begun due to the Circuit Court of the District of Columbia deciding that the federal government could not function as a developer. Stein to MacMahon, 6 November 1936, CSP/CUL.

47. Wright, *Rehousing Urban America*, xii; ibid., 69.

48. "Garden Apartments," *Architectural Forum* 72 (May 1940): 309–322, 309.

49. This arrangement did not apply to the second floor flats, which had entrances only from the service side of the building, though these did have balconies overlooking the interior parks. C. S. Stein, "The Gardens of Soochow: Chinese Pavements Photographed by Clarence S. Stein," *Pencil Points* 19 (July 1938): 427–430, 428.

50. BHV had a much smaller percentage of its open spaces dedicated to active recreation. This appears to have been a combination of the community's choice, lack of support for such facilities through FHA, and the onset of the war, which limited funding for such amenities. While Stein lamented the lack of playgrounds and a pool, in retrospect he admitted in *Toward New Towns* that the private space could be increased at the expense of public space, resulting in reduced maintenance costs and a more pleasant experience for the resident. Bauer, "Description and Appraisal," 54.

51. Dorothy F. Wong, Robert Nicolais, and Loretta Hess, "National Historic Landmark Application for Baldwin Hills Village (Village Green)" (unpublished report, August 1999).

52. Elizabeth Mock, ed., *Built in USA—1932–1944* (New York: Museum of Modern Art, 1944), 56; Bauer, "Description and Appraisal," 57–58.

53. Stein to Schilling, 24 March 1939, Box 2, CSP/CUL. Stein had already visited Washington several times in January and February 1939 to address the government concerns and had offered

his California associates suggestions for reassessing the costs and making changes to the design to bring the costs projected in the Job Program in line with the amount the USHA was willing to loan the LA County Housing Authority.

54. George A. Fuller Company, *Housing: Building Construction 1882–1944* (New York: George A. Fuller, 1944); Melville Dozier to Stein, 22 July 1939, Box 2, CSP/CUL. The site totaled 607 dwelling units. Adding to the monotony of the units was the elimination of the varied roof lines. Dozier reported, "The row houses now permitted by USHA are plainer than those considered when you were here, for the sake of economy, that is, the breaks in ridge alignment have been eliminated."

55. Stein to Lewis Wilson, 11 February 1939, Box 2, CSP/CUL.

56. C. S. Stein, "Harbor Hills Housing," *Pencil Points* 22 (November 1941): 677–683, 677. The 102-acre site only yielded 27 acres usable for housing due to ravines that crossed through the property. An early site plan for Harbor Hills dated July 1938 located all development north of North Drive (on the earlier site plan, Palos Verdes Drive), avoiding the problem of a major road cutting through the project. This early plan also included more cul-de-sacs and loop roads organically arranged with the housing clustered along these drives and oriented toward an interior park. The chevron pattern of residential development was not evident in this version of the site plan. See figure 5.21.

57. Stein, "Harbor Hills Housing."

58. Stein to MacMahon, 4 February 1941, Box 36, CSP/CUL; "Building for Defense—Prefabricators Put on a Show," *Architectural Forum* 75 (September 1941): 188–189, 188; Frederick Gutheim, "Indian Head Experiment in Prefabrication," *Pencil Points* 22 (November 1941): 724, 724; "Building for Defense," 188; Gutheim, "Indian Head," 724.

59. Stein to MacMahon, 1 May 1941, Box 36, CSP/CUL. On the Stowe project, he clarified, "It is high up above the Ohio River and below is the fierce ugly beauty of industrial Pittsburgh" (Stein to MacMahon, 22 May 1941, Box 36, CSP/CUL). Stein was able to employ initially ten and then twenty-five draftsmen and architects on these two jobs and earned "over ten thousand dollars [with] most expenses paid" (Stein to MacMahon, 20 and 22 May 1941 and 11 June 1941, Box 36, CSP/CUL). Stein to MacMahon, 1 and 13 May 1941, Box 36, CSP/CUL.

60. "Stowe Township, PA," *Architectural Forum* 77 (July 1942): 83–84, 83.

61. Stein to MacMahon, 12 October 1941, Box 36, CSP/CUL.

62. See Architect's Contract dated 19 July 1941 and letter from Stein to E. and C. Stotz dated 25 July 1941, Box 4, CSP/CUL. Stein was to receive half the architect's fee of $8,500. Stein to MacMahon, 25 July 1941, Box 36, CSP/CUL. In fact, within ten days of signing the contract with the federal government, Stein and his Pittsburgh associates had produced site and unit plans. At the meeting seeking preliminary approval for the project design, the architects were shocked to learn that Carmody had ordered postponement of this project. See Stein to MacMahon, 29 July 1941 and 8 and 15 August 1941, Box 36, CSP/CUL.

63. Stein to Harris, 21 May 1943, Box 4, CSP/CUL. The Louisiana design team on the project was the architecture firm of Walker and Gillette with J. M. Phillips, town planner. Nola Mae Wittler Ross, "History of Maplewood—Calcasieu Parish, Louisiana," *American Press*, 3 June 1990, retrieved January 25, 2010, http://files.usgwarchives.org/la/calcasieu/newspapers/maplewoo. txt. Maplewood was approximately 8 miles from Lake Charles and 3 ¾ miles from the smaller town of Sulphur. With a population of three thousand, Sulphur was about the projected size of Maplewood. John W. Harris Associates, Inc., "Maplewood" (unpublished report, 1946), Box 4, CSP/CUL.

64. C. S. Stein, "Notes on Pine Gardens" (unpublished, May 16, 1943), Box 4, CSP/CUL.

Stein also criticized the distribution of the one-, two-, and three-bedroom homes stating that Harris Associates had too few one- and two-bedroom units. The reduction of lot width on some of the lots was predicated on the width increasing for the larger homes in the community. Mott also appeared to "strongly agree" with Stein that Center Boulevard should not be connected to a major highway. Stein had proposed that the street bounding the eastern edge of the project function as a through street instead. Based on review of early aerials of the project, it appears that Center Boulevard did ultimately function as a through street, perhaps in part due to Harris's decision to run power for the community along this street and/or the fact that Harris Associates was unable to secure the properties that would allow the eastern street to connect to the highway. See C. S. Stein, "Connection with Highway 90" (inter-office memo circa June 1943), Box 4, CSP/CUL.

65. Stein to Harris, 1 July 1943, Box 4, CSP/CUL.

66. Stein to Arthur Mayer, 17 June 1945, Box 9, CSP/CUL. The town was expected to double in size after the war.

67. Harmon to Wade Sutton, Chief Underwriter, FHA, New Orleans, 14 August 1943, Box 4, CSP/CUL. Memo from Dehm (an employee of Harris Associates) to Harris, received 20 August 1943, Box 4, CSP/CUL. Several of Harmon's criticisms pointed out defects of the design—such as a section of the parking area that conflicted with the delivery drive for the stores and circulation issues in the parking area due to its one-way design and limited access. Harmon also noted that the gas station should be a free-standing building rather than being incorporated with the shops. For his part, Harris refers to Stein's "excellent plan" and the compliments the builder received on its design in a letter to Stein (Harris to Stein, 11 May 1946, Box 4, CSP/CUL).

68. C. S. Stein, "Housing and City Redevelopment During and After the War" (lecture, Citizens' City Planning and Housing Council of Rochester, NY, November 17, 1941), Box 6, CSP/CUL, 1–2.

69. FHA, "Planning Neighborhoods for Small Houses," Technical Bulletin No. 5 (1936; rev. ed. Washington, DC: Government Printing Office, 1938), 24. Radburn was the only development explicitly referenced in the publication. The description under the drawing stated: "The Radburn type plan showing a series of culs-de-sac grouped in a superblock around a central park. The traffic highways border the superblock. The houses face the front yards and parks rather than the streets. The cul-de-sac roadways are service drives and give access to the rear of the houses. Traffic passed by rather than among the houses" (24). "Green Acres, A Residential Park Community," *Architectural Record* 80 (October 1936): 285–286, 285.

## 6. The Regional City and Town Planning

1. Stein to MacKaye, 6 December 1927, BMP/DCL; Lewis Mumford, "Address of Lewis Mumford," *American Institute of Architects, Journal of Proceedings* (1925): 27–30, 29–30, Box 6, CSP/CUL.

2. Stein to MacMahon, 3 February 1933, CSP/CUL. President Roosevelt signed the Norris Act establishing the TVA on May 18, 1933. In a statement urging passage of the act, he described the agency's responsibilities as follows, "It should be charged with the broadest duty of planning for the proper use, conservation, and development of the natural resources of the Tennessee River drainage basin and its adjoining territory for the general social and economic welfare of the Nation. This authority should also be clothed with the necessary power to carry these plans into effect" (as quoted in David Lilienthal, *TVA: Democracy on the March* [1944; reprint

Chicago: Quadrangle Books, 1966], 52). For more on the TVA, see also Walter L. Creese, *TVA's Public Planning: The Vision, the Reality* (Knoxville: University of Tennessee Press, 1990). In a letter to Stein dated April 11, 1934, MacKaye reported enthusiastically about the activities of the TVA—"Knoxville is a little buzzing side-edition of Washington.... It takes me back to the honeymoon of the U.S. Forest Service a generation ago under Teddy [Roosevelt] and G. P. [Gifford Pinchot].... Tracy Augur is a real find, and I shall be happy with him as my immediate boss" (BMP/DCL). MacKaye had the job of outlining the regional plan for the entire Tennessee Valley and called it "the best job of my life." MacKaye to Stuart Chase, 20 July 1935, BMP/DCL. The other divisions were "Forestry, Agriculture, Minerals, Manufacture, and 'Social-Economic' matters."

3. Stein described the school, located at 116 East Sixteenth Street as "a school sponsored by the Federation of Architects, Engineers, Chemists, and Technicians" and "run by the draftsmen union." See Stein to Mumford, 24 August 1937, CSP/CUL, and Stein to MacKaye, 27 August 1937, BMP/DCL; C. S. Stein, "Community Building Studies under the leadership of C.S S., Revised" (unpublished notes, August 22, 1937), BMP/DCL.

4. Stein to MacKaye, 9 November 1937, BMP/DCL.

5. C. S. Stein, "Housing: The Next Chapter" (lecture, MIT, Boston, MA, October 27, 1937), 34, Box 6, CSP/CUL; C. S. Stein, "Community Planning—The Architect's Approach" (lecture, New York University, April 27, 1938), 1, Box 6, CSP/CUL.

6. Stein, "Housing: The Next Chapter," 24.

7. Ibid, 7.

8. Certificate of Incorporation for Civic Films, Inc., 10 June 1938, Box 7, CSP/CUL. The cost of making the film was fifty thousand dollars.

9. Stein to Mumford, 15 June 1938, Box 7, CSP/CUL. As Gillette documents in his 1977 article on the film, Henwar Rodakiewicz elaborated on Lorentz's outline while Mumford wrote the narrative for the film. Materials in Stein's files on the film reinforce the significant role Mumford had in drafting the script with promotional materials for the film attributing the "narrative" to Mumford, the "scenario" to Rodakiewicz, and the "original outline" to Lorentz. Further, the "Approved Script" is attributed to Lewis Mumford (Box 7, CSP/CUL). Gillette, "Film as Artifact." Gillette also addresses other creative differences between the filmmakers and planners, particularly the amount of emphasis to place on the new towns and the amount and nature of the narrative that framed the images. For a more recent analysis of *The City* that focuses on space as depicted in the film, see Erica Stein, "The Road to Heaven Twists: *The City*, Urban Planning, and Experiential Space," *Media Fields Journal* 3 (2011): 1–10; Stein to MacKaye, 26 August 1938, BMP/DCL.

10. In collaboration with Alfred E. Poor and Oliver Reagan, Stein designed a relatively modest building located in the Community Interests Zone on the northern side of the fair grounds. The architect applied his experience with synagogues and churches to the Temple of Religion, a nondenominational structure featuring a 150-foot tower, an auditorium for musical performances, and areas for quiet reflection, including a cloistered garden. The final design was of an austere colonnaded front façade with the ornamentation reserved for the tower located at the rear of the building through the cloistered garden. *Official Guide Book, New York World's Fair 1939*, 27.

11. Federal Writers' Project of the Works Progress Administration in New York City, *The WPA Guide to New York City* (1939; reprint New York: Pantheon Books, 1982), 630; promotional material for *The City*, circa September 1939, Box 7, CSP/CUL.

12. Promotional material for *The City*, circa September 1939, Box 7, CSP/CUL; C. S. Stein, "The Case for New Towns," *Planners' Journal* 5 (March–June 1939): 39–41, 41; Harland Bartholomew, "Response to 'The Case for New Towns,'" *Planners' Journal* 5 (March–June 1939): 42, 42.

13. "Camera over the U.S.A," *Theatre Arts Monthly* 23 (August 1939): 890–895, 892–893.

14. Gillette, "Film as Artifact." See Stein to William A.M. Burden, president of the Museum of Modern Art, 5 December 1957, Box 7, CSP/CUL; and Stein to Julius A. Stratton, President, MIT, 23 January 1958, Box 7, CSP/CUL. In December 1957, Civic Films, Inc. gave the film to the museum as a gift and used the proceeds it had earned to establish the Robert D. Kohn Fund at MIT's Department of City and Regional Planning "to bring experienced city developers to America to discuss practical problems in the creation of contemporary cities." Having done that, the nonprofit disbanded.

15. Stein to Mumford, 6 October 1943, Box 4, CSP/CUL. At the time Buttenheim was also the long-standing editor of *The American City*. Stein to Mumford, 6 October 1943, Box 4, CSP/CUL. Stein substituted the word *redevelopment* for *planning*, which he felt had been overused and diminished to simply reflect studies without implementation. As he explained to MacKaye, "Redevelopment seems a good deal better to me. 'Re' suggests that we are going to do things over, 'development' gives the idea of change and continued movement, adjustment and revision" (Stein to MacKaye, 7 October 1943, BMP/DCL). As Stein noted in the proposal, in order for the state to be competitive after the war, a comprehensive plan for redevelopment needed to outline the "orderly and simultaneous resettlement of workers and their working places in moderate sized communities decentralized throughout all the desirable parts of the state and tied together as great rural-urban communities by park-lined freeways" (C. S. Stein, "Appendix to Report to Governor Dewey on 'A Proposal for a Division of Planned Development in the Executive Department,'" 13 December 1943, 4, Box 8, CSP/CUL). Stein to Chauncey Hamlin, Niagara Frontier Planning Group, 2 February 1948, Box 8, CSP/CUL. Stein was reflecting back on the outcome of the report several years later.

16. Stein to Bauer, 14 January 1944, Bancroft Library, University of California, Berkeley. Stein to Major John O. Walker, 9 November 1944; Stein to Frank Palmer, 5 February 1944, Box 16, CSP/CUL.

17. Stein to Eberlin, 11 March 1944; Stein to Palmer, 27 March 1944, Box 16, CSP/CUL.

18. C. S. Stein, "Prospectus of Clarence S. Stein and Associates New Towns and Neighborhoods," 14 August 1944; C. S. Stein, "Minutes of a conversation of Clarence S. Stein with Roland Wank on 2 June 1944," 4 June 1944, 1, Box 16, CSP/CUL.

19. Hollinshead to Stein, 22 April 1944, Box 4, CSP/CUL. See proposals entitled "Gary" dated 5 and 20 July 1944 and an organizational chart of the Harris-Gary Corporation dated 9 July 1944, Box 4, CSP/CUL. In response to a document Harris prepared for Carnegie-Illinois outlining the business arrangement between Stein and Harris Associates, the architect drafted a letter countering practically every aspect of the contractor's proposal reminding him that "ours are two cooperating organizations" and that Stein's architectural firm conduct all preliminary planning investigations as well as the "town and site planning" and "complete architectural services." Unless these conditions were met, Stein clearly stated that he "would not be interested in being associated with the job" (Stein to Harris, 28 July 1944, marked "not sent," Box 4, CSP/CUL).

20. C. S. Stein, "Housing and City Redevelopment During and After the War" (lecture, Citizens' City Planning and Housing Council of Rochester, NY, November 17, 1941), 5, Box 6, CSP/CUL. The cooperation of government and industry as part of the war effort, he argued, was evidence that such partnerships were possible. C. S. Stein, "Preparedness for Post War Urban Redevelopment," *American City* 57 (February 1942): 68–69, 68.

21. C. S. Stein, "City Patterns ... past and future," *New Pencil Points* 23 (June 1942): 52–56; Mumford to Stein, 5 April 1950, Box 16, CSP/CUL.

22. Stein to Mumford, 5 September 1946, CSP/CUL. Philip Glick, General Counsel of PHA

documented that liquidation of the towns was a subject of congressional Appropriations Committee hearings as early as 1942. See Philip Glick, General Counsel, Public Housing Administration, "General Counsel's Opinion No. 28," 24 March 1948, Box 9, CSP/CUL.

23. Augur and Stein consulted on the towns; Bigger was chief of planning. Walker, Crane, and Hartzog were town planners respectively for Greenbelt, Greendale, and Greenhills. Reeder was chair of the committee and former manager at Greendale. American Institute of Planners, "Report of Committee on the Greenbelt Towns," 26 December 1947, 1, Box 8, CSP/CUL. This report was probably drafted in response to Public Regulation No. 1, issued in 1947 by Raymond Foley, administrator of the new Housing and Home Finance Agency (HHFA), promoting subdivision of the towns to facilitate sale of all properties owned by the agency.

24. American Institute of Planners, "Report of Committee on the Greenbelt Towns," 26 December 1947, 2, Box 8, CSP/CUL. Establishing plans to guide build-out of the towns was considered one strategy to facilitate development that better supported the cost of running the towns. Elbert Peets, who originally worked on the design of Greendale, drew up plans for the town's expansion, and Alexander Bing expressed interest in being the developer. See Arnold, *The New Deal in the Suburbs*; Stein to Dillon Myer, Commissioner, PHA, 16 October 1947, CSP/CUL. In 1945, Greenbelt alone had been valued at almost $19 million (see Arnold, *The New Deal in the Suburbs*). A letter from Stein to Walter E. Kroening of the Housing and Home Finance Agency, Public Housing Administration dated January 21, 1948, notes that "New York Life is really interested in Greendale" (CSP/CUL).

25. Stein to Mayer, 16 October 1947, CSP/CUL. Commissioner Egan did intervene with Foley, his boss at the HHFA, resulting in the Greenbelt Towns being specifically exempted from Public Regulation No. 1 with more favorable conditions for their sale designed to protect them. Senator Taft worked to get a law passed in 1948 that provided FHA insured loans for those wishing to purchase greenbelt homes, thus making it easier for existing residents to buy them. Stein to MacMahon, 22 June 1948, CSP/CUL; Stein to Stephenson, 18 April 1949, Box 4, CSP/CUL.

26. Public Law 65, Chapter 127, 81st Cong., 1st sess. (19 May 1949). Infrastructure and public facilities, such as community pools and parks, were conveyed to the appropriate local government agencies. Julian Whittlesey partnered with Mayer in the architecture firm of Mayer and Whittlesey formed in 1935. He had been part of the Housing Study Guild and worked on the town of Greenbrook, New Jersey. Stein to Egan, 12 July 1949, Box 9, CSP/CUL. See also Stein, Mayer, and Whittlesey to Egan, 30 May 1949, Box 9, CSP/CUL.

27. C. S. Stein, "Disposal of Greenbelt Towns" (unpublished notes, October 3 and 4, 1949), Box 9, CSP/CUL. At Greenbelt, all the row houses and some apartment units were sold to the Greenbelt Veterans Homeowners Corporation, which granted contracts to the Foundation for Cooperative Housing (FCH) to develop more than seven hundred acres of land (see Roger Willcox to Cyril McC. Henderson, Municipal Manager, Corporation of the District of Kitimat, 2 January 1953, Box 3, CSP/CUL). Willcox, who worked as Stein's assistant on the new town of Kitimat, British Columbia, transitioned directly from that project to head the FCH in early 1953. Both Whittlesey and Stein functioned as advisors and board members of the new nonprofit. Very few houses were developed and lots sold, and by the mid-1950s, the remainder of the vacant property was sold to private developers. For further discussion of Greenbelt and what happened to Greendale and Greenhills, see Albert Mayer, *Greenbelt Towns Revisited* (Washington, DC: Department of Housing and Urban Development, 1968).

28. Mumford to Stein, 12 July 1947, Box 16, CSP/CUL. Stein to Mumford, 16 January 1948, BMP/DCL. Other than Stein, MacKaye was the only previous long-term RPAA member to attend the meeting, though Harold Buttenheim, who had been involved with the group, also at-

tended. In total, twelve architects and planners participated. At the meeting, Osborn emphasized the significance of national, long-term planning and the engagement of rural groups interested in preserving farmland and open space. See "Memorandum of New Town Conference, December 1947 to April 1948," Prepared by Paul Oppermann, Box 7, CSP/CUL. Citing the RPNY's budget of $250,000 annually, Stein proposed an annual budget to start at $100,000. Portions of this section are adapted from Larsen, "Cities to Come."

29. C. S. Stein, "A Program for the Regional Planning Association of America," (unpublished, April 18, 1948), Box 8, CSP/CUL.

30. Bauer to Stein, 13 April 1948, Box 8, CSP/CUL; Mayer to Stein, 26 October 1948, and Kohn to Stein, 23 August 1948, Box 8, CSP/CUL; Stein to Mumford, 30 May 1948, Box 8, CSP/CUL.

31. See "Minutes of Meeting of the Regional Planning Association of America" (unpublished, April 22, 1948), Box 8, CSP/CUL; C. S. Stein, "Memo to 'The members' of the RPAA" (unpublished, 18 September 1948), Bancroft Library, University of California, Berkeley.

32. The group decided to change their name to the Regional Development Council of America in January 1949. By April 1951, there were 64 dues paying members with the majority—21—in the New York City area. Overall membership was at 103. See list of members of the RDCA, April 1951, Box 8, CSP/CUL. Paul Oppermann, a member of the American Institute of Planners, worked as a consultant in Washington, DC, and served on the Bureau of Community Facilities of the Federal Works Agency. Matthew Nowicki was an architect and planner from Poland who was acting head of the North Carolina State College Department of Architecture at the time. Carl Feiss had been a student of Henry Wright's and served in a variety of capacities with the federal government, including chief of the Community Planning and Development Branch of HHFA. T. J. Kent was a planner and the department head of Civic Planning at the University of California, Berkeley. An architect and principal project planner for the NYCHA, Elisabeth Coit had edited *Public Housing Design* for the Federal Public Housing Authority. At the time, Eric Carlson was assistant editor of *The American City*. Also a student of Wright's, architect and planner Chloethiel Woodard Smith had served as chief of Research and Planning for FHA in the 1930s and was already known as an authority of Latin American planning. Roger Willcox, a friend of the Stein family for many years, worked at the time for the Regional Plan of New York.

33. Fritz Gutheim, "Preliminary Report to R.P.C.A. re Proposed Suggestions to the Hoover Commission" (unpublished report, December 7, 1948), Box 8, CSP/CUL. At the time, the RPCA, or Regional Planning Council of America, was the title of the organization. Gutheim to Herbert Hoover, Chairman, Commission on Organization of the Executive Branch of the Government, First Draft, no date, Box 8, CSP/CUL. See Philip Funigiello, "City Planning in World War II: The Experience of the National Resources Planning Board," in *Introduction to Planning History in the United States*, ed. Donald A. Krueckeberg (New Brunswick, NJ: The Center for Urban Policy Research, Rutgers University, 1983): 152–169.

34. C. S. Stein, "On Legislation Required for Urban Development as Well as Re-Development" memo drafted for an unknown audience dated 29 December 1948, Box 8, CSP/CUL; Announcement for an upcoming RDCA meeting on 9 February 1949, Box 8, CSP/CUL. RDCA, "A Division of Planned Development for New York State" (unpublished minutes, February 9, 1950), Box 8, CSP/CUL; S. R. Mozes, "The Growth of State Planning in New York State" *IFHP Bulletin* 1 (1963): 4–20, Box 11, CSP/CUL.

35. Different members of the RDCA assumed responsibility for presenting specific topics to the group. Ben Kizer, who had been promoting a Columbia Valley Authority, testified in Washington regarding the Columbia Valley Administration Bill (H.R. 4286, introduced on April 14,

1949). He led the discussion on the topic, "The Columbia River and How it Makes a Region" at the October 14, 1949 RDCA meeting. Fritz Gutheim, "Preliminary Report to R.P.C.A. re Proposed Suggestions to the Hoover Commission" (unpublished report, December 7, 1948), Box 8, CSP/CUL. The councils were intended to be "broadly representative of the region," including politicians and public officials from relevant agencies representing the area, citizens, and special interest groups. RDCA, "Minutes" (unpublished, October 20, 1950), Box 180, LMP/UPA. See also C. S. Stein, President, RDCA, "Report on meeting of 20 October 1950" (unpublished, June 4, 1951), Box 8, CSP/CUL; C. S. Stein, "Report" (unpublished, June 4, 1951), Box 8, CSP/CUL. Mumford acknowledged at the meeting that he believed such a framework required a "top-notch administration decentralized from the top down under central control from Washington. It all needs a type of coordination we've never seen."

36. C. S. Stein, "On Legislation Required for Urban Development as Well as Re-Development" memo drafted for an unknown audience dated 29 December 1948, Box 8, CSP/CUL. Truman reorganized the federal housing agencies in late July 1947 creating the HHFA to oversee the Home Loan Bank Board, the FHA, and the Public Housing Administration. According to Nathaniel Keith, at the time assistant to the housing administrator of the HHFA, the National Public Housing Conference was the "main coordinating group" of the various agencies advocating for the Housing Act of 1949. See Nathaniel Keith, *Politics and the Housing Crisis since 1930* (New York: Universe Books, 1973); Hugh Pomeroy, "Memo on Redevelopment and Development Legislation—Federal and State," 5 December 1948 (Box 8, CSP/CUL), drafted by Pomeroy during an RDCA meeting, the memo reflected the organization's position. RDCA, "Minutes" (unpublished, December 22, 1948), CSP/CUL, Box 8. Due to the predominance of industry as an employer during this time, much of the discussion centered on the location of industry. An RDCA meeting on March 27, 1950, focused on the government's role in locating industry in Great Britain as a possible model for the United States (RDCA, "The British Industrial (Trading) Estate" (unpublished minutes, meeting of March 27, 1950, issued June 1950), Box 10, CSP/CUL.

37. Stein to Johnson, 3 February 1949, Box 18, CSP/CUL; Keith, *Politics and the Housing Crisis*; Housing and Home Finance Agency, "A Handbook of Information on the Provisions of the Housing Act of 1949" (Washington, DC: Office of the Administrator, July 1949), 2; ibid, 3. At their meeting of May 13, 1949, members reiterated their concerns about the proposed legislation—a focus on compartmentalized projects rather than those comprising a comprehensive, long range plan and "the basic weakness ... so far redevelopment is tied to housing." See RDCA, "Minutes of the May 13, 1949 meeting" (unpublished, dated November 26, 1949), Box 8, CSP/CUL.

38. Nathaniel S. Keith to Stein, 9 March 1950; RDCA, "Memo" (unpublished, January 17, 1950), Box 8, CSP/CUL.

39. Augur to Stein, 9 November 1950; Memo from Stein to Mumford, Subject: Notes on Proposed RDCA Memo, 4 December 1950; and Memo from RDCA, signed by President C. S. Stein, to Charles E. Wilson, Director of Defense Mobilization, Subject: "Building for Productive Defense," 6 February 1951, Box 8, CSP/CUL.

40. For more on dispersal see K. C. Parsons, "Shaping the Regional City, 1950–1990: The Plans of Tracy Augur and Clarence Stein for Dispersing Federal Workers from Washington, DC," in *Proceedings of the Third National Conference on American Planning History* (Cincinnati: Society for American City and Regional Planning History, 1989): 649–691; Subcommittee of the Committee on Public Works United States Senate, *Hearings on S. 4232: A Bill to Authorize a Program to Provide for the Construction of Federal Buildings Outside of, but in the Vicinity of and*

*Accessible to the District of Columbia, and for Other Purposes,* 81st Cong., 2nd sess., 13, 14, and 18 December 1950, Written Statement of C. Stein incorporated into the Record, 178. This quote also appeared in an article in *The American City* in February 1951 entitled "Regional Development Council Urges New Towns for D.C. Region," no author. Committee on Public Works United States Senate, *Report No. 216 to accompany S. 218,* 82nd Cong., 1st Sess. 11 April 1951, 6.

41. Stein testified on February 19, 1951. See Committee on Banking and Currency United States Senate, *Defense Housing Act: Hearings on S. 349,* 82nd Cong., 1st sess., 1951; Foley to Stein, 17 April 1951, Box 8, CSP/CUL; Albert Mayer, "A Call to the Planners," *Journal of the American Institute of Planners* (fall 1951): 161–162, 162.

42. Stein to Miller, Director, Planning and Housing Division, Columbia University, 22 April 1947, Box 14; "City and Regional Planning at M.I.T." (M.I.T. Office of Publications, circa 1955), n.p., Box 10, CSP/CUL.

43. Draft letter from Stein to Perkins, October 1950, Box 8; Stein to Bannister, 26 December 1950, Box 15, CSP/CUL.

44. The other members of the team were Dr. Edwin S. Burdell, president of Cooper Union in New York, who chaired the committee; Arthur McVoy, director, Department of Planning, Baltimore, Maryland; and Joseph L. Fisher, associate director, Resources for the Future, Inc., Washington, DC. See Killian to Stein, 28 October 1955, Box 10, CSP/CUL. According to the report prepared by the committee in November 1955, MIT had the second oldest program in the country, just behind Columbia, and the largest number of alumni of any planning school. See President's Special Committee to Review the Program, "A Summary of the Program and Objectives of the Department of City and Regional Planning at M.I.T." dated November 1955, Box 10, CSP/CUL; C. S. Stein, "Memorandum on Planning Education at M.I.T.," 11 November 1955, 2, Box 10, CSP/CUL; Ibid, 4–5.

45. Bauer to Stein, 15 December 1955; President's Special Committee to review the Program, "A Summary of the Program and Objectives of the Department of City and Regional Planning at M.I.T.," November 1955, 7, Box 10, CSP/CUL;. Excerpt from Report on Athens Meeting—June 11–16, 1962, Urbanism Commission, U.I.A., Box 14, CSP/CUL.

46. See C. S. Stein, "California Institute of Technology Visits with Hardie Phillip" (unpublished notes, February 21, 1947), Box 1, CSP/CUL. Portions of this section are adapted from Larsen, "Cities to Come."

47. See Lewis Mumford, "Memorandum on Planning," circa March 1947; and "Memorandum on Planning II," 6 March 1947 (Call #0220/2, Department of Special Collections and University Archives, Stanford University Libraries). Memo from the Business Manager's Office, Stanford University, to the President's Office, 13 September 1950 (Call #SU 216, Department of Special Collections and University Archives, Stanford University Libraries). Stein to Alf E. Brandin, Business Manager, Stanford University, 1 May 1951, Box 4, CSP/CUL. MacMahon also developed ties to Stanford. She appeared during the summer of 1951 in the title role of "The Mad Woman of Chaillot" at the Stanford Theater. In the mid-1950s, she was appointed "artist-in-residence" for three summers, and she and Stein lived on campus. She is recognized as the first professional actress to receive such an appointment at a major university. See Jeanne Stein, "Aline MacMahon Had the Wit to Sense What Audiences Liked Her to Project," *Films in Review* 16 (December 1965): 616–632.

48. Minutes of Advisory Committee on Land and Building Development, Stanford University, 14 January 1952, 1 (Department of Special Collection and University Archives, Stanford University Libraries).

49. Stein to Sterling, 16 January and 14 April 1952 (Call #SC 216, Department of Special

Collection and University Archives, Stanford University Libraries). In his report, Stein mentioned that more detailed studies were necessary in order to begin the development process. Brandin to the President's Office, Attention: Robert J. Wert, 9 September 1952 (Call #SC 216, Department of Special Collection and University Archives, Stanford University Libraries). Brandin to Stein, 27 April 1953, Box 4, CSP/CUL.

50. C. S. Stein, "Regional City" Alcan (unpublished report, July 26, 1951), Box 9, CSP/CUL.

51. West to Stein, 13 and 31 July 1951; Stein to West, 27 July 1951; Stein to A. W. Whitaker Jr., vice president and general manager of Alcan, 5 October 1951, Box 2, CSP/CUL. For his efforts, Stein was paid fifteen thousand dollars plus expenses for a six-month period to "direct and coordinate all physical and functional planning" with the option for him to continue his contract. In return, he agreed to devote all his professional efforts to Kitimat during this period. Mayer and Whittlesey were appointed as "master physical plan Planning Consultant[s]" on September 12, 1951. See "Kitimat Townsite Report—Diary" (unpublished, dated September 24, 1951 through May 9, 1952), Box 3, CSP/CUL.

52. Peter and Cornelia Oberlander, "Critique: Canada's New Towns," *Progressive Architecture* 37 (August 1956): 113–119. The Oberlanders defined single enterprise communities as follows: "The town is tied to the single enterprise that generated it in the first instance" (113). By the time they wrote the article in the mid-1950s, approximately 160 single enterprise communities had been documented in Canada. "Industry Builds Kitimat," *Architectural Forum* 101 (July 1954): 128–147, 139.

53. Industry Builds Kitimat," *Architectural Forum* 101 (July 1954): 128–147, 139. Pixie Meldrum, "Kitimat: The First Five Years" (Corporation of the District of Kitimat, 1958).

54. Willcox left the project in early 1953 to found the Foundation for Cooperative Housing (FCH). The new organization had secured contracts to develop residences for the Greenbelt Veteran's Housing Corporation in Greenbelt, Maryland, as well as cooperative units for the United Nations International Cooperative Community. See Willcox to Cyril M. Henderson, municipal manager, Corporation of the District of Kitimat, 2 January 1953, Box 3, CSP/CUL.

55. "Kitimat Townsite Report—Brief Biographical Sketches of Consultants" (unpublished report, May 22, 1952), Box 3, CSP/CUL. MacKaye and Ross, "Suggestions re Development of Kitimat Regions, British Columbia," (unpublished report, January 26, 1952), 1–2, Box 3, CSP, CUL.

56. Due to the higher development costs associated with its remote location, Alcan offered to any employee who constructed his home a second mortgage and a monthly bonus "roughly equal to principal and carrying charges of the second mortgage" ("Industry Builds Kitimat," *Architectural Forum* 101 [October 1954]: 158–161, 160). In 1954, the town council adopted zoning regulations consistent with "the most important principles of the master plan" (Meldrum, "Kitimat," 16).

57. See Albert Mayer and Julian Whittlesey, "Kitimat Townsite Report" (unpublished report, February 29, 1952), 20, Box 3, CSP/CUL; and Albert Mayer and Julian Whittlesey, "Kitimat Townsite Report—Neighborhood 'A'—The First Community to be Built: Description of Plan and its Underlying Principles, Detailed" (unpublished report, no date), 7–2, Box 3, CSP/CUL. No specific figure was given for the number of families on the larger superblock. Mayer and Whittlesey, "Kitimat Townsite Report—Neighborhood 'A'," 7–2 and 7–3, Box 3, CSP/CUL.

58. See the neighborhood community center plan in "Industry Builds Kitimat," *Architectural Forum* 101 (August 1954): 120–127, 126. Stein and Willcox, "Memorandum on Neighborhood Center Design Requirements" (unpublished report, December 3, 1952), 2, Box 3, CSP/CUL; "Industry Builds Kitimat," *Architectural Forum* 101 (July 1954): 128–147.

59. Mayer and Whittlesey, "Kitimat Townsite Report," 10; C. S. Stein, "Kitimat Townsite Report—Planning Objectives for Kitimat," (unpublished report, May 11, 1952), 5, Box 2, CSP/CUL.

60. Stein began showing signs of strain in late 1952 and early 1953. MacKaye looked after him while MacMahon worked in Hollywood in January and February 1953. He resumed shock treatment during this time. Though Stein hoped the situation was temporary, under doctor's orders, he terminated his association with Alcan in February 1953. See MacKaye to MacMahon, 5 February 1953 and Stein to J. B. White, vice president, Alcan, 5 February 1953, CSP/CUL. Still, Stein continued providing some input to the town site report in April and June 1953. Oberlander and Oberlander, "Canada's New Towns," 113.

61. Meldrum, "Kitimat," 18. Mayer and Whittlesey visited the town in 1955 and specifically noted "the level of crudeness and incompleteness" evident in the first neighborhood as a significant concern (see Mayer and Whittlesey to James E. Dudley, Planner, and Cyril McC. Henderson, Municipal Manager, Corporation of the District of Kitimat, 25 October 1955, Box 3, CSP/CUL). Interestingly in their 1956 assessment of Kitimat, Peter and Cornelia Oberlander argued that the strong regulations within Kitimat could force developers to build just outside the town, most likely along the new road connecting Kitimat with the nearby town of Terrace, resulting in a "rash of ribbon development" (114). "Industry Builds Kitimat," *Architectural Forum* 101 (July 1954): 128–147, 145.

62. C. S. Stein, "Regional City" (unpublished lecture, Ottawa, Canada, October 1950, Revised April 1953), Box 9, CSP/CUL. In a letter to Ken Wilhelm, Santa Clara Farm Bureau, dated 9 October 1956, Stein acknowledged "that Kitimat and the places they are rebuilding in England are not regional cities. They are New Towns. Towns of that kind with large agricultural areas between them is what would make a Regional City" (Box 8, CSP/CUL). C. S. Stein, "Method of Planning Kitimat for Comprehensive Operation and Development" (unpublished report, April 21, 1953), Box 3, CSP/CUL. In May 1957, Whittlesey visited Kitimat to assess difficulties with developing the City Center, in part due to poor implementation of the plan. Mayer and Whittlesey were clearly still considered the consultants on the project, and Whittlesey was retained to redesign the City Center plan while accommodating the structures and parking that had already been installed. His letters back to Stein and Mayer express his exasperation, not only with the lack of coordination and oversight by Alcan's administration but also with the poor site planning, grading, and drainage throughout the project. See letters to Mayer and Stein dated 3 and 13 May 1957, Box 3, CSP/CUL.

63. Charles Bennett and Milton Breivogel, "The Plan for the San Fernando Valley, Developed by the Los Angeles Planning Commission," *Pencil Points* 26 (June 1945): 93–98, 93–94.

64. C. S. Stein, "San Fernando Valley" (unpublished notes, April 11, 1951), 3–4, Box 8, CSP/CUL.

65. C. S. Stein, "N.E. Los Angeles County—Visit with Milton Breifogel, Holden and Catherine Bauer" (unpublished notes, August 3, 1955), Box 8, CSP/CUL.

66. Santa Clara County, "Generalized Development Plan," 27 January 1954, Box 8, CSP/CUL. Stein to Ken Wilhelm, Santa Clara Farm Bureau, 28 November 1956, discussing Stein's recommendations regarding "Planned Development and Preservation of Agriculture in Santa Clara County," Box 8, CSP/CUL. During the summer of 1956, Stein visited farm land with Wilhelm, discussed planning issues in the area with Paul Oppermann, director of planning for nearby San Francisco, met with large landholders in the county, was the featured speaker in front of 125 "agriculturists, wives, and children" regarding the application of the Regional City approach, and studied local planning documents and state laws regarding annexation and land use. See "Minutes of Talk with R. Ken Wilhelm, of Santa Clara County Farm Bureau," dated

25 July 1956; "Conservation of Agricultural Land—Talk with Paul Oppermann," dated 28 July 1956; Stein to Breivogel, director of planning, The Regional Planning Commission, Los Angeles County, 12 September 1956; and C. S. Stein, "Santa Clara's Future" (unpublished notes, October 14, 1956), Box 9, CSP/CUL. C. S. Stein, "The Regional City and the Water-Shed District Are Parallel Conceptions" (unpublished notes included in a letter to Gordon Stephenson. October 10 and 21, 1954), Box 10, CSP/CUL. Stein had been following the efforts of the Soil Conservation Division of the U.S. Agricultural Department to develop Small Water-Shed Districts. These included ongoing meetings with Ken Ross, who had consulted on Kitimat, and Edward Graham of the Soil Conservation Service. Stein was especially excited about passage of soil conservation legislation in the summer of 1954 that he broadly viewed as a means to establish regional agencies to promote rural-urban partnerships for balanced development (Public Law 566-83d Congress, Chapter 656-2d Session, H.R. 6788, dated 4 August 1954).

67. Stein in consultation with Mayer and Smith, "Proposals Regarding the West Side Renewal Project" (unpublished report, March 4, 1959), 8–9, Box 10, CSP/CUL. Ibid, 10–11.

68. City Planning Commission and Department of City Planning, City of New York, "Planning Progress 1959" (New York, n.p. 1959), 11. Retrieved from http://www.nyc.gov/html/dcp/pdf/history_project/planning_progress_report_1959.pdf. C. S. Stein, "A Note on Small Parks throughout New York City" (unpublished, January 22, 1963), 1, Box 10, CSP/CUL. As a continuing member of the Citizen's Housing and Planning Council, a group Stein had been involved with since its inception in 1937, the community architect participated on an Open Space Committee that produced a document entitled, "Wanted: An Effective Park Plan for New York City," which outlined the organization's statement and recommendations on the matter. These closely paralleled Stein's position.

69. Stein to Robbins, 1 July 1959, Box 10, CSP/CUL. See also William Reid, Chairman, NYCHA, to Maxwell Hahn, Executive Vice President of the Field Foundation, 13 November 1959, Box 10, CSP/CUL, requesting that the foundation fund Stein and Mayer's study.

70. Stein to Robbins, 1 July 1959, Box 10, CSP/CUL. Stein's affiliation with the Lavanburg Foundation extended back to the philanthropic organization's founding in 1927 when Stein was retained as a consulting architect on the Lavanburg Homes. In the mid-1950s, he served as chairman of the Lavanburg Foundation's Committee on Cooperative Housing. Stein and Mayer, "Attachment No. 1—Proposed Research-Design Project in Large Scale Housing" (unpublished report, circa November 1959), 1, Box 10, CSP/CUL; ibid, 4. Minutes of the Lavanburg Foundation, "Research Design Project concerning open and communal spaces originally submitted by New York City Housing Authority November 13, 1959 and considered at Lavanburg meeting early in December," Box 10, CSP/CUL; Roger W. Straus Jr. of Farrar, Straus & Company, Inc. to Oscar Straus and Carl Stern, Lavanburg Foundation Board, 10 March 1960, Box 7, CSP/CUL. Among the reasons Stein noted for his resignation was "I can accomplish more in the fields of Community and Regional Development and Housing by myself or with those who are sympathetic or have confidence in my judgment" (notes dated 1 August 1961, Box 7, CSP/CUL).

71. Thomas B. Thompson, assistant commissioner for Development, Public Housing Administration, Housing and Home Finance Agency to Albert Mayer, 7 December 1961, Box 10, CSP/CUL; Keith, *Politics and the Housing Crisis*, 144; "Grant Application pursuant to Section 207 of Public Law 87-70, the Housing Act of 1961, for the purpose of aiding in the financing of low-income housing demonstration project," signed by officials of the NYCHA, 6 June 1963, Box 10, CSP/CUL. Bloom, *Public Housing that Worked*, maintains that this period was a particularly relevant one for revitalizing landscape design at the agency's projects—especially given the

high amount of open space (over 80 percent) on these properties and the increasing number of children living there (see especially 163).

72. Stein, *Toward New Towns*, 219.

## 7. International Initiatives and Building a Legacy

1. His depression was considered serious enough that it was treated with electroshock therapy at the Neurological Institute in New York City for a month before Stein then continued his recuperation at Silver Hills in New Canaan. Based on consultations his sister Lillie had with his doctors, the concern was that he was overwhelmed by his work and should retire. He in fact returned to work in late 1946. See letters to MacMahon dated 30 July and 5 August 1945 (Box 36, CSP/CUL).

2. An architect and planner, Abercrombie led the professionals who put the plans together. For more on postwar planning in Great Britain, see Frederic J. Osborn, *Green-Belt Cities*, new ed. with a forward by Lewis Mumford (1946; reprint London: Evelyn, Adams & Mackay, 1969); Frederic J. Osborn and Arnold Whittick, *The New Towns: The Answer to Megalopolis* (London: Leonard Hill, 1969); Peter Self, "The Evolution of the Greater London Plan, 1944–1970," *Progress in Planning* 57 (2002): 145–175; Peter Hall, *Cities of Tomorrow*, 4th ed. (Malden, MA: Wiley-Blackwell, 2014); and Stephen V. Ward, *Planning the Twentieth-Century City* (Chichester, UK: John Wiley & Sons, 2002). Unwin was technical adviser to the Greater London Planning Commission appointed by Minister of Health Neville Chamberlain in 1927. The report of the commission, authored by Unwin and completed in 1933, also recommended a regional governmental agency to oversee planning. Though approved in 1935, not much came directly from this report. Once he became prime minister, Chamberlain established the Barlow Commission in 1937 to examine challenges associated with the significant residential and industrial densities found in large cities. The report contained an impressive amount of data documenting the social and economic disadvantages in these areas and made recommendations regarding, "national planning, dispersal, and guidance of the location of industry" (Osborn, *Green-Belt Cities*, 47). Published in 1940, the Barlow Report provided the foundation (along with two other reports that addressed respectively compensation for land and safeguarding the countryside) for the County of London Plan and the Greater London Plan. C. S. Stein, "Planning Technique and the London Plan," *Architectural Review* 96 (September 1944): 79–80, 79.

3. The reduction of population in London proper, estimated at just over 1 million, would be absorbed in the eight new towns (with an average population of 50,000 each) and expansion of existing towns. A relatively small number (approximately 100,000) would move well outside the municipal area. Osborn, *Green-Belt Cities*, 48.

4. Stein to Mumford, 15 April 1946, CSP/CUL.

5. The dramatic competition to be the host city for the new UN headquarters involved several cities with New York narrowly beating Philadelphia in the eleventh hour. The architect Wallace Harrison, a senior aide to Nelson Rockefeller, found the site. The younger Rockefeller convinced his father John D. Rockefeller to buy it and donate it, thus securing New York City's bid. Harrison, architect of the Trylon and Perisphere at the World's Fair, headed the international team that designed the project. Fairbank, *Liang and Lin*, 150.

6. Neither project was awarded to the architects.

7. Stein to Mumford, 15 April 1946, CSP/CUL.

8. Designated on November 11, 1946, the project was delayed for more than seven months

due to a court case brought by residents of the area who argued that the government had not followed proper procedure in designating the town. See the Minister of Local Government and Planning, *Town and Country Planning, 1943–1951* (London: His Majesty's Stationery Office, 1951), especially 126. Stephenson worked for the precursor agency, the Ministry of Works and Buildings in the Reconstruction Group beginning in 1942; then in the Ministry of Town and Country Planning when it was formed in 1943 through his resignation in 1947, when he took an academic position at Liverpool University. During his time with the ministry, among other responsibilities, Stephenson drafted the "community planning standards" in the Greater London Plan for the inner urban, suburban, and outer country rings around the city. In July 1945, he, along with four others, was asked to prepare the plan for Stevenage. Gordon Stephenson, "Building in Cities—The Challenge to Architects," *Architecture in Australia* 55 (July 1966): 123–124. When he attended MIT on fellowship, Stephenson also heard Stein lecture. He began the city planning graduate program there in 1936, the first year MIT awarded advanced degrees in the profession, and completed his studies in two years. Gordon Stephenson, *On a Human Scale: A Life in City Design*, ed. Christina DeMarco (South Fremantle, Australia: Fremantle Arts Centre Press, 1992), 87.

9. Stein to Robert Alexander, 26 January 1951, Box 14, CSP/CUL. The *Town Planning Review* had been established in 1910, one year after the program in Civic Design was founded at Liverpool University. Abercrombie, a professor there at the time, was the first editor of the journal.

10. Stephenson to Stein, 8 March 1949, Box 4; Stein to MacMahon, 8 July 1947, Box 15, CSP/CUL. On July 25 Stein sent to Mumford a first outline, stating the reasons for writing the book—"These experiments in planning and doing, social, economic and structural, have influenced activities not only in America but elsewhere. They promise if properly understood and analyzed, to offer much more" (outline dated 17 July 1947, Box 1, CSP/CUL).

11. The plan developed in 1947 was intended to reduce trip time along these major transit routes in Scandinavia's largest city. Rasmussen chaired the Regional Plan Committee, which conducted the study behind the plan. Though Denmark established powers to implement the plan through the Urban Development Act of 1949, those outside the city limits did not necessarily do so. Thus development occurred within the areas that were supposed to remain open as recreational and passive parks for the nearby urban residents.

12. In 1949, Wilhelm-Olsson oversaw a competition to design Vastra Frolunda, a new town near Goteborg for thirty thousand people based on guidelines he had prepared. Similar to the County of London and Greater London Plans, Stockholm adopted a regional master plan in 1952 that called for redevelopment to create a less congested center city combined with initiatives to decentralize industry and to build new communities in the outlying areas. Stein to Yngve Larsson, 4 January 1950, Box 16, CSP/CUL.

13. For more on the influence of the Radburn Idea on Greater Stockholm's "new towns," see K. C. Parsons, "American Influence on Stockholm's Post World War II Suburban Expansion," *Planning History* 14, no. 1 (1990): 3–14. As Parsons indicates, the Radburn Idea was not consistently followed throughout Vallingby perhaps due to the challenging topography. Further, though the Swedes adapted the neighborhood unit, the center of the community focused on the commercial area rather than the school—though the school was located nearby. In addition, the mix of housing types and densities was much more varied than at Radburn. C. S. Stein, "Stockholm Builds a New Town," *Planning Proceedings of the American Society of Planning Officials Conference* (1952), 57–64, 58. William-Olsson to Stein, 10 January 1950, CSP/CUL. William-Olsson did acknowledge the prevalence of higher-density living and municipal land ownership as significant differences from conditions at Radburn.

14. Gordon Stephenson, "Editorial Notes," *Town Planning Review* 20 (October 1949): 185. See also Stephenson, *On a Human Scale*. Stephenson and his wife Flora, also an architect and planner, helped Stein edit the drafts for publication. Stein to MacKaye, 2 August 1949, BMP/DCL. Stein, *Toward New Towns*, 44. Of course, Radburn's superblocks are significantly larger than those at Hampstead Garden Suburb. See K. C. Parsons, "British and American Community Design: Clarence Stein's Manhattan Transfer, 1924–74," *Planning Perspectives* 7, no. 2 (1992): 181–210. Stephenson, "Editorial Notes," 185. The projects featured in this issue were Sunnyside Gardens, Radburn, Chatham Village, Phipps Gardens, and Hillside Homes. The remainder of Stein's articles appeared in the January 1950 issue and addressed Valley Stream, the Greenbelt Towns, and Baldwin Hills Village.

15. Stephenson began design work in 1950, with the first phase (301 units) under construction in 1951 and the second phase (197 units) underway in 1953. Stephenson to Stein, 16 September 1950, Box 4, CSP/CUL. Stephenson, *On a Human Scale*, 123. The "Wrexham Experiment" as Stephenson called it, was successful in demonstrating cost savings in design and construction during a period when British housing costs were skyrocketing. Stephenson designed the residential project in the largest industrial center in Wales with three other architects who had partnered with him on the Physics and Civic Design buildings at Liverpool University in 1949–1950.

16. Stephenson, *On a Human Scale*, 98. Ibid, 98–99.

17. With the formal establishment of the Stevenage Development Corporation, a chief architect and planner—Clifford Holliday—was appointed by the corporation in 1947. This was the model that was followed by the other British new towns—rather than the architects and planners working directly under the Ministry of Town Planning as they did initially on Stevenage.

18. C. S. Stein, "The Proposed Town Center of Stevenage" (unpublished report, September 5, 1950), 2, Box 2, CSP/CUL.

19. In a letter to Stein dated 16 September 1950, Stephenson notes, "I edited your draft and changed very little and it was circulated to members of the corporation as a document by all 3 together with prints of the diagram" (Box 4, CSP/CUL). Stephenson to Stein, 16 September 1950, Box 4, CSP/CUL. Stein continued corresponding with Stephenson and Holliday to develop more detailed aspects of the plan through the spring of 1951.

20. T. Hampson, "The Stevenage Town Centre," *Town and Country Planning* (January 1959): 13–16, 13. Osborn and Whittick, *The New Towns*, 179.

21. For more on Mayer's work in India, see Laurel Harbin and Kristin Larsen, "American Regionalism in India: How Lessons from the New Deal Greenbelt Town Program Translated to Post-World War II India" (paper presented at the 16th International Planning History Society Conference in St. Augustine, Florida, July 21, 2014); Andrew Friedman, "The Global Postcolonial Moment and the American New Town: India, Reston, Dodoma," *Journal of Urban History* 38, no. 3 (2012): 553–576 ; Sanjeev Vidyarthi, "Reimagining the American Neighborhood Unit for India," in *Crossing Borders: International Exchange and Planning Practices*, eds. Patsy Healey and Robert Upton (New York: Routledge, 2010), 73–93; Tridib Banerjee, "U.S. Planning Expeditions to Postcolonial India: From Ideology to Innovation in Technical Assistance," *Journal of the American Planning Association* 75, no. 2 (2009): 193–208.

22. Albert Mayer, "Techniques of New Town Design," *American Institute of Planners* (1949): 19–20, 19, Box 10, CSP/CUL. Prime Minister Nehru had charged Mayer to design a modern city for the postcolonial era while also accommodating refugees from nearby Pakistan. Mayer's contract for work on the master plan had been finalized in December 1949. In addition to his partners Julian Whittlesey and Milton Glass, Mayer retained Eberlin for his engineering skills; James Buckley, an expert on city economics and transportation; and landscape architect Clara

Coffey. While Stein had already provided feedback on the project in February, Mayer formalized the arrangement in a March 2, 1950, letter to Stein, broadly outlining the type of feedback they were seeking and apologetically listing a fee of $1,200 for his time (Mayer to Stein, 2 March 1950, Box 2, CSP/CUL). Mayer, "Techniques of New Town Design," 20.

23. Memo from Stein to Mayer and Whittlesey, "Capital of East Punjab: Suggestions from Farmers' Market, Los Angeles, Applicable to Local Markets," 22 February 1950, Box 2, CSP/CUL. Memo from Stein to Mayer and Whittlesey, "East Punjab Capital: Comments on Preliminary General Plans," 21 March 1950, Box 2, CSP/CUL.

24. Mayer to Shri Varma, Chief Engineer, Chandigarh, 25 March 1950, 4, CSP/CUL. This village ideal reflected the Gandhian rural village as a collective, cooperative, and cultural unit (see Friedman, "The Global Postcolonial Moment"). Mayer to Shri Varma, Chief Engineer, Chandigarh, 25 March 1950, 1, CSP/CUL. Norma Evenson, *Chandigarh* (Berkeley: University of California Press, 1966), 13. Evenson criticizes Mayer's emphasis on the neighborhood unit as failing to treat the government center with the proper sense of monumentality required for its design. Overall though, she admired Mayer and Nowicki's work on the city.

25. Whittlesey to Stein, 21 June 1950, Box 9, CSP/CUL.

26. Nowicki to Stein, 21 August 1950, Box 16, CSP/CUL. Of Nowicki's death Mumford observed, "He had every indication of becoming one of the great architects of our age.... His going leaves an irreplaceable and unfillable gap in all our lives" (Mumford to Stein, 3 September 1950, Box 16, CSP/CUL).

27. Between 1948, when the country was founded, and 1955, the population doubled with the addition of more than 700,000 immigrants (Harold Robinson, "Israel's Expandable House," report circa 1955, Box 13, CSP/CUL). Within the first 4½ years of gaining nationhood, the overall plan was drafted. When Stein met Glikson, the country's architect/planners were working on this plan. Stein to Karl J. Belser, Director, County of Santa Clara Planning Department, 16 May 1959, Box 14, CSP/CUL. Artur Glikson, *Regional Planning and Development: Six Lectures Delivered at the Institute of Social Studies, at The Hague, 1953* (Leiden: A. W. Sijthoff's Uitgeversmaatschappij N.V., 1955), 72–73.

28. Glikson to Stein, 7 January 1956, Box 13, CSP/CUL. While a small village was on-site, the proposed medium-sized town of Beersheba was considered a new town, much like Stevenage, in this case functioning as the regional center of the Negev. Glikson was listed as chief architect of this neighborhood unit. Stein to Harold Robinson, Regional Housing Advisor, International Corporation Administration, Washington, D.C., 12 March 1956, Box 13, CSP/CUL. Artur Glikson, "Some Problems of Housing in Israel's New Towns and Suburbs," translation of a paper published in *Handasa We Adrikhalut* (Journal of the Association of Engineers and Architects, Israel) (May–June 1958), 3, Box 13, CSP/CUL. MacMahon joined Stein on this trip, which also included stops in Iran to visit town building initiatives there. Though the visits were brief, Stein managed to meet with top architects and planners in both countries, seeing Shiraz, Teheran, and Isafaham before traveling to Tel Aviv, also visiting Jerusalem, Nazareth, Beersheba, Haifa, and Acre. See Stein to Bauer, 22 April 1959, Box 14, CSP/CUL. Stein, "Planning in Israel" (unpublished notes, September 6, 1959), Box 13, CSP/CUL.

29. C. S. Stein, "Honors and Awards" (unpublished notes, circa 1967), Box 10, CSP/CUL. American Institute of Planners, Citation for the Distinguished Service Award, dated 29 October 1958, Box 10, CSP/CUL. Wyndham Thomas, Town and Country Planning Association, to Stein, 5 November 1959, Box 10, CSP/CUL. Albert Mayer, *The Urgent Future* (New York: McGraw-Hill, 1967).

30. With the overall series title of "Architecture as Total Community: The Challenge Ahead"

the seven articles appeared in the March, April, May, July, August, September, and October 1964 issues of the journal. See especially Mayer in consultation with Stein, "New Towns: And Fresh In-City Communities," *Architectural Record* 136 (August 1964): 129–138. Stein continued to promote a federal Department of Urban and Regional Development, an integrated agency overseeing housing, community facilities, redevelopment, recreation, conservation, and transportation to coordinate balanced communities and resolve urban problems on a regional basis. The 1968 and 1970 Housing Acts expanded the new town program. Many of its elements reflected goals Mayer and Stein highlighted in their articles, though the overreliance on the private sector, lack of sufficient funding, and minimal oversight did not meet with their approval. These factors, along with the recession of 1973, brought the program to a standstill.

31. Stein, *Toward New Towns*, 221.

32. Another sign of this recognition is the designation of these communities as National Historic Landmarks—Radburn (2005), Chatham Village (2005), Baldwin Hills Village (2001), and Greenbelt (1996)—with Sunnyside Gardens and Phipps Garden Apartments both listed on the National Register of Historic Places.

33. C. S. Stein, "Regional City Proposal—A Program for Further Development" (unpublished, February 22, 1955), 4, Box 10, CSP/CUL. Stein defined "community" as "a group with common interest or activity" acknowledging that "both cities and regions are made up of many different communities having different functions, serving different needs and therefore having different sizes. The population and area served by each should be determined by a balance between the size at which its activity is carried out most effectively and most economically" (C. S. Stein, "The Regional City" (unpublished, June 4, 1951), 4, Box 10, CSP/CUL). C. S. Stein, "Cities to Come—Introduction" (unpublished, February 1957), 5, Box 10, CSP/CUL.

34. Talen, *New Urbanism*, rightly points out that the RPAA membership focused on "the notion of the ecological region" (213). As Stein practiced it, regionalism was not a "separate culture" from those who focused on "the specifics of internal urban form" (215). In fact, Stein combined this broader regional vision with conceptual—via the Regional City—and pragmatic—via the Radburn Idea—approaches.

35. Wheeler, "The New Regionalism." As often occurs in historical examinations of the RPAA membership's contributions, Stein is not included in discussions regarding regional endeavors, though he played an essential role, not just as facilitator but as contributor.

36. Philip R. Berke, and Maria Manta Conroy, "Are We Planning for Sustainable Development?" *Journal of the American Planning Association* 66, no. 1 (2000): 21–33, 23. Benton MacKaye, "Regional Planning and Ecology," *Ecological Monographs* 10 (July 1940): 349–353. Stein, *Toward New Towns*, 219.

37. John Randolph as quoted in Joseph Schilling and Jonathan Logan, "Greening the Rust Belt: A Green Infrastructure Model for Right Sizing America's Shrinking Cities," *Journal of the American Planning Association* 74, no. 4 (2008): 451–466, 454. Philip R. Berke, "The Evolution of Green Community Planning, Scholarship, and Practice," *Journal of the American Planning Association* 74, no. 4 (2008): 393–407, 397. Berke outlines how the RPAA reinforced key characteristics of the green community, including "human health, natural systems, spiritual renewal, and livability" (see page 397). I would argue that the community building Stein and the RPAA advocated also fulfilled Berke's fifth and final characteristic "fair share," which addresses the benefits of increased density and a reduced environmental footprint, in their advocacy of a more effective balance between circulation, development, and open greens to enhance quality of life.

38. Stein, *Toward New Towns*, 219.

39. Larsen, "*Cities to Come*," 46; Stein, *Toward New Towns*, 219.

40. Henry S. Churchill, "Subdivisions for Investment or Speculation," *Architectural Record* 81 (May 1937): 3–7; Richard J. Neutra, "Peace Can Gain from War's Forced Changes," *New Pencil Points* 23 (November 1942): 28–40, 33. His article though gave primary responsibility for the design of Radburn to Wright, noting the cooperation of Stein along with Bing and Emmerich. Stein, *Toward New Towns,* 224. See Nicholas D. Bloom, *Suburban Alchemy: 1960s New Towns and the Transformation of the American Dream* (Columbus: Ohio State University Press, 2001), especially 19.

41. Cynthia Girling and Kenneth Helphand, *Yard, Street, Park* (New York: John Wiley & Sons, 1994), 69.

42. Andres Duany, "Preface," in Raymond Unwin, *Town Planning in Practice* (1909; reprint New York: Princeton Architectural Press, 1994): v.

43. C. S. Stein, "Memorandum to the Subcommittee on Housing and Rents, Senate Banking and Currency Committee in Reference to S-351, Authorizing Sale of Greenbelt, Greendale, and Greenhills without Competitive Bidding," 23 March 1949, Box 9, CSP/CUL. Jill Grant, *Planning the Good Community: New Urbanism in Theory and Practice* (New York: Routledge, 2006), 19–20.

44. See Edward Goetz, "Potential Effects of Federal Policy Devolution on Local Housing Expenditures," *Publius: The Journal of Federalism* 25 (summer 1995): 99–116; R. Allen Hays, *The Federal Government and Urban Housing: Ideology and Change in Public Policy* (Albany: State University of New York Press, 1995); Alex F. Schwartz, *Housing Policy in the United States,* 3rd ed. (New York: Routledge, 2014); Charles J. Orlebeke, "The Evolution of Low-Income Housing Policy, 1949 to 1999," *Housing Policy Debate* 11, no. 2 (2000): 489–520; M. A. Turner and G. T. Kingsley, *Federal Programs for Addressing Low-Income Housing Needs: A Policy Primer* (Washington, DC: Urban Institute, 2008). Schwartz notes that this federal tax incentive program has resulted in the development of 2.5 million housing units since the program's inception to the end of 2011 (135).

45. See Congress for the New Urbanism and U.S. Department of Housing and Urban Development, *Principles for Inner City Neighborhood Design* (Washington, DC: Department of Housing and Urban Development, 2000); Susan J. Popkin, Bruce Katz, Mary K. Cunningham, Karen D. Brown, Jeremy Gustafson, and Margery A. Turner, *A Decade of HOPE VI: Research Findings and Policy Challenges* (Washington, DC: Urban Institute, 2004). These livability principles are transportation choice; equitable, affordable housing; economic competitiveness; revitalization of existing communities; leveraging federal support and interagency coordination; and celebrating healthy, safe, and walkable communities.

# BIBLIOGRAPHY

Abrams, Charles. *The Future of Housing*. New York: Harper & Brothers, 1946.

Ackerman, Frederick. "Where Goes the City-Planning Movement?" *Journal of the American Institute of Architects* 7 (December 1919): 518–520.

Adam, Thomas. "Transatlantic Trading: The Transfer of Philanthropic Models between European and North American Cities during the Nineteenth and Early Twentieth Centuries." *Journal of Urban History* 28, no. 3 (2002): 328–351.

Adams, Thomas. "The New York Regional Plan—The Making of the Plan." In *Planning Problems of Town, City and Region: Papers and Discussions at the International City and Regional Planning Conference Held in New York City, April 20 to 25, 1925*, edited by International Federation for Housing and Town Planning Congress, 212–233. Baltimore, MD: Norman, Remington, 1925.

American Ethical Union. "Providing Summer Outings." *The Standard* 8 (July 1921): 29.

American Federation of Labor Housing Committee. "Should the Administration's Housing Policy Be Continued? Pro." *The Congressional Digest* 15, no. 4 (1936): 117–118.

American Institute of Architects, Committee on Community Planning. "Report of the Committee on Community Planning to the Sixty-First Annual Convention." April 6, 1928, 1–3. Box 5, CSP/CUL.

American Institute of Architects, Committee on Economics of Site-Planning and Housing. "Report of the Committee on Economics of Site-Planning and Housing to the Sixty-Fifth Annual Convention—April 1932," 1–6. Box 5, CSP/CUL.

American Institute of Planners. "Report of Committee on the Greenbelt Towns." December 26, 1947. Box 8, CSP/CUL.

Anderson, Larry. *Benton MacKaye: Conservationist, Planner, and Creator of the Appalachian Trail*. Baltimore: Johns Hopkins University Press, 2002.

Angel, Marc D., and Jeffrey Gurock. "Jews." In *The Encyclopedia of New York City*, edited by Kenneth Jackson, 620–623. New Haven: Yale University Press, 1995.

"Apartment House Planning Requirements Including Basic Dimensions." *Architectural Record* 77 (March 1935): 169–181.

Arnold, Joseph L. *The New Deal in the Suburbs*. Columbus: Ohio State University Press, 1971.

Ascher, Charles S. "The Extra-Municipal Administration of Radburn: An Experiment in Government by Contract." *National Municipal Review* 18, no. 7 (1929): 442–446.

Augur, Tracy. "Radburn—The Challenge of a New Town." *Michigan Municipal Review* 4 (February and March, 1931); reprint, New York: City Housing Corporation, circa 1931. Box 1, CSP/CUL.

# Bibliography

Bamberg, Angelique. *Chatham Village: Pittsburgh's Garden City*. Pittsburgh: University of Pittsburgh Press, 2011.

Banerjee, Tridib. "U.S. Planning Expeditions to Postcolonial India: From Ideology to Innovation in Technical Assistance." *Journal of the American Planning Association* 75, no. 2 (2009): 193–208.

Bartholomew, Harland. "Response to 'The Case for New Towns.'" *Planners' Journal* 5 (March–June 1939): 42.

Bauer, Catherine. "Description and Appraisal ... Baldwin Hills Village." *Pencil Points* 25 (September 1944): 46–60.

———. *Modern Housing*. Boston: Houghton Mifflin, 1934.

———. "Planned Large-Scale Housing: A Balance Sheet of Progress." *Architectural Record* 89 (May 1941): 89–105.

Bauman, John F., and Edward K. Muller. "The Planning Technician as Urban Visionary: Frederick Bigger and American Planning, 1881–1963." *Journal of Planning History* 1, no. 2 (2002): 124–153.

Behrendt, Walter C. *Modern Building: Its Nature, Problems, and Forms*. New York: Harcourt, Brace, 1937.

Bennett, Charles, and Milton Breivogel. "The Plan for the San Fernando Valley, Developed by the Los Angeles Planning Commission." *Pencil Points* 26 (June 1945): 93–98.

Berke, Philip R. "The Evolution of Green Community Planning, Scholarship, and Practice." *Journal of the American Planning Association* 74, no. 4 (2008): 393–407.

Berke, Philip R., and Maria Manta Conroy. "Are We Planning for Sustainable Development?" *Journal of the American Planning Association* 66, no. 1 (2000): 21–33.

Bettman, Alfred. "How to Lay Out Regions for Planning." In *Planning Problems of Town, City and Region: Papers and Discussions at the International City and Regional Planning Conference Held in New York City, April 20 to 25, 1925*, edited by International Federation for Housing and Town Planning Congress, 287–301. Baltimore, MD: Norman, Remington, 1925.

Biles, Roger. "Nathan Straus and the Failure of U.S. Public Housing, 1937–1942." *The Historian* 53, no. 1 (1990): 33–46.

Birch, Eugenie L. "Radburn and the American Planning Movement: The Persistence of an Idea." *Journal of the American Planning Association* 46, no. 4 (1980): 424–439.

Birch, Eugenie L., and Deborah S. Gardner. "The Seven-Percent Solution: A Review of Philanthropic Housing: 1870–1910." *Journal of Urban History* 7, no. 4 (1981): 403–438.

Bloom, Nicholas D. *Public Housing that Worked: New York in the Twentieth Century*. Philadelphia: University of Pennsylvania Press, 2008.

———. *Suburban Alchemy: 1960s New Towns and the Transformation of the American Dream*. Columbus: Ohio State University Press, 2001.

Bobeczko, Laura, and Richard Longstreth. "Housing Reform Meets the Marketplace." In *Housing Washington*, edited by Richard Longstreth, 159–180. Chicago: Center for American Places at Columbia College Chicago, 2010.

Boyd, John T, Jr. "Garden Apartments in Cities." *Architectural Record* 48 (July 1920): 53–74.

Brownlow, Louis. *A Passion for Anonymity: The Autobiography of Louis Brownlow, Second Half*. Chicago: University of Chicago Press, 1958.

———. "Radburn. A New Town Planned for the Motor Age." *International Housing and Town Planning Bulletin* (February 1930): 4–11.

# Bibliography

Buder, Stanley. *Visionaries and Planners: The Garden City Movement and the Modern Community*. New York: Oxford University Press, 1990.

"Building for Defense—Prefabricators Put on a Show." *Architectural Forum* 75 (September 1941): 188–189.

"*Building the World of Tomorrow*": *Official Guide Book, New York World's Fair 1939*. New York: Exposition Publications, 1939.

"Buildings First Year at War." *Architectural Forum* 78 (January 1943): 71, 73.

Butler, Charles. "The Temple Emanu-El, New York." *Architectural Forum* 52 (February 1930): 150–154.

"Camera over the U.S.A." *Theatre Arts Monthly* 23 (August 1939): 890–895.

Carlhian, Jean P. "The École des Beaux-Arts: Modes and Manners." *Journal of Architectural Education* 33, no. 2 (1979): 7–17.

Cautley, Marjorie Sewell. "Planting at Radburn." *Landscape Architecture Magazine* 21, no. 1 (1930): 23–29.

Chafee, Richard. "The Teaching of Architecture at the École des Beaux-Arts." In *The Architecture of the École des Beaux-Arts*, edited by Arthur Drexler, 61–109. New York: Museum of Modern Art, 1977.

Churchill, Henry S. "Subdivisions for Investment or Speculation." *Architectural Record* 81 (May 1937): 3–7.

City Housing Corporation. "Radburn Garden Homes." N.p., circa 1929.

——. "Radburn: Protective Restrictions and Community Administration." 1929.

City Planning Commission and Department of City Planning, City of New York. "Planning Progress 1959." New York, 1959. http://www.nyc.gov/html/dcp/pdf/history_project/planning_progress_report_1959.pdf.

Commission of Housing and Regional Planning. *Report to Governor Alfred E. Smith*. May 7, 1926.

Committee on Banking and Currency, U.S. Senate. *Defense Housing Act: Hearings on S. 349*. 82nd Cong., 1st sess., 1951.

Committee on Housing Exhibition. "The Planned Community." *Architectural Forum* 58 (April 1933): 253–274.

Committee on Public Works, U.S. Senate. *Report No. 216 to accompany S. 218*. 82nd Cong., 1st Sess. April 11, 1951.

Congress for the New Urbanism and U.S. Department of Housing and Urban Development. *Principles for Inner City Neighborhood Design*. Washington, DC: Department of Housing and Urban Development, 2000.

Cotten, Anne Boyer. "Clarence S. Stein and his Commitment to Beauty: Architect First, Community Planner Second." Master's thesis, Cornell University, 1987.

Crawford, Margaret. *Building the Workingman's Paradise: The Design of American Company Towns*. London: Verso, 1995.

Creese, Walter. *The Search for Environment: The Garden City Before and After*. 1966; reprint Baltimore: Johns Hopkins University Press, 1992.

——. *TVA's Public Planning: The Vision, the Reality*. Knoxville: University of Tennessee Press, 1990.

Cret, Paul. "The École des Beaux-Arts and Architectural Education." *Journal of the American Society of Architectural Historians* 1, no. 2 (1941): 3–15.

Curl, Edward P. "Private Capital in Large-Scale Housing." In *Housing Officials' Yearbook*,

# Bibliography

*1937*, edited by Coleman Woodbury, 110–122. Chicago: National Association of Housing Officials, 1937.

Doctors, Steven I. "The Collaborative Divide: Crafting Architectural Identity, Authority, and Authorship in the Twentieth Century." Ph.D. diss., University of California, Berkeley, 2010. https://escholarship.org/uc/item/13t043q2#page-6.

"Does Housing Offer a Career to Architects? Large-Scale, Privately Financed Housing." *Architectural Record* 83 (April 1938): 81–86.

Duany, Andres. "Preface." In *Town Planning in Practice* by Raymond Unwin, v. 1909; reprint New York: Princeton Architectural Press, 1994.

Eldst, Paula. *Governor Alfred E. Smith. The Politician as Reformer.* New York: Garland, 1983.

Emmerich, Herbert. "World War II Housing." *Journal of Housing* 12 (July 1955): 231–233.

Emmons, Paul. "Diagrammatic Practices: The Office of Frederick L. Ackerman and 'Architectural Graphic Standards.'" *Journal of the Society of Architectural Historians* 64, no. 1 (2005): 4–21.

Ethical Culture Society. "The Workingman's School and Free Kindergarten." N.p., 1881.

Evenson, Norma. *Chandigarh.* Berkeley: University of California Press, 1966.

Fairbank, Wilma. *Liang and Lin: Partners in Exploring China's Architectural Past.* Philadelphia: University of Pennsylvania Press, 1994.

Federal Housing Administration. "Planning Neighborhoods for Small Houses." Technical Bulletin No. 5. 1936, rev ed. Washington, DC: Government Printing Office, 1938.

Federal Works Agency. *First Annual Report, Federal Works Agency.* Washington, DC: United States Government Printing Office, 1940.

"The Federal Works Agency." *Architectural Forum* 73 (November 1940): 14.

Federal Writers' Project of the Works Progress Administration in New York City. *New York Panorama: A Companion to the WPA Guide to New York City.* 1938; reprint New York: Pantheon Books, 1984.

——. *The WPA Guide to New York City.* 1939; reprint New York: Pantheon Books, 1982.

Fishman, Robert. "The Metropolitan Tradition in American Planning." In *The American Planning Tradition: Culture and Policy*, edited by Robert Fishman, 64–85. Baltimore: Johns Hopkins University Press, 2000.

Friedman, Andrew. "The Global Postcolonial Moment and the American New Town: India, Reston, Dodoma." *Journal of Urban History* 38, no. 3 (2012): 553–576.

Friedmann, John, and Clyde Weaver. *Territory and Function: The Evolution of Regional Planning.* Berkeley: University of California Press, 1979.

Fuller Company, George A. *Housing: Building Construction 1882–1944.* New York: George A. Fuller, 1944.

Fulton, William. "The Garden Suburb and the New Urbanism." In *From Garden City to Green City: The Legacy of Ebenezer Howard*, edited by Kermit C. Parsons and David Schuyler, 159–170. Baltimore: Johns Hopkins University Press, 2002.

Funigiello, Philip. "City Planning in World War II: The Experience of the National Resources Planning Board." In *Introduction to Planning History in the United States*, edited by Donald A. Krueckeberg, 152–169. New Brunswick, NJ: Center for Urban Policy Research, Rutgers University, 1983.

"Garden Apartments." *Architectural Forum* 72 (May 1940): 309–322.

Gillette, Howard, Jr. *Civitas by Design: Building Better Communities, from the Garden City to the New Urbanism.* Philadelphia: University of Pennsylvania Press, 2010.

# Bibliography

——. "Film as Artifact: *The City* (1939)." *American Studies* (fall 1977): 71–85.

Gilmartin, Gregory F. *Shaping the City: New York and the Municipal Art Society*. New York: Clarkson Potter, 1995.

Girling, Cynthia, and Kevin Helphand. *Yard, Street, Park: The Design of Suburban Open Space*. New York: John Wiley and Sons, 1994.

Glikson, Artur. *Regional Planning and Development: Six Lectures Delivered at the Institute of Social Studies, at The Hague, 1953*. Leiden: A. W. Sijthoff's Uitgeversmaatschappij, 1955.

Goetz, Edward. "Potential Effects of Federal Policy Devolution on Local Housing Expenditures." *Publius: The Journal of Federalism* 25 (summer 1995): 99–116.

Goldfeld, Abraham. *The Diary of a Housing Manager*. Chicago: National Association of Housing Officials, 1938.

Goodhue, Bertram Grosvenor. "The Architecture and the Gardens." In *The Architecture and the Gardens of the San Diego Exposition*, edited by Carleton Monroe Winslow, 3–9. San Francisco: Paul Elder, 1916.

Gournay, Isabelle, and Elliott Pavlos. "Americans in Paris." *Journal of Architectural Education* 38, no. 4 (1985): 22–26.

Grant, Jill. *Planning the Good Community: New Urbanism in Theory and Practice*. New York: Routledge, 2006.

"Green Acres, A Residential Park Community." *Architectural Record* 80 (October 1936): 285–286.

Gries, John M., and James Ford, eds. *Slums, Large-Scale Housing and Decentralization*. Washington, DC: President's Conference on Home Building and Home Ownership, 1932.

Gutheim, Frederick. "Indian Head Experiment in Prefabrication." *Pencil Points* 22 (November 1941): 724.

Hackett, Horatio. "How the PWA Housing Division Functions." *Architectural Record* 77 (March 1935): 148–152.

Hall, Peter. *Cities of Tomorrow*, 4th ed. Malden, MA: Wiley-Blackwell, 2014.

Hamlin, Talbot F. "Housing Is Architecture." *Pencil Points*, 20 (February 1939): 81–97.

Hampson, T. "The Stevenage Town Centre." *Town and Country Planning* (January 1959): 13–16.

Harbin, Laurel, and Kristin Larsen. "American Regionalism in India: How Lessons from the New Deal Greenbelt Town Program Translated to Post–World War II India." Paper presented at the 16th International Planning History Society Conference in St. Augustine, Florida, July 21, 2014.

Harrison, Michael. "William Alexander Harvey (1874–1951): Bournville and After." Paper presented at the International Planning History Society Conference, Catalonia, Spain, July 14–17, 2004.

Harvey, William Alexander. *The Model Village and Its Cottages: Bournville*. London: B. T. Batsford, 1906.

Hayden, Dolores. *Building Suburbia: Green Fields and Urban Growth, 1820–2000*. New York: Vintage Books, 2003.

Hays, R. Allen. *The Federal Government and Urban Housing: Ideology and Change in Public Policy*. Albany: State University of New York Press, 1995.

Hegemann, Werner, and Elbert Peets. *The American Vitruvius: An Architect's Handbook of Civic Art*. 1922; reprint New York: Princeton Architectural Press, 1988.

Hinman, A. G., and G. C. Woodbury. "Landscape Architecture's Role in Modern Housing Projects." *American Landscape Architect* 1 (October 1929): 9–15.

# Bibliography

Hitchcock, Henry-Russell, and Philip Johnson. *The International Style*. 1932; reprint New York: W. W. Norton, 1966.

"Hommage a Laloux." *Pencil Points* 18 (October 1937): 621–630.

"A House for the Motor Age." *Architectural Record* 65 (February 1929): 197.

Housing and Home Finance Agency. "A Handbook of Information on the Provisions of the Housing Act of 1949." Washington, DC: Office of the Administrator, July 1949.

Howard, Ebenezer. *Garden Cities of To-Morrow*. 1902; reprint Cambridge, MA: MIT Press, 1965.

Hudson, Robert B. *Radburn: A Plan of Living*. New York: American Association for Adult Education, 1934.

Hunt, D. Bradford. "Was the 1937 U.S. Housing Act a Pyrrhic Victory?" *Journal of Planning History* 4, no. 3 (2005): 195–221.

"Improvements to FHA." *Architectural Forum* 64 (March 1936): 208.

"Industry Builds Kitimat." *Architectural Forum* 101 (July 1954; August 1954): 128–147; 120–127.

Jenkinson, Michael. "Tyrone the Creation of a Model Ghost Town." *American West* 5, no. 2 (1968): 39–42, 78–79.

Johnson, David A. *Planning the Great Metropolis: The 1929 Regional Plan of New York and Its Environs*. New York: Taylor and Francis, 1996.

Josephson, Matthew, and Hannah Josephson. *Al Smith: Hero of the Cities*. Boston: Houghton Mifflin, 1969.

Kahn, Ely Jacques. *Ely Jacques Kahn*. New York: McGraw-Hill, 1931.

Kantor, Harvey A. "Charles Dyer Norton and the Origins of the Regional Plan of New York." *Journal of the American Institute of Planners* 39, no. 1 (1973): 35–44.

Keith, Nathaniel S. *Politics and the Housing Crisis since 1930*. New York: Universe Books, 1973.

Klaber, Eugene Henry. *Housing Design*. New York: Reinhold, 1954.

Knepper, Cathy D. *Greenbelt, Maryland: A Living Legacy of the New Deal*. Baltimore: Johns Hopkins University Press, 2001.

Lang, Michael H. *Designing Utopia: John Ruskin's Urban Vision for Britain and America*. New York: Black Rose Books, 1999.

——. "Town Planning and Radicalism in the Progressive Era: The Legacy of F. L. Ackerman." *Planning Perspectives* 16, no. 2 (2001): 143–167.

Larsen, Kristin. "Cities to Come—Clarence Stein's Post-War Regionalism." *Journal of Planning History* 4, no. 1 (2005): 33–51.

——. "Clarence Stein's Formative Experiences and Unbuilt Projects—Transforming Classical Training into Modern Design and Planning Sensibilities." *Public Versus Private Planning: Themes, Trends, and Tensions*, 1321–1336. Chicago: Proceedings of the 2008 International Planning History Society Conference.

——. "Planning and Public–Private Partnerships: Essential Links in Early Federal Housing Policy." *Journal of Planning History* 15, no. 1 (2016): 68–81.

——. "The Radburn Idea as an Emergent Concept—Henry Wright's Regional City." *Planning Perspectives* 23, no. 3 (2008): 381–395.

Lilienthal, David. *TVA: Democracy on the March*. 1944; reprint Chicago: Quadrangle Books, 1966.

"Limited Dividend Roll Call." *Architectural Forum* 62 (January 1935): 98–101.

"Low Cost Houses." *Architectural Forum* 75 (October 1941): 211–212.

Lubove, Roy. *Community Planning in the 1920s: The Contribution of the Regional Planning Association of America*. Pittsburgh: University of Pittsburgh Press, 1963.

# Bibliography

MacKaye, Benton. "An Appalachian Trail: A Project in Regional Planning." *Journal of the American Institute of Architects* 19 (October 1921): 325–330.

———. *The New Exploration: A Philosophy of Regional Planning.* Harpers Ferry, WV: Appalachian Trail Conference; and Urbana-Champaign: University of Illinois Press, 1928.

———. "Regional Planning and Ecology." *Ecological Monographs* 10, no. 3 (1940): 349–353.

———. "The Townless Highway." *The New Republic*, March 12, 1930: 10–11.

MacLeish, Archibald. *Housing America.* New York: Harcourt, Brace, 1932.

Magnusson, Leifur. "A Modern Copper Mining Town." *Monthly Labor Review* 7, no. 2 (1918): 278–284.

Maltby, Richard. "New Cinema Histories." In *Explorations in New Cinema History: Approaches and Case Studies*, edited by Richard Maltby, Daniel Biltereyst, and Philippe Meers, 3–40. Malden, MA: Wiley-Blackwell, 2011.

Mayer, Albert. "A Call to the Planners." *Journal of the American Institute of Planners* (fall 1951): 161–162.

———. *Greenbelt Towns Revisited.* Washington, DC: National Association of Housing and Redevelopment Officials, 1968.

———. "Techniques of New Town Design." *American Institute of Planners* (1949): 19–20.

———. *The Urgent Future.* New York: McGraw-Hill, 1967.

Mayer, Albert, in consultation with Clarence Stein. "New Towns: And Fresh In-City Communities." *Architectural Record* 136 (August 1964): 129–138.

McCullough, Robert L. *A Path for Kindred Spirits: The Friendship of Clarence Stein and Benton MacKaye.* Chicago: Center for American Places at Columbia College Chicago, 2012.

Meldrum, Pixie. "Kitimat: The First Five Years." Corporation of the District of Kitimat, 1958.

Miller, Donald. *Lewis Mumford: A Life.* Pittsburgh: University of Pittsburgh Press, 1989.

Minister of Local Government and Planning. *Town and Country Planning, 1943–1951.* London: His Majesty's Stationery Office, 1951.

Mock, Elizabeth, ed. *Built in USA—1932–1944.* New York: Museum of Modern Art, 1944.

Mozes, S. R. "The Growth of State Planning in New York State." *IFHP Bulletin* 1 (1963): 4–20.

Mumford, Lewis. "Address of Lewis Mumford." *American Institute of Architects, Journal of Proceedings* 1925): 27–30. Box 6, CSP/CUL.

———. "A Modest Man's Enduring Contributions to Urban and Regional Planning." *AIA Journal* 65, no. 12 (1976): 19–29.

———. "The Plan of New York." In *Planning the Fourth Migration: The Neglected Vision of the Regional Planning Association of America*, edited by Carl Sussman, 224–259. Cambridge, MA: MIT Press, 1976.

———. "Regions to Live In." *Survey Graphic* 54, no. 3 (1925): 151–152.

———. *Sketches from Life: The Autobiography of Lewis Mumford.* Boston: Beacon Press, 1982.

"The National Housing Act." *Architectural Forum* 60 (June 1934): 468–470.

National Housing Agency. *War Housing in the United States.* Washington, DC: U.S. Government Printing Office, 1945.

Neutra, Richard J. "Peace Can Gain from War's Forced Changes." *New Pencil Points* 23 (November 1942): 28–40.

"A New FHA Low Cost Housing Plan." *Architectural Forum* 63 (November 1935): 520–521.

New York State Board of Housing. *Preliminary Report of the State Board of Housing to Governor Alfred E. Smith.* December 15, 1926.

"The NHA Becomes Law." *Architectural Forum* 61 (July 1934): 66.

Nicolaides, Becky, and Andrew Wiese, eds. *The Suburb Reader.* New York: Routledge, 2006.

# Bibliography

Oberlander, Peter, and Cornelia Oberlander. "Critique: Canada's New Towns." *Progressive Architecture* 37 (August 1956): 113–119.

O'Hara, Christine Edstrom. "The Panama-California Exposition, San Diego, 1915: The Olmsted Brothers' Ecological Park Typology." *Journal of the Society of Architectural Historians* 70, no. 1 (2011): 64–81.

Oliver, Marshall. "The Way Out." *Architecture* 67, no. 5 (1933): 247–252.

Oliver, Richard. *Bertram Grosvenor Goodhue*. Cambridge, MA: MIT Press, 1983.

Orlebeke, Charles J. "The Evolution of Low-Income Housing Policy, 1949 to 1999." *Housing Policy Debate* 11, no. 2 (2000): 489–520.

Osborn, Frederic J. *Green-Belt Cities*. New ed. with a forward by Lewis Mumford. 1946; reprint London: Evelyn, Adams & Mackay, 1969.

Osborn, Frederic J., and Arnold Whittick. *The New Towns: The Answer to Megalopolis*. London: Leonard Hill, 1969.

Parsons, Kermit C. "American Influence on Stockholm's Post–World War II Suburban Expansion." *Planning History* 14, no. 1 (1990): 3–14.

——. "Benton MacKaye's Collaboration with the Regional Planning Association of America: Its Influence on the Appalachian Trail and Regional Planning (1921–1931). Paper presented at the One-Day Public Conference on Benton MacKaye and the Appalachian Trail 75th Anniversary Celebration of Vision, Planning, and Grass-Roots Mobilization, in Albany, NY, October 24, 1996.

——. "British and American Community Design: Clarence Stein's Manhattan Transfer, 1924–74." *Planning Perspectives* 7, no. 2 (1992): 181–210.

——. "Clarence Stein's 1919–1928 Contributions to New York State and National Housing Reform." Paper presented at the Annual Conference of the Association of Collegiate Schools of Planning, Pasadena, CA, November 1998.

——. "Collaborative Genius: The Regional Planning Association of America." *Journal of the American Planning Association* 60, no. 4 (1994): 462–482.

——. "C. S. Stein's Apprenticeship with Bertram Grosvenor Goodhue: The Mining Town of Tyrone, New Mexico 1915–1919." Paper presented at the Seventh Biennial Conference of the Society for American City and Regional Planning History, Seattle, WA, October 24, 1997.

——. "Financing Affordable Housing in the 1990s: Lessons from Alexander Bing's Innovations at Sunnyside and Radburn in the 1920s." Paper presented at the Annual Conference of the Association of Collegiate Schools of Planning, Phoenix, AZ, November 6, 1994.

——. "Growing Up in New York and Paris: Clarence Stein's Urban Roots and Values." Paper presented at the Eighth Biennial Conference of the Society for American City and Regional Planning History, Washington, DC, November 1–4, 1999.

——. "Shaping the Regional City, 1950–1990: The Plans of Tracy Augur and Clarence Stein for Dispersing Federal Workers from Washington, DC." *Proceedings of the Third National Conference on American Planning History*. Cincinnati: Society for American City and Regional Planning History, 1989, 649–691.

——, ed. *The Writings of Clarence Stein*. Baltimore: Johns Hopkins University Press, 1998.

Perry, Clarence. "The Neighborhood Unit: A Scheme of Arrangement for the Family-Life Community." In *Neighborhood and Community Planning*. New York: Russell Sage Foundation, 1929.

——. *Wider Use of the School Plant*. New York: Russell Sage Foundation, 1910.

Perry, Elizabeth I. "Women's City Club of New York." In *The Encyclopedia of New York City*, edited by Kenneth Jackson, 1269. New Haven: Yale University Press, 1995.

# Bibliography

"A Planned Community Appraised." *Architectural Forum* 72 (January 1940): 62–63, 34.

Plunz, Richard. *A History of Housing in New York City*. New York: Columbia University Press, 1990.

Popkin, Susan J., Bruce Katz, Mary K. Cunningham, Karen D. Brown, Jeremy Gustafson, and Margery A. Turner. *A Decade of HOPE VI: Research Findings and Policy Challenges*. Washington, DC: Urban Institute, 2004.

Post, Langdon. *The Challenge of Housing*. New York: Farrar & Rinehart, 1938.

Public Works Administration Housing Division Staff. *Urban Housing: The Story of the PWA Housing Division, 1933–1936*. Washington, DC: Federal Emergency Administration of Public Works, 1936.

Radest, Howard B. *Toward Common Ground: The Story of the Ethical Societies in the United States*. Garden City, NY: Fieldston Press, 1969.

Radford, Gail. *Modern Housing for America: Policy Struggles in the New Deal Era*. Chicago: University of Chicago Press, 1996.

Recchiuti, John L. *Civic Engagement: Social Science and Progressive-Era Reform in New York City*. Philadelphia: University of Pennsylvania Press, 2007.

Regional Planning Association of America. "A Housing Policy for the Government." *Octagon* 5 (June 1933): 6–7.

Resettlement Administration. *Greenbelt Towns: A Demonstration in Suburban Planning*. September, 1936.

Riley, Robert B. "Gone Forever: Goodhue's Beaux Arts Ghost Town." *AIA Journal* 50, no. 2 (1968): 67–70.

Rogers, Cleveland. "Robert Moses, An Atlantic Portrait." *Atlantic Monthly* 156 (February 1939).

Rosenfield, Isadore. "Phipps Garden Apartments." *Architectural Forum* 56 (February 1932): 110–124, 183–187.

Ross, Nola Mae Wittler. "History of Maplewood—Calcasieu Parish, Louisiana." American Press, June 3, 1990. http://files.usgwarchives.org/la/calcasieu/newspapers/maplewoo.txt.

Rowe, Peter G. *Modernity and Housing*. Cambridge, MA: MIT Press, 1993.

Saylor, Henry H. "The Hillside Housing Development." *Architecture* 71 (May 1935): 245–251.

Schaffer, Daniel. *Garden Cities for America: The Radburn Experience*. Philadelphia: Temple University Press, 1982.

Schilling, Joseph, and Jonathan Logan. "Greening the Rust Belt: A Green Infrastructure Model for Right Sizing America's Shrinking Cities." *Journal of the American Planning Association* 74, no. 4 (2008): 451–466.

Schnadelbach, R. Terry. "Phipps Apartment Houses, Sunnyside Queens, New York: The Landscape Architecture of Marjorie Sewell-Cautley." Paper presented at the Beatrix Farrand Conference on Women in Landscape Architecture, University of California, Berkeley, CA, November 8, 2002.

Schwartz, Alex F. *Housing Policy in the United States*. 3rd ed. New York, NY: Routledge, 2014.

Scott, Mel. *American City Planning Since 1890*. 1969; reprint Chicago: American Planning Association, 1995.

Self, Peter. "The Evolution of the Greater London Plan, 1944–1970." *Progress in Planning* 57 (2002): 145–175.

Shand-Tucci, Douglass. *Ralph Adams Cram: An Architect's Four Quests—Medieval, Modernist, American, Ecumenical*. Amherst: University of Massachusetts Press, 2005.

Silver, Christopher. "Neighborhood Planning in Historical Perspective." *Journal of the American Planning Association* 51, no. 2 (1985): 161–174.

# Bibliography

Southworth, Michael, and Eran Ben-Joseph. *Streets and the Shaping of Towns and Cities.* Washington, DC: Island Press, 2003.

Spain, Daphne. "Octavia Hill's Philosophy of Housing Reform: From British Roots to American Soil." *Journal of Planning History* 5, no. 2 (2006): 106–125.

Spann, Edward K. *Designing Modern America: The Regional Planning Association of America and Its Members.* Columbus: Ohio State University Press, 1996.

Stein, Clarence S. "Address of Clarence Stein." *American Institute of Architects, Journal of Proceedings* (1925): 30–32. Box 6, CSP/CUL.

——. "Amsterdam—Old and New." *Journal of the American Institute of Architects* 20 (October 1922): 310–328.

——. "A Building on the Board." *Pencil Points* 10 (August 1929): 535–544, 581.

——. "The Case for New Towns." *Planners' Journal* 5 (March–June 1939): 39–41.

——. "The City of the Future—A City of Neighborhoods." *American City* 37 (November 1945): 123, 125.

——. "City Patterns ... past and future." *New Pencil Points* 23 (June 1942): 52–56.

——. "Community Planning—The Architect's Approach." Lecture, New York University, April 27, 1938. Box 6, CSP/CUL.

——. "Form and Function of the Modern Museum." *Museum News*, October 15, 1935: 6–8.

——. "The Gardens of Soochow: Chinese Pavements Photographed by Clarence S. Stein." *Pencil Points* 19 (July 1938): 427–430.

——. "Harbor Hills Housing." *Pencil Points* 22 (November 1941): 677–683.

——. "Henry Wright, 1878–1936." *American Architect and Architecture* 149 (August 1936): 23–24.

——. "Hillside Homes." *American Architect* 148 (February 1936): 16–33.

——. "Housing and City Redevelopment during and after the War." Lecture, Citizens' City Planning and Housing Council of Rochester, NY, November 17, 1941. Box 6, CSP/CUL.

——. "Housing and Common Sense." *The Nation* 134 (May 1932): 541–544.

——. "Housing and the Depression." *Octagon* 5 (June 1933): 3–5.

——. "Housing for Defense." *Common Sense* 10 (April 1941): 106–108.

——. "Housing: The Next Chapter." Lecture, MIT, Boston, MA, October 27, 1937. Box 6, CSP/CUL.

——. "Housing and Reconstruction." *Journal of the American Institute of Architects* 6 (October 1918): 471.

——. "Investment Housing Pays." *Survey Graphic* 29 (February 1940): 75–77, 127.

——. "An Outline for Community Housing Procedure." *Architectural Forum*, 56 (March, April, May 1932): 221–228, 393–400, 504–514.

——. "A Plan for the State of New York." In *Planning Problems of Town, City and Region: Papers and Discussions at the International City and Regional Planning Conference Held in New York City, April 20 to 25, 1925*, edited by International Federation for Housing and Town Planning Congress, 282–286. Baltimore, MD: Norman, Remington, 1925.

——. "Planning Technique and the London Plan." *Architectural Review* 96 (September 1944): 79–80.

——. "Possibilities: Four Opinions by Housing Experts II." *Women and the City's Work* 6, no. 4 (1920): 4–6.

——. "Preparedness for Post War Urban Redevelopment." *American City* 57 (February 1942): 68–69.

——. "The Price of Slum Clearance." *Architectural Forum* 60 (February 1934): 154–157.

# Bibliography

———. "The Problem of the Temple and Its Solution." *Architectural Forum* 52 (February 1930): 155–211.

———. "The Radburn Plan." Lecture at the Tenth Anniversary of Radburn, Meeting of the New Jersey Federation of Official Planning Boards, November 30, 1939. Box 6, CSP/CUL.

———. "Stockholm Builds a New Town." *Planning Proceedings of the American Society of Planning Officials Conference* (1952), 57–64.

———. *Toward New Towns for America.* Cambridge, MA: MIT Press, 1957.

———. "Transportation or Housing." *Journal of the American Institute of Architects* 6 (July 1918): 363.

———. "A Triumph of the Spanish-Colonial Style." In *The Architecture and the Gardens of the San Diego Exposition*, edited by Carleton Monroe Winslow, 10–18. San Francisco: Paul Elder, 1916.

———. "The Wagner-Steagall Housing Act of 1937." *American Architect and Architecture* 151 (November 1937): 36–37.

———. "Why We Changed Our Name." *Citizen's Housing and Planning Council, Housing News* 6, no. 6 (1948): 1, 4.

Stein, Clarence S., and Catherine Bauer. "Store Buildings and Neighborhood Shopping Centers." *Architectural Record* 75 (February 1934): 175–187.

Stein, Erica. "The Road to Heaven Twists: *The City*, Urban Planning, and Experiential Space." *Media Fields Journal* 3 (2011): 1–10.

Stein, Jeanne. "Aline MacMahon Had the Wit to Sense What Audiences Liked Her to Project." *Films in Review* 16 (December 1965): 616–632.

Stephenson, Gordon. "Building in Cities—The Challenge to Architects." *Architecture in Australia* 55 (July 1966): 123–124.

———. "Editorial Notes." *Town Planning Review* 20 (October 1949): 185.

———. *On a Human Scale: A Life in City Design*, edited by Christina DeMarco. South Fremantle, Australia: Fremantle Arts Centre Press, 1992.

Stern, Robert A.M. "PSFS: Beaux-Arts Theory and Rational Expressionism." *Journal of the Society of Architectural Historians* 21, no. 2 (1962): 84–102.

"Stowe Township, PA." *Architectural Forum* 77 (July 1942): 83–84.

Straus, Michael W., and Talbot Wegg. *Housing Comes of Age.* New York: Oxford University Press, 1938.

Subcommittee of the Committee on Public Works United States Senate. *Hearings on S. 4232: A Bill to Authorize a Program to Provide for the Construction of Federal Buildings Outside of, but in the Vicinity of and Accessible to the District of Columbia, and for Other Purposes.* 81st Cong., 2nd sess., 13, 14, and 18 December 1950.

Sussman, Carl. "Introduction." In *Planning the Fourth Migration: The Neglected Vision of the Regional Planning Association of America*, edited by Carl Sussman, 1–45. Cambridge, MA: MIT Press, 1976.

Sutcliffe, Anthony. *Paris: An Architectural History.* New Haven: Yale University Press, 1993.

Szylvian, Kristin. "Defense Housing in Greater Pittsburgh: 1945–1955." *Pittsburgh History* (spring 1990): 17–28.

———. "The Federal Housing Program during World War II." In *From Tenements to the Taylor Homes: In Search of an Urban Housing Policy in Twentieth-Century America*, edited by John F. Bauman, Roger Biles, and Kristin Szylvian, 121–138. University Park: The Pennsylvania University Press, 2000.

# Bibliography

Talen, Emily. *New Urbanism and American Planning: The Conflict of Cultures*. New York: Routledge Taylor and Francis Group, 2010.

Thomas, John L. "Holding the Middle Ground." In *The American Planning Tradition: Culture and Policy*, edited by Robert Fishman, 32–63. Baltimore: Johns Hopkins University Press, 2000.

Turner, Margery A., and G. T. Kingsley. *Federal Programs for Addressing Low-Income Housing Needs: A Policy Primer*. Washington, DC: Urban Institute, 2008.

"Twelfth Night in Mr. Goodhue's Office." *Pencil Points* 3 (January 1922): 21–26.

United States Housing Authority. *Annual Report of the United States Housing Authority for the Fiscal Year 1939*. Washington, DC: Government Printing Office, 1940.

Unwin, Raymond. *Nothing Gained By Overcrowding!* Letchworth, UK: Garden City Press, 1912.

——. *Town Planning in Practice*. 1909; reprint New York: Princeton Architectural Press, 1994.

Vidyarthi, Sanjeev. "Reimagining the American Neighborhood Unit for India." In *Crossing Borders: International Exchange and Planning Practices*, edited by Patsy Healey and Robert Upton, 73–93. New York: Routledge, 2010.

von Hoffman, Alexander. "The End of the Dream: The Political Struggle of America's Public Housers." *Journal of Planning History* 4, no. 3 (2005): 222–253.

Ward, Stephen V. *Planning the Twentieth-Century City*. Chichester, UK: John Wiley & Sons, 2002.

Way, Thaisa. *Unbounded Practice: Women and Landscape Architecture in the Early Twentieth Century*. Charlottesville: University of Virginia Press, 2009.

Wheeler, Stephen. "The New Regionalism: Key Characteristics of an Emerging Movement." *Journal of the American Planning Association* 68, no. 3 (2002): 267–278.

"Wichita's New Art Museum Designed to Symbolize the Southwest." *The Art Digest*, October 15, 1935, 14.

Wong, Dorothy F., Robert Nicolais, and Loretta Hess. "National Historic Landmark Application for Baldwin Hills Village (Village Green)." Unpublished report, August 1999.

Wood, Edith Elmer. "The Development of Legislation." In *Public Housing in America*, edited by M. B. Schnapper, 71–78. New York: H. W. Wilson, 1939.

——. *The Housing of the Unskilled Wage Earner: America's Next Problem*. New York: MacMillan, 1919.

——. "The International Conference—London." *Journal of the American Institute of Architects* 20 (May 1922): 165.

——. *Slums and Blighted Areas in the United States*. 1936; reprint College Park, MD: McGrath, 1969.

Wright, Chester M. "Washington Monthly Newsletter." *Pencil Points* 16 (April 1935): 181–184.

Wright, Henry. "The Apartment House: A Review and a Forecast." *Architectural Record* 69 (March 1931): 187–195.

——. "The Autobiography of Another Idea." *Western Architect* 39 (September 1930); reprint: New York: Regional Planning Association of America, 1930, n.p. Box 18, CSP/CUL.

——. "Institute Business." *Journal of the American Institute of Architects* 14 (November 1926): 499–500.

——. *Rehousing Urban America*. New York: Columbia University Press, 1935.

# INDEX

*Italicized* pages numbers indicate illustrations, maps, and tables. Page numbers followed by n and nn indicate notes.

# Index

# Index

# Index

# Index

# Index

# Index

# Index

# Index

# Index

# Index